JOURNALISTS BETWEEN HITLER
AND ADENAUER

Journalists between Hitler and Adenauer

FROM INNER EMIGRATION TO THE MORAL RECONSTRUCTION OF WEST GERMANY

VOLKER R. BERGHAHN

PRINCETON UNIVERSITY PRESS

PRINCETON & OXFORD

Copyright © 2019 by Princeton University Press

Published by Princeton University Press
41 William Street, Princeton, New Jersey 08540
6 Oxford Street, Woodstock, Oxfordshire OX20 1TR

press.princeton.edu

Jacket image: Bomb attack on Hamburg-Altstad, Germany: March 20, 1945.
Passersby on Speersort in front of the burning press house
© ullsteinbild-H. Schmidt-Luchs / The Image Works

LCCN 2018946391
ISBN 978-0-691-17963-6

British Library Cataloging-in-Publication Data is available

Editorial: Amanda Peery
Production Editorial: Ali Parrington
Jacket Design: Leslie Flis
Production: Erin Suydam
Publicity: Jodi Price
Copyeditor: Marilyn Martin

This book has been composed in Arno

Printed on acid-free paper. ∞

Printed in the United States of America

10 9 8 7 6 5 4 3 2 1

CONTENTS

JOURNALISTS BETWEEN HITLER AND ADENAUER

Journalists and Freedom of Expression in the Twentieth Century

JOURNALISTS BETWEEN HITLER AND ADENAUER is, in its broadest perspective, a study of the situation of journalism and its practitioners as they grappled in the twentieth century, and are grappling to this day, with the age-old question of the freedom of expression and, more particularly, their own freedom to report on current events and articulate their views in editorials and op-ed pieces of their media outlets. However, when conceptualizing this book I did not have in mind a philosophical study of the perennially precarious position in which the freedom of opinion has found itself ever since the arrival of the Gutenberg press and all the way down to modern times. I obviously needed to achieve a clear focus and to anchor my analysis in tangible empirical material.

Accordingly, I chose what to my mind was a particularly intriguing and crucial case in point and decided to write a history of German journalism and journalists from the late Weimar Republic and the Hitler dictatorship up to developments in the West German press in the early postwar decades. As this was in itself still a huge field of inquiry, I took a further step: instead of writing a more general analysis of journalism in this period, I turned to biography and determined to look at the life and work of a few very prominent journalists: Paul Sethe, its "grand old man," who worked for *Frankfurter Allgemeine Zeitung* (FAZ) and later for Axel Springer's *Die Welt* before finishing his long career at *Die Zeit* and *Der Stern*; Marion Countess Dönhoff of *Die Zeit*, widely deemed to have been the "doyenne" of the West German quality press; and finally Hans Zehrer, a particularly fascinating and controversial figure during the Weimar period, who became the editor in chief of *Die Welt* and the intellectual mentor of Axel Springer, West Germany's powerful press mogul of the postwar media metropolis Hamburg.

The period at the core of this book, from 1932 to the mid-1960s, thus provides the time frame of an effort to investigate three key questions: how, to begin with, did these three Hamburgian journalists live, work, and survive under the Nazi dictatorship, and how did they interpret the end of the Third Reich in 1945? Secondly, what kinds of ideas and visions did they develop for the reconstruction of a defeated and devastated German society? Yet, while much of this book is about their experiences under Hitler and later during the era of Federal Chancellor Konrad Adenauer, as well as the insights they gained into contemporary developments and transmitted to their readers, this is also a study of the intellectual and political history of postwar Germany and its major media empires. It is this third and more expansive theme that finally provides the setting for some concluding considerations of the recent evolution of journalism and freedom of expression in the age of mass communication and social media.

What the three journalists had in common was that they had been adults and *anti-Nazis* in the Weimar Republic who had been enjoying liberal press freedoms under Article 118 of the Constitution. According to this article, "every German" had "the right, within the limits of general laws, to express his opinions freely, by word of mouth, writing, printed matter, or picture, or in any other manner. This right must not be affected by any conditions of his work or appointment, and no-one is permitted to injure him on account of his making use of such rights." It continued: "No censorship shall be enforced, but restrictive regulations may be introduced by law in reference to cinematographic entertainment. Legal measures are also admissible for the purpose of combatting bad and obscene literature, as well as for the protection of youth in public exhibitions and performances." Since none of the three worked for papers promoting such entertainment, they were primarily dependent on their employers, the proprietors who had the ultimate legal right to hire as well as to dismiss them if they did not follow the owners' political and cultural preferences. However, their freedom became threatened when from 1930 onward they witnessed the rise of Nazism and then Hitler's seizure of power in January 1933. Sethe, Zehrer, and Dönhoff (though she was not yet a journalist) continued to keep their distance from the regime thereafter. Unlike millions of other Germans, they never became members of the Nazi Party, nor did they emigrate or join the early underground resistance, most of whose members had by 1935 been caught by the Gestapo and sent to concentration camps or condemned to death and executed. Instead "my" three journalists went into "inner emigration," a concept that I define a bit later.

However, this is not the end of their story. Having lived, often quite dangerously, under the Hitler dictatorship to the bitter end, after 1945 they began to wrestle with the question of what kind of society they wanted to see emerge from the rubble of World War II and how, as journalists and public intellectuals, they intended to explain their experiences and insights to their West German readers. What makes the cases of Sethe, Dönhoff, and Zehrer so intriguing, though, is that they were not so much concerned with the rebuilding of a war-torn economy and with *material* recovery; nor were they primarily focused on political reconstruction in a narrow sense of the word, that is, of building a viable and stable parliamentary-constitutional democracy. Realizing that an abjectly criminal regime, responsible for the murder of millions of innocent men, women, and children, had destroyed literally all ethical and moral norms and values, these three journalists saw the task in front of them as much more fundamental. They wanted to restore precisely those moral and ethical axioms that Hitler had so totally demolished. To them, these axioms were the foundation without which a new West Germany would be built on sand, foundations that the Germans must never abandon again.

To the best of my knowledge, there is no similar study in the English language that raises and closely examines the difficult questions of the impact of the Hitler dictatorship on journalists before 1945 and then extends the analysis to the revival of journalism in the Western zones of occupation and, from 1949, the Federal Republic, thereby also dealing with the problem of continuity and discontinuity in modern German history and with societal change and learning. What encouraged me to undertake this research was not only that it proved to be an underdeveloped field of intellectual and media history in the English language, but also that my interest in the life and work of those three journalists became keen after I was given access to largely untapped archival sources. No historian can resist such an opportunity. First, I was fortunate that Dönhoff's voluminous papers had just been catalogued and were made available to me by her executor. In the case of Paul Sethe's papers, I encountered a similar stroke of good luck: Sethe's daughter had a treasure trove of letters at her apartment in Munich that had never been evaluated. The Zehrer papers, though they had been deposited by his family at the Federal Archives in Koblenz and accessible to researchers for some time, also contained much original material. In addition, there were two volumes of diaries that Zehrer had kept during his final years at *Die Welt* and that his heirs gave me permission to consult.

As this is a book about journalism and journalists, I had the additional advantage that the many articles and books that Sethe, Dönhoff, and Zehrer published were accessible online or through Interlibrary Loan, making it possible for me to trace their intellectual journeys through their private papers as well as their published writings. Finally, I was able to rely on a number of studies in German. As far as Marion Dönhoff is concerned, there are no fewer than three biographies, by Alice Schwarzer, Klaus Harpprecht, and Haug von Kuenheim.[1] Several anthologies on the history of *Die Zeit* have also helped me to formulate my approach.[2] There is nothing biographical on Paul Sethe, not even in the German language, apart from a number of obituaries and references relating to him in histories of the *Frankfurter Zeitung* (FZ), FAZ, and *Die Welt*. Sethe had started his career as editor in chief of a local paper in Solingen, in the Ruhr industrial region, in the 1920s, and after an agonizing journey through subsequent decades spent the happiest years of his life in the 1960s when he was welcomed and esteemed by Gerd Bucerius, the publisher of *Die Zeit* and *Der Stern*. Before joining the Bucerius media empire, Sethe had been a political editor at *Die Welt*, the daily that Axel Springer had bought from the British occupation authorities in 1953. It had been Hans Zehrer, the editor in chief of *Die Welt*, who had recruited Sethe in 1955 after he had fallen out with Chancellor Adenauer, his colleagues on the FAZ board, and the financiers and owners of the paper. On Zehrer, there is at least Ebbo Demant's book of 1971, as well as a string of articles and references in books on his Weimar journalism; but there was, as I found, more to be said on his life and his strange intellectual trajectory from Weimar Berlin to postwar Hamburg and finally back to Berlin.[3]

After the discovery of these fresh sources, it was but a small step to develop a plan for a study that was basically biographical, but not in the traditional sense. Rather than writing full biographies I decided to limit myself to several crucial issues that Sethe, Dönhoff, and Zehrer had been wrestling with as members of a particular generation. What intrigued me was that they were all born before 1914 and experienced the Weimar Republic as adults and opponents of Hitler before they were suddenly, in 1933, confronted with the huge quandary of how to react to the brutal dictatorship that the Nazis succeeded in establishing in Germany and later throughout Continental Europe so amazingly swiftly.

Of course the expansion of my project into a generational one raised the question of representativeness. How could I make claims about those three journalists as part of a generational cohort without a much larger sample, even if this cohort was limited to a relatively small group of public intellectuals? However, as I immersed myself in the careers of Sethe, Dönhoff, and Zehrer, I discovered that, although their lives diverged in many other respects, there were a number of tangible commonalities in their lives as journalists. These, I decided, would allow me to draw some larger conclusions relating to their quest, encapsulated in their writings and political positions, for what I call the "moral reconstruction" of post-Nazi Germany. This perspective, reflected in the book's title, also explains why it essentially ends in the late 1960s. I chose this terminal point partly because by that time the postwar reconstruction effort in which the three had become so deeply involved could be said to have largely succeeded. A further consideration was that Zehrer and Sethe died in 1966 and 1967, respectively. In the case of Dönhoff, who lived until 2002, I decided go beyond the 1960s time frame because it would enable me to highlight certain biographical continuities that had existed before but became distinctly more visible in the 1990s toward the end of her life. It would also allow me to discuss how Dönhoff responded to fresh threats to the moral foundations she began to see and then wrote about, enabling me to offer in the conclusion some larger considerations about journalists and the media at the end of the twentieth century and the beginning of the twenty-first.

Admittedly, my generational approach to capturing the lives and work of three individuals is peculiar in that it diverges from received notions of generational analysis in terms of cohorts and subcohorts born into a particular period. If I have called this particular generation the "Generation of '32," it is not because they were born in 1932. Rather I see the three journalists as members of a group that was defined and shaped by their adult experience of the Weimar Republic and the rise of the Nazi dictatorship. Together with many other Germans, this then confronted them, as mature individuals, with the existential question of how to react to the new post-1933 circumstances. Their response was to go into "inner emigration"—a concept with which I hope to open up a field of research that has not received as much attention as other alternative reactions to the Hitler dictatorship, such as forced emigration abroad, underground resistance, or collaboration with the Nazi regime. The decision not to leave, to go underground, or to join the Nazi movement but to stay in Germany and to become "inner emigrants" is, I postulate, best viewed as a spectrum along which they moved from a limited involvement with the regime to survive economically while continuing to reject Nazism, at the one end, to increasingly passive resistance and ultimately active participation in anti-Nazi movements, at the other end.

As far as I can see, our knowledge about inner emigrants and their dilemmas remains scant. To be sure, compared with those who joined the Nazi regime, they represented a small minority, and yet it seems worthwhile to take a closer look at their experiences and responses. After all, they knew that their position was very precarious and that a wrong move or angry outburst against the regime could have dire consequences, involving, in the extreme, torture and execution. Because these threats were hanging over them, their words and actions provide insights into life under the Hitler dictatorship, but also into the lessons they learned and applied after 1945. The question that is therefore ultimately at stake is that of what one could do if one was living in a parliamentary-democratic system that suddenly became an autocracy or even a dictatorship. So, apart from the generational concept that I deploy to shape the biographical narrative of the next three chapters, there is also the concept of inner emigration through which I approach the lives and work Sethe, Dönhoff, and Zehrer.

Clarifying the "Generation of '32"

Analyzing societies in terms of generations and generational conflict has been a field that many historians and social scientists have viewed as a promising avenue toward understanding socioeconomic and cultural change, and Karl Mannheim was among the very first to think more systematically about the concept in his seminal essay of 1928.[4] Accordingly, researchers, journalists, and politicians in mostly Western countries have identified and discussed divergent generations and their interactions, usually in comparison with their predecessors but also with later generations. There are many examples of the application of this approach to modern American society, the most recent being the study of the "millennial" generation. Yet nowhere else have scholars been more preoccupied with the concept and its problems than in Germany. To a considerable degree this is probably due to the huge upheavals and dislocations that German society experienced in the twentieth century. This, in turn, stimulated efforts to refine Mannheim's work and also to provide empirical backup for fresh lines of argument. Researchers began to disentangle the broad early hypotheses that had been put forward, adapting them to more specific circumstances and moving away from the original notion that a generation spanned a period of some thirty years.

Social scientists and social historians now deal with shorter periods when taking up Mannheim's proposition that traumatic events, such as wars or economic depressions, can telescope a generation into ten or fifteen years. No less important has been the hypothesis that, in very general terms, all human beings are part of a particular generation that they cannot relinquish, as they might decide spontaneously to give up their membership in a sports association or private club. In this respect, generational belonging is said to be similar to being part of a socioeconomic class into which an individual has been socialized from birth and within which he or she has been shaped. And yet, however much individuals perceive themselves to be part of a specific generation, they do not form a clearly identifiable community with all others from their generation.

Accordingly, generations have been broken down into cohorts or even subcohorts.[5] The advantage of this kind of approach has been that it has facilitated a better understanding of group consciousness in psychosociological terms. Researchers have also discovered subgroups that are marked by a retrospective longing and the wish to reconstitute a lost age. At the same time, there have been cohorts and subcohorts that have been driven by a desire to build an allegedly better future upon the ruins not only of a bygone era but also of the currently existing socioeconomic and cultural order.[6] A considerable amount of more recent work in this field has also been devoted to examining intergenerational negotiation and conflict that can even escalate into physical violence, even if it has not been easy to determine which cohort in fact triggered the escalation of civilized intellectual exchange into violent confrontation.[7]

In Germany, Ulrike Jureit has been at the forefront of recent attempts to conceptualize these problems.[8] In "New Perspectives on Generational Research," Kirsten Gerland, Benjamin Möckel, and Daniel Ristau have argued that generations can be taken as projects, as loci of longing, or as periods in which intergenerational negotiation takes place.[9] They see these efforts as characterized by memory, experience, and expectations. However, according to the three authors, generations can also be differentiated by perceived obligations (*Verpflichtungen*) arising from the past and to be implemented in the future. It is this latter perspective that—as we shall see—is particularly helpful in understanding the life and work of "my" three journalists of the "Generation of '32."

It is also helpful to what follows that scholarship has been quite rich with respect to the "Generation of '45" and the "Generation of '68." Dirk Moses was among the first to wrestle with the "45ers," as he called them.[10] He focused on those born between 1922 and 1932. This was a cohort that was deeply influenced by the experience and memory of the Nazi youth organizations and their ideological indoctrination. They had reached the age of 17 or 18 by 1944 and at the end of World War II were then recruited into the armed forces, where they saw brutal fighting and more indoctrination. It was the West German sociologist Helmut Schelsky who called this cohort, who had lived through the momentous rupture of 1945 and the years of chaos and dislocation in the late 1940s, the "Skeptical Generation."[11] Other researchers have spoken more pointedly of the "Flakhelfer" or even the "Auschwitz" generation. They were the ones who, in 1945, felt betrayed by the Nazi regime and later embarked on the search for a new moral and constitutional order.[12] It is important to mention them here, as the journalists among them will be discussed in more detail in chapter 4. What differentiated the 45ers from the 32ers was that they wanted not only to restabilize society on moral foundations but also to reform it, though not revolutionize it.

A new generation emerged in the 1960s, the 68ers, who set out to challenge the 45ers.[13] They criticized their predecessors for having, as adults, treated the Nazi past and the members of the generation who had lived and worked under Nazism too sympathetically, for having failed to vigorously confront their elders about their role in the Third Reich. Instead—thus the reproach— the 45ers had remained silent, allowing the older generation to resume many of the positions that they had lost during the Allied occupation.[14] The 68ers claimed to want to correct this earlier failure by refusing to remain silent about compromised individuals and about the authoritarian mentalities and practices that had been carried over into the Federal Republic, resulting in Adenauer's autocratic "chancellor democracy."[15] Ironically, this reproach was misdirected with regard to Sethe, Dönhoff, and Zehrer, whose criticism of Adenauer's policies and style of government will be examined in the next three chapters.

This is why mention must finally be made of Christina von Hodenberg's book that concentrated on the 45ers in the media.[16] She is interested in the socialization and professional ethos of this particular generational subgroup. Devoting much of her research to their ideological positions and activities in the 1950s and 1960s as well as their contributions to the reconstruction and stabilization of West Germany, von Hodenberg finds that many journalists among the 45ers, like others of their generation, had tolerated the return of elder colleagues. To be sure, they had no sympathy for former dyed-in-the-wool Nazi ideologues among them, many of whom had a record of brutality to boot. It was a different matter with those elders who had been opportunists and had contributed to the regime with their pens, though not as leaders of Nazi organizations or even perpetrators of massive crimes.

It is against this background that my book proposes to encourage the study of the allegedly silent Generation of '32. By this I mean journalists who were born from around the turn of the twentieth century to 1914. The question is how this particular generation of journalists experienced the end of the Weimar Republic and how they responded when they were suddenly confronted in 1933 with a dictatorship that, with breathtaking speed and brutality, was turning the country into a one-party state that many of them—not knowing the future— believed could not possibly last. I realized, of course, from the start that I could not possibly provide a study of the 32ers that was statistically representative. But in order to make a start, I decided to examine the trajectories of three journalists who became "inner emigrants" after 1933 and emerged as influential voices after 1945, interacting with the 45ers and to some extent becoming their role models. However, since the reactions of this cohort were immensely variegated, the best way to start was to approach it biographically in an effort to begin to capture the complexities of journalism under the Nazis as well as after 1945.

Defining "Inner Emigration"

This leaves me with the difficult problem of defining "inner emigration," which requires a preliminary note. Teaching in Britain and the United States for many decades, I was struck by how firmly undergraduates tended to be set in a conventional black-and-white mental frame when it came to "the Germans." They knew that a few had actively resisted the Nazi regime and, when caught, had been tried, imprisoned, or even executed. And they knew that others, especially German Jews, had to flee in order to survive. As for the rest, they supposed that all joined the Nazi movement, collaborated, and sustained a criminal regime to the bitter end.[17] These students had never heard of inner emigrants. Those who fell into this particular category are best illustrated by reference to Zehrer. Having opposed Hitler's seizure of power and having lost his job as a journalist, he, with good reason, to be discussed in chapter 3, began to fear for his life. Encouraged by friends and colleagues, he left Berlin and ultimately moved to a hovel on the remote North Sea island of Sylt near the Danish border, where he survived on a meager budget until 1945.

In other words, there were Germans who either fell completely silent or became associated with the regime in some more remote professional capacity, while finding covert ways to oppose it, until some of them, such as Sethe and Dönhoff, became involved in forms of active resistance. Others in this category, while still refusing to join the National Socialist German Workers' Party

(NSDAP) and its affiliates, found it too difficult to join the active resistance because of family or other responsibilities that they believed they could not jeopardize. Simple fear was also a significant factor. After all, it was generally known what it meant to be arrested and put on trial or to be sent into the legal black hole of a concentration camp. However, after 1945 a number of scholars and intellectuals began to write about these "refuseniks," among them Friedrich Krause and Karl O. Paetel, who had found refuge in the United States.[18]

The motivation for this book is echoed in Krause's preface, in which he argued against "the fairy tale" that "all Germans had been Nazis and [are] hence culpable."[19] He added: "We were sitting in safety [in New York] and were not exposed to the enormous pressure of a God-less party machinery." In his contribution Paetel focused on Germans who participated in an "inner-German resistance."[20] The conditions of open terror, he added, had led many anti-Nazis to remain mum. Still, their decision to refuse collaboration was an "expression of their resistance."[21] They decided to resort to metaphors and historical parallels that were "indirect, and yet they were clear enough for anyone who was prepared to hear the intermediate tones." In short, inner emigration was "the common code of the entire anti-Hitler movement." It was, Paetel concluded, "more far-reaching, but [hence] also less sharply contoured" when compared to the codes of the "old anti-fascist underground movement." However, it was "closer to reality, precisely for this reason."

There were, third, those described in an extract from Frank Thiess's writings as "inner-German emigrants" who could rely on an "inner space that Hitler, however hard he tried, was never able to conquer."[22] Many of them were completely isolated and suffered economically. But their predicament "gave them a treasure trove of insights and experiences" that could be "of the highest value for their future work." It was, Thiess asserted, a richer experience than "if I had witnessed the German tragedy from the boxes or the parquet of a foreign country." He hastened to add that he had no wish to criticize those who had left the country, as for most of them it had been a "life-or-death" decision. Accordingly, he ended on a conciliatory note, hoping for a trans-Atlantic alliance and taking the admonitions and "angry greetings from beyond the ocean" as a "sign of a deep inner bond between the two camps of emigrants." He did not "expect to be rewarded for not having left Germany. For us it was natural that we stayed."

Another writer to take up the question of inner emigration was the journalist and professor of political science at West Berlin's Free University Richard Löwenthal.[23] He had become interested in concepts of nonconformism and resistance and viewed inner emigration as a form of *Widerständigkeit*, that is, as an expression of "a will to societal refusal" due to "ideological dissidence." To him its significance lay in the quest "to salvage the cultural traditions of the earlier Germany from the years of terror by affecting the consciousness of important minorities." With this broad understanding of resistance, he proposed to "integrate a variety of forms of *Widerständigkeit*" into his concept "of refusal that involves a withdrawal of loyalty," whether individual or institutional. Peter Steinbach, as a scholar of the anti-Nazi resistance, was more skeptical.[24] According to him, dissidence was "unspectacular" and a "precondition of resistance" that lies in an individual's "intellectual independence, an intact morality and humanity, in faith and being a Christian, in enlightenment and reason, in decency and responsibility," upon which "all resistance is ethically and morally founded."

It might therefore be argued, also with reference to the journalists at the center of my study, that those who saw themselves as inner emigrants operated within a spectrum that extended from grudging cooperation to passive resistance that could become more active as the war unfolded. Postulating the existence of such a spectrum facilitates placing a person at a particular point along it and studying his or her back-and-forth movements over time, either in the direction of greater compliance or toward the opposite end of passive or even active resistance. Still, trying to define "inner emigration" within this spectrum of what might be called a "gray zone" rather than a black or white one, is fraught with many difficulties, and the rest of this introduction is designed to demonstrate this by examining the cases of three other journalists and asking how far they fit into this gray zone or whether they should be put outside the spectrum of inner emigration.[25] In other words, it is an attempt to grapple with the difficulties of this term before the life and work of Sethe, Dönhoff, and Zehrer are examined in greater detail.

Three "Inner Emigrants"?: Ernst Jünger, Margret Boveri, and Henri Nannen

Paetel's essay referred to a separate volume in the Krause series titled "Ernst Jünger, the Metamorphosis of a German Writer and Patriot," and later he reprinted an extract from Jünger's memorandum "Der Friede" (The peace).[26] The mention of Jünger in the volume raises the question of where to put him along the spectrum of inner emigration and to use his case, together with two others, to test whether there were limits to including an individual on the inner emigration spectrum.

Jünger's reputation was that of an arch-militarist whose writings in the Weimar years had had a hugely negative impact on the life of the Republic. Born in 1895, after a brief spell in the French Foreign Legion as a 17-year-old, he had fought on the Western Front. He was wounded several times and awarded not only the Iron Cross, First and Second Class, but also the highest Prussian army decoration, the Pour le Mérite, for his bravery. He wrote about his very personal experiences in a best-seller titled *In Stahlgewittern* (*Storms of Steel*).[27] The popularity that this book gained him enticed him to write *Der Kampf als Inneres Erlebnis* (Combat as an Inner Experience), a more general study of the face of modern war.[28] In it he declared that war was "the father of all things" and described how World War I had "hammered, chiseled and hardened" the combatants into men. It was the glorification of war in this particular piece and his many other essays that literally influenced millions of mainly right-wing veterans in the Weimar Republic, enabling them to view their wartime sacrifices as having been worthwhile and for a just cause.[29] No less important, it confirmed their belief that the parliamentary-democratic Constitution had to be replaced by an authoritarian regime that would overthrow the "shameful" Versailles peace settlement. In the late 1920s Jünger placed his hopes for a "state of the front soldiers" temporarily in Hitler's hands. But once the Nazis had come to power in 1933 and were showing their real face, Jünger, after returning to a military career, began to change his mind. A novel that he published in 1939 under the title of *Auf den Marmorklippen* (*On the Marble Cliffs*) was taken by many of his readers as a veiled anti-Hitler statement.[30]

After the invasion of France in 1940 Jünger kept a diary containing such a mishmash of entries that it has been difficult for scholars to fathom his thoughts about war and the Nazi occupation. Some have viewed him as an arrogant Wehrmacht captain who had no qualms about the occupation and enjoyed life in Paris. A Francophile, Jünger sat in cafés, met with fascist and accommodationist French intellectuals and artists, and had a number of love affairs. However, his diaries also contain references to the brutal aspects of life in occupied Paris. He learned of the execution of hostages and the recruitment of forced labor. He saw Jews wearing the Star of David and heard about their deportations. Because he was responsible for censorship and liaison with Parisian producers of culture, one of his sources of information was Otto von Stülpnagel, the commander of the Occupied Zone, who, having resorted to draconian repression, came close to a nervous breakdown and had to be relieved by his cousin, Heinrich von Stülpnagel. But Jünger was apparently never quite at ease, either, and, surrounded by so much violence, began to suffer from insomnia.[31]

From the summer of 1941, after the Nazi invasion of the Soviet Union, he began to hear rumors about brutal warfare and mass murder in the East. Apparently in an effort to gain firsthand knowledge, he undertook a longer trip to the Caucasus in 1942–43 that seems to have changed him from a *bon vivant* to an opponent of Hitler, whom he disdainfully nicknamed "Kniébolo" (not translatable; possibly a play on "Diabolo"). Hannes Heer, having scrutinized the relevant documents of Jünger's trip to the East, came to the conclusion that Jünger had experienced a "crisis" after talking to Wehrmacht officers and members of the SS Security Services (SD) who had witnessed the mass murders that were being perpetrated in the region.[32] To Heer, the experience remained no more than an "episode," so a "possible switch to another path," namely that of outright resistance, never occurred.

Jünger's story seems to be more complicated, though. While he did not join the active military resistance to remove Hitler and believed that the Nazi regime had to suffer total defeat to avoid the rise of another legend of the Stab in the Back (based on the post-1918 right-wing charge that the Imperial army had not been defeated but had allegedly been betrayed by the Left and Jewish profiteers at the home front.[33] In fact it was an anti-socialist and anti-Semitic lie that helped undermine the Weimar Republic. Having returned from the East to Paris, Jünger was in touch with a number of high-ranking officers who had committed themselves to the assassination of Hitler and the overthrow of his regime. One of them was Cäsar von Hofacker, a cousin of Claus von Stauffenberg, the man at the center of the conspiracy. He tried to win Jünger for the cause, though apparently without intending to recruit him directly; rather he hoped to rely on him after a successful coup as a celebrated writer who would speak up to justify the assassination of Hitler.

It may be that Hofacker had learned through Hans Speidel, the chief of the general staff to General Heinrich von Stülpnagel in Paris and later to Field Marshal Erwin Rommel, the commander of the Atlantic defense district, that Speidel had encouraged Jünger to compose a memorandum to be published after the overthrow of Hitler.[34] Titled "Der Friede" (The Peace), it was not found after the failure of the 20 July 1944 plot, in the wake of which Speidel was arrested. Meanwhile, Heinrich von Stülpnagel, thinking that the coup in Berlin had succeeded, had summarily interned hundreds of SS and SD officers, including their chief, Carl Oberg, as well as Otto Abetz, the German ambassador. When this news reached his superiors, he was ordered to Berlin for report. Knowing that he would be arrested as a traitor, he tried to commit suicide but survived, losing his eyesight in the process. Shortly after his arrival in Berlin, he was hanged with the blood-soaked dressing still around his head.

Speidel, having covered his tracks better than his superior, was interrogated, but was released unharmed. Nor did Jünger have his belongings searched, among which were his peace memorandum and diaries. He survived and published "Der Friede" in April 1945 as an appeal for renewal.[35] The document was more straightforward than many others but contained one illusion: that Germany would emerge as a third power between the United States and the Soviet Union. No less significant, he dedicated the document to the memory of his "dear son" Ernstel, who had resisted tyranny and "languished in its prisons," from which his father succeeded in freeing him.[36] Ernstel was subsequently recruited into the army at age 18 and sent to the Marble Mountains of Carrara, where he fell on 29 November 1944. Although Jünger's position on the 1944 plot remained opaque, I would nevertheless argue that Jünger had become part of the "inner emigration" and by 1943 had, in fact, moved to a position that could have cost him his life if "Der Friede" and his diaries had been discovered. After all, as he put it, by that time "the play of hide-and-seek" had become "more difficult and over large stretches knowledge about one another" was "very precise."[37] In other words, "the air has become tougher, but also more transparent and this means that the yardsticks have become more clearly discernible." It seems that this was an opaque way of discussing the dilemma of his situation at the end of the Hitler regime.

However, neither this observation nor the publication of his peace memorandum was of much help to Jünger after 1945. Memories of his books and essays of the 1920s were still very much alive among Social Democrats and others who had fought his militarism and anti-Republican politics. He was vigorously attacked as being one of the gravediggers of Weimar Germany, and neither his *On the Marble Cliffs* nor the publication of his diaries counted for much in the balance. Like many other Germans with an inner emigration past, he resented having to undergo de-Nazification, a response that was reinforced by his latent anti-Americanism. He retreated to Wilfingen, near Sigmaringen in the Southwest, and refused to follow the advice of Armin Mohler, his rightist private secretary, to participate in the reconstruction of Germany and Europe in a spirit of conservatism that we shall encounter again in Zehrer.[38] Instead he tended his garden and wrote several rather esoteric novels.[39] He met with his mainly Southwest German Francophile friends, among whom were Theodor

Heuss, the first president of the Federal Republic, Hans Speidel, and Carlo Schmid, the Francophile intellectual in the Social Democratic Party (SPD). But he was also in touch with Carl Schmitt, the Nazi jurist. Jünger kept up a voluminous correspondence with his many German and French friends and acquaintances. Toward the end of his life, he accepted an invitation from Chancellor Helmut Kohl to attend a Franco-German commemoration of the First World War on the battlefields of northern France. He died in 2001 at age 103. His was a life with incredible twists and turns, reflecting the tumultuous course of the twentieth century. He has been called an *Einzelgänger* (loner) and therefore continues to pose a great challenge to a biographer. This explains why so much has been written on him by historians and also by Germanists who have scrutinized the strange journey of this soldier and intellectual.[40]

The case of Jünger provides a good example of the complexities of conditions inside Germany during the Nazi period. Unlike some academics who successfully kept silent about their involvement in the regime, Jünger had a past that was too well known for it to remain hidden after 1945. He tried to defend himself, but when this proved futile he concentrated on writing allegorical novels. As Daniel Morat has shown,[41] his correspondents included Schmitt and the philosopher Martin Heidegger, who, while also keeping silent in public, continued to exchange views about the past that showed how little they had learned from it. Judging from his wartime record, Jünger's trajectory is less clear. He remained close to his brother Georg Friedrich, whose transformation from a militaristic nationalist to an anti-Nazi was in many ways similar to Ernst's. As early as the mid-1930s Georg published a long poem that he titled "The Poppy."[42] In it he took a strong anti-war position and, referring in the mid-1930s to Hitler's preparations for war, spoke of "the mourning dead" resting in a "silver fountain of peace" where they can no longer hear the noise of battle and "the infantile song of glory-less intoxication."[43]

Next is the case of the journalist Margret Boveri, who also made an explicit attempt to grapple with a definition of "inner emigration." She claimed to have heard of the concept from Theodor Heuss.[44] Before the Nazi seizure of power he had been teaching at the Hochschule für Politik (HfP) in Berlin, where Boveri was one of his students. After voting for Hitler's Enabling Act in March 1933, Heuss, who had been a member of the Reichstag for the pro-Republican Deutsche Demokratische Partei (DDP), considered himself an "inner émigré" but did not fall completely silent. Instead he wrote reviews and articles on cultural themes for Joseph Goebbels's highbrow paper *Das Reich*. After 1945 Heuss encountered considerable difficulties when the American occupation authorities discovered this. They deemed him a collaborator whose application to become the co-publisher of the *Rhein-Neckar-Zeitung* they rejected at first. It was approved only after some slightly devious string-pulling by more lenient American officers.[45]

Writing in 1965, Boveri defended Heuss's posture in the Third Reich.[46] She thought it was perfectly understandable, so long as he had assumed that the regime would not last and that, following its early collapse, the refugees who had gone abroad would come back and unite with the "inner émigrés" and the active resistance to rebuild the country. She added, no doubt correctly, that this stance became more and more unrealistic when Hitler succeeded in consolidating his power and ruled with an iron fist for the next twelve years, only to be defeated in World War II by the Allies. What men like Heuss had badly underestimated was the enormous dynamism of the Nazi movement and Hitler's policies. By 1940 they found themselves swept away by the rapid political and socioeconomic changes around them, many of which were so piecemeal that they were grasped only when it was too late. After the conquest of Poland and most of western and northern Europe by 1940, even non-Nazi conservatives like the famous historian Friedrich Meinecke were swept off their feet by the "splendid victories" of the Wehrmacht.[47] These military successes were the context in which many educated Germans, believing that the regime was now here to stay, very mistakenly came to believe that it needed to be given more intellectual substance during its quest to "reorder" Europe.[48]

Boveri next went beyond the prevalence of such impulses to discuss the shifting attitudes toward the Nazi regime when pressures on and risks to anti-Nazis grew exponentially from the mid-1930s onward and even more when a defeat of Nazi Germany appeared on the horizon from 1941–42 onward. Therefore, she mentioned the constant and increasing danger of being denounced by fellow-citizens or of stumbling into a Gestapo trap by coincidence. As she put it, the dividing line between inner emigration and collaboration was never sharply drawn for Germans who continued to be critical of Nazism after 1933. As sanctions against all kinds of "subversive" behaviors proliferated and became more draconian, "mere unenthusiastic standing aside," she wrote, could end "in a prison sentence or concentration camp internment."

Boveri's biography, like Jünger's, is thus another test case for gauging how far her attempt to specify inner emigration, which she claimed for herself during the Nazi period, in fact applied to her. As we will see, her case is raised here because it highlights the historian's dilemmas when operating in this peculiar territory. Dealing with Nazi ideologues and enthusiastic followers or, alternatively, with members of the active resistance and with rescuers of Jews and, third, with men like Jünger, is challenging enough but is still relatively easy in comparison to assessing Boveri's behavior. Indeed the question must be asked whether she in fact qualifies as an inner emigrant in light of her puzzling movements along the cooperation-resistance spectrum. Fortunately, we have an excellent biography of her by Heike Görtemaker on which the following analysis relies quite heavily.[49]

Born on 14 August 1900, Boveri fits neatly into the Generation of '32's temporal framework. Her father was an internationally renowned zoologist who held a chair at the University of Würzburg; her mother, Marcella Isabella O'Grady, had been born in the United States into a well-to-do family.[50] O'Grady attended Vassar College as an undergraduate and subsequently obtained her graduate training at MIT and Harvard. The couple were married in Boston and subsequently moved to Germany. Their daughter Margret grew up in a privileged bourgeois household but from early on had problems accepting her hyphenated German-American identity. She never warmed to her mother's elite education, though in a complex way she probably took her mother as a role model. Margret began her studies close to home, at Würzburg University, registering for a range of humanities and science subjects and believing that it was possible to build a bridge between what C. P. Snow called the Two Cultures. At the same time, she had come under the influence of the German Youth Movement and its romanticism while keeping her distance from American pragmatism and rationalism, as well as her mother's support of the traditions of constitutional democracy. She witnessed her father's close friendship with Wilhelm Röntgen, the inventor of the X-ray machine, and imbibed the two men's deep conviction that German culture was superior to all others.

By 1926 Margret decided that she was German rather than German-American. For a while she thought of a career in teaching, but she had developed a strong interest in international affairs.[51] Relocating to Berlin, she began to take courses at the university and the newly established HfP, where she studied with Heuss and Arnold Wolfers. Her teachers at Berlin University were the historians Otto Hoetzsch and Hermann Oncken. The latter eventually accepted her proposal to write her doctoral dissertation on pre-1914 British foreign policy. In domestic politics she disdained the narrow petty-bourgeois ideology and activism of the Nazis. When in 1933 the latter forced the closure of the HfP, Arnold Wolfers quickly found a position at Yale University and apparently urged Boveri to emigrate to the United States. But she refused to take a dim view of Germany's future under Hitler and tried to take advantage of the vacancies that Nazi anti-Semitism created in the media. She placed an ad in which she highlighted not only her doctorate but also her status as an "Aryan" and hoped to be taken on by the prestigious FZ.

While some of Margret's work was accepted for publication, it did not result in a permanent staff appointment. Although life was difficult, she was sufficiently well-heeled through her family to undertake a tour of North Africa by car. It may have been an escape from what she saw happening in Germany during the violent early months of the regime. By May 1933 she wrote to Emil Dovivat, the director of the German Institute of Journalism, that she felt depressed by the "many sad individual lives" around her and feared that something that had existed whole until now would become completely splintered. To Wolfers at Yale she confessed that every day had become torture to her. And yet she insisted that things could change only if those who did not allow themselves to be "synchronized" (*gleichgeschaltet*) by the regime stayed on and bore "this entire bitterness." In short, Boveri was not prepared to leave the country. In December 1933 she joined the synchronized Reichsverband Deutscher Schriftsteller (Reich Association of German Writers).[52]

By January 1934 Boveri took the view that whoever wanted to continue to live in Germany without closing their eyes and ears and, for that matter, all their senses (at which, she added, "most people are now becoming virtuosi"), would have to be clear about his or her attitude.[53] She felt that she could not join the Nazi Party or the opposition, adding, somewhat puzzlingly, that she had remained a "liberal" and that the system of government was hence irrelevant to her. Although the era of individualism was over in Boveri's view, she had remained an individual. By contrast, her friends and mentors, such as Heuss and the feminist Gertrud Bäumer, had grown "somehow old" and were merely interested in salvaging their vocation and inheritance in the face of the Nazi onslaught.

While Rudolf Kircher, the editor in chief of FZ, procrastinated about employing her, Boveri was finally picked up by Paul Scheffer, the editor in chief of the formerly Jewish-owned and liberal *Berliner Tageblatt* (BT).[54] There she developed a close professional relationship with Karl Korn, to whom she felt a special intellectual affinity. Like the FZ, the BT was a paper that Joseph Goebbels and his press watchdogs were prepared to keep on a long leash. The FZ continued to cover international news and was also widely read abroad as an organ that helped foreigners to read the tea leaves of Hitler's diplomacy and military strategy in the 1930s. Meanwhile, the BT targeted an educated readership in the German capital. Still, given the repressive political environment of the Third Reich, the paper's position and that of its editors remained precarious. In June 1935 Boveri was arrested out of the blue and her apartment searched.[55] She was interrogated and spent a frightening twenty-four hours in solitary confinement before she was released without being charged.

In previous months she had resolved that she would not allow herself to be thrown off balance like some of her colleagues, who, she learned, lived in a constant state of nervous anxiety. But after her experience in a Gestapo cellar she was, as she confessed later, also terrified. Of course it was known in general terms what happened to people who were arrested and not released shortly after. She appreciated that she had constantly done things that she should have kept away from, even if none of her activities amounted to serious crimes. Fortunately, not only was Boveri discharged, but also her books and papers that the Gestapo had carted off were returned to her, leaving her to wonder what the police had been hoping to find out. It seems they merely wanted to scare her, as dictatorships also tend to do.

After a longer trip abroad, Boveri returned to Berlin in July 1938 and found the political climate depressing.[56] Nor can she have missed the stepped-up persecution of the Jews during that year, culminating in the November Pogrom. Observing all this, she wanted to retreat to her parents' home away from the cauldron of Berlin to finish a book about her recent travels. When the BT was closed down in 1939, Boveri took the train to Frankfurt at the end of August to explore a more permanent position with FZ.[57] She spoke with Dolf Sternberger and Paul Sethe and was finally received by Erich Welter, the deputy editor in chief. In the end she was made the FZ correspondent for Scandinavia and moved to Stockholm. Her experience of living among the Swedes was not a good one. She heard and read a lot of criticism of her country, with which she still strongly identified. Her reporting therefore poses a further puzzle for the historian. How is one to interpret her intellectual transformations when war was looming and finally started in September 1939? While many of her colleagues had become increasingly critical and moved toward more firmly oppositional positions, Boveri became more collaborationist.

If she had been skeptical of Hitler's foreign policy in earlier years, by 1939 she had come to admire how he had, she believed, outmaneuvered the British in August 1939.[58] When the war broke out and the Wehrmacht destroyed Poland within a few weeks and in 1940 swiftly defeated France, Belgium, and the Netherlands after conquering Denmark and Norway, she was swept away by the more general wave of blind patriotism. In a letter of 31 December 1939 to her colleague Herbert Küsel, with whom she had had disagreements before, she rejected his criticisms of her political attitudes.[59] If one joins some cause, she wrote, one cannot exclude oneself. Otherwise one forfeited, if nothing else, the right to condemn those who are obliged to do things that are unsupportable. As far as morals were concerned, Boveri argued, she could take up critical positions, even if she might not be happy with everything she did or wrote.

In the view of her biographer, she was walking a very narrow mountain path with a precipice on either side that left Boveri uncertain about what to do. She was now being wooed by *Das Reich*, a paper increasingly under Goebbels's heel, but hesitated to sign up, preferring to keep FZ as her journalistic base.[60] Perhaps it was to get away from these political pressures that she accepted an appointment as the FZ correspondent in the United States. Still strongly pro-German, she decided to travel to the United States via Moscow and Japan. On her long journey by train, she registered the many Jewish refugees passing through Moscow.[61] When she took the boat across the Pacific, the American fellow-passengers with whom she shared her meals took her to task about Germany's inhuman policies toward Jews and about the conclusion of the Nazi-Soviet Pact. Apparently Boveri remained unmoved, so the table conversations eventually turned to other, less controversial, topics. Such encounters continued once she had settled in New York and began to report on developments in America. The basic thrust of her articles was to counter local criticisms of Nazi Germany with pieces on racism in the American South and the country's homogenized culture, which to her was so inferior to that of Europe.[62] If in her youth she had refused to identify with the society in which her mother had grown up, this rejection now surfaced with renewed vigor.

After the Japanese surprise attack on Pearl Harbor and Hitler's declaration of war against the United States, Boveri was briefly interned as an enemy alien but later allowed to return to Berlin via Lisbon.[63] However, her political stubbornness continued, even as she witnessed and experienced the deteriorating situation and the increasingly terroristic policies of the Hitler dictatorship. When, on Hitler's orders, the FZ was shut down in 1943, she lost her job and was ordered to join the Nazi *Völkischer Beobachter* (VB). At the same time she met with the diplomat Adam Trott zu Solz, though she did not know of his connections to the conservative resistance that was planning to kill Hitler.[64] She also spoke with armaments minister Albert Speer about the overall situation, as German cities were increasingly reduced to rubble by Allied carpet bombing. She was vexed by self-doubts as to whether she should continue to write, but her patriotism remained firm. After a short spell as a correspondent on the Iberian Peninsula, she returned once again to Berlin.

On a visit to Switzerland, Boveri heard what she still refused to believe: that Germany was losing the war. She was also exposed to the hatred of Germany in Switzerland, where rumors that had begun in the spring of 1944 about the deportation and murder of the Hungarian Jews circulated.[65] With the FZ no longer in existence, she wrote for *Das Reich*, by then an organ of Goebbels's propaganda campaigns of total war. Back in Berlin, she spent the weekends at her *dacha* on Lake Teplitz but was back in her city apartment during the week. When it suffered bomb damage, she organized the repairs and reproached colleagues who had decided to leave the city to avoid the constant air raids. She came to believe that the roofs of Berlin were good platforms from which to observe the nightly duels and fireworks between Allied planes and German anti-aircraft guns. Apparently without emotion, she looked at the dark skies, like Ernst Jünger had done from the roofs of occupied Paris when the Allies had gained air superiority.

There was no shift, like Jünger's, in Boveri's views toward more active resistance as the Third Reich fell apart. She now expected defeat, but her attitudes at this time raise the question of the credibility of her claim that she had spent the Third Reich in inner emigration. Her career in Nazi Germany certainly fits into the spectrum of collaboration and resistance that I outlined earlier. Yet, while some fellow-journalists fell completely silent or moved more closely toward the active resistance end of the spectrum, we have to place Boveri more toward the opposite end. She continued to defend her country and remained detached from the misery around her, refusing to confront the injustices and crimes committed before her eyes. Ultimately she presents an enigmatic case, probably exacerbated by difficulties to connect with others at a more personal level. The journalist Günther Gillessen, who knew her, called her "*menschenscheu*" (diffident).[66] Her case not only allows us to study the intellectual trajectory of a prominent journalist of the Generation of '32 but also helps locate the point at which to place inner emigrants along the spectrum of cooperation and resistance. Boveri, too, lived in the previously mentioned gray zone, but at the collaborationist end of the spectrum.

This leaves one last test case that shows how thin was the line that separated members of the Generation of '32 from outright collaboration. It is that of Henri Nannen, who after World War II became the editor in chief of the magazine *Der Stern* and whose postwar journalism will be discussed in chapter 4. How is one to assess his life and work before 1945?

Born on 25 December 1913, he grew up in a lower-middle-class family in the East Frisian town of Emden.[67] His father rose to the position of police commissar and, having entered the SPD after 1918, also served on the town council for a while. Although he left the Party in 1931 and claimed to have voted for the Nazi Party in the early 1930s, the Nazis dismissed him in 1934, together with some of his "unreliable" colleagues, under the terms of the Law for the Restitution of the Civil Service, as the Nazis cynically called it. It was the same law that also led to the unceremonious termination of many Jewish academics and Republican civil servants. It is also relevant that in the 1920s Henri fell in love with Cäcelie (Cilly) Windmüller, who hailed from a Jewish family. They remained inseparable until Henri, having passed his *Abitur*, moved to Munich in 1933 to study art and art history. He stayed in touch with Cilly until 1937, when she, increasingly terrified by Nazi persecution, moved to Palestine, where she stayed for the rest of her life. Her father, Adolf, who was a patriotic German, and his wife stayed in Emden and were deported to Łódź in Poland in 1940. It is not known where they eventually perished.

Nannen was at least once beaten up by Nazi hoodlums, apparently for his continued friendship with Cilly, and also had run-ins with the authorities. But, with the regime firmly in the saddle, he began to think of his future more opportunistically.[68] He wanted to write on art and eventually became an editor of an art magazine published by F. Bruckmann in Munich, to which he contributed some really terrible, fawning articles on Nazi art, but—as an admirer of Emil Nolde, Paul Klee, Max Beckmann, and Käthe Kollwitz who protested the removal of "degenerate" artists from museums—he joined the long lines of visitors to view the infamous "Degenerate Art" exhibition in Munich. All the while, the local Nazi organization in Emden kept an eye on him, and more than once did he get into trouble with the authorities. Consequently, he faced the dilemma of many Germans in the 1930s who did not want to "belong" and kept away from Party membership. But he also did not want to be an outsider, leave the country, or join the underground. As he put it after the war: "I was no resistance fighter, no hero," but also no Nazi.[69] To have at least some Nazi affiliations to show, he joined one or two cultural associations and also began to write a few radio features. He even thought of a career in film after he had met Leni Riefenstahl, who took an interest in this very tall and attractive young man. Hooked on air travel, he finally became a member of the Luftsportverband, which opened a door for him at the beginning of the war. In 1939 he was drafted into the Third Company of the Airforce News Regiment 3 to write articles for the Luftwaffe's propaganda arm. An energetic and experienced journalist, he was promoted quite fast and began to dream of a career as an air force officer.

By July 1940 Nannen was attached as a "technical writer" to a dive-bomber squadron, where he also trained as a gunner before he was sent to the Soviet Front for the next two years.[70] It was a dangerous life. He survived a crash landing and gained several decorations, including the Iron Cross 2nd Class and the "Crimea Shield." By the end of January 1944 he found himself on the Italian Front as part of an "active propaganda" detachment of the Army High Command 10.[71] With the German defenses against the Allies and Italian partisans crumbling, his unit retreated into the Alps, where, by the end of the war, he finally reached Oberfischbach in Bavaria, where his family had found refuge in a small farmhouse. Much more important than his movements during those final years and the people he worked with in psychological warfare is, in the current context, how he behaved as a war propagandist producing—as his biographer put it—"annihilation prose from the country of silence"[72] and how he coped with the mass murder that he saw or heard about, just as Jünger had done during his travels in the Caucasus. His anti-Nazism became stronger, but he did not turn into a resister in the face of the atrocities that he witnessed.

In November 1941 Nannen wrote a long letter to a friend that, if caught by the censors, would have gotten him into serious trouble. In it he describes the plight of Soviet POWs, who were being marched to the rear areas, totally starved and without even the ability to forage the bark from trees because it was frozen.[73] When these soldiers collapsed from exhaustion, they were shot on the spot and left lying at distances of a few meters between them. Nannen wrote that he was glad not to be with the infantry, whose soldiers saw such scenes all the time. Next he wrote about the behavior of the White Russian police in Minsk and Borisov, who had evacuated the ghettos. They had forced Jewish men, women, and children to dig their own graves. The Jews had to line up alongside their graves and, shot in rows, fell into the ditches. If one of them had not been killed, the next victim would tumble on top of him. Nannen wrote: "One officer told me of such a mass murder during which one Jew had gotten up again shouting: 'Dear Sir, please, good Sir, shoot me dead!' This is what happens to thousands, in Minsk alone it is supposed to have been seven thousand." He concluded with a sentence that reflected his total disorientation and the continuing search for scapegoats, in this case not the Jews as portrayed in Nazi propaganda, but Perfidious Albion: "Small wonder that even the oldest pilots are longing for the day when they can again fly against England." Referring to the many German graves that he had also seen, he hoped that he would not have to die in this way. To him it was a terrifying thought, as his death would come too soon and end a life that was still unshaped (*unfertig*). Indeed, he wrote, he had even been able to put some order into it. So, while Henri Nannen did survive, his earlier dissidence had evaporated, and it is doubtful that he can be placed inside the spectrum of inner emigration. At the same time, he never forgot what he had seen and heard in the East. What he could do after 1945 was to apply the lessons he had learned from his meandering life in the 1930s and early 1940s to his work as a journalist after the ordeal was finally over.

The Structure of *Journalists between Hitler and Adenauer*

Moving beyond the broad definitions of the Generation of '32 and inner resistance, which have now been explored more specifically with respect to Jünger, Boveri, and Nannen, the rest of this book deals with different journalists, who responded to the events in Germany differently than those just discussed. Chapter 1 deals with the life of Paul Sethe, born in 1901, from the time of his early journalism for a local paper in the Rhenish city of Solingen all the way to that of his work for major national newspapers in Frankfurt and Hamburg. The second chapter looks at the intellectual and political journey that Marion Countess Dönhoff, born in 1909, took from growing up on an East Prussian noble estate to becoming the revered editor in chief of *Die Zeit*. Chapter 3 provides a fresh analysis of Hans Zehrer, born in 1899, examining his journalism and politics at the end of the Weimar Republic. Ousted after the Nazi seizure of power, he "emigrated internally" to Sylt. He left the island after 1945, first as the editor in chief of *Allgemeines Sonntagsblatt*, founded by Bishop Hanns Lilje in Hanover, and later of *Die Welt* in Hamburg.

The fourth chapter then moves beyond the biographical and analyzes the broader context of the three journalists' work in Hamburg as one of several media centers in West Germany. But no less importantly and in line with the title of this study, I also explore the question of press freedom during the Adenauer years and of how far journalists were able to enjoy it. After all, the West German Basic Law guaranteed the freedom to write and speak, within the limits of the law, without fear of being arrested and imprisoned. The Nazi era, when these freedoms had been suppressed, was over. Yet there was another constraint: after the war the Federal Republic, having abolished Nazi regimentation of the press, adopted a capitalist economy. This meant that the ultimate freedom to publish rested with the publishers and owners of a particular paper. If the latter did not like a journalist's opinions, this employee either had to follow the owner's editorial and ideological-political guidelines or leave his or her job to express opinions in another paper sympathetic to, or tolerant of, these views. This is the legal background of the emergence of a free press in West Germany. Many journalists who had experienced "un-freedom" and brutal censorship during the Nazi period now found themselves in the era of the Cold War, with its new conformist pressures, which were personified by Chancellor Adenauer, for he in many ways embodied the autocratic style that continued to pervade post-1945 West German political culture. Accordingly, journalists were locked in another, though nonlethal, confrontation with both government and proprietors.

The problem that they faced was put into a nutshell when Sethe left *Die Welt* after disagreements with Axel Springer about the paper's politics. Press freedom, he averred, was in effect the freedom of some two hundred wealthy people who owned the country's press. He added bitterly that this was being expressed not by Karl Marx, but by Paul Sethe. Earlier on, as one of the editors of FAZ, he had also experienced the party-political pressures that Adenauer had exerted on the paper's owners. Bucerius, the publisher of *Die Zeit*, was different in this respect. He attended editorial meetings and argued with his editors about the layout and contents of a particular issue without insisting that his views must prevail. Not surprisingly, Sethe had finally found a place for his journalism, which he had not been able to practice since 1933. This is why the conclusion will raise some big and topical issues about the media and the evolution of contemporary society.

1

Paul Sethe

RESISTANCE AND ITS POST-HITLER MORAL AND JOURNALISTIC CONSEQUENCES

IT IS AGAINST the background of the larger issues of modern German history and journalism outlined in the introduction that I now turn to the first major figure of the Generation of '32: Paul Sethe. Because of his death in 1967, he is now largely forgotten, although he was one of the best-known journalists during the founding years of the Federal Republic. In the eyes of Gerd Bucerius, he was even the "grand old man" of West German journalism in his time.[1] At the same time, Sethe poses a considerable challenge to the historian who tries to evaluate his professional record because of his work as an editor of the *Ohligser Anzeiger und Tageblatt* (OA) until December 1933 and of *Frankfurter Zeitung* (FZ) between 1934 and 1943.[2] After all, whereas in the OA he expressed views that were critical of Hitler before 1933, the FZ's journalism occupied a rather more ambiguous position in the Third Reich. There is also the question of whether deep down in his heart he was more of a scholar of serious history than a journalist writing in the daily hustle and bustle of the newspaper business. As we will see, he wrote several big books on historical themes after 1945 and, judging from his output, putting pen to paper certainly seems to have come to him with ease. What he produced was generally thoughtful and aimed at a nonexpert educated readership.

Family and Academic Training

Paul Sethe was born on 12 December 1901 in Bochum, a major industrial city in the heart of the Ruhr coal and steel region, and grew up in a Protestant

Paul Sethe, 1901–1967. Photograph courtesy of Florian and Nathalie Scriba.

middle-class family.[3] His father was a publican and restaurant owner (*Gastwirt*) but also took up other business activities. There is little information on the son's youth. He went to primary school in Bochum between 1908 and 1911 and seems to have hoped to finish his secondary education with the *Abitur* certificate. However, writing to his sister Herta after 1945, he remarked in a slightly bitter tone: "Too bad that the Old Sethe did not send me to a gymnasium; [it is] a double pity that I did not study ancient history and embark upon an academic career."[4] But that happened at the end of World War I with its revolutionary turmoil, and his parents may have wanted him to get a more applied education rather than a classical one with ancient Greek and Latin.[5] So Paul was sent to an *Oberrealschule* at which he excelled sufficiently to be admitted to Bonn University in the spring of 1920. He moved on to the University of Münster in the autumn of 1921.

However, he had to take a leave of absence until the autumn of 1922, when he resumed his studies at Bonn, which continued until Easter 1923. It was a

time of rampant inflation and economic hardship, and he probably had to
interrupt his studies again for financial reasons. Both before and after his leave
he pursued a broad curriculum, majoring in history, German literature, and art
history, but also taking courses in philosophy, law, and economics. As inflation began to spin out of control, Sethe had to leave, apparently without an
academic qualification. He was fortunate enough to find a job on the editorial
staff of the OA, a small local paper published in one of the suburbs of Solingen,
the city of world-famous steel cutlery. He held this job until the end of 1933
and, starting as a political editor, eventually rose to the position of editor in
chief. Yet he never abandoned his plan to complete his studies, perhaps in the
hope of realizing his earlier dream of a university career. Reregistering at Bonn
University in the spring of 1930, he was accepted for a doctorate in history and
passed his oral exams at the end of January 1932. While his official sponsor was
Fritz Kern, a conservative full professor and medievalist, it was in fact Dr. Hans
Hallmann, a *Privatdozent* at Bonn, who "trained and shaped" his scholarship.[6]

In 1927 Hallmann had written a book on the naval ambitions of Wilhelm
II and the crisis in Anglo-German relations during 1895, after the Kaiser had
sent a telegram of support to Ohm Krueger, the leader of the Boers, the Dutch
settlers in South Africa who had rebelled against the British.[7] Subsequently,
Hallmann had begun another book on the origins of the German naval
buildup in the late 1890s.[8] Sethe was assigned a topic that had become a bone
of contention among naval historians after 1918, that of why the Royal Navy
had adopted the strategy of a wide blockade in the northern North Sea during World War I rather than confronting the Imperial Navy in a decisive battle
further south in the German Bight. His doctoral dissertation was published
in late 1932.[9] In it Sethe emerges as a perceptive analyst of a complex problem
of naval history. He clearly also had a knack for telling quite an intriguing
story—a skill that is also reflected in his later books on larger themes of German and European history.

The book is an illuminating study of perception and misperception in international diplomatic and military relations as well as of bureaucratic rivalries
among generals and admirals, based on a careful evaluation of three multi-
volume editions of official documents from Britain, Germany, and the United
States that appeared between 1919 and 1931.[10] Starting with a discussion of
the conflicts inside the Wilhelmine navy both before and during the war, the
issue was whether to deploy the German battle fleet against the Royal Navy
in the North Sea strait in 1914 in an all-out confrontation, as advocated by
Alfred von Tirpitz, the builder of the battleship fleet. By contrast, Hugo von

Pohl, the chief of the admiralty staff, in rightly judging the fleet to be inferior to the Royal Navy, refused to take a risk that he believed would lead to a disaster.[11] Pohl's passivity ironically derived from Tirpitz's earlier "risk theory," which Tirpitz had proclaimed in 1900[12] and was sharply criticized by Wolfgang Wegener, another naval officer, in the 1920s.[13] Sethe believed that the Wegener debate would rumble on for years, as indeed it did even beyond 1945 because Tirpitz's aims had been so far-reaching.[14] Ultimately, he was thwarted because the Royal Navy responded to the German threat by engaging Germany in a naval arms race that the Imperial Navy lost. Thus the German plan to shift the international balance of power was never realized.[15] Worse, the admirals began to live in the fear of a British pre-emptive strike such as the Danish fleet had experienced when it was "Copenhagened" in 1807.[16]

But this strike never came after the British Admiralty moved the fleet to the far North at Scapa Flow.[17] Critical of this particular strategy, some British planners wanted to lure Pohl out of the safety of Wilhelmshaven to do battle; they were stopped each time by Winston Churchill, the first lord of the Admiralty, and Admiral John Jellicoe.[18] The conflict within the Royal Navy was finally settled after the Gallipoli adventure, when Britain failed to occupy the Turkish Dardanelles. As Sethe put it succinctly:[19] "The Dardanelles became the grave of the big British offensive in the North Sea." Accordingly, Britain practiced its wide blockade while the war of attrition in the trenches of the Western Front continued. It was the appearance of fresh American troops in the spring of 1918 that finally brought Germany to its knees, leading to the fall of the Hohenzollern monarchy and to the German revolution of November 1918.[20]

Sethe's doctoral dissertation has been summarized here in some detail because it proved him to be a perceptive analyst of a major issue of the history of World War I. His conclusions said even more about the quality of a mind that had learned to differentiate, as would also been seen repeatedly in his later career as a journalist. For him the war was catastrophic not only for Germany, but also for Britain and her empire in that it prolonged the conflict beyond the time frame that might have made a British victory possible. Worse, the passions of total war pushed the country after 1918 into a "quite un-English peace of Versailles whose consequences today belong to the most onerous worries of the Empire."[21] Thinking of Britain's troubles in Ireland, Asia, and Africa, Sethe concluded that, while the wide blockade had helped defeat the German enemy, it had also inflicted life-threatening wounds on the victor "that were becoming fully visible only today," in 1932, while the prolongation of the war by three years had covered the rest of "Europe with a sea of blood and tears."

Writing for the *Ohligser Anzeiger* and the
Crisis of the Weimar Republic

Sethe's pessimistic conclusion must be linked to his journalism and politics at the end of the Weimar Republic. What were his perceptions at this time both of the fallout from the war and of the contemporary situation that he was facing at the OA? His papers contain at least a few leads, thanks to a letter that Hallmann wrote to Elfriede Sethe, Paul's widow, in 1967, shortly after her husband's death.[22] In it his former mentor quoted from two letters that Sethe had written to him in 1932. In the first he had expressed his deep gratitude that Hallmann had encouraged him to research his dissertation topic. He had, he said, received many insights in the seminars that he had taken with him. To him these hours had been important beyond his doctoral degree and had enabled him to transfer much of what he had learned to his work at his newspaper. What had also been instilled in him was the urge to look for what lay beneath the surface of historical events. His eyes had been sharpened to discern what was genuine and essential in this world, and the insights he had gained had also become a constant reminder of the responsibility he had before the country's history. What he had gleaned from these seminars would thenceforth guide his actions, even in a position as modest as the one he held in Solingen-Oligs. And last, but by no means least, there was his "longing for a new harmony between *Geist und Macht*" that Hallmann had spoken about in the concluding session of his seminar on Machiavelli and Fichte.

The other remark by Sethe in Hallmann's letter to his widow dates from June 1932 and was composed in rather a different key.[23] Sethe confessed that he no longer felt much joy in being a journalist. He was depressed about the overall situation in Germany. Even worse was his sense that the onslaught of the "masses in politics" since around 1930 had undermined the philosophical foundations of his journalism. While the major papers in the big cities might still be able to deal with pressures from all sides, pessimism was particularly widespread in the provinces. In fact, the freedom of the press seemed to him to be a worthless constitutional guarantee. A "revolution of the primitive" had set in and it subverted Solingen's politics and its newspapers. People, Sethe concluded, merely wanted to be confirmed in their beliefs. Whoever took a different point of view was deemed a traitor. What he wanted to see highlighted in the current intellectual crisis was the "destruction of the freedom of the press from below." Therefore, he had attended a public meeting of the Nazi Party at which he was threatened with three years of hard labor in a quarry. After that, so the warning continued, he would receive a more humane treatment than he in fact deserved. Those were the things that were being said in Solingen about him as a man "who is certainly not suspect of being an adherent of Marxist ideology." Some of his colleagues, he wrote, had already made their peace with Nazi politics in the hope of gaining recognition and job security. But then there was "the rest of us who do not dispose of so much Jewish[!] flexibility" and for whom "new conflicts of interest arise every day." Being no more than a journalistic auxiliary and a "servant of business," Sethe was evidently becoming more and more resigned. The alternative was to move to another career, which—he informed Hallmann—he was now pondering.

At the end of Sethe's letter, he advised his former mentor in Bonn not to encourage young people to go into journalism. It was not a career for "parsivals," as it was impossible to work in this machinery, even as a small cog, except with a strong dose of skepticism. Worse, in a future Third Reich, moral humiliations would be demanded of journalists; no one would be able to resist this for long and without damage to one's soul. How long, Sethe asked Hallmann, would it be before, living in a "total state," they would be writing the opposite of what was on their minds? Thinking of the academic position of his mentor, he asked how long it would take the universities to fall into line. If Sethe still harbored any of his earlier dreams of becoming a professional historian, it seems that he had given them up by force of circumstance. He remained a thoughtful journalist instead.

Assuming that Hallmann had correctly excerpted the passages from those two letters and that they accurately reflect their author's state of mind at this crucial juncture of German history, these words are significant in terms of both Sethe's attitudes toward the Nazi period and his post-1945 journalism. They will help us assess his subsequent work and actions during the Third Reich and the lessons he drew from those twelve years for his writing in West Germany.[24] While the significance of Sethe's letter of 1932 for an understanding of his postwar career can therefore hardly be overestimated, we must first ask where he stood at the end of the Weimar Republic and then during the early Nazi period.

Sethe's Politics and Journalism during 1932–1933

As far as Sethe's attitudes toward domestic politics in 1932–33 are concerned, his papers contain a letter from Curt Georgi, the former publisher of the OA and hence Sethe's boss in Solingen during a crucial period, until the latter left for Berlin and the FZ in 1934. Although the letter was written on 13 November 1945 and might hence be regarded as a *Persilschein* ("laundering certificate") to facilitate Sethe's smooth passage through the de-Nazification process,[25] both its scrappiness and the many details mentioned in it indicate that it represented more than a document for submission to a tribunal. These details had once led Georgi to conclude that during his years at the paper Sethe had been "pressured here in Solingen and Ohligs like no other editor."

He added that Sethe had raised his voice even before the Nazis' rise and that this had not been without consequences for him once Hitler had seized power. According to Georgi, it had been soon after January 1933 that he received a warning from the Nazi police president of nearby Wuppertal relating to an article that had appeared in the OA. In fact, Georgi as the publisher had also been sent a complaint from the regional bureau of the Reich Propaganda Office in Düsseldorf that criticized Sethe's negative attitude toward the Nazi Party. Finally, Georgi mentioned that two local Nazi leaders, Messrs. Keller and Potthoff, had visited him in order to voice their dissatisfaction with Sethe's editorial policies. When Georgi replied that Sethe, as the editor in chief, was responsible for what was published in the OA, the two asked for another meeting with both him and Sethe. This second meeting was held at Georgi's home on a Sunday morning, and at it Sethe did not cave in. Instead he admitted that he did not agree with the Party's aspirations. More specifically, he had objected to some Nazi speakers who, in line with the Party's quest for autarky, had called Solingen's export of goods "crazy," although it was well known how dependent the city was on exports.

Experiencing these pressures as the publisher, Georgi had come to realize that it had become impossible for Sethe to stay in his position. He quoted a passage from Sethe's farewell article of 30 December 1933, in which he had expressed his belief in a strong state that was rooted in the people and founded on the ideology of National Liberalism(!). Sethe added that Weimar's foreign minister, Gustav Stresemann, the "liberator of the Rhineland," had envisioned this kind of Germany. In a letter of recommendation that Georgi wrote on 31 December 1934 and quoted in his message of November 1945, Georgi remarked that "Dr. Sethe was the creator and guardian of the best liberal ideas"—noble in his attitudes as well as patriotic and social "in the best sense of the word."[26] This is therefore the point at which we must consider Georgi's postwar statements by evaluating the OA, at least for the crucial months before and after the Nazi seizure of power

Before examining Sethe's editorials, a few introductory remarks must be made about the locality. Solingen was a town in the southern Ruhr region that was famous for its steel-processing industries. This meant that many of its manual workers supported the Metal Workers' Union and the Social Democrats as well as the Communist Party. But there was also a sizeable middle-class population in which the Protestants among them tended to vote for the German People's Party (DVP) or the German Nationalist People's Party (DNVP), while the Catholics tended to support the Center Party, a party that cut across class lines and attracted support from Catholic industrial workers and the middle classes. With workers in the majority, local politics had veered toward the extreme left during the Weimar years. Ohligs, a suburb to the West of the city center, was more middle-class and, although OA marketed itself as "non-partisan,"[27] its readership appears to have been largely bourgeois and Protestant.

Starting with the Reichstag elections of May 1924, table 1 shows the percentages garnered by the major parties in Solingen to 1933:[28] The least remarkable fact emerging from these percentages relates to the well-known supposition that the rise of the Nazis came primarily at the expense of the Protestant middle-class parties, with the left-liberal DDP and Gustav Stresemann's DVP virtually disappearing by 1932. The right-wing DNVP under Alfred Hugenberg had its percentages cut back by more than half in 1930, but then held fairly steady, and this can also be said of the Catholic Center Party. The more surprising figures relate to the SPD, which, unlike in the rest of the Reich and following its greatest success in 1928, hovered at around 10 percent in Solingen. Meanwhile, the Communists received between 38 and 41 percent and invariably more than the NSDAP at the height of its electoral success in 1932.[29] It was only in the elections of 5 March 1933, when the Communists had already been banned following the Reichstag Fire at the end of February and Social Democrats and trade unionists had also been arrested and terrorized, that the right-wing parties, including the Nazis, surpassed the Communist Party (KPD). The final vote was 52,743 for the Right as against the Left's 42,674,[30] which led the OA to proclaim on 6 March 1933 that "Greater Solingen is no longer red."[31] Up to that point, the Solingen city government had been dominated by the Communists.

Sethe tailored his "non-partisan" but in effect middle-class paper to this larger sociopolitical environment. Each issue had, apart from sections with local, regional, and national news, pages that covered features for women, gardening, industry and commerce, and sports, as well as a full page with photos on a variety of topics, emulating the *Illustrierte* that had appeared in the 1920s. The OA did not carry many ads and therefore seems to have relied on subscriptions from a loyal local readership, and perhaps also on subsidies from

TABLE 1. Reichstag Election Results, 1924–1933

Party	5/1924	5/1928	9/1930	7/1932	11/1932	3/1933
KPD	32.8	38.1	40.4	38.4	41.4	35.9
SPD	14.8	16.1	11.0	9.5	9.6	8.9
Ztr	10.8	9.1	8.5	8.8	8.9	8.3
DDP	6.2	4.2	3.2	0.5	0.5	0.4
DVP	22.9	12.1	1.1	4.7	1.1	1.8
DNVP	8.0	6.8	3.0	3.4	3.5	4.2
NSDAP	0.7	0.4	16.3	34.0	30.1	38.2

Source: Compiled from a table of Solingen election results in Ralf Stremmel, *Politische Plakate, 1870–1960* (Solingen, 1992), 176.

Note: KPD = Communist Party; SPD = Social Democratic Party; Ztr = (Catholic) Center Party; DDP = Deutsche Demokratische Partei; DVP = German People's Party; DNVP = German Nationalist People's Party; NSDAP = National Socialist German Workers' Party.

local businesses. Some of its readers were Protestants and inclined toward the DVP. But, as we will see in a moment, the editor in chief evidently also had his Catholic middle-class readership in mind, as his 1932–33 lead articles contained frequent references to the policies and strategies of the Center Party.[32] Thus, in looking back to the years of the Reich chancellorship of Heinrich Brüning, a Catholic, Sethe praised Brüning's struggle to obtain a moratorium on German reparation payments, even if it had been his successor, Franz von Papen, another Catholic, who benefited from it.

Brüning had been hoping that his austerity program at home was beginning to turn the depressed economy around. But, as Sethe wrote retrospectively on 31 December 1932, what the former Reich chancellor had not sufficiently considered had been the impoverishment of millions of Germans and the impact this had on their voting behavior.[33] At the same time, he now felt much satisfaction that the presidential elections of spring 1932 had made certain that "a party leader [i.e., Hitler] will not be [the] dictator [of Germany] as long as the Marshal [i.e., Reich president Hindenburg] is alive." Sethe was, of course, proven wrong in March 1933, when Hitler was given dictatorial powers by the Reichstag through the passage of the Enabling Act, but at this earlier point he was evidently still opposed to Hitler as Reich chancellor. It was only in February 1933 that the OA temporarily changed its tune, though on the assumption that Hindenburg remained in possession of his presidential powers under Article 48 of the Weimar Constitution, which would have enabled him to dismiss Hitler at any time, just as he had sacked Brüning and Papen and was about to do with Reich chancellor Kurt von Schleicher.[34]

Leaping from the end of Brüning's chancellorship to the period after Papen's demise, Sethe was very clear on 26 November 1932 that he was firmly opposed to the rumored reinstallation of Papen: "We would consider [this] a national calamity," he wrote. Instead he claimed that many opponents of Nazism were by then prepared "to give a chance to the leader of the rightist movement [Hitler] to which he has had a claim for some time," though still dependent on Hindenburg's Article 48 powers. Knowing that there had been negotiations between Hitler and Hindenburg about this, Sethe believed in December 1932 that their failure had been due to errors and misunderstandings.[35] This latest deadlock now led the OA editor in chief to set his hopes on Schleicher, whom he viewed as the "wizard" behind the scenes. Since the general had been the "father" of earlier chancellorships, Sethe wanted him to come to the "front" and to take the chancellorship himself. It would, he thought, bring "tangible relief of the political atmosphere" and reinforce the "first weak signs of an economic recovery." He also hoped that there would be no fresh elections and that it would be possible for Schleicher to create an axis of support that extended from the trade unions and the SPD to the Strasser wing of the Nazi Party, sidelining Hitler and Goebbels, who were dead opposed to entering such a coalition under Schleicher's chancellorship.[36] However, when Hitler confronted Gregor Strasser about his straying from the Party's line, the latter resigned from his powerful position at the head of the Nazi organization. Schleicher's strategy collapsed.

Although Sethe was not privy to all these backstage maneuvers, his editorial of 10 December 1932 reported that Strasser had implored Hitler to accept Hindenburg's offer of a seat in the Cabinet, adding that Hitler had to choose between Strasser and "radicals" like Joseph Goebbels, who urged the "Führer" to wait. Sethe concluded that the "force of the inner self-cleansing of the [Nazi] Party" would "determine its future fate." But with Strasser ousted and Schleicher's strategy undermined, Sethe expected, rather dejectedly, yet another national election. The campaigning for it would "accelerate the radicalization of the National Socialists" and deepen the chasm "between Hitler and Hindenburg." To him it was self-evident that renewed political turmoil would trigger a "fresh [and] serious disturbance of the economy." Frustrated by these developments, he urged Schleicher to act rather than trying indirectly to build bridges to all sides. "What," he asked, "does Herr von Schleicher want?" He did not want Hitler to be the sole ruler but rather aimed at the establishment of a "strong and socially just state." Clearly out of the loop, Sethe warned Schleicher against shattering the Nazi Party, as this would deprive him of a pillar for his bridge-building. But it also began to dawn on Sethe that Hitler, with Strasser out of the way, was setting his sights on gaining a huge victory in the Lippe-Detmold regional elections in mid-January and, buoyed by it, would continue to pursue his struggle to gain the Reich chancellorship thereafter. Focused on Schleicher, the OA editor was completely surprised when it became known that Papen had met with Hitler at the residence of a Cologne banker, Kurt von Schroeder.[37]

On 7 January 1933, Sethe thought that all he could do was to warn Papen that he was skating on thin ice. At the same time, Sethe raised his voice in favor of the local export-oriented steel industry, knowing that there were strong tendencies in the Nazi Party to promote autarky and independence from the world market. But instead of openly taking issue with Hitler's economic policies, he criticized the circle of intellectuals who were writing about a "closed trading state" and a retreat to the European Continent in *Die Tat*.[38] He mocked them for believing in "miracles" and juxtaposed their advocacy of self-sufficiency with his own demand to restore Germany's links with the world economy.

On 10 January, Sethe mentioned the appearance of "heavy industry" on the scene. While Hitler was laying his bets on a breakthrough in the Lippe-Detmold elections as the path to the chancellorship, the hostility of the managers of heavy industry in the Ruhr region toward Schleicher was now "the most important event of recent weeks." These managers were, Sethe wrote, suspicious of Schleicher because he was a "social general." To Sethe it was odd that industry, fearful of "socialism," would launch its offensive on the side, as he put it, of the "National Socialist German Workers Party," whose economic program, moreover, contained much foggy thinking that industry should be wary of. In fact, when it came to work-creation programs, the Nazis had gone beyond what Günther Gereke, Schleicher's labor minister, had initiated. In short, at least those Nazis who read the OA are unlikely to have been pleased by Sethe's views on current commercial as well as social policies. He was not one of them.

Following the Lippe elections, in which the NSDAP took 39.5 percent of the vote, with 6.1 percent for the DNVP, but also 30.1 percent for the SPD and 11.2 percent for the Communists,[39] it was clear to Sethe that it was merely a matter of time before Hindenburg would use his presidential powers to dismiss Schleicher. The OA editor in chief now hoped that Hindenburg and Hitler, as he put it on 17 January, would "act jointly in order finally to effect a fortification of our domestic conditions." The crucial question now was whether Schleicher—who was still chancellor—was prepared to govern in a "really authoritarian" fashion without—and, in extremis, even against—the Reichstag or would hand "the chancellor's office to Hitler." The first solution, Sethe argued on 24 January, might be described as a "state emergency." The second would facilitate the reconstitution of a parliamentary majority consisting of the NSDAP, the DNVP, the DVP, and the Center Party. But it was unlikely that such a coalition would ever come about, not least because the DVP and the Center Party were opposed to the Nazis' struggle against what their propaganda called the "chimera of exports." Sethe finally speculated that, as a third solution, Hitler might form a minority government that would comply with the letter of the Constitution and would not require its breach, as envisaged under a "state emergency"model. No less important, the second approach to the crisis would resolve "the problem of involving the National Socialists in the leadership of the state" by drawing them into government responsibility. Although Sethe did not abandon Schleicher completely, on 26 January he seems to have tilted toward a broad coalition of rightist parties with Hitler as chancellor. Still, the participation of the Center Party remained the big question for Sethe, and since Hindenburg was not presented with a government majority in the Reichstag, he was unlikely to appoint Hitler to lead it.

Maneuvering in the Early Days of the Nazi Regime

On 30 January Sethe published another piece on this topic titled "From Schleicher to Hitler?" knowing that Schleicher had been forced to resign and that a Papen-Hitler deal with Hugenberg had meanwhile been struck behind the scenes. Apparently disappointed, Sethe reproached the former chancellor for having sat tight in the face of his enemies' attacks. Relying blindly and erroneously on Papen's "loyalty," Schleicher had partly caused his own downfall. Sethe also mentioned the resistance of the large-scale landowners, spearheaded by Elard von Oldenburg-Januschau, and the *Osthilfe* scandal of the government's giving subsidies to the agrarians that had suddenly hit the headlines.[40] Nominating Hitler as chancellor therefore seemed to him the only alternative that Hindenburg, despite "his most serious doubts" about the Nazi leader, was now bent on adopting, if the latter offered him "a majority" in the Reichstag. Such a majority could be put together only if the Center Party was included. But the Catholics had instead again "implored" the president "to govern within the framework of the Constitution," leading Sethe to ask how any solution would be possible unless the Center Party "finally consents to a Hitler chancellorship." This was surely worth a "few sacrifices" to the Nazis.

The fact that Hitler, Papen, and Hugenberg presented Hindenburg with a cabinet without the Catholics and hence did not have a parliamentary majority took Sethe once more by surprise. After all, as he editorialized on 31 January under the heading "Decision after Detours," the three politicians had been at loggerheads just a few weeks ago and had now demonstrated a "turnability (*Wendigkeit*)" that "no one had expected." Still, it must have been reassuring to Sethe that Papen had been put at Hitler's side as vice chancellor and "very proactive watchdog." Since the OA editor in chief also pointed to conservative General Werner von Blomberg as Reichswehr minister and to the extensive economic powers that Hugenberg had been given, it seems that Sethe had bought into an argument that was widespread among conserva tives at this moment: that, while Hitler had provided Hindenburg with the longed-for mass base, the former had been safely "caged" by the conservative ministers in his Cabinet, all of whom adhered to an authoritarian solution to the crisis and thus aimed to perpetuate the presidential regime under Article 48.[41]

The problem was that Hugenberg, keen to form a coalition government with Hitler, had agreed to the latter's demand to hold national elections and had done so literally at the last minute, just before they were led into Hindenburg's chambers to be sworn in. It was one of those puzzling contingencies that spurred the Yale historian Henry A. Turner to postulate that it was not major structural factors that brought Hitler to power but intrigues and last-minute deals.[42] It was also a decision that Hugenberg's DNVP came to regret very quickly. Encouraged by the Lippe-Detmold success, Hitler clearly hoped that he could obtain the absolute majority in another Reich election and—as Sethe put it on 2 February—to achieve "complete, almost dictatorial freedom of action" once he could revive the defunct parliamentary pillar of the Constitution that would make him independent of Hindenburg's rule under Article 48. Sethe was skeptical that this would happen, although he knew that Goebbels, as the newly appointed propaganda minister, now had both the Party's and the Reich's official public relations apparatus at his disposal. No less important, Wilhelm Frick, now minister of the interior, was in charge of the police, supported by Hermann Goering at the head of the Prussian police. In pursuit of gaining an absolute majority in the national elections, now set for 5 March, the Nazis inundated the country with their propaganda. Meanwhile, Frick and Goering reinforced the ordinary police with an "auxiliary police" made up of Nazi Storm Troopers who were given armbands marked "*Hilfspolizei*" as the sign of their official legitimation.[43]

Thenceforth and up to these elections, Sethe and his paper focused on two themes. They reported on attempts by the DNVP, the DVP, and the (Protestant) Christlich-Soziale Volksdienst[44] to form a united electoral front of the bourgeois parties. This effort failed rather ignominiously. Worse, the Center Party refused even to tolerate a minority Hitler government, as Sethe reported on 10 and 18 February. At the same time, the OA carried quite a few items about street fighting and its many casualties in Solingen as well as in other parts of the country. What it did not mention was the radical change in the balance of power and the role that the auxiliary police were now playing in the violent politics that erupted after the Nazi seizure of power by unleashing a reign of terror and intimidation on the Left. Communists, Social Democrats, and trade unionists were arrested, roughed up, and arbitrarily imprisoned. On 21 March the OA carried an item on "the first concentration camp" that had been built in Munich[-Dachau], with a capacity of "5000 human beings," and reported that the Communist leaders among the inmates would not be "released for the time being."[45] In other words, it was wellknown even in Solingen how the Left was being treated during those early weeks of lawlessness, covertly promoted by the new government and condoned by many virulently anti-"Marxist" middle-class voters who believed that the Left deserved what they now were getting. On 21 February, it is true, Sethe reported approvingly that Frick had spoken up against an official ban on the KPD but mentioned the possibility that Communist Reichstag deputies might have their seats rescinded. Evidently opposed to Nazi radicalism, he averred that the KPD had been playing an important role in the disintegration of "Marxism" and was hence indispensable to a victory of the Right. Outright bans should be left for a later phase. While the OA continued to report in a less than enthusiastic vein, were these remarks veiled hints of disapproval on the part of the paper?

On 28 February the OA reported that the Reichstag building had gone up in flames and that the fire had been started by a Dutch communist and "unkown comrades." Historians have debated endlessly whether Marinus van der Lubbe, who was arrested clambering around the building, could have set the fire on his own or whether it had been secretly laid by the Nazi Storm Troopers.[46] Whoever the arsonists were, the incident was a godsend to the Hitler government. Goebbels exploited to the full the widespread middle-class fears of Communism, and Hindenburg was persuaded to sign an emergency decree stepping up the witch-hunt against the Left and outlawing the KPD. In his editorial of 1 March Sethe wrote that it looked increasingly as if the Communist Reichstag faction would be prevented from voting. In that case, the "large parliamentary majority for the government" would be secured. This, in turn, would open the door to a "far-reaching enabling act" giving the government "unlimited freedom of action." Consequently, it was only *"force majeure* that could bend the straight line of a path, calculated for the next four years," to produce what the German people were dreaming of: a genuine internal peace. As for the opponents, the new regime would, "where possible, take away from them all freedoms of action." However, Sethe realized that, apart from excluding the Communists from a Reichstag vote, a two-thirds majority was needed for the passage of an enabling act. He now urged the Center Party not to reject cooperation out of hand. Still, the first step for him was to fight the Communists as the "decisive way out of the political and constitutional difficulty" of securing a two-thirds majority.

On 4 March, the day before the election, Sethe again demanded the destruction of Communism "with unlimited violence." He thought the SPD was paralyzed and the Center Party would also be pulled down because it had failed to see the signs of the hour. If the elections did not yield a majority for what was a NSDAP/DNVP coalition, the government would have to resort to measures "very close to the limit of the Constitution." But Sethe also warned of the misuse of power by "overheated radicals" in the Nazi Party and reiterated his hope that the electorate would open the door to a stable right-wing majority. On 5 March the voters heeded the call of the Cabinet to the extent that they gave the NSDAP 43.9 percent (17,277 million votes) and Hugenberg's DNVP/Kampfbund Schwarz-Weiss-Rot 8.0 percent (3,137 million), putting the coalition just over the threshold at 51.9 percent.[47]

Writing on 6 March, Sethe announced that Weimar democracy had been overthrown at the polls and that the (plainly rigged) elections had mobilized some five million new voters, including former supporters of the Left. "We do not deny," he continued, "that we had wished for a stronger performance of Hitler's bourgeois partners." But as the coalition had won over 50 percent of the votes, there would be no more votes of no confidence in the Reichstag, and industry would at last be free of "the pressure of eternal political crises." While the Center Party had held onto its voters, it had lost—Sethe noted—its former key position. He did not know whether the defeated parties would undergo an "inner cleansing" process. Moreover, the new beginning would not happen without some "harshness." But—and here Sethe again voiced some unease over recent developments—he hoped that the "German force of freedom of conscience would not be buried." This was his concern and admonition, but also "our hope and our faith" in the process for the "welfare of the nation."

It is even more difficult to penetrate Sethe's thoughts during the following weeks, when Hitler quickly established his rule and on 23 March succeeded in getting the required two-thirds majority for the Enabling Act (including the Center Party deputies), which gave him full executive powers, independent of the Reichstag and of Hindenburg, to transform the Weimar political system into a one-party dictatorship within less than a year. On the one hand, it was not beneath Sethe to write a nasty article on 9 March about Otto Braun, the former Social Democrat prime minister of Prussia, whom he accused of a "terrible spiritual failure" that was responsible for his dismissal.[48] But he also mentioned that there were circles on the Left who were hoping for a renaissance. If this were to occur, it would have to be with another set of leaders who spoke the "language of the folk." On the following day he devoted a longer piece to the theme of "Workers and the State." To him, the solution was not to destroy the working-class organizations, as the government was in fact beginning to do. These organizations should not be "fought and raped" but rather "won over and convinced." Nor was Sethe prepared to contemplate the formation of an axis between the trade unions and the military, as *Die Tat* had advocated in 1932.[49] Such a path would quickly result in a "democratic-parliamentary watering down and paralysis." The way forward was instead to "depoliticize" the unions and to integrate them into the state as "true professional associations." In other words, Sethe was contemplating an authoritarian corporatism (*Ständestaat*) that had been bandied about by the non-Nazi Right for some time. He also recommended the training of young people at this time of mass unemployment and mentioned that the DINTA Institute had done useful preparatory work in this respect.[50]

There was no comment from the editor in chief on the passage of the Enabling Act, but on 24 March the OA published extracts from Social Democrat leader Otto Wels's courageous and memorable speech in the Reichstag in which he had opposed the act's ratification and then reprinted beneath it Hitler's mendacious rebuttal. On 18 March the OA carried an article by Werner Schwant titled "Hindenburg and Frederick the Great," and it published an unsigned piece on 27 March, the Day of Potsdam, after Hindenburg (in full Imperial uniform and with his many decorations) and Hitler (with top hat) had appeared on 21 March for a very hypocritical celebration of unity between the Old Germany and the New. On 1 April Sethe wrote on the occasion of Bismarck's birthday, ending with the hope that the "spirit" of the Reich's founder would hover over the new Reich. In a similar vein, on 4 April he marked the town-hall inauguration of Dr. Helmut Otto, the new Nazi mayor of Solingen, as a "celebration of the folk." Focusing on the four Social Democrat deputies who sat silently, he reminded his readers that the SPD had once been the great hope of Solingen. He admitted that they had fought a few upright and honest fights, even if it had now become difficult to exercise individual fairness when assessing their work. Many, whose political records showed they were "innocent," were now suffering together with others who bore a measure of guilt for their earlier actions. He remarked that the Center Party had at least pledged its local cooperation. The task was therefore to build a bridge to the opponents of yesterday. He concluded that Otto was a man of action who would remove the debris of the past.

Such pronouncements must be juxtaposed against statements that could be read as more direct criticisms of the Hitler regime. As early as 7 February, Sethe had warned against the danger that bans against the press posed and said that they amounted to arbitrariness and the assertion of political advantage. Censorship merely generated insecurity. If there had to be some censorship, it should be applied with moderation. Nor was it sufficient to impose bans against one side and merely to admonish and educate the other side. While the government had to show a strong hand against one half and had to hit agitators without mercy, though also with justice, the other half of the opponents should not be suppressed. By 1 April Sethe's tone had changed even more markedly. He mentioned that the resignation of Ernst Oberfohren from the DNVP leadership in protest against the growing *Gleichschaltung* by the Nazis had been a "clarion call."[51] Among members of the DNVP and also the Stahlhelm veterans association there was a growing recognition of the "seriousness of the situation." He now unceremoniously identified both Papen and Hugenberg as "defeated" men in Hitler's Cabinet. This, Sethe continued, had also had an impact on the freedom of the press, which looked increasingly "like a fossil from a past liberal era." There was talk that the population no longer wanted this freedom, and this made him wonder if "the development in Germany would take the same path as in Italy," where Mussolini had come to power in 1922 via a coalition before gradually transforming the country into a Fascist dictatorship. Not knowing the future, Sethe did not feel he should resort to any prophesies. However, he found that "at this moment the tendency is increasingly toward handing over all power to one party," which he clearly did not welcome.

If Sethe had stuck his neck out a bit too far with his references to the Oberfohren crisis and his assessment of press freedom, he counterbalanced these statements on 10 April with an editorial titled "The March into the Unitary

State," in which he welcomed this development as a decision of the National Revolution advanced by "deed." Referring to the recently promulgated law, he wrote that Prussia and the other federal states of the Weimar Republic had been integrated so as to enable all Germans to feel "only as Germans" in the future. Classes, he added, had disappeared, but the estates had remained and the fight against corruption had set in. Finally, on 20 April, Sethe celebrated Hitler's 44th birthday by heaping praise on "the great unifier of the nation." Less a "popular tribune" than a statesman, he said, the Nazi leader had allegedly ended the fragmentation of the country into small states. The OA editor in chief wished that God might give Hitler a long life and—rather more ambiguously—hoped that the day would come when "the freely elected duke of the German folk can stand with it [the folk] on free grounds."

If it seems clear from Sethe's editorial policies and articles in the OA during the final months of the Weimar Republic that he was opposed to Hitler and his movement and, as Georgi had written in his letter of November 1945, not only tried to uphold the international and domestic positions of Gustav Stresemann and the DVP but also preferred a Schleicher Solution in December 1932 and January 1933. Meanwhile, millions of other Germans were also looking for a way out of the crisis that would transform the parliamentary Weimar republic into an authoritarian system.[52] When a Hitler Solution emerged on 30 January, Sethe seems to have hoped for a reconstitution of a parliamentary majority government after the elections of 5 March while turning his eyes away from the brutal methods by which the new government was being established. Indeed, when Hitler succeeded in getting a dictatorial mandate through the Enabling Act, Sethe, like so many other educated Germans, kept silent. Only toward the end of March and in April did he express his worries about the development, but couched them as indirect criticisms of an emergent "unitary state."

There seems to be a connection here with the previously mentioned letter that he had written to Hallmann in June 1932, in which he had hinted that running a local paper had become more and more difficult. Despite some initial optimism, the Nazi seizure of power made things much worse and did so at breakneck speed not only for all known anti-Nazis but also for more cautious journalists like Sethe. Goebbels's Propaganda Ministry was quickly consolidated, and the press became "synchronized" and censored. Next to the Goebbels empire, the Reich Press Chamber was created on 22 September 1933 to become yet another organization interfering with editorial policy.[53] The emergence of a welter of Nazi organizations resulted in interdepartmental rivalries and confusion. It seems, therefore, that the developments relating to Sethe's increasing difficulties with the Nazi regime, which Georgi recalled shortly after 1945, are likely to have taken place later in 1933, when the Nazi Party and the Hitler regime were in firm control at all levels of government.

Like many other Germans, Sethe could have made things easier for himself by joining the NSDAP. But he refused and did so up to 1945. It is possible that an unsigned article in OA that appeared on 20 March 1933 under the title of "*Märzlinge*," referring to those who had rushed to sign up for membership in March 1933, was written or at least inspired by him. It argued that those who stayed away were not "the worst lot." On the contrary, "the new state needed their energies and experiences even then, or rather even more so now." The author even expressed some sympathy for these outsiders if they could not "reconcile their character or sense of decency with an entry into the dominant party," which was quite risk-free and promised success but also raised suspicions. Given the pressures that the regional Nazi functionaries were putting on Sethe ever more bluntly by the autumn of 1933, it is not surprising that he came to feel that his situation would be better at one of the papers published in the big cities. Consequently, he began to look for employment in Berlin or Frankfurt, especially after yet another decree of 4 October 1933 had made him as the editor in chief of OA "responsible for total content and attitude of the textual part" of the paper.[54] Its Paragraph 14 required him not to publish material likely to weaken the strength of the Reich at home or abroad, and he was also not to undermine the nation's cohesion, military preparations, economy, or culture.

It is not clear how, after leaving the paper at the end of December 1933, he landed a job with the prestigious FZ that he held from 1934 onward. Apparently someone in Frankfurt had followed Sethe's journalism and political skills and had paved the way for his move.[55] It also seems that it was around this time that he got married to Elfriede Wiebel, who hailed from a large family in the small town of Halver, just west of Lüdenscheid and close to the Wupper River valley. Sethe was certainly correct that the FZ was able to provide him with more shelter from the regime than a provincial paper. The positions that the prestigious daily had taken up in 1932 had been very critical of Nazism and Hitler. Thus Rudolf Kircher, its editor in chief, had opined in early November 1932 that next to Communism, the NSDAP was the main danger to the Weimar Republic.[56] On 1 January 1933 the FZ reported that Hitler's offensive had been stopped and that Schleicher was now launching a counteroffensive. A bit later it played down the electoral success that Hitler had won in Lippe-Detmold on 17 January; it was not representative of the national picture. On 30 January

Benno Reifenberg, another editor, expressed doubts as to whether Hitler had in the past shown the human qualifications required for high office.[57] No less courageously, he reminded FZ readers of the supporting telegram that the Nazi leader had sent to two members of the Brownshirts who had been arrested for the brutal murder of a communist at Potempa.[58]

By early February, the FZ had apparently moved, if reluctantly, to an acceptance of the idea of "taming" Hitler by surrounding him in his Cabinet with conservative non-Nazi ministers. The assumption was that the Party would soon demonstrate its lack of competence once it had been given responsibility. Two days after Hitler's nomination to the chancellorship, the paper judged his policies to be a mixture of dilettantism and passion that did not leave much room for hope. It also expressed fears in light of the lawless repression to which the Storm Troopers and the "auxiliary police" especially had been resorting. For the moment, these reservations were quite strong, but as the regime consolidated its power with amazing speed, Kircher's relationship with Nazism as editor in chief became more chameleonlike, and he began to talk about the need to build bridges. If there was any resistance, it was "between the lines." As Günther Gillessen put it in his history of the FZ, ingenuity, cunning, ambiguity, and audacity—but also caution, timidity, humiliation, deception and self-deception, and also silence—became widespread.[59] As Sethe remembered after 1945, "One of the most gifted" colleagues at the paper "never wrote a single line in order not to expose himself to the danger of helping Hitler."[60] Only loyal Nazi journalists scribbled away, never mincing their words.

Serving as Editor at *Frankfurter Zeitung*

While newspapers such as VB and the regional Party press remained tightly supervised by their masters and the Goebbels ministry, the FZ, with Kircher's growing willingness to be flexible, was kept on a longer leash and marketed as Germany's national voice on the international stage.[61] This meant that it reported on events and developments abroad and in its news coverage and editorials did not spread blatant Nazi propaganda. The calculation was that foreign readers would continue to rely on it for information on what was happening inside the Third Reich and on statements about Hitler's foreign policy. A closer look behind the façade reveals a story that reflects the complexities of political and economic relations in the early years of the Third Reich. In the summer of 1934, the FZ had been "Aryanized" when the Jewish owners of the paper announced that, over their protest, control had been handed over to a group of minority shareholders.[62] This group was led by Hermann Hummel, who was a member of the board of the I. G. Farben chemical trust. It was the power and influence that I. G. Farben could bring to bear that gave the FZ additional room for maneuver. Although the corporation was deeply involved in Hitler's rearmament program, its board was for a long time hesitant to fully buy into his policies of creating an autarkic economic bloc. Rather it continued to view itself as a company that was involved in the world market, as it had been before 1933.[63]

It is also significant that Wendelin Hecht, the top executive of the I. G. Farben–owned Imprimatur Ltd., managed, with the help of Farben CEO Carl Bosch, to return the FZ to profitability.[64] When Sethe joined its staff, the paper printed some 64,000 copies, up from 55,000 in 1932, far behind the much higher circulation of the VB and other Nazi papers; by 1939, the FZ made a profit of a little over a million marks. This meant that the FZ was indeed widely read abroad and that another campaign in 1937 to increase foreign subscriptions, in the course of which American Jews and non-Jews received a circular urging them to subscribe, had been quite successful.

Klaus Hildebrand and other scholars have shown how Hitler tried hard to reassure the British and Americans that his policies toward them were not aggressively expansionist and did not challenge their interests around the globe.[65] If Germany had any territorial claims, they were all in the East and, as far as the Soviet Union was concerned, ultimately aimed at confronting and destroying Bolshevism.

The FZ's long leash did not imply, however, that Hitler and Goebbels were personally happy to have a newspaper to burnish the regime's reputation abroad. In 1986 Gillessen published his history of the FZ in the Third Reich, titled *Auf verlorenem Posten* (On a lost outpost).[66] But whether or not this title accurately described the FZ's predicament, its editors certainly resisted relentless government pressure on them regarding its news coverage and commentaries. Under the censors' watchful eyes, this was their constant struggle. Jewish editors were kept on until 1935, despite growing anti-Semitic persecution. Benno Reifenberg, who in January 1933 had written that Hitler was not qualified to assume the chancellorship and who, being "half-Jewish" under the 1935 Nuremberg Laws, was in the Nazis' crosshairs as deputy editor in chief,[67] was replaced by Erich Welter in November 1935. Welter, no confirmed Nazi either, had held the same position at *Vossische Zeitung* in 1932 and stayed in his new post until the beginning of the war.[68] With like-minded colleagues such as Dolf Sternberger, Jürgen Tern, Fritz Saenger, and Sethe at his side, Reifenberg was able to remain an editor until Goebbels ordered the closing of the FZ in August 1943. In the meantime, direct censorship increased. In 1934 an issue was suppressed that had discussed a speech given by vice chancellor Papen at Marburg that had been very critical of Hitler. Up to 1937, the paper received some fifty admonitions but was able to continue. In April 1939 it experienced a major change when Hitler was given the paper and its printing house, the Frankfurter Societäts-Druckerei, as a gift on the occasion of his 50th birthday.[69]

Up to that point, Sethe seems to have benefited from the privileged position that the FZ enjoyed. While it was no doubt known that he had been critical of Nazism before 1933 and had been having "problems" with the local Nazi organizations in Solingen in 1933, he used the FZ's greater license to report on political and military news. According to Gillessen, he remained a Bismarckian National Liberal. Occasionally Sethe was sent on special assignments, as in December 1936, when a plebiscite was held in the Saarland on whether its people wanted to join Germany.[70] In his report he decribed the Saarlanders' choice as a dilemma. If they had stayed under the administration of the League of Nations, they would have been "German" without living inside Germany under National Socialism, though in the shadow of France, which to Sethe implied a "colonial regime."

With his background in military history and strategy, Sethe became the main correspondent during the German campaign against France in the spring of 1940, regularly filing, in Gillessen's words, "big articles on the course of the operations, above all the fast pincer and encirclement movements in the direction of the Channel Coast."[71] These reports, Gillessen continued, could be transmitted in the language of the military expert. However, "Sethe occasionally found it difficult to preserve the necessary balance and, in his admiration of the military feats, not to be swayed by 'fiery victory songs'" that his colleagues ridiculed. While Gillessen's criticisms must be taken seriously, it is also true that there were many other non-Nazi Germans in 1940 who got carried away by the "splendid victories" of the Wehrmacht.[72] Yet Sethe's military journalism may also have been a protection, because it enabled him to avoid direct political comment. It is likely that this kind of reporting extolling military successes continued up to the autumn of 1941. Although Sethe was also an editor of other articles and acted as a *Gegenleser* (critical checker), for example, of the pieces that Richard Sorge filed from Tokyo while being a secret Soviet agent,[73] there are a number of articles from 1941–43 that are initialed with either "se" or "P.S."[74]

In some of these articles Sethe he posed as a historian who drew on the past in order to make indirect comparisons with the current situation. Thus, on 16 November 1941, Sethe recalled the dismissal of Colonel General Hans von Seeckt, the chief of the Weimar Reichswehr, in October 1926[75] and then related the incident to a conflict that was raging within the Reichswehr between conservatives like Seeckt and a number of junior officers, Schleicher among them, who wanted to modernize the army.[76] Sethe argued that Seeckt had "helped preserve the spirit of the old [Prusso-German] army" and maintain it in the difficult circumstances of Weimar politics "until it could be united with the forms of the new age," namely, Hitler's introduction of the draft in 1935. Was this an underhand statement that this spirit was being violated by Germany's barbaric warfare in the occupied territories of the Soviet Union?[77] Or was Sethe trying to highlight the professional expertise of the generals against the widely known constant interference by Hitler?

A few weeks later, on 25 December 1941, Sethe went all the way back to the Middle Ages, but in conclusion reminded his readers of the large amounts of blood that had been "needlessly" spilled during the current campaign against the Red Army. In his view, it had been the excesses of empire that had ultimately undermined the entire medieval Reich edifice and had caused its demise. His next piece, signed "P.S." and dated 16 March 1942, might similarly be taken as an implicit criticism of the setbacks that the Wehrmacht had meanwhile suffered in the Soviet Union. It was a review of a book on Russia's Ivan the Terrible. Sethe concluded that this study was a "most valuable contribution to the image of Ivan that is familiar to us." While this book neatly supported the image that Nazi propaganda was spreading about Stalin, could it also be read as a reference to Hitler's tyranny?

Writing on the occasion of the Easter holidays of 1942, Sethe averred that one could now gauge from hindsight "what this [past] winter has meant for us." It had been tough at the front, but the population back home had also found it difficult to cope with the war's trials and tribulations. There had been deep snow and long periods of freezing temperatures. Having to work under severe stress during the winter months, according to Sethe, the population had been subjected to many hard tests. People back home knew that their fathers, sons, and brothers were fighting brutal defensive battles, while snow fell in ever-new waves. This struggle, Sethe continued, had frequently been compared with that of Frederick the Great, for whom the Seven Years' War of the eighteenth century had not been about "victory or defeat, but about victory or total collapse." What was at stake in 1942 in Sethe's mind was complete annihilation. Millions would die a horrible death, while the survivors would live on in unimaginable poverty. Achieving victory would not, as in Frederick's time, merely secure the existence of the state but also meant "the final rise to a high goal."

As Gillessen pointed out at the end of his long quote from Sethe's Easter article, "none of these lines were freely written."[78] Rather they amounted to compromises that had to be struck between the author and those who held political power, just as many compromises were regularly made between an author and his *Gegenleser*. By 1942 Sethe had stopped talking of great Wehrmacht victories. Instead he wrote about how much the war in the East had begun to cost Germany. To quote Gillessen again, the reader noticed "from the changed form in which the argument was presented that Hitler had no choice."[79] There was no plan, no policy any more, and "the fate of the nation was now chained to the catastrophic course" of Hitler's *va banque*.

However, it was not just the distressing new realities of the war that Sethe now laid out to FZ readers. As before, he went back into history and tried to connect the medieval German Reich with the tasks of the future. In an article titled "The Other Reich" of 15 August 1942, "se" argued that, while Hitler had united the Germans, the country had by then become the power that would reorder Europe. This job, he warned, could not be done by merely relying on military victories. Great responsibilities were lying ahead and, he wrote, "when we meet this obligation vis-à-vis the whole of Europe, we'll be able to say that we have been true to the millennial tradition" of the ancient Reich. Again the question arises of how this article is to be interpreted. Was it a plea to move ahead with the highly centralized New European Order that Hitler and other Nazis were discussing at this time?[80] Or was it a reminder of the decentralized medieval entity that had been dissolved when the Habsburg emperor Francis II relinquished the crown of the Holy Roman Empire in August 1806?

In December 1942, "se" took up yet another historical theme when he criticized the eminent historian Theodor Mommsen because he had never given up his struggle against Bismarck. This time, and evidently in a veiled reference to Hitler, Sethe warned against making the mistake of believing that the "man of genial scientific cognition" was also the man who had a broad understanding of political reality. Two days later, Sethe had in his crosshairs the historian Heinrich von Sybel (1817–95), who had once defined himself as a "liberal conservative," but Sethe then wondered what one was to make of Sybel's view of the role of the state in society. Although he did not offer much detail, he knew that Sybel's work also related to mid-nineteenth-century arguments about liberalism and notions of state-building. To quote the historian Georg Iggers, Sybel's "law of freedom" demanded that the state act in "the sense and the interest of freedom."[81] Is this what Sethe had in mind when he chose this topic at the end of 1942?

Sethe's papers finally contain a presumably uncensored letter to a former colleague dated 13 December 1942. He predicted that this "*orloog*" would be long, difficult, and full of risks.[82] He was not too worried about the North African campaign and believed that, while dangers might threaten Germany from that region at a later date, this conflict could be won even without Italy. Instead it was "the Russians" that preoccupied him most of all. As before, the task was to defeat the Soviets before the Americans had reached their full strength. Given the manifest Soviet capacity to produce in the Urals, he did not wish to rely on "uncertain hopes" that Stalin would be defeated once the Wehrmacht had reached the Archangel-Astrachan line. Ultimately, Sethe concluded his letter, it had in any case become a "matter of faith" rather than of "mathematical calculation." It seems, therefore, that, with the German defeat at Stalingrad around the corner, Sethe doubted the Wehrmacht's invincibility in the East—a view that he could express only in private, while his articles in the FZ continued to contain references to supposedly instructive historical case studies.

Thus, on 16 December 1942 Sethe commemorated the bicentennial of the birthday of field marshal Gebhard von Blücher, calling him a "great soldier and perfect knight, close to the heart of the people." When Blücher had helped to defeat Napoleon at Waterloo, the victory had been due not just to raw violence but also to the "higher ethical forces" that the field marshal embodied. No less significant, the FZ journalist and historian put him on a par with Prussia's great reformers Heinrich Friedrich vom Stein and Wilhelm von Humboldt. Sethe next chose the first day of 1943 to remember another date. This time "se" went back to the ancient Greeks, examining the "greatness and downfall of Themistocles on the two-thousandth anniversary of his death." Finally, in August 1943 he returned to the French Revolution, reminding his readers of the demise of the Gironde and the chaotic conditions in France 150 years before. Are these historical examples to be seen as Sethe's exhortations to FZ readers to hold out and not give up their belief in an ultimate German victory? Was he, though never a member of the NSDAP, a collaborator, as was asserted after 1945?[83] Or are his articles indications of a shift from a passive anti-Nazism within the spectrum of the gray zone toward a preparedness to join the active resistance, as will be discussed in a moment?

Shortly thereafter, the paper that had been the poster child of Goebbels's pseudointernationalism was shut down. Not surprisingly, it had incurred the wrath not only of the propaganda minister but also of dyed-in-the-wool Nazi journalists and the ideological watchdogs in the many and constantly prolif-erating Nazi agencies concerned with agitation and thought control. After the many prior admonitions and endless censorship,[84] there were finally attacks in *Das Schwarze Korps*, the paper of Heinrich Himmler's SS, under the editorship of Gunter d'Alquen, that bluntly accused the FZ of voicing the anti-Hitler posi-tions of liberals and Jews.[85] Tellingly, D'Alquen also charged FZ journalists for having become masters of the method of hiding their messages between the lines, in his view a method designed to undermine the regime.

When the shutdown became public, the *New York Times* wrote rather dis-dainfully on 28 August 1943 that the FZ had "in recent years . . . merely [had] the framework of its old conservative-democratic self, as it displayed toned-down Nazism in well-chosen nomenclature and tasteful typography."[86] The article also referred to the FZ's tensions with *Das Schwarze Korps*, which "had the habit of taking the Frankfurt daily's worldliness to task and accusing its editors of 'playing ball with the foreigners.'" Another factor in the decision to scrap the paper was no doubt the fact that the country had by then been put on a footing of total war. Influencing international opinion was no longer impor-tant. Rallying the Germans was now the main task of Goebbels's propaganda machine. Increasingly, scarce newsprint came to be allocated to the Nazi press and its ever-more-desperate sloganeering. Hitler also weighed in. In a speech made at the end of that fateful year, he railed, in his customary way, at Jews and Marxists before commenting on the "left-bourgeois *Frankfurter Zeitung*."[87] A group of FZ journalists was ordered to join the staff of the VB. Appreciat-ing what this meant, Sethe evaded the transfer, at least for the time being.[88] Although his moves in the spring of 1944 are not entirely clear, it seems that he succeeded in obtaining an attachment to the propaganda department that the Wehrmacht had been running independently of the Goebbels ministry and the SS indoctrination bureaucracy.[89] This shelter enabled him to delay his move to the VB in Berlin and to stay in Frankfurt. His papers contain clip-pings of articles that he wrote for the *Frankfurter Anzeiger* (FA) in the winter of 1943–44, again with a focus on historical themes.[90]

On 25 November 1943, "p.s." returned to the Wilhelmine period, claiming that the Hohenzollern monarchy had failed to forge a "genuine *Volksgemein-schaft*" and hence "an indestructible alliance between" the bourgeoisie and the workers, which had led to the kaiser's downfall. Now such an alliance was more necessary than ever, as Germany's enemies were threatening both the property of the former and the labor of the latter. Such a union, Sethe added, was the best guarantee that, unlike in 1918, the existence and the greatness of the German Reich could be salvaged. When the anniversary of the founding of the Bismarckian empire came up on 18 January, Sethe reminded his readers that the German national state had been established in 1871, but that it had been an elite project. Regrettably, "millions of Germans [had] remained excluded" from the settlement, and only a few politicians had tried to integrate those multitudes. Then came Sethe's inevitable reference to the situation of 1944. Things had now changed, he claimed, and this in itself was "sufficient cause to be thankful when we remember 18 January 1871 today." Unable to let go, "P.S." traced the onerous and tearful steps taken along the path toward the founding of Imperial Germany.

In summarizing Sethe's articles in FZ and FA, the earlier question remains: What is one to make of his writings during World War II? Was he a *Schreibmaschinentäter* (typewriting perpetrator), the term that the journalist Otto Köhler used as the title of his postwar book on journalism in the Third Reich?[91] But does this term fully capture what Sethe wanted to say when, time and again, he focused on historical events and personalities? It may be that the shift toward his pessimistic articles occurred well before the winter of 1941–42. In 1968, Karl-Heinz Janssen, his colleague at *Die Zeit*, edited a collection of Sethe's portraits of prominent politicians, officers, and clergymen, as well as profiles of West Germany's parties, complemented by articles that he had published on major topics of West German politics.[92] When this volume was reviewed in the left-liberal *Frankfurter Rundschau*,[93] its author reported that Sethe had visited Poland after the German occupation of 1939 and returned shaken and sickened by what he had seen and heard about SS activities in the rear areas, where tens of thousands of Polish intellectuals, priests, Jews, and politicians had been murdered.[94] Later Sethe undertook a tour to the Nazi-occupied Soviet Union, where he was attached to the headquarters of Field Marshal Gerd Rundstedt.[95] He found the time there, as he put it rather neutrally, "intensely interesting"; but it would be very surprising to know that he did not hear anything about what was going on in the rear areas of Rundstedt's Army Group South, which was supposed to conquer the Ukraine and the Caucasus.[96]

This raises the question of what Sethe learned during the summer or autumn of 1941 about the atrocities that the SS's Einsatzgruppe C committed in the Ukraine. Aware of what was going on in the rear areas, Rundstedt had issued an order on 24 September 1941 that Wehrmacht soldiers were prohibited from participating in mass shootings of Jews. Nor were they to be bystanders and to take photos of what they were witnessing. Did Sethe, as a good journalist and military historian, ask Rundstedt's staff not merely operational questions but also questions about mass killings, especially after what he had learned in Poland in 1939? Although he did not mention his tour in the article, when he wrote about Rundstedt in 1948, he was certainly highly critical of the field marshal's wartime record.[97] A few years earlier, in November 1945, Sethe had made a similar point in a letter to Georgi.[98] He had, he admitted, been a witness to many good qualities of the Prussian nobility on Rundstedt's staff. But Rundstedt was the "liveliest example" of the blind obedience of many officers. Hitler may have been a plebeian beside this aristocrat who despised National Socialism. Yet in decisive moments, the field marshal had always stood to ramrod attention before his leader.[99]

On the Fringes of the Anti-Nazi Resistance

In the late spring of 1944, Sethe could no longer avoid his move to Berlin. Arriving at the VB's office there, he was immediately viewed with suspicion by the other editors, not least because he was still not a member of the Party. According to a later testimony, his Nazi co-workers refused to sit at the same table with him during the lunch hour. [100] However, being on the FZ editorial board, with expertise in military history, Sethe had become acquainted with men in the armed forces and the foreign office charged with press relations. One of them seems to have been Harro Schulze-Boysen, who had joined the Air Force Ministry in 1934. Subsequently, he was on the editorial staff of the ministry's magazine, *Luftwehr*. In May 1939 he was promoted to lieutenant and transferred to the information bureau of the intelligence department of the Luftwaffe, where he had access to foreign and military news. From the start, Schulze-Boysen had been a determined opponent of the regime, and as he learned more about its abject criminality, he became one of the leaders of the Red Orchestra resistance group.[101] He regularly corresponded with his parents about the evolving political and military situation but never told them about his resistance activities. The members of the group were caught as early as 1942, tried, and quietly executed. Among them was Mildred Harnack, the American wife of Arvid, the son of the famous theologian and church historian Adolf von Harnack.

As Harro Schulz-Boysen's father, a retired navy captain, had merely been told about his son's death, he tried to find out more after the war and turned to

Sethe.[102] He had heard that Sethe had been sent to attend the trials against the men charged with the failed attempt on Hitler's life in July 1944 and wondered if he also had information on the Red Orchestra trials. Sethe had not, but he asked his colleague Brigitte Beer, adding that any information was important not only for Schulze-Boysen senior "but also for our country" in that it would be "a fresh proof that Hitler and Germany were not the same." When the Red Orchestra later became the subject of public and scholarly interest because it had been in touch with Leopold Trepper, a Polish communist who was the resident of the Soviet intelligence organization in Brussels, Sethe came to believe that the Schulze-Boysen/Harnack group had been a Soviet spy cell engaged in treasonous activities, although Harro's father "passionately" disputed this.[103] Instead he claimed that his son had admitted this connection only in order to remove his father and brother from suspicion, and thus save them from prosecution. While this correspondence provides a glimpse of what it meant to face a lethal dictatorship and the anguish of the families of active resisters, recent research has shown that the Berlin group tried to smuggle military documents to Switzerland and to make them available to the British secret service before the arrival of Allan Dulles as the resident of the American Office of Strategic Services (OSS), and that its main aim was to bring down the Nazi dictatorship at whatever cost.[104]

Sethe also seems to have been in touch with Rudolf von Scheliha, a diplomat who, after the invasion of Poland, had been put in charge of the information department of the German Foreign Office.[105] His assignment was to read the international press and to counter Allied propaganda about the atrocities that the Nazi regime was committing in Poland. A determined opponent of the regime, Scheliha may have mentioned what was happening in Poland. Perhaps he even facilitated the trip that Sethe undertook to that country in 1939 and from which he returned deeply shaken.[106]

It is against this background and that of what he had written between the lines in the FZ that his acquaintance with Fritz Bartsch becomes relevant. There is quite detailed information about this relationship in a letter that Bartsch wrote to Elfriede Sethe in June 1967, shortly after her husband's sudden death.[107] The two men had been colleagues at the FZ. But in 1941 Bartsch had left the paper to work in a variety of jobs. It was not until after the FZ had been shut down in 1943 that they met again in Berlin. Bartsch was by then the executive director of *Tele*, an illustrated European magazine published in Sweden. He lived in the "Esplanad," one of Berlin's best hotels, where in the spring of 1944 the two men regularly met for an evening meal after

Sethe's move from Frankfurt. The waiter gave them special privileges, including a bottle of wine to wash down the bad news that they were exchanging. In return, Bartsch passed on copies of American, British, and French papers to the hotel manager, who eagerly devoured the news in them, notwithstanding the fact that reading or listening to foreign news was strictly forbidden. By this time there were heavy penalties for such "subversive" and "defeatist" activities.

When the news of the failed coup of 20 July reached the two men, Bartsch recalled that this was "a bad day for us, especially for me." To begin with, they could not meet at the usual time, since "the area had been cordoned off." When Sethe finally made it by 8 p.m., they did not really enjoy their meal. The reason for their gloom was that Bartsch had repeatedly met with Carl Goerdeler, the former mayor of Leipzig and one of the key conspirators, when the latter visited Berlin. As late as 14 July, Bartsch had walked with Goerdeler along the platform of Berlin's Anhalter Station before the latter boarded the train to Leipzig. No doubt the Gestapo watched the two men, with Goerdeler remarking as they said good-bye: "Bartsch, times are serious. I hope we'll see each other again in good health."

They didn't. Goerdeler first went into hiding, but he was soon found, tried in Roland Freisler's People's Court, and executed. Meanwhile, Bartsch had gone on a frantic trip first to Leipzig and then to Vienna. The Gestapo finally arrested him among the beer-swilling crowds in Munich's Hofbräuhaus. He was taken back to Berlin and interrogated about Goerdeler. He rightly feared being hauled before Freisler's People's Court and condemned to death as the other defendants had been. Upon learning of his friend's predicament, Sethe tried to save him. He contacted Günter Lohse, one of his many "joint good acquaintances," who had been working in the Foreign Ministry's press department since 1940 and—though "half-Jewish"—had survived the war in his job.[108] In the summer of 1944, Sethe, who must have known Lohse from his time at the FZ, asked if something could be done to ensure that Bartsch would not be called upon to testify before the People's Court, incriminating not only Goerdeler but also himself. Lohse approached one of the state prosecutors involved in the investigations, whereupon this man agreed to pull out Bartsch's file and to mark it with a note "to be submitted after the war." He apparently also prevented the suspect's harsh interrogation. After all, other suspects had collapsed under torture, and no one knew anyone's capacity to withstand extreme pain until it was actually tested—no doubt yet another apt observation on the dangers of living under Nazism. Bartsch remained imprisoned until the end of the war but survived to tell his story, concluding with the words: "Perhaps it is thanks to Paul Sethe and Loose [sic!, with an apology that he may have misspelled the name] that I am still alive."

When meeting over their dinners at Esplanad before the failed coup, Bartsch and Sethe had also discussed the fact that Goerdeler had been drawing up lists with names of people to be nominated to various positions after a successful regime change. It is from Bartsch that Sethe learned that he had been mentioned as the editor in chief of the national newspaper that Goerdeler wanted to establish after a successful coup. Years after the war, Sethe claimed that it was as good as a done deal to appoint him.[109] But this story, too, is more complicated:[110] Although Sethe had been trying to meet Goerdeler, the conversation between him and Goerdeler never took place, and the offer was therefore never formally made. In a letter to his sister of 1 February 1946, Sethe wrote that he did not want to join VB in Berlin after the end of the FZ.[111] Instead he stayed in Frankfurt writing for the FA. He then added: "If only I had not done this!," meaning that he might have met Bartsch earlier, and the latter might "have given in to my pressure for a conversation with Goerdeler." Of course it is impossible to imagine what would have happened in that case. But, as Sethe confessed, "I would myself probably feel better—if I were still alive." Returning to this topic a little later, he added that he had not made the connection (*eingelassen*) with Goerdeler because the latter did not have the time or the inclination to talk.[112] Consequently, Bartsch had merely told Goerdeler about Sethe. Sethe wrote that the notion that "I was supposed to become his 'editor in chief,' I learned only in Frankfurt in August [1945]. Nevertheless, I am more proud of this than I would have been [as the recipient of one of the highest decorations] a *Ritterkreuz*."

Sethe returned to this subject in his early postwar correspondence with his former FZ colleague, Brigitte Beer, in which he again corrected rumors about his relationship with Goerdeler.[113] He could see now why Goerdeler was reluctant to meet with him. With the Gestapo on his heels, Goerdeler did not want to endanger more people than were already on his appointment list for the post-coup reconstruction. Sethe concluded his message to Beer by stressing that he had not been involved in the 20 July uprising. Nor had his name appeared on any of Goerdeler's lists, so he had avoided arrest, which in turn had enabled him to save Bartsch. Life under Hitler had many contingencies. Yet, as an opponent of Nazism, Sethe continued to agonize over his role, the more so since his FZ colleagues had been gossiping about him. It also seems that Sethe did not completely keep his mouth shut until he was warned that he was endangering Bartsch.[114] As he put it in the letter to his sister of

February 1946:[115] "And the mea culpa is on my mind and oppresses me very much. It is a terrible feeling of shame."

Flight from Berlin and Early Postwar
Search for a New Career

The end of the war also confronted Sethe with the question of a greater guilt when Allied officers began to interrogate him about his career and his work for the FZ. He had made a wise decision to leave Berlin before the arrival of the Red Army, although his former colleague Margaret Boveri criticized him for abandoning the ship. But it is highly likely that he would have been arrested by the Russians and deported as some of his colleagues were if he had stayed. Later he learned that one of them had been sent off to the Urals for tree-logging work, where he had perished in November 1947. Among other victims was the Berlin correspondent of the *Magdeburgische Zeitung*, an "old party friend of mine" from the DVP and an "icy enemy" of Nazism.[116] What apparently had gotten this colleague into trouble was that his name had appeared on invitation lists of the Ribbentrop Foreign Ministry, causing Sethe to wonder if his name had also been found in those files. As late as February 1945, he had attended a reception there together with Fritz Saenger, then the head of the German News Agency (DNB). The two had been sitting at the back of the room near the fireplace making scathing remarks about Ribbentrop, who "comported himself like a complete ass." Not surprisingly, Sethe thought that his name on such a list would have sent him to Siberia, too.

Having left Berlin, Sethe got as far as Oebisfelde, a small town to the east of Wolfsburg, right on the border between the Soviet and the British Zones of Occupation, where he stayed from 11 April until 6 June 1945 and was interrogated by the Americans. He quickly realized how difficult it was to explain "to a foreigner that I came from the *Völkischer Beobachter* and yet hated Hitler." His experiences with his interrogators were rather mixed. When one of the American officers asked him about the FZ, his answers were admittedly somewhat rude and impatient.[117] But another interrogation went well and ended with the officer's remark that Sethe's answers were believable. In the next interview it was apparently accepted as logical when the journalist said, "I had helped Hitler's opponents."[118] He added: "But I was not logical, but Prussian," and this meant that "at age 43" he could not shed the skin of his earlier socialization. Finally he was once more interviewed about the FZ, this time for three hours. The questioning was "merciless," and Sethe became rather depressed. Yet the officer let him go. More interrogations followed, apparently also by the French, who were very hostile. Overall, what irked Sethe most about these experiences was the feeling of being put into the same group as "this [Nazi] scum, to remove which I would not have shied away from as a great risk, if only I had seen an opportunity to do so."[119]

After Sethe had been released to make his way to his wife and daughter back home in Halver, he became increasingly critical of Allied policies. On 2 June 1946 he noted that the tribunals let the guilty ones go, while the innocent were being punished. He felt that the country was still quite a long way away from the rule of fairness and reason and had lost faith in sensible Allied government.[120] On another occasion he noted a point that is significant in terms of his subsequent struggle in the 1950s:[121] "Nor do I know, whether it is right, that a democracy starts with not granting press freedom." Still, at this point he was hopeful that, given time, this would "perhaps" change and that the public's attitude would become more critical of the hypocrisy, rumor-mongering, and distrust of information policy in light of experiences under Nazism. By December 1947 he had not only turned against the reeducation efforts of the Allies but also proved very stubborn when it came to defending long-held views that he thought were not National Socialist. In the letter to his sister of 1 February 1946, in which he used the term "mea culpa" and dissociated himself from the Nazi "scum," he mentioned that in Oebisfelde he had met a "captain" who had been more reasonable than the Germans.[122] Sethe had confessed to him that, since there had been war, he would have been obliged to support the constituted government "if the existence of the Reich had been at stake." Listening to his case, the captain, while not approving of Sethe's statement, had nonetheless accepted it as a "fair" explanation of his motives and was hence not angry: "What you have written against Britain would interest us only if it were written in a base tone." Asked who those "other" Germans were, Sethe mentioned the conductor Wilhelm "Furtwaengler, and Goerdeler and Beck and [Kurt] Schumacher," the latter of whom had emerged as a physical wreck from eleven years in a concentration camp to become the admired leader of the postwar SPD.[123]

Sethe's encounters with Allied officers show how difficult it was for a man with his political past to clarify what was in his own mind about where he stood after 1945 and also to explain to members of the victorious powers the complexities of life under a dictatorship as well as his own twisted path within it. As he wrote on 1 February 1946, "If the Americans" made generalized judgments, it merely proved "once more" that they were born into another society and did not understand the conditions of life under Hitler.[124]

Sethe's papers, furthermore, contain rambling accounts of his thoughts and feelings in early 1946 about those conditions and Germany's future.[125] If there was an identifiable guilt, it had been incurred during the tumultuous months of 1933:[126] "This is when it began. Everything else thereafter was enforced (*Zwang*)." Looking back on his meetings with Bartsch, Sethe insisted again that he had never wanted to join the VB. But he also lapsed into a more rebellious mood and turned against a denial of Germany's earlier history, the castigation of Frederick the Great, and the "lie of our war guilt [of] 1914." He was of course familiar with this charge from the debates among historians of the 1920s, but "the veracity of these claims does not seem to me to have become greater in the meantime." In 1943, though not before, he continued, he should have voiced his attitudes "much more loudly"—only to backpeddle in the next sentence by stating that "one does not attack the flag in [the moment of] misfortune—[this was] the fatal mistake of the [Weimar] Republic in 1919." Nor was it right, in the hour of misfortune, to "spit on the nation's past."[127] Of course the older generation would have to examine this past, which might then have to be revised. However, he demanded that this be done reverently and felt some of the pain that would befall one "who detaches himself from the great names of the past."[128]

On 15 November 1945, Sethe doubted that Germany would get back on its feet.[129] He did not think it possible that the country would be able to free itself on its own from the crimes of the past. He spoke of "our collective guilt" and believed that "we have forfeited the right to freedom." After all, the hatred and disdain of the rest of the world was now "limitless." Nor was it possible to argue that "these feelings were not deserved." Of course there were innocent people, but "as a whole we have deserved our terrible fate." In March of 1946 he vacillated between feelings of "heavy guilt" and hope for a "coming generation," but then concluded that he had "learned to be resigned."[130] There were moments when these feelings were so strong that, he wrote, "it would have been better, if one atomic bomb had hit Germany." Indeed his pessimism was "insuperable":[131] "Yes, if only the 20 July [1944] had succeeded." On 6 June 1946, he even went so far as to ask: "Why does one not send the Germans to Auschwitz? We are beyond salvation."[132] Going again to the theater in Düsseldorf, he was overcome by "a melancholic longing for the countless occasions" when he had been there with his wife Elfriede.[133] Yet, he asked, "When will this [normal life] come back? Oh, this Hitler!"

Turning from the past to a dispiriting present, Sethe's anti-Communism remained as strong as it had been when he involved himself in the case of Harro Schulze-Boysen or, for that matter, remembered the KPD in Solingen during the Weimar years.[134] He disliked the agitation that focused on the "Fascists" and "coldly" aimed at leaving its opponents "leaderless."[135] As to the Russians, he did not think that they would start a war for which they were not prepared during the next "5–10 years."[136] To be sure, should Soviet tanks ever roll westward, he believed, they would not stop until they had reached Lisbon. But he thought it most likely that the Russians would seek compromises and "perhaps" would even join a zonal agreement with the Western occupying powers. However much this notion anticipated his attitudes toward the East in the 1950s, Sethe remained distrustful of the KPD and the Soviet Union.

Instead he seems at first to have leaned toward the SPD and saw Kurt Schumacher as one of its key figures until he attended one of his speeches in March 1946, which left him with ambivalent feelings.[137] The SPD leader spoke in convoluted prose that produced no more than weak applause. There was little enthusiasm in the hall, and Sethe left with the impression that the working class was completely exhausted after years of dictatorship. To be sure, there were also high points in Schumacher's speech, but Sethe nevertheless came away thinking that the SPD could not possibly pursue its policies against the millions of veterans who had fought in the East, nor against further millions of Eastern refugees. In the end, his party-political sympathies do not appear to have changed much from his liberal conservatism of the Weimar years. As he wrote to his sister on 7 December 1946:[138] "I have voted liberal-democratic. [But] it's nothing good either. [They are] betraying their ideas every day and deliver us to the bureaucracy." In short, he was still the bourgeois intellectual increasingly anxious to write for the middle-class papers that began to reappear under the Allied licensing system.

Many of his thoughts occurred to him while he was with his family in Halver, no doubt enjoying the peace, but, while tending the garden, also discovering that a simple life was "difficult for an intellectual person."[139] Like many of his former colleagues, he tried to rebuild his former networks. He had offers and, while accepting some, turned down others. Without going into the details of his efforts to restart his journalistic career,[140] suffice it to say that by the spring of 1946 Sethe began to write again. He found employment with the *Badische Zeitung* in Freiburg, where he moved with his family.[141] Apparently he was offered the opportunity to become the successor of Karl Silex as the paper's editor in chief but declined. Two years later he found a position farther north as deputy editor in chief at *Allgemeine Zeitung* in Mainz. Erich Welter, who had been deputy editor of the FZ until 1943 and after 1945 a consultant in Mainz, apparently saw to it that Sethe became a member of the editorial and management board of the newly established *Frankfurter Allgemeine Zeitung* (FAZ).[142]

Founding the *Frankfurter Allgemeine Zeitung*

Having examined the life and work of Paul Sethe, first up to 1945 with its many twists and turns and ambiguities, and then between 1945 and 1948, in the remainder of this chapter we will be concerned with the no less interesting question of what insights he had gained from his experiences and what lessons he tried to apply to his postwar career as a journalist. Three concerns of his stand out on which I shall concentrate here. The first was his work to promote a general public recognition of what the men of 20 July had stood for and of their legacy to the West Germans. In particular, he wanted to highlight the significance of their ethical values for the rebuilding of postwar society. The second issue is also directly taken from his experience with Nazism, that is, his fight for civil liberties, the freedom of the press in particular. Third, there is Sethe's National Liberalism from his Weimar days, with the emphasis in his case on nationalism and his belief that, as far as foreign policy was concerned, the first task of the West German government once it had been constituted in 1949 was to reunify the country.

As to Sethe's struggle to give the anti-Nazi resistance a proper place in society, it is well known that the men of the July 1944 plot were for a long time despised by ordinary West Germans. Among soldiers and those on the home front the attempt to kill Hitler had been vigorously rejected after Goebbels's propaganda machine had convinced them that the coup had been a stab in the back of the Wehrmacht at a time when the *Endsieg* was just around the corner.[143] These convictions survived the defeat, and the disdain had been extended to all men and women who had been caught, imprisoned, or executed as "traitors." This prejudice, and indeed hatred, was directed even against the widows and orphans of those who had lost their lives in one of the many resistance movements, as Dorothea von Meding has shown.[144] When the anti-Nazi activities of their fathers were known, the children often had a terrible time in school unless they were sent, like Jan von Haeften, whose father and uncle were both executed in connection with 20 July, to Salem, a private school in a remote Bavarian *Schloss*.

Immediately after the war, Sethe was understandably concerned, first of all, to learn more about Goerdeler and the history of the 1944 plot. Hearing from actual participants who had survived, he found out about the plans to overthrow the regime that General Ludwig Beck and others had made as early as 1938.[145] But the Munich Agreement between Hitler and the British prime minister Neville Chamberlain had stopped these efforts. As Sethe wrote to his sister in 1945, Goerdeler and others had been planning a second time to strike in early 1940. Again the operation came to nothing when key generals refused to participate. Sethe was also critical of subsequent attempts in 1941 and later and of the "fateful procrastination" of commanding officers.[146] Also, in light of the earlier analysis of his contacts with Bartsch, it is not surprising that he rather impatiently wrote after 1945 that Beck's caution had reflected the "decadence of Prussiandom." As we have seen, he was no less scathing in his remarks about Rundstedt.[147] Instead he invoked Gerhard von Scharnhorst's "volcanic" activism during what in Sethe's view were the truly great days of Prussiandom during the Napoleonic wars.

While he kept his distance from the Red Orchestra and the communist resistance, he began to extol representatives of "Another Germany," who were not the officers and conservative civilians of the 1944 plot but Social Democrats.[148] Therefore, in 1963 he received a letter from Marianne Krell about a commemorative meeting for the Social Democrat leader Carlo Mierendorff.[149] She asked about a rumor relating to Mierendorff's friend Theodor Haubach, on whom the People's Court had initially not imposed the standard death penalty. Sethe replied three weeks later, reporting that only after Haubach had spoken at the end of the trial had Freisler gotten so enraged by his defiant words that Haubach, too, was sent to the gallows.[150] There is also a letter from Annedore Leber, to whom Sethe had written in 1946 about her husband, Julius, after Sethe had witnessed how Leber had stood upright and unbent before the court. Annedore replied:[151] "You will be able to gauge for yourself what your letter means to me," adding the hope that they would soon meet in person.

It is probably fair to say that Sethe was most supportive of the conservative resistance. As was typical of so many educated middle-class Germans, he had been suspicious even before 1933 of the "masses" whom the Nazis had seduced and abused for their destructive aims. His conservatism may also explain why he felt that "aristocrats had rarely been Nazis; no estate was as pure as this one, presumably because its instinctive response against Proletheus [!] was strongest" among them. While, Sethe's view of the German nobility was too rosy, as will be shown in chapter 2, deep down in his heart of hearts Sethe continued to see himself as a middle-class intellectual and serious historian who, from among the array of high-brow magazines that had begun to appear in West Germany, would praise the *Göttinger Universitätszeitung* as an "honorable spiritual counterweight against National Socialist reminiscences."[152] He advocated for the commemoration of the 1944 plot and was therefore among a number of journalists who raised their voices in favor of making its anniversary an annual event.[153] He, too, believed that what Germany needed was a "historical-moral self-examination," as Bernhard Guttmann, until 1935 one of the foreign correspondents of the FZ, had put it after the war.[154] Looking back on both Nazi crimes and the resistance movements against them, he bemoaned the absence of the men of 20 July and hoped that the Germans would learn to look up to them as "their true role models."[155]

If Sethe, in commemorating the anti-Nazi resistance, was concerned with helping lay the ethical foundations of a society that was not only physically, but also morally, devastated by Hitler's regime and the war, he was also motivated by his memory of having had to write under conditions of censorship as well as the constant fear of arrest and imprisonment, and even death. Consequently, he came to see not only freedom of expression more generally but also the freedom of the press as a sine qua non of postwar West German political life. It was an axiom whose proof would be tested by whether he was free to express his views on the reunification of a country that had become divided into East and West Germany with the unfolding of the Cold War. Sethe's determination to establish this principle came to dominate his professional life at the FAZ, reaching a dramatic climax in 1955.

With the creation of the Federal Republic and the end of the Allied press licensing system, it did not take long for discussions to begin about the revival of the time-honored FZ under its old title. But this quickly proved unfeasible because the Simon family, the paper's former owners, had initiated restitution claims. Erich Welter, the driving force behind the project, though himself skeptical of going back to the past, happened to be a member of the Wirtschaftspolitische Gesellschaft (Wipog), a gathering of businessmen founded to exchange ideas about current political and economic problems, among them Otto Seeling of Deutsche Tafelglas A.G. in Fürth near Nuremberg, Alexander Haffner of the shoe-manufactruing Salamander A.G., and Max Schmid of Zellstoff Waldhof in Mannheim. More important from Welter's perspective, they became interested in an "expansion of [Wipog's] publicity" and in raising the capital for a conservative newspaper.[156] The initiative attracted the support of several hundred members, and this, in turn, facilitated the hiring of a number of journalists who had occupied leading positions in the newspaper world, first during the Weimar years and later in the Third Reich. One of them was Karl Korn, who had been editor of a provincial paper before moving in 1934 to the FZ, where he had worked as political editor until 1943. By age the most senior colleague was Erich Dombrowski, who had worked for BT during the Weimar years and had been editor in chief of the *Frankfurter Generalanzeiger* from 1936. Finally there were Hans Baumgarten, who had been in charge of two economics papers in the 1930s, and Paul Sethe.[157]

Wipog eventually raised some 50,000 marks as well as obtaining a loan of 700,000 marks, and the FAZ was born. Its executive director, responsible for the business side, was the deputy chairman of Wipog, Otto Klepper, who had been Prussian finance minister during the Weimar Republic. He looked after the paper's financial viability now that the Federal Republic had become a "social market economy" in which blew the harsh winds of competition and in which private enterprises had to meet the bottom line. The leadership structure was unusual in that Welter, Dombrowski, Baumgarten, Korn, and Sethe appeared on the masthead not only as editors but also as publishers (*Herausgeber*), with Wipog in the background.

However, this did not mean that the five journalists were independent of the administrative and supervisory structure that was created under the stipulations of the Commercial Code. In fact, they were in a contractual relationship to the legal entity of the FAZ publishing company. While the *Herausgeber* were responsible for the content of the paper, those who had raised the money were not barred from interfering directly or indirectly with the political orientation of the paper. When the Basic Law became the (provisional) constitution of the Federal Republic, its Article 5 formally guaranteed freedom of the press, but the bearers of this freedom were not explicitly mentioned. Instead, since the freedom to own property was also protected by the Basic Law, the owners came to see themselves as the bearers of press freedom and the editors as their employees.[158] Court rulings soon confirmed this. Consequently, it did not take long for individual investors, such as Seeling and Haffner, to raise their voices, arguing that the representation of industrial interests in the paper was "somewhat slow and lame."[159] Haffner added that it was not enough merely to view business as the midwife at the FAZ's birth. Further negotiations between Haffner and his group and Klepper, supported by three representatives of Wipog, yielded the agreement that the society was the exclusive owner of the FAZ publishing house and that its mission with respect to policy and economic policy

was enshrined in the FAZ's not being tied to any political party. So, while the
Wipog acted as the trustee of the investors and providers of loans, the latter
were also represented in the FAZ administrative council and thus had another
lever with which to influence the overall outlook and content of the paper.
Finally, they had to contend with Klepper, who, as a former Weimar minister
and refugee from Nazism, had returned with strong opinions on how West German socioeconomic and political life should be reconstructed.[160]

The details of the resulting tensions and the financing of the FAZ will be
examined in chapter 4 in connection with similar problems relating to *Die Zeit*
and *Die Welt*,[161] but the focus here is on Sethe and his role at the paper. As will
be seen in a moment, ultimately his disagreements with his four colleagues
on the board became so irreconcilable and the pressure on him from both the
Adenauer government in Bonn and private industry so great that he stepped
down in 1955 and began to work for Axel Springer's *Die Welt* in Hamburg.
However, the uproar that this caused had a longer history that went back to
the immediate postwar period and involved differences of opinion over the
strong convictions that Sethe held on West German foreign policy and the
debate on German reunification.

So, while there seems to be a continuity in Sethe's views on relations with
Russia that dated back to his support of Stresemann in the 1920s and were also
reflected in his early postwar statements on Soviet intentions with respect to
Western Europe,[162] he had not been the first to write about this question in
the FAZ. Instead Dombrowski had put the cat among the pigeons when he
published an article titled "German-Russian Possibilities to Talk" on 1 April
1950.[163] In it he suggested that talks with the Soviets might be facilitated by the
reestablishment of trade relations, especially in light of the fact that the Federal
Republic was no more than a "pound of meat" in the larger East-West conflict.
The public reaction to this proposal was overwhelmingly negative, even if German industry, the steel industry of the Ruhr region in particular, in looking
for markets may have taken a more favorable view of Dombrowski's piece.[164]

A few months later, the industrial landscape changed dramatically with the
outbreak of the Korean War. Suddenly West German steel was very much
in demand, accelerated by the embryonic discussions on German rearmament.[165] Still, the issue of independent political contacts with the Soviet
Union did not disappear from public discussion, and this was seen by some
of Dombrowski's critics as an "incomprehensible misstep" (*Entgleisung*).[166]
Worse, Klepper was dragged into the blame game and the whole issue came
to be linked to the Nauheim Circle of neutralists around Professor Ulrich

Noack.[167] Dombrowski subsequently defended his position by insisting on the need to gain time, which would be enhanced by "mediating [and] conciliatory gestures." In the end, his colleagues and the paper's Wipog supporters stopped the fracas by agreeing that the East-West conflict must be treated "firmly and unambiguously in the confrontation with the Bolshevik system." This position immediately put a damper on an East German proposal of October 1950 to hold all-German elections and also on another one that Otto Grotewohl, the East German prime minister, made in October 1950, even if Sethe had the impression that the Soviets were perhaps prepared to make concessions on the much-vaunted German Question.

Klepper reacted quite differently to an article that Sethe had written without his knowledge on the Franco-German relationship. Being very much in favor of reconciliation, the former felt that the article had been lacking in "tact" and had therefore damaged Bonn's relationship with Paris. He then rapped Sethe over the knuckles by postulating that he, who had "tactlessly disturbed" that relationship, had committed "a sin" against Germany's fate.[168] It is possible that Baumgarten and Dombrowski had encouraged Klepper to speak up after they had come out quite strongly in favor Franco-German cooperation as the core of West Germany's European policy. They did not want to wait for Britain, which had stayed away from the Schuman Plan negotiations to create the European Coal and Steel Community. Sethe, by contrast, while also favoring European economic integration, wished to complement cooperation with Paris with an entente with London.

On another occasion, Klepper was prepared to defend Sethe, however.[169] After the latter had been depicted as an ally of SPD leader Kurt Schumacher, a sharp critic of Adenauer, Klepper refuted the charge. To him it was most important to talk about the positive contributions the paper was making to the budding Republic. Above all, a quality paper like the FAZ should "in principle be critical of the government" that happened to be in power. Considering the persistence and inaccuracies of these attacks on the FAZ, the incident provides a foretaste of the criticisms that Sethe soon had to endure.

Tensions over the FAZ's Political Orientation and Freedom of Expression

There was—it must be stressed—an initial period when the five editors tolerated whatever differences of view arose among them and allowed free expression of their opinions in their articles. However, as the party system consolidated, it was perhaps inevitable that some of the five should veer more toward the Christian Democratic Party (CDU), while others, without being party members, had, as journalists, been constantly on the lookout for information and contacts with the Free Democrats (FDP) or the reformist wing of the Social Democrats. This applied to both domestic and foreign policy matters. As far as external affairs were concerned, the big and thorny issue was whether West Germany should firmly hitch its wagon to the United States as the main protector of Western Europe during the escalating Cold War. The alternative to this unshakably pro-American policy was a more flexible approach that did not, as a matter of principle, block what was on everyone's mind: the quest for a reunified Germany. Millions of voters, especially those who had settled in the West as refugees or expellees from eastern Europe, continued, throughout the 1950s, to hope not only for a coming together of East and West Germany but also for a reconstitution of the country within the borders of 1937 that would have given many of them the opportunity to return to the territories lost to Poland and the Soviet Union in 1944–45.[170]

But the really sensational news came on 10 March 1952, when Joseph Stalin himself offered a reunification of the Federal Republic and the German Democratic Republic (GDR).[171] In return, the Soviet dictator insisted that Germany not be rearmed and not be integrated into the American-dominated North Atlantic Treaty Organization (NATO). Chancellor Konrad Adenauer rejected this initiative out of hand and refused even to explore how serious the Soviet dictator was about it, insisting that the integration of the country into the Western alliance and into the emerging European community must continue without distractions.[172] He was not only unwaveringly convinced that his government had no choice but to align itself with the United States militarily as well as politically and economically; he was also autocratically trying to suppress all criticism of his foreign policy. Sethe became the one among the FAZ editors who fundamentally disagreed with Adenauer on this issue, and he voiced this by publishing three articles on 12, 14, and 22 March on Stalin's offer.[173] Alexander Gallus has undertaken a careful analysis of Sethe's early responses and has stressed that they were circumspect and anything but enthusiastic.[174] What Sethe asked for, while acknowledging a persistent Soviet military threat to the West, was that exploratory talks be held to find out whether Stalin was serious. With time, his language became more explicit, though. The first of his three pieces, on 12 March, was no more than an appeal to test whether relations between East and West had in fact reached "a turning point."[175] Two days later, he rejected a renewed expulsion of the Poles from the territories east of the Oder-Neisse Line and envisioned a reconciliation between the two societies. By 22 March his appeal not to reject Stalin's offer appeared under the headline "We Are Approaching a Question of Fate."[176]

When Adenauer read Sethe's early musings on German national unity and how it might be achieved, he responded gently and, mediated by the FAZ representative in Bonn, invited him to his office for a discussion.[177] When Sethe remained unmovable and insisted on his right to express his opinions freely, the chancellor began to put pressure on the FAZ board, some of whose members, he knew, were also opposed to Sethe's writings. The policy of mutual tolerance began to fray. And it did not help Sethe's position internally that in 1953 he published a piece critical of Adenauer's policy with respect to the Saarland that Klepper, and probably some colleagues, also disapproved of.[178]

Things got more difficult for Sethe when political rumors began to circulate whose sources were obscure. As this was still the height of Cold War anti-Communism, he was suspected of being a neutralist who wanted to sell out the Federal Republic to the Soviets and had covertly collaborated with East Germany. An earlier article of his from his time with the Mainz *Allgemeine Zeitung* of 16 March 1949 was dug up in which he had expressed some sympathy for the neutralist position of Ulrich Noack's Nauheim Circle.[179] It did not matter that by 1952 Sethe had come to recognize that the neutralism of this circle was unrealistic. He thought that the partnership with the United States and the West was indispensable and merely wished to explore how much room for maneuver there might be for Germany with respect to talking to the East. After all, thoughtful people in Washington had themselves begun to think about how the dangerous Cold War with its nuclear arms race might be de-escalated.[180] In short, there were nuances that got lost in the confrontationist propaganda and Adenauer's single-mindedness. Among the retrospectives that Sethe produced in later years there is one piece indicating that he received back-channel information from East Berlin, and that may have contributed to the rumors about his being a mole. On 16 June 1967 he wrote to Henri Nannen, the influential editor in chief of *Der Stern* magazine, that Georg Dertinger, the East German foreign minister, had told him in November 1952 "that the Russians had mandated him [Dertinger] to draw up a plan for the reunification of two non-socialist Germanies."[181] If this news circulated among the five editors at the time, it explains why their earlier willingness to accept differences of opinion among them came under stress. Worse, there were insinuations and the reproach that in 1941–42 Sethe had written "pro-Nazi articles on the course of the Russian campaign."[182]

Whatever methods Sethe's political opponents inside the FAZ (with Baumgarten and Dombrowski now most prominently among them) resorted to in order to undermine their colleague's position, Adenauer also knew how to deploy economic levers for his purposes. With the obstreperous FAZ journalist now firmly in his crosshairs, he began to encourage business interests to exert pressure on the newspaper.[183] It was no secret that since its founding businessmen had given direct financial support, made donations, or had placed advertisements. Being in sympathy with Adenauer's strict *Westbindung*, they now began to protest either privately or even publicly. Although the earlier precarious financial position of the FAZ had seen some consolidation, businessmen could still inflict pain, especially when the initial backers from the medium-sized enterprises in the South and Southwest were reinforced by the managers of the big corporations in the Rhineland and Ruhr regions.

Even if Stalin's offer had not been taken up because of American opposition, thenceforth German unity continued to be a constant theme in the media, also because other journalists and papers, such as Rudolf Augstein of *Der Spiegel* and the editors of *Die Zeit*, kept pushing.[184] There were also a number of prominent politicians in the SPD and FDP and even within Adenauer's CDU who were unhappy about the chancellor's refusal, as Sethe revealed in an article he wrote in December 1952.[185] Thomas Dehler, the minister of justice in the Cabinet, was also wondering if there were alternatives to the chancellor's orthodoxy.

In June 1953, shortly after Stalin's death, the people of East Germany staged an uprising, raising hopes that it would trigger an American intervention and the beginning of the much-vaunted rollback of the Soviet Union from its possessions in Eastern Europe.[186] Instead Soviet tanks were dispatched to Berlin and other major cities, and the uprising collapsed, also because the United States and NATO had decided that an intervention threatened to unleash another world war and the possible use of atomic weapons. However, Stalin's death in the spring had created not only a popular ferment in the Soviet empire but also a power struggle from which Nikita Khrushchev emerged as the new strong man in the Kremlin.

These developments encouraged Sethe to renew his proposal to put out feelers to the Soviets. His hope was that this would pave the way for negotiations on German unity, by now even at the price of giving up claims to territories beyond the eastern borders of East Germany.[187] Adenauer's response was to increase the pressure on the FAZ's editorial board to curb Sethe and, if this proved impossible, to oust him. It was also irritating to the chancellor that Sethe resumed his earlier criticism of Adenauer's policy toward the Saarland, opposing any solution that would "tear away" this territory from the Federal Republic.[188]

Again it was not only politicians but also the business community that appeared on the scene. It seems that Adenauer succeeded in mobilizing the powerful Bundesverband der Deutschen Industrie under the leadership of Fritz Berg, although this question requires further investigation.[189] There is more tangible evidence relating to direct pressure from one of the business circles that had helped get the FAZ on its feet in the early 1950s.

This pressure came in two phases. The first began in November 1953 when Adenauer, angry with Sethe, asked Anton Storch, his minister of labor, to see Haffner in Stuttgart to discuss Sethe's articles with him, including those on the Saarland issue. In a four-hour meeting, Haffner told Storch that he had reproached the Adenauer critic most severely but that Sethe was a "strange man" who constantly felt he had to be on the opposing side.[190] This is why Haffner and his colleagues had resolved to send Sethe for several months on a tour of the United States and other countries and decided that no articles of his on issues of principle would appear in the FAZ during that time. This initiative to silence Sethe came to nothing.

The second wave swept into the FAZ board in the spring of 1955, with Haffner once more in the lead. When he was talking, accompanied by Ziervogel, to members of the circle who had given their financial support to the FAZ, it was no longer a matter just of the independence of the editors but also of the paper's basic position.[191] After all, it had been founded by industry and commerce (*Wirtschaft*) because those entities thought that "the entire daily press" was guided by socialism or had at least been "socialistically infected." To counter these tendencies, a paper was to be established that "protected bourgeois politics, economy and culture" or that was, "if you prefer, anti-collectivist." Such a paper, Haffner continued, would make sense only "if it stood on the same foundations as the bourgeois government" of Adenauer. This ideological position had been extensively discussed with the editorial board at the time, and there hence existed no doubts about these fundamentals. However, parts of the editorial board and Sethe as well as Herbert von Borch, the FAZ correspondent in the United States, had violated the paper's founding principles. Furthermore, it was not acceptable that divergent views kept appearing on the same page. According to Haffner's "friends," the "flexibility" of opinions could go only so far, and the paper should not deal with basic political issues by printing an oppositional article at the same time as a pro-government one. If, Haffner added, it had been the mission of the FAZ to "draw as many [readers] as possible from the socialist into the bourgeois camp," his circle now feared that a reversal of this trend might occur if the government was constantly criticized for its mistakes. With Adenauer pursuing a "policy of strength" toward the Soviet Bloc, it looked as if parts of the FAZ were "afraid" of this policy. The paper was promoting negotiations with the Soviets, just as with the oppositional Social Democrats. For Haffner the question was how to escape the dilemma that had arisen between freedom of expression and the paper's basic mission, which had now divided the editorial board into two camps. If a consensus could not be achieved with the board, it was time for the "publisher" to become involved. He certainly did not think that a publisher would be able to live with the fact "that the articles in his paper contravened his own political convictions." The publisher of the FAZ, he concluded bluntly, was the FAZ Ltd., whose shareholders were "the promoters" in conjunction with the Mainz Newspapers Company, and he took it as given that the two were united on fundamental principles.

After this renewed and very revealing warning shot, the crisis came to a head in the summer of 1955. On 5 August, Albrecht Pickert, a member of the board of Hein, Lehmann and Company in Düsseldorf wrote to the FAZ's managing director, Werner G. Hoffmann.[192] He expressed his personal dismay but also the "profound uneasiness" of a "larger circle of friends and colleagues" about the FAZ's "foreign policy stance." What they were missing, Hoffmann thought, was a coherent concept with respect to the country's external relations, and he noted that Baumgarten's and Sethe's editorials were "diametrically opposed in their tendency." Worse, the supporters of the "foreign policy of our government" repeatedly had to distance themselves from the FAZ's attacks on Adenauer, which were "rarely open and mostly indirect and covert." By contrast, his policies were "supported by our entire industry," even if they, too, occasionally had a "positive critique of individual issues."

This situation, Pickert continued, had increasingly led to a "noticeable burdening of the relationship between the FAZ and [the] *Wirtschaft.*" Time and again, the latter had shown "endless patience" in trying to facilitate compromise between the two sides. However, "during the last few weeks that attitude of the paper had created a situation that required a straight-forward clarification in the interest of the honest name of German industry," Pickert wrote. He then mentioned several examples that had irritated the FAZ's supporters and hinted darkly that some of the paper's connections extended across the Iron Curtain. In the end, Hoffmann was asked to inform the editors, especially Welter, of these complaints.[193] It seems that Welter was mentioned because he had meanwhile become the editor in chief. Simultaneously in charge of the economic section of the paper, Welter had geared its editorial staff firmly to the axioms of the economics minister, Ludwig Erhard, as a key member of the Adenauer government.[194]

With Baumgarten and Dombrowski at loggerheads with Sethe over the direction of West German foreign policy and the need to align the FAZ with the chancellor's strategy, Welter now pursued the same kind of synchronization with regard to the FAZ's political department that he had applied to the economics section of the paper. Sethe, on the other hand, viewed this practice as a violation of the freedom of the press. For him it was no longer just a question of an exclusive orientation toward the West versus flexibility and openness toward the Soviet Bloc but also a question of a journalist's fundamental right to freely express his views. After all, he had personally experienced the suppression of this freedom in the Third Reich, and from this experience he had taken away the lesson that this freedom must never be undermined again by an autocratic government or the pressures of economic interest groups.

In the end, Welter sided with Baumgarten and Dombrowski. Sethe became convinced that there was no future for him at the FAZ and resigned. Although Korn's vote was not necessary, his role in this picture is unclear.[195] Nor did it matter that the majority of the editorial staff and his younger colleagues sided with Sethe against the *Herausgeber*, who had come to believe that pluralistic tolerance had to be constrained if the paper wanted to remain a leading voice of the West German bourgeoisie, as Haffner and his Circle had postulated. Sethe's ouster created quite a stir and was widely discussed throughout 1955–56. In this debate it became even more evident that freedom of the press à la Sethe was not unlimited. Consequently, he received a good deal of encouragement from people who had been getting no less worried than he about the seemingly increasing authoritarianism of the Adenauer government and the business community. All these pressures and the attitudes reminded him and some of his supporters of the Nazi years.

While Sethe's colleagues never fully divulged their side of the story and Baumgarten vigorously denied that there had been economic pressures from behind the scenes, Sethe's correspondence with Fritz Erler provides insight into the drama from the victim's point of view. It was Hartmut Soell, an academic historian and a prominent Social Democrat deputy in the Bonn Parliament, who not only assembled all of the then-available evidence on the conflict among the FAZ editors and the political and economic pressures they were under but also published two long letters by Sethe of 4 February and 28 March 1956 and Erler's replies of 23 February and 4 April 1956.[196] In his first letter the former FAZ *Mitherausgeber* provides a point-by-point summary of the tensions within the board and the outside influences that Adenauer brought to bear in the months and weeks before Sethe resigned.[197] Stressing that his colleagues never spoke of such pressures but merely invoked their consciences and purely "objective" (*sachliche*) reasons for their stance,[198] Sethe recounts the intervention of Anton Storch, labor minister in the Adenauer Cabinet, who had spoken to Haffner about Sethe's articles in the FAZ.[199] Sethe also quoted from a letter of June 1955 he had received from the Cologne banker Robert Pferdmenges, the chancellor's private adviser, in which the latter declared, "My friends and I" had been "very dissatisfied" with Sethe's pieces.[200]

The accused had made his main point straightaway in the first paragraph of his letter to Erler. Sethe insisted that the case was not of interest because of him as a person but "because of the symbolic character with respect to the extent [*Mass*] of press freedom in the Federal Republic."[201] In his second letter Sethe asserted that the FAZ had become the paper of a "small minority" who were no longer certain of the support of the "overwhelming majority" of the editorial staff as a whole.[202] This minority had not only violently assaulted (*vergewaltigt*) him psychologically but also subjected the staff to a "dictatorship." When Sethe had made it a condition of his staying with FAZ that "in future similar decisions not be made by three people but by the editorial staff as a whole (perhaps limited to members with a longer professional experience)," his demands had been rejected. In conclusion, Sethe came back to his insistence on freedom of expression and even suggested that journalists might be employed in the manner of university professors, who enjoyed the protection of tenure. When he was told that this idea was "fantastic," he felt he had no choice but to lapse into resignation and leave.[203] Referring to the freedom of the owner, as interpreted in the Basic Law, he wrote that only the person "'who is wealthy, is [also] free.'" He added that this "is not by Karl Marx, but by Paul Sethe."[204] No less important for an understanding of his motives was the fact that it was an observation that "contains the fruit[s] of the experiences of thirty-five years" of journalism before and after 1945.

Joining Axel Springer's *Die Welt*

Along with gaining insights as a journalist living under the Hitler dictatorship that had led him to promote the memory of the 20 July 1944 plot, Sethe had also resolved that he would uphold the freedom of expression as an absolute good against Adenauer's authoritarianism, which his colleagues on the FAZ board had meekly accepted. In his letter to Sethe of 23 February 1956, Erler went even further when he wrote that he had always taken it as "a sign of an incipient totalitarian mentality if someone internally yields to a pressure and does not even realize that he has fallen" to this pressure.[205] Since these weak-kneed colleagues were neither wealthy in their own right nor the actual owners of the paper, Sethe had also taken aim, with his blunt dictum on freedom and wealth, at the businessmen behind the FAZ who had been throwing their economic weight about.

Sethe was not unemployed for long. On 26 September he received a letter from Hans Zehrer, the editor in chief of Axel Springer's *Die Welt* in Hamburg, whose biography and journalism are the subjects of chapter 3 of this book.[206] At this point his correspondence with Sethe in the autumn of 1955 is of interest. Zehrer began his letter with references to the two occasions when, to the best of his memory, they had met before, for the first time during "the turbulent times [of] 1946" and again at the founding of the "Kuratorium Unteilbares Deutschland," an influential association promoting German reunification that was led by Wilhelm Wolfgang Schütz. At this point Zehrer merely spoke of the "heavy blow" that Sethe's departure from the FAZ had constituted. He had assumed—as it were erroneously—that Sethe would stay and become the paper's correspondent in Vienna, and he felt envious about this assignment. However, Sethe's departure had left a "gap that could not be filled" politically and even less so in light of the "not very strong situation of the West German press."

Four weeks later, and apparently after Sethe had replied to his letter, Zehrer asked him if there might be a possibility of cooperation.[207] His idea at this stage was to pay for Sethe to take a trip around the world, at the end of which Sethe would become the exclusive representative of *Die Welt* in the United States. Zehrer also mentioned the congenial team spirit of the paper and concluded that he and his colleagues would be very glad if "you came to us." Two weeks later, a deal had been struck and Sethe had agreed to join the editorial staff in Hamburg.[208] Zehrer was delighted and greeted him "cordially." He added that their agreement would raise the "journalistic rank and status" in West Germany's press and "serve the freedom and independence of expression." Sethe started his new job on 17 November 1955.[209]

His move came at a propitious moment with regard to the positions that Sethe had fought for in previous years, while the turmoil about the orientation of the FAZ continued, exacerbated by the controversy over the creation of a West German army. This time Adelbert Weinstein, the paper's military expert, had come under fire over the question of whether the new Bundeswehr should be a universal-service army or a much smaller professional force. Weinstein favored the latter.[210] There was also controversy about the stationing of tactical nuclear weapons on German soil after Carte Blanche, a NATO exercise in North Germany, had resulted in millions of (simulated) casualties. It was clear that a war with nuclear weapons was unthinkable. Instead planners began to look for a de-escalation of the East-West arms race, and the idea of talking to the Soviets received a fresh boost after Nikita Khrushchev had made his speech before the twentieth congress of the Soviet Communist Party in February 1956, in which he criticized Stalin's erstwhile dictatorship. Renewed talk of détente almost inevitably raised the issue of West Germany's relations with the East, even more so when Adenauer accepted an invitation to visit Moscow in September 1955. The chancellor returned to Bonn with an agreement in his pocket on mutual diplomatic recognition and the return of German POWs who had been held in Siberian camps since the war. Thenceforth key bureaucrats in the West German foreign office and various politicians felt encouraged to begin to think outside the framework that Adenauer's *Westbindung* principles had set since 1949.

Like other papers, *Die Welt* had been critical of the chancellor's stubborn refusal to test Stalin's offer of March 1952, so the public debate on German reunification rumbled on. Sethe therefore used the new freedom that he had won to resume his quest for improving West Germany's relations with the East.[211] Having walked along the Via Dolorosa up to his move to *Die Welt* himself in 1955, he did so by publishing an article about Karl Georg Pfleiderer and what he called the "Path of Suffering of a Planner" that the latter had been forced to take during Adenauer's exclusive policy of *Westbindung*.[212] After all, as early as June 1952 the diplomat had had the temerity of putting forward the "Pfleiderer Plan," followed two years later by his proposal to send a delegation of Bundestag deputies to Moscow.[213]

Having been removed from the Bonn Foreign Office to the embassy in Belgrade, in a letter Pfleiderer thanked Sethe profusely for his article on 18 April 1956.[214] Although times were clearly changing, Pfleiderer did not feel, that this was the moment to revive his plan, which he believed had by now become "sterile." Instead he wanted to put "completely new cards" on the table at home and abroad. For as long as there was no indication "in the German people" that they were prepared to "draw revolutionary conclusions from a revolutionary situation," progress in the "question of reunification" could not be expected. After adding some further thoughts on the need for improved relations with Poland, the chastened diplomat signed his letter "with most esteemed and most cordial greetings," as "Your most sincerely devoted Hans-Georg Pfleiderer."

Over the next four years, Sethe contributed articles to *Die Welt* on a variety of topics. In particular, he was at liberty to discuss his ideas on East-West relations and German reunification. Given Zehrer's welcoming words, he must have been happy to be able to speak his mind in a newspaper that had meanwhile established itself as a Hamburgian voice in competition with that of the FAZ. Yet fresh trouble was looming for Sethe, this time from Axel Springer, the owner of *Die Welt*. After buying the paper from the British in 1953, Springer was at first primarily interested in the economic prosperity and growth of his press empire. But soon he was reinventing himself to become a publisher keen to influence high politics.[215] This gradual process was no doubt stimulated by the changing international climate. By the late 1950s, a slew of "plans" were being publicized that promoted the idea of détente and negotiation with the East.[216] By the end of 1957, Springer's thinking on reunification had focused on the notion that, if he were able to go to Moscow to talk to Khrushchev, he could persuade the Soviet leader to open the door to German reunification.

It is not clear how enthusiastic Zehrer was about this somewhat megalomaniac endeavor, but in January 1958 Springer and his entourage, including Zehrer, flew to Moscow, although Khrushchev had never given them a date for a meeting or extended an official invitation.[217] The group spent two humiliating weeks in a hotel without news of a meeting from the Kremlin. Increasingly angry and frustrated, Springer was about to return home when he was given an appointment. But instead of listening to Springer's proposals, Khrushchev apparently treated his visitors as journalists who had come for an interview, so the whole journey became a complete flop. Worse, Soviet policies, possibly buoyed by the successful launching of *Sputnik*, became more hardline and indeed aggressive, especially with respect to West Berlin, whose survival as an island inside East Germany had been under threat ever since the 1948 blockade. There was also the growing instability of East Germany, from which refugees were now escaping in droves, mostly via East Berlin, whence they took the suburban train to the Western sectors and were flown out to the Federal Republic to restart new lives without the repressive policies of the Ulbricht regime. The unsustainable loss of often highly skilled personnel was stopped in August 1961. Ulbricht built the Berlin Wall, and the East German border with the Federal Republic in the West was also made more and more impenetrable. [218]

Sethe's Separation from Springer and
Move to *Der Stern* and *Die Zeit*

Deeply offended by Khrushchev's rejection, Springer now geared his press empire to the pursuit of an acerbic campaign against Communism and the East German regime in particular, thereby contributing to the destabilization of the GDR. Thus, when the Berlin Wall was built, it was not only a major set-back to Adenauer's hardline Eastern policy, even if the chancellor had begun to soften it from 1958 onward, but also the nail in the coffin of Springer's reunification efforts. As a result he became even more defiant of the Soviet Bloc and planned to move his headquarters from Hamburg to a brand-new nineteen-story office building in Kochstrasse, right next to the wall. He also "synchronized" the editorial policies of his newspapers, including his mass-circulation *Bild-Zeitung* as well as *Die Welt*, for an anti-communist crusade.[219] The result was that Sethe was once more under pressure to toe the new edi-torial line in *Die Welt*. This pressure was not indirect, as it had been at the FAZ. After all, Springer was the exclusive owner-publisher, and under the interpretation of press freedom that the courts had developed in the 1950s he was entitled to give directions from the top. Chapter 3 examines the reaction to this shift of Zehrer, whose stake in *Die Welt* as the editor in chief was even higher than Sethe's.[220]

The latter's growing unhappiness emerged in a letter that he wrote to Springer in January 1959.[221] After some complimentary remarks about the publisher's "foreign policy program," he confessed that "the course of the paper" that had "in part been initiated" by Springer himself looked to him as if "we are slipping into the camp of the Cold War." Whatever tensions had arisen in the face of recent Soviet demands, it would be unfortunate if the West failed to arrive at a "concrete policy of negotiations." His blood, he added, "was freezing" when he thought of what might otherwise happen next. If noth-ing else, "the walls before reunification would grow mountain-high." *Die Welt* would run the risk of supporting a policy "that was sterile," as recent years had shown. To Sethe, it was unwise to change course "like a speed boat," which would merely lead to a loss of political influence so dear to Springer himself. In short, Sethe was "very depressed" not only because of the general political situation but also because of "the development" of *Die Welt*, even though in principle he was still willing to support the publisher's overall program.

The rest of 1959 merely saw an escalation of Springer's anti-communism. By the spring of 1960, Sethe had become so unhappy that he handed in his resignation and decided to radicalize the statement that he had made to Erler in 1956. "Press freedom," he now opined, "is the freedom of 200 wealthy people to spread their opinions."[222] A few days later, he received Springer's reply, in which he listed two things that "pained" him.[223] First of all, he saw Sethe's departure "a bit as a defeat at the human level." True, Sethe had again argued that differences of opinion between two intellectually adult people "cannot be bridged by friendship and respect," not even temporarily. Nevertheless, the publisher thought that he had failed in that he "could not be more convincing," be it in the realm of facts or in the human sphere. However, these feelings did not change his sense of excitement whenever Sethe entered the room. In fact, he believed that one day, when "politics is again open towards the front," they would again be on the same page. Almost five years later, on 30 November 1965, it was Sethe's turn to recall his feelings whenever he had gone upstairs to Springer's office, "often in an obstinate mood, sometimes also resentful"; but he had always left the room pensively, "often convinced, [and] occasionally raptured."[224]

Even before leaving *Die Welt*, Sethe had received a letter from Rudolf Augstein, the owner and editor of *Der Spiegel*, offering him the headship of a new department responsible for producing "historical-political features," together with a salary of 4.000 marks and the same benefits as he had enjoyed with Springer.[225] For the moment, Sethe agreed in principle to write articles on contemporary politics with the approval of the editor in chief, while Augstein consented to Sethe's being free to publish in Mainz's *Allgemeine Zeitung*, the paper he had worked for before joining the FAZ. It is not clear if this agreement was ever implemented. However, Augstein was thinking of founding his own newspaper in addition to *Der Spiegel* at this time and seems to have had Sethe in mind as its editor in chief.[226] When this project went nowhere, Sethe was picked up by *Die Zeit*, the liberal weekly, and *Der Stern*, Henri Nannen's popular illustrated magazine, both published in Hamburg.

The next seven years of Sethe's long and meandering journalistic career probably were the happiest in his life. Ideologically, the conservative liberalism of *Die Zeit* was more in harmony with his own outlook on politics. Gerd Bucerius, the publisher, welcomed him as part of the team. As he wrote to Sethe on 30 April 1963: "I am so glad that we have now come to an agreement" and that "Nannen has accepted my formula without reservations."[227] He added: "It is quite moving also for me that the 'grand old man of German journalism' has joined our compound. We are all very glad about this." Sethe took charge of the influential section with reviews of political and historical books. Under the roof of the press empire that Gerd Bucerius had built up, he also published broader features on historical themes in *Der Stern*. Sethe's private papers contain a list of almost three dozen illustrated articles that he produced for this magazine, covering mainly major historical themes of the twentieth century.[228] He continued to see himself as a scholar whose work appealed to an educated lay readership and published several widely read books.[229] At his desk in Hamburg's *Pressehaus* or in his study at his home in the northeastern suburb of Wellingsbüttel, Sethe devoted much of his time and energy to editing the section "Das politische Buch" in *Die Zeit*.

There were too many books that Sethe sent out for review or reviewed himself for them to be discussed here. But the promotion of the debate that the Hamburg historian Fritz Fischer unleashed with his books and articles on the origins of World War I and Imperial Germany's war aims deserves fuller examination, partly because it says much about Sethe's journalism and scholarly interests. It is also mentioned because this controversy saw a revival in recent years in connection with the commemorations on the occasion of the centenary of World War I and with Christopher Clark's hypothesis that the Europeans "sleepwalked" into the catastrophe.[230]

What is so intriguing is that earlier Sethe had been in touch with Gerhard Ritter, the doyen of West German historiography at Freiburg University, with whom he was apparently largely in agreement about the course of pre-1914 German history as well as the one-sidedness of Adenauer's foreign policy. Thus on 27 March 1952, soon after the publication of the Stalin Note, Ritter joined Sethe in expressing his opposition to Bonn's exclusive *Westbindung*. In another letter to Sethe of 20 July 1953, he suggested that Germany and Europe might be able to offer "the Russians" a "kind of reinsurance treaty" such as Otto von Bismarck had concluded with the Tsarist empire in the 1880s.[231] The next letter to arrive on Sethe's desk was dated 17 October 1955, shortly after the latter's ouster from the FAZ, in which Ritter very much regretted Sethe's departure.[232] He then added a remark relating to an article in *Der Spiegel* whose author had maintained that it had been "intolerable" how Sethe had "celebrated" the Wilhelmine period and had "worshipped" (*vergötzt*) the politically questionable Prof. Gerhard Ritter." Ritter finally thanked Sethe for having helped to spread Ritter's ideas. The latter reciprocated with a favorable review of the second volume of Ritter's *Staatskunst und Kriegshandwerk*.[233]

The relationship with Ritter soured when on 17 November 1961 Sethe wrote a review of Fritz Fischer's book under the heading "When Germany

Aimed at World Power."[234] He did not explicitly side with the arguments of the Hamburg historian but expected them to unleash extensive debate. Still, he felt that this was the one book to "shake us, even to throw us off balance." Referring to German war aims and "unrestrained German power politics," he concluded that these reflected an overestimation of Wilhelmine Germany's power and an underestimation of that of its opponents. On 24 November, *Die Zeit* published a letter from Fischer in which he tried to correct Sethe's misapprehension that the book was about the "sole guilt" of Germany.[235] Rather, Fischer insisted, he had been concerned with the *responsibilities* of the top decision-makers. Ritter, who had vigorously opposed Fischer's interpretation from the start as totally tendentious, protested to Sethe, who then apologized for an "unfortunate" mistake that had slipped in at the proofing stage.[236] However, the dams of older, more apologetic interpretations had broken, and a flood of arguments inundated scholarly journals and the quality press, with Ritter among the critics, asserting gloomily that the Hamburg historian's work represented the "culmination point of the self-darkening of German historical consciousness."[237]

Sethe, by contrast, stressed that he had opened the pages of *Die Zeit* in the hope that Fischer's book would "provoke lively discussions among the experts" and inform "the large circle of educated laypersons," who, he hoped, would learn from recent scholarship.[238] Later Sethe admitted that, given his background and socialization as a historian at Bonn University, he had adhered to views of the war's outbreak that were uncritically circulated in Weimar Germany. Now the compelling evidence that Fischer had unearthed had persuaded him to take a much more critical view of the responsibility of Germany's leaders for the catastrophe of July 1914. By the mid-1960s, Sethe seems to have veered back toward Ritter[239] when he published a rather critical review of the work of Fischer's assistant Immanuel Geiss.[240] And on 5 February 1965 he praised Ritter's third volume of *Staatskunst und Kriegshandwerk*, on World War I, which had left him "deeply moved."[241]

In this context, mention should be made of a review that Sethe wrote at about the same time of William Shirer's bestselling *The Rise and Fall of the Third Reich*, criticizing the American journalist for telling many "half-truths."[242] Evidently pained by Shirer's success in the United States and learning that Ritter was composing volume 4 of *Staatskunst und Kriegshandwerk*, he wondered if the Freiburg historian would consider publishing it in English in the expectation that it would have a much greater impact.[243] While relations between Sethe and Ritter improved, Sethe kept in touch with Fischer and advised him to publish a shortened version of his by then much-cited book, whose third impression had almost been sold out by February 1967.[244] An early high point of the Fischer Debate occurred at the International Historians' Congress in Vienna in 1964, at which the Hamburg historian presented his arguments about German war aims and 1914 to a packed auditorium. Sethe subsequently wrote a summary of the lecture in *Die Zeit* and also reprinted it after some of Fischer's conservative German opponents had refused to shake hands with him on the stage in full view of their colleagues from all over the world.[245] In short, by the mid-1960s the Fischer controversy had become very nasty, and yet it was typical of Sethe and his view of quality journalism that he continued to see it as his job to inform the general public on a crucial historical topic.[246] Indeed, it is not too far-fetched to say that this attitude reflected another lesson he had learned from the lack of press freedom and public debate under Nazism.

Somewhat later, Sethe received a letter from Professor Golo Mann, the son of the celebrated novelist Thomas Mann, who had become a well-known historian living in Kirchdorf on Lake Zurich.[247] Critical of Fischer's book, Mann expressed relief that he did not have to listen to the "Babylonian confusion of languages" relating to the debate on 1914 at the 1964 congress of historians. After reading Fischer's text, he professed that "the man was intellectually just not up to the task that he has taken on, however desirable this actually was." Sethe took a different view of Fischer's achievement and continued to use the pages of *Die Zeit* to educate West Germans about their tortuous history.

Beyond the question of Sethe's willingness to learn from the past, there was also his continued preoccupation with the country's present and future, regarding which his voice was no less influential. After all, by the early 1960s the reunification question was slowly tilting toward positions that he had advocated since 1952. With the election of John F. Kennedy to the US presidency in 1960, détente had been firmly put on the agenda of international politics. Having failed to persuade Adenauer to test Stalin's Note of March 1952, by the 1960s domestic and international developments were moving toward Sethe's position. In West Berlin, Willy Brandt took the first cautious steps toward a dialog with the East whose early success was embodied in an agreement with the East German government to issue visitors' permits to West Berliners to enable them to visit family members in the East, separated from them by the Wall since 1961. After Adenauer had finally retired from the chancellorship in 1963, the door of West German foreign policy began to open more widely toward *Ostpolitik*, this time with the general approval of Washington, where détente toward the Soviet Union had become an official strategy.[248] After writing a string of earlier publications on his favorite historical topics, Sethe's last book, published in 1966, was titled "Opening to the East: World Political Realities between Bonn, Paris, and Moscow."[249]

By that time the spirit of the anti-Nazi resistance and the 20 July 1944 plot had become more widely recognized as having produced a movement upon whose moral principles West Germans should build their postwar society. Thus, on the twentieth anniversary of the 1944 plot, Sethe published a review of a book that Heinrich Fraenkel and Roger Manvell had written on this topic.[250] In it he complained that "wide circles" outside West Germany still had a warped image of the attempt on Hitler's life. He praised the book but confessed that his own memory of July 1944 had filled him with "depression," probably because he had been reminded of his struggles with Nazism and his role on the fringes of the plot. The weak spots of the coup, he wrote, paled in comparison to the "audacity of morals and richness of spirit" of the men who gave their lives in their fight against the Hitler regime.

On 10 June 1966, possibly in response to criticisms by some academic historians of the all-too-conservative notions of politics of Goerdeler and his co-conspirators, Sethe pointed to the fractures in the 1944 resistance movement.[251] He thought that its Social Democrat members could not possibly have been in agreement with the conservatives on constitutional issues. But he hastened to add that "our admiration and our esteem for the men of 20 July is not diminished" by such differences of opinion. As will be seen in the next chapter, relating to the life and work of Marion Countess Dönhoff, Sethe's colleague at *Die Zeit*, she, too, believed that there were profound moral lessons to be learned from those who had given their lives to destroy an immoral and criminal dictatorship. For both of them the task of West German reconstruction was not just political and economic; it was also about the establishment of fundamental values, freedom of expression being only one of them.

By 1964 Sethe had become a regular commentator on domestic and foreign political issues of the day. He wrote, for example, on the British Profumo scandal, on Nikita Khrushchev, on Tito, and on the "demystified Empress" Soraya of Persia.[252] Among domestic themes there were pieces on politicians such as Eugen Gerstenmaier, Max Brauer, and Herbert Wehner, as well as on parliamentarism and federalism.[253] Above all, Sethe continued to press for keeping alive the question of reunification—though no longer within the 1937 borders but as a simple merger of East and West Germany. In one of his first articles after his move to *Die Zeit* he countered the view of Karl Jaspers, now a professor of philosophy at Basle, that the Germans had forfeited their claim to unity.[254] Two months later, Sethe asked whether, since 1960 had been a year of "world-political ferment," 1961 might be "a year of decision." [255] In November 1961, two months after the Berlin Wall had gone up, he returned to the question of contacts with the Soviets, arguing that negotiating was not tantamount to "capitulation."[256] On 4 February 1966, in reviewing a book by Schütz, the spiritus rector of the Kuratorium Freies Deutschland, he raised the question of whether reunification was still possible.[257]

Sethe's subsequent affirmative thoughts on this subject are to be found in his book "Opening to the East."[258] In a letter of 21 November 1966 no less a person than Rainer Barzel, the leader of the Christian Democratic Union/ Christian Social Union (CDU/CSU) parliamentary faction in the Bundestag, congratulated Sethe on his plea "for a policy that makes sense."[259] Sethe is likely to have been even more pleased by a letter that he received shortly before his death from Egon Bahr, Brandt's adviser, the architect of Ostpolitik, and the protagonist of the strategy of "change through rapprochement."[260] After years of having criticized Bonn's official policy on reunification and Adenauer's resistance to Brandt's and Bahr's recipes, Sethe could now look back on his journalistic career with some sense of achievement. But if one includes in an assessment of his professional life his work during the Weimar Republic and the Third Reich, it had been quite an arduous path with many setbacks, disappointments, and agonizing decisions.

It is because Sethe represents arguably the most telling case among the journalists at the center of this book that his vita has been examined first. His life was in many ways the most complex, starting with his becoming a scholar as well as a journalist and with his liberal-conservative editorial policies at the OA both before 1933 and after, when Hitler began to build his brutal dictatorship. He encapsulates the dilemmas of the Generation of '32, for whom Weimar's freedom of expression became ruthlessly suppressed. Sethe went into inner emigration, but his editorials for OA and later for FZ also showed how Germans who did not leave the country, went underground, or joined the NSDAP moved back and forth along a spectrum. At one end of it Sethe faced the question of commitment to active resistance. Later he reproached himself for not having been more courageous. But it is out of this self-criticism that his determination grew not only to spread the memory of those who were executed for their beliefs but also to put postwar West German journalism and freedom of expression on a firm foundation. His career suffered setbacks for the principles that he stood for, but he never diverged from them until he died from a massive heart attack on 21 June 1967.

2

The Intellectual Journey of Marion Countess Dönhoff

Preface

Marion Countess Dönhoff has rightly been deemed the "most outstanding [female] journalist among the Germans of the twentieth century."[1] She had a long and very influential career, first as an editor and later as the editor in chief and finally the publisher of the Hamburg weekly *Die Zeit*. She died in 2002 aged 92 and was buried, as she had always wanted to be, close to the mansion of the Hatzfeldts, the family into which her brother had married, in Crottorf in the Siegerland region east of Bonn.

Marion Dönhoff fits the generational time frame set out in the introduction.[2] She belongs to what I defined as the Generation of '32 in the sense that she was born in the decade and a half before 1914 and had experienced the end of the Weimar Republic as a politically conscious adult. Moreover, she, too, was confronted with the difficult question of how to react to the dictatorship that Hitler established so swiftly starting in January 1933. There are several differences, though, in her life in comparison to those of Sethe and Zehrer: some ten years younger than they, in 1933 she was still a university student writing her doctoral dissertation and did not become a journalist until after 1945. For an understanding of her career, both during the Nazi period and after the Second World War, it is also important that she was a woman in what was still very much a male-dominated world. These are significant factors when it comes to assessing her role as an "inner emigrant." Here she, an anti-Nazi of the first hour, moved more and more toward active resistance and, as will be seen, was lucky that the local Gestapo let her go after a brief interrogation following the failed July 1944 plot to kill Hitler. After 1945 she became a journalist who

Marion Countess Dönhoff, 1909–2002.
Photograph courtesy of Marion Dönhoff Stiftung.

wrestled with explanations of what had happened under Nazism and of what kind of society should be built out of the ruins of the German and European catastrophe.

However, although she died in 2002, this chapter primarily covers her life and work up to the late 1960s. However, it also covers two larger themes that point to certain continuities in her thought. She wrote about these most clearly in the 1990s, but they must be related to her socialization into a Prussian noble family, after which they became a basso continuo throughout her life. As I explained in the introduction, I chose the narrower postwar time frame not only because the two other journalists at the center of this book died in 1966 and 1967, but also because this seemed to me to be the moment when the process of founding the Federal Republic as a society and a polity had reached a certain closure, except for Dönhoff, who lived on. Beyond this shorter time frame and with respect to the generational analysis on which this book is based, it is now generally agreed that a new generation had emerged by the late 1960s, identified in recent scholarship as the "68ers." They began to challenge the postwar settlement and the political, moral, socioeconomic, and cultural axioms that the Generation of '32—and Sethe, Dönhoff, and Zehrer in particular—had tried to establish on the ruins of the Nazi dictatorship. I shall touch upon this generational challenge in more detail in chapter 4.

Family Life and Career in Times of Peace and War

Marion Dönhoff was born on 2 December 1909 into a noble family with a distinguished pedigree.[3] In the eighteenth century there were still two clans in Germany, one Polish and the other Prussian. But the former had died out, leaving the latter in possession of Friedrichstein, an imposing mansion about twelve miles east of Königsberg with some 3,700 hectares of land and forests, including the Quittainen estate sixty miles farther west. The traces of the Polish lineage were still visible even in the twentieth century in the first names of members of the clan, among them Bogislaw, about which I shall have more to say in a moment. Suffice it to say that Marion's father, August Count Dönhoff, was married to Ria, née von Lepel. They were also related via one of Marion Dönhoff's grandmothers to the no less distinguished Lehndorff family, whose Steinort estate, where their forebears had lived since 1400, was next to Friedrichstein.

The Dönhoffs had accumulated considerable wealth that enabled August, born in 1845, to maintain the mansion and estate in style. Like his father, he had joined the diplomatic service and, following his retirement, traveled extensively, leaving the management of the estate to inspectors and the large household to his wife. Later August became an influential member of the German Conservative Party, the bastion of the agrarian Prussian aristocracy, and was among the founders of the radical right-wing Fatherland Party in 1917. Before her marriage to August, Ria Dönhoff had been a lady-in-waiting (*Palastdame*) to Empress Auguste Victoria, the wife of Wilhelm II. Though she had married up, having savored the world of the high aristocracy in Berlin had made her very status conscious. Thus she expected her many domestic servants and other personnel to address her as "Excellency." Ria bore August seven children, among whom Heinrich, born in 1899, was the eldest and Marion the youngest after Christa, Yvonne, Dietrich, Christoph, and Maria. August died in 1919, so Marion did not really get to know him, and there is no record of his politics after the defeat of Germany in 1918. Still, it is safe to assume that a conservative spirit pervaded Friedrichstein. It was against this spirit that Marion and her brothers began to rebel in the 1920s.

Marion's rebellion set in during her school years.[4] First there were the early years, when she had private teachers at home and was under the strict discipline that family tradition imposed. Looking back, she thought that it was not her teachers who influenced her perceptions of the world, but the spirit of a close-knit rural community, no matter how stratified it continued to be. Later she went to a public school in Königsberg, where the family kept an apartment, before she spent her high school years at an all-girls *Lyceum*. Intelligent and highly motivated, she was then allowed to transfer to an all-boys *Gymnasium* in Berlin. Being the only woman was no doubt a challenge but reflected the more liberal thinking about education in the Weimar Republic. In 1929 she obtained her *Abitur* certificate, which was the ticket to admission to her later university studies and laid the foundations for her earning her doctorate and, after 1945, for her rise as an esteemed journalist.[5] However, her conservative mother gave her permission to go to university only after she had attended a finishing school where, rather grumpily, she learned to cook and knit.

Marion's years at Friedrichstein, away from the next city, were not dull. She was close to her siblings, especially to her brother Heinrich, who was ten years her elder. She also saw much of her cousins Heini and Sissi von Lehndorff. The trio spent many hours together riding and grooming their horses. Marion also cheerfully participated in hunting parties, in those days a popular pastime of the aristocracy. It was only much later that she came to disdain all blood sports. Having grown up in a strict "Prussian" household, she had learned self-discipline and hard work. She adhered to the austere sociocultural traditions and the elitist exclusiveness of her class, but, unlike many other aristocrats, she did not look back nostalgically on the Wilhelmine monarchy but rather tended to identify with the Republic. The Protestant faith was instilled in all the Dönhoff children very early on, and Marion, being the youngest, regularly had to say prayers before and after their joint meals. However, hers was not a routinized religiosity. As she put it in September 1926, religion was something "miraculous and truthful" to her.[6] She added that she wanted to be free and "have faith in her God." After all, humans of all cultures practiced some kind of *religio* through which they sought to transcend their mortality.

Meanwhile, Marion's mother was more rigid in her outlook and attitudes, and she tried to keep the family together following her husband's death. She expected formal dress at evening dinners, to which guests regularly came from the surrounding estates, from Königsberg, or from as far away as Berlin. Beyond such formality, Marion, growing up in the spacious mansion among many precious art objects and books, developed a keen love for her father's collections and especially for literature. She scoured the shelves of the library and discovered Thomas Mann's novels and Rainer-Maria Rilke's poetry but also the books of Leon Tolstoy and other famous Russian writers.

Intellectually, Marion was a modern woman, railing in March 1929 at the narrow-mindedness of "our cast."[7] An attractive woman, she kept up her reserve toward the young noblemen who showed an interest in her. Meanwhile, her sister Yvonne married Alexander von Kuenheim at age eighteen, and Maria, with Down syndrome, found a haven in Pastor Boldelschwingh's well-known mental asylum in Bethel, near Bielefeld, where, having escaped the Nazi "mercy killing" program, she died at age 65. Marion stayed in close touch with her brothers Heinrich and Christoph. Her brother Dietrich had married her cousin Sissi von Lehndorff, Marion's best female friend. Going home during breaks from her *Gymnasium* in Berlin, she found the long train journeys tedious and began to take a plane to Königsberg, where she was collected by Ludolf, the senior coachman at Friedrichstein. More alluringly, motor cars were also at their disposal in the 1930s when Marion became a sports car enthusiast. With a princely annual income of some 3,900 marks, plus a few perks, she acquired a white two-seater convertible and began to travel. In 1937 and again in May 1939 she went on long tours of the Balkans and Italy together with Yvonne. After the war she could be seen speeding in a Porsche from her home in the western suburb of Blankenese to the head office of *Die Zeit* in the center of Hamburg.

With the *Abitur* certificate in her pocket, she was invited to visit the United States and also went to see her brother Christoph in Kenya. Although she vigorously disagreed with the racist views of the Massai peoples he espoused, they never fell out. With few exceptions, family ties proved stronger than differing opinions among most of the aristocracy. The motorcars that were kept on the Dönhoff and Lehndorff estates would take the children on trips to the Baltic Sea coast and other sites, teaching them on at least one occasion that modern mobility also had its grave dangers when one day, on the way home after dark, one of their cars plunged into a deep river. Marion was able to free herself and reached the surface, while two small children drowned. It was a traumatic blow to all of them.[8]

Beyond the region there were the contacts between the larger clans, often related in the most convoluted ways and again finely stratified.[9] Without having to refer to the *Gotha Almanach*, children learned who was who, how they were cousins, and of what degree. This solidarity proved particularly important during the Nazi period, when some of Marion's cousins and friends became involved in the anti-Nazi resistance movement, while others joined the Nazi Party or Himmler's SS. Inevitably, this already created tensions within the Dönhoff family before Hitler's seizure of power, but Marion refused to be distracted from her plan to go to university, if only to escape from East Prussia and live a more intellectual and cosmopolitan life. She registered as a student at Frankfurt University to study economics, living with the Metzeler banking family and encountering Nazi students on campus, whom she disdained. After passing her examinations for a diploma in economics in May 1934, she had the good fortune that Professor Edgar Salin, who had moved from Frankfurt to Basle, took her under his wing so that she was able to escape the increasingly oppressive political climate of Frankfurt.[10]

Originally Marion wanted to do doctoral research on an international topic, but Salin persuaded her to undertake a close study of the economic development and administrative practices of the Friedrichstein estate. With the family archives virtually untouched, the project proved to be a very worthwhile assignment and invaluable for her career following the completion of her doctorate in 1935. Her brother Heinrich had meanwhile taken overall charge of the Dönhoff properties, while Marion began to manage Quittainen estate to the west.[11] However, when he decided to marry Dorothea Countess Hatzfeldt, whose family hailed from the Siegerland west of Cologne and was Catholic, strict inheritance rules obliged him to give up the Friedrichstein estate. It is still intriguing to read about the traditionalism of this aristocratic world and the power of its socializing practices, including hunting, which Marion Dönhoff came to dislike only after the war.

As war loomed in the later 1930s, it was more and more likely that her eldest brother Heinrich, more conservative than his sister though not a Nazi, would embark on a military career when called up, as indeed he did in 1939. He apparently quite enjoyed training with his mounted regiment at Insterburg, but when he participated in the invasion of Poland, he apparently witnessed disturbing brutalities. Having recovered from a serious injury sustained during the Polish campaign, he returned to his battalion and soldiered on. He was not killed in action but perished in November 1942 on his way to Smolensk on board a military plane that crashed near Kovno (Kaunas) in Lithuania. To make things worse, Karl August and Christoph von Dellinghausen, the two sons of Marion's sister Christa (who had died in childbirth in 1924), had also fallen early in the war. Marion was devastated, and, having taken charge of both Friedrichstein and Quittainen, tried to get permission to visit Heinrich's grave.[12]

Hitler's invasion of the Soviet Union in June 1941 and the fighting in the East thwarted Marion's plans to go to Kovno at the end of 1942. But she thought, perhaps somewhat naïvely, that her chances had improved a few months later. Requiring a special permission, she turned to Friedrich Werner Count von der Schulenburg, whom she had known in 1940 during his tenure as German ambassador to Moscow.[13] In October 1943 she asked him for his help so that she could visit the site on the anniversary of Heinrich's death. Schulenburg wrote to the German chargé d'affaires in Riga, who, he was convinced, would issue the requisite documents. He added: "Countess Dönhoff is an especially nice young lady (she is unmarried) and has visited me twice in Moscow; this is why I'd like to do her a favor." He would be particularly grateful if his colleague would accelerate the process. She did not need any currency or a place to stay since she would go for one night only and would be staying with an acquaintance. There was no need to worry about her safety while traveling to Lithuania. The Dönhoff Papers contain a thank-you note by Marion to Schulenburg in which she reports that she has had no news from Riga. It seems the trip never materialized.

However, Dönhoff's correspondence with Schulenburg is also interesting for an earlier exchange that resulted in her two visits to Moscow in 1940 during the Nazi-Soviet Pact years.[14] In her first handwritten note of 26 May 1940 she thanked Schulenburg for some caviar that he had sent her and announced her plan to fly to Moscow in June. She added that the days at the estate were filled with business until late in the evening and with "ever new worries." Her main connection with the outside world and "the great events" of this time was through the afternoon and evening news. She confessed that there was something unreal and frightening, as she was trying to grasp "the great developments concerning the future of Europe—if this notion still exists, while the shop here continues as if these matters were of no concern to us. But this is what everyone experiences today." Two weeks later she expressed her delight with his latest letter, adding that she had continued to ponder "the Volga Plan" as something that might still be implemented once the situation had calmed down. But she knew that all this lay in the more distant future.

The mention of Schulenburg's Volga Plan is puzzling. We know that he was among those German diplomats who hoped that the alliance with Stalin would last and that trade and economic relations that had been established after the conclusion of the Nazi-Soviet Pact in August 1939 could be intensified. However, with France defeated in June 1940, it was very likely that Hitler would turn east in an attempt to conquer "living space" and exploit the material and manpower resources of the Soviet Union after another swift victory of the kind that the Wehrmacht had just won in western and northern Europe.[15] It was Hitler's invasion with its unpredictable consequences that Schulenburg feared and therefore hoped to prevent at all cost. When this failed, the invasion also scuttled his Volga Plan. He returned to the Foreign Office, where he chaired the "Russia Committee" and by 1943–44 had become a committed opponent of the Nazi regime, though he did not belong to the inner circle of the July 1944 conspiracy. Since he was deemed to be less implicated in the failed coup, his trial was delayed, while the Foreign Office, in an attempt to obtain his release, argued with the Gestapo that Schulenburg's judgment had been impaired by his old age.[16] It was to no avail. He was condemned to death on 23 October and hanged in Berlin's notorious Plötzensee Prison on 10 November 1944.

This was also the fate of Marion Dönhoff's favorite cousin, Heinrich von Lehndorff. He had taken over the management of the Steinort estate from his uncle Carol, but during the war had also become actively involved in the resistance movement. Apparently he took this crucial step after he had observed the mass murder of Jews near Borissov and then learned that General Fedor von Bock, the commander of the Army Group Central, had ignored pleas from his junior officers to launch a protest.[17] Marion may have known about these atrocities from her cousin, but when she was asked after 1945 if she had ever heard anything about the extermination camps during the war, she professed ignorance. As in the case of Hans Scholl, on leave from the front in Munich in 1942, it was time and again the witnessing of anti-Jewish outrages and mass executions committed by both SS and Wehrmacht units that convinced some army officers that the only way to stop the carnage and to end the war was to assassinate Hitler and to stage a coup.

When the coup was finally attempted and it quickly became clear that Claus von Stauffenberg's bomb had not killed Hitler, Heinrich immediately became a suspect.[18] On 21 July the Gestapo drove into the Steinort courtyard to arrest him. Seeing their arrival from the main building, he fled into the adjacent woods. His wife tried to get help, but she was understandably in a panic, and it seems that in the resultant confusion there were misunderstandings and help never came. Even more dramatically, Heinrich, fearing that his wife, Gottliebe, in advanced pregnancy, would be incarcerated (as she was, then gave birth in prison) and that his children would be taken to a secret location with new names (as in fact happened), returned to Steinort and gave himself up. Carted off to Berlin, he was tried and executed, aged 35.[19] Gottliebe survived and, having been reunited with her daughters after the end of the war, found a place to live in Bremen. She may have expected more support from the Dönhoffs, but she and her family were eventually taken in by the Plettenbergs at their estate near Unna in Westphalia. Traumatized by her ordeal, Gottliebe tried to overcome her depression by turning to religion. Vera, one of her four daughters, is known to have made some critical remarks about the Dönhoffs, but these must be seen against the backdrop of the chaos at war's end and the flight to Western Germany. Marion, too, was destitute when she finally arrived in Westphalia after her escape on horseback from Friedrichstein. Later the families met again at reunions, but they were never close.

This difficult-to-reconstruct chain of events after the failed 1944 coup raises a broader question of where to place Marion politically seeing that at least two members of her family had become prominent Nazis. There was, first of all, her brother Christoph, who had joined the NSDAP in Kenya in 1935. After his return from East Africa, he had directed the legal department of the Nazi organization for Germans abroad (the Auslandsorganisation) in Paris before being drafted into the Waffen-SS in 1944.[20] However, while disagreeing fundamentally, Marion and he did not argue to the point of separation. Rather, true to the Dönhoff tradition, their affection for each other remained strong. Nor did Marion ever talk in public about his career. The other family member to become a Nazi was Bogislav Dönhoff, who is mentioned in subsequent correspondence. However, as was the case with so many family "secrets" circulating more widely among the German nobility, they were discussed only in private after the war. In the case of the Dönhoffs, these secrets appear in correspondence between Marion and one of her many cousins, Fürst zu Ysenburg und Büdigen, whose landed properties were situated in the region northeast of Frankfurt.[21] The two began their discussion after her cousin, whom she called "Pucky," had written to her on 25 June 1979 about the role of Social Democracy in Sweden and the Federal Republic and about Willy Brandt's Ostpolitik. (I shall come back to the substance of this exchange toward the end of this chapter in connection with Dönhoff's support of Brandt and a reconciliation between West Germany and her eastern neighbors.[22]) But then their exchange quickly devolved into an acrimonious but very revealing tit-for-tat about their clan's involvement with Nazism.

Replying three days after she received Pucky's letter of 25 June, Marion said she wondered if her cousin had learned anything from the past before she became even more personal:[23] "Dear Pucky, if you were to be ashamed of a member of your family, it would be the brother of your mother who was on 'Du' terms with the representatives of a system that made a pact with Moscow in 1939 and who put my mail under surveillance for a year in order to denounce me personally to the Gestapo." She felt that this relative could have written Pucky's letter.

The Fürst replied on 5 July, insisting that he did not wish to prolong their correspondence but did want to make one point relating to the Nazi past.[24] After all, there were "Bogi[slav] Dönhoff and his wife Nena," who were known for their "extreme Nazi views," which posed a danger to everyone. He assumed that the "Dönhoff family was not enthralled by these members." Bogi had been a "very weak person" who was under the influence of Nena, who was "extraordinarily evil" in her other attitudes as well. But this, he added, is what happens "if one marries someone from quite different circles who probably thought to create a position for herself in this fashion." In the end, he thanked Marion somewhat sarcastically for her "best greetings" at the end of her letter, signed so graciously with her full noble name of Marion Countess Dönhoff. This is why he would like to respond to her "especially cordially," as their correspondence had, at least for him, its peculiar charm. He signed this letter "Very cordially, as ever, your still old cousin Pucky."

While his endeavor to uphold the façade of civility is telling with regard to the modes of social intercourse among the West German aristocracy, it also indicates that the split that the Hitler regime had caused throughout German society between enthusiastic Nazis and anti-Nazis also ran through the Dönhoff family with reverberations that went well beyond 1945. The correspondence is reminiscent of the story of the Pomeranian von Thadden-Trieglaff clan, in which, at the one extreme, Elisabeth von Thadden was executed for her anti-Nazi resistance, while another family member, Adolf von Thadden, became the leader of the West German neo-Nazi National Democratic Party (NPD) in the 1960s.[25] As far as Marion's position during the Hitler dictatorship is concerned, it is safe to assume that she hated Nazism from the start but, instead of joining the active resistance, went into "inner emigration" to manage the family's estates in East Prussia at least for the time being. It is possible that her brother Heinrich thought that it was too dangerous for her, as a woman, to join an underground movement.

Anti-Nazi Resistance and the July 1944 Plot to Kill Hitler

At the same time, while Dönhoff withheld her views from her pro-Nazi brother Christoph, she was close enough to Heinrich von Lehndorff and Friedrich von der Schulenburg not to keep her opinions about Hitler to herself with them.

Consequently, rumors about her views and contacts were rife in East Prussia. She had frequently been traveling to Berlin, where she met with Peter Count Yorck and his wife, Marion, as well as other members of the 1944 conspiracy. She may also have been involved in the recruitment of Heinrich Count Dohna von Tolksdorf.[26] As a member of the East Prussian regional government, he was expected to play a key role after the coup had succeeded. This seems to indicate that Dönhoff also knew about the plot in general terms. On at least one occasion she visited Jakob Burckhardt, the former League of Nations commissioner for Danzig, in Switzerland and apparently gave him information about the anti-Nazi resistance in broad outline to pass on to foreign diplomats. Fritz-Dietlof von der Schulenburg had meanwhile also shed his initial enthusiasm for Hitler and become a member of the conservative resistance. In June 1944 he had visited Marion Dönhoff on her estate, and she was due to go to Berlin on 20 July to see him again. At the last minute, she decided against the trip and sent Schulenburg a telegram. However, it could not be delivered and was returned by the post office, so the Gestapo never saw it. It was such strange coincidences that saved her from becoming a serious suspect. According to her biographer Klaus Happrecht, she was a messenger and mediator who worked for Peter Yorck and other conspirators.[27]

However, after the coup had failed, Marion was taken to the Gestapo headquarters in Königsberg, where she was interrogated. It was not the events in Berlin that had put her into danger but her uncle Bogislav. As the previously mentioned correspondence between Dönhoff and her cousin Pucky zu Ysenburg und Büdingen revealed, "Bogi" had become a Nazi and, after moving to the Quittainen estate, befriended Erich Koch, the Gauleiter of East Prussia.[28] Evidently suspicious of Marion's activities, he had been checking her mail and had recorded the senders' addresses. These lists had been taken to Koch's office to be used in her interrogation. But she quickly realized that this was all they had and thus found it easy to refute any allegations. Before she was released, she was asked if she had anything to say about her Nazi uncle, whereupon she replied: "I consider the whole thing an act of personal revenge."[29] Following the failed coup, there is also the question of whether her brother Christoph or someone else close to the family with Nazi contacts informed the Lehndorffs and other families of where the arrested men were being held. As Heinrich had feared, his children were indeed given new names, but the older ones among them made certain that their real names were not forgotten. After they had been liberated by American troops, they were reunited with their families.

Years later, Gordon Craig, a historian at Stanford and a friend, recalled that Marion surmised that her duties on the estate ruled out any role for her in the resistance movement and that "therefore her name was on none of the lists of people earmarked for [a] position in the post-Hitler government."[30] As mentioned in chapter 1, this was also Paul Sethe's good luck when his name was mentioned as the editor in chief of the post-coup newspaper but was not in the inventory of positions that Goerdeler kept. Most of the men on this list were executed. In 1984 Dönhoff admitted in an interview that "I shouldn't have liked to have shot him [Hitler] myself. But I always said, 'The fellow has got to be killed, of course!' I don't know whether I would have done it myself if there had been no other alternative."[31] On a later occasion, she asked herself what in fact she had done; she answered by remarking opaquely that she "did what all rational people would do in such situations."[32] It is a comment that is significant in terms of the meaning of "inner emigration," involving an individual's agonizing move within the "gray zone" toward passive and later perhaps even active resistance. Paul Sethe, as we have seen, also faced this dilemma and later reproached himself for not having been more courageous but having done what "all rational people would do in such situations," knowing that the alternative was to accept torture and execution.

After Dönhoff had avoided arrest in 1944, her oppositional frame of mind certainly became more unbending; but in the climate of the ubiquitous death and chaos of the final months of the Nazi regime there was little scope for demonstrating that she had in fact moved firmly to the resistance end of the inner emigration spectrum.[33] Uncertain if she would have shot Hitler had she been given the opportunity, Marion found that all she could do while preparing for her flight on horseback to the West was to mourn the loss of her executed friends and relatives. Besides their fate on the gallows, other deaths were added. Along with the two sons of her sister Christa who had fallen, her brother Heinrich had died in an air crash. His two sons and a daughter had been orphaned when their mother, Dorothea, passed away. As she put it in retrospect:[34] "Nothing is worse than to lose all your friends and to be the only one left." In light of all these tragedies, it is hardly surprising that the rehabilitation of the men of the 20 July plot and spreading the knowledge of their sacrifice would be one of her most important missions after the war. This is why I shall turn first to the work that she began on their behalf during the postwar decades before examining the other causes that she took up once she had moved to Hamburg and started her career as West Germany's most influential female journalist.

Flight to West Germany, Mourning, and
Defending the Anti-Nazi Resistance

With the Red Army approaching Friedrichstein, Marion embarked upon a very dangerous flight on horseback in the winter of 1944–45 which, by early spring, finally took her to Schloss Vinsebeck, close to the Egge Montains in Westphalia.[35] It was owned by the Metternichs, who took her in. The three Dönhoff orphans were sent to the Hatzfeldts, their mother's family, at Crottorf in the Sieg river valley. Dieter, Sissi and their three children found shelter at the estate of Count Görtz in Brunkensen near Alfeld south of Hanover. This is where Marion Dönhoff joined them from Vinsebeck. Apparently it was Carl-Hans Count von Hardenberg who, himself a survivor and living nearby, encouraged her to write down what she knew about the 1944 conspiracy. By the autumn of 1945, she had produced a typescript entitled *In Memoriam 20. Juli 1944: Den Freunden zum Gedächtnis gewidmet*, some three hundred copies of which were subsequently circulated to family and friends.[36] She began by explaining the rationale behind this essay. It was the time of the first anniversary of the 20 July plot, the day "on which Germany lost its best and most genuine patriots at one stroke." Those who knew of the background of these events were urged to "guard the inheritance" and at the same time "make it accessible to those who did not have the privilege of being close to the [conspiratorial] circle of friends."

This was the moment, she continued, "to say something about the spiritual background and inner posture" of the men of July 1944. While killing Hitler had been their main motive, she wrote, the "precondition[s] of their work" should also be considered: the task of the "spiritual transformation of the human being, the rejection of materialism, and the transcending of nihilism as a form of life." Hitler's opponents, she averred, were not merely the antipodes of the Nazis. It was rather that human beings were once again to be put into a Christian world order that was "rooted in the metaphysical" so that they would be able to "breathe again the full width of the space that lies between Heaven and Earth." Moreover, they would be "liberated from the confines of a world that views itself in absolute terms because blood and race and the law of causality" had been taken "as the ultimate wisdoms."

Anticipating later scholarly arguments about the origins of fascism, Marion Dönhoff went on to postulate that the abandonment of God had begun in France and Britain after 1789 and had culminated in the "orgies of Hitler's rule." The spiritual leaders that she now had in mind had developed a "form of life" that differed from that of the nineteenth century, one that was in complete harmony with practical life. Fundamentally, they had conceived of this new form of life in both European and Christian terms. Fascism and democracy, collectivism and individualism, had been mere slogans. It had been no less disturbing that humans had become "tools of technology" as well as "creatures of abstract political ideas." They were no more than a "function of science" and "servants of economic laws" that had been transformed into absolutes. By contrast, the task of the future was to free humans from all prejudices and to erect in front of them a genuine *humanitas*, a true image of humans in their dignity and proud self-confidence. To Dönhoff these postulates were not abstractions. The men of 20 July had had tangible aims, one of which was to reconstruct Germany from scratch as a state of the rule of law built on Christian foundations. At the international level, the idea of economic self-sufficiency would have to be abandoned. Instead Germany was to be integrated into the community of European nations as well as the global economy and society.

On subsequent pages Dönhoff discussed the first attempts by opponents in the officer corps to overthrow the Hitler regime during the crisis of 1938–39. There was also the constant danger of denunciation and the threat of being sent to a concentration camp or even being executed. But this did not deter the conspirators. It was from those spiritual foundations that they had moved toward rebellion. In the end, Marion left no doubt that those friends who gave their lives did not do so to fill "the meat-pots of Europe," as decreed by Hitler. Instead, they died "for the reconstitution of the honor and dignity" of the Germans. Insisting that success was never the only yardstick of judgment, she wrote that the spirit in which the men of July 1944 had taken action was no less important. Her hope was therefore that these men would serve as an admonition to the defeated nation and that, irrespective of their conspiracy's not having ushered in a new beginning, their spirit would live on. Achieving wide recognition of these ideas now became a cause to which she devoted the rest of her life.

Having been hired by the newly established weekly *Die Zeit*, Dönhoff moved to Hamburg, renting at first a small room in the house of Erik Blumenfeld, a friend of Gerd Bucerius, one of the weekly's publishers.[37] In her early articles she took up more general philosophical and ethical themes. Signed with her initials "M.D.," one of her first pieces appeared on 21 March 1946.[38] In it she commemorated the dead of World War II. The task of the postwar period, she added, was a "spiritual transformation of the *Mensch*." The image that humankind had of humans had to be "fundamentally renovated."

To achieve this, human energy was insufficient; it was dependent on some transcendental power. "The dying of the dead" was to be made "fruitful in a superior sense" so that the dead would be remembered "in the full consciousness of the responsibility that this war, that has affected everyone in the same way," has been put "on the shoulders of the survivors." In conclusion, Marion pleaded for a "new order in the spirit of fraternity to be built on the ruins of a fragile world."

In weighing this very early publication of March 1946, we can see that her mention of Christianity and faith was nothing unusual. She had been religious person in the 1920s, out of her free will. Later her executed friends had found consolation toward the end of their lives in their belief in the existence of a transcendental world. Here the roles of theologians like Dietrich Bonhoeffer, Pater Delp, and Eugen Gerstenmaier had been particularly important; of these only Gerstenmeier survived the mass executions at the end of the war.[39] Their farewell letters were among the earliest documents of the period, published by families and friends. After 1945 Marion Dönhoff was not a regular church-goer; she expressed her faith more spontaneously. Thus, in December 1952 she wrote to Carl Burckhardt two days after the Christmas holidays that she had made it her habit, when in Bonn or elsewhere after a busy day, to take a fifteen-minute "break in a church. That is wonderfully relaxing."[40] It must also be remembered that there was a more general upsurge in church attendance. The fact that the Catholic Church and the Vatican had been maneuvering rather ambivalently when dealing with Mussolini's and Hitler's versions of fascism and that the Protestants had split into the pro-Nazi "German Christians" and the anti-Nazi "Confessing Church" was quickly swept under the rug.[41] Many ordinary Germans were looking for moral leadership from the churches and were prepared to ignore their failure to raise their voices against injustice and oppression before 1945. The many solemn services that were conducted by both denominations in the Western zones of occupation had something soothing for people who sought to forget or tried to cope with their losses of loved ones and the ubiquitous misery. Indeed historians have only just begun to fathom the extent of the mourning for a lost husband, son, or close relatives that took place in all too many families.

After her more general commemoration of the dead in March 1946, Dönhoff took the opportunity of the second anniversary of the 1944 plot to write a piece titled "The Secret Germany of the Men of 20 July,"[42] followed in October by a more focused one titled "Born on 22 June 1909. Executed on 4 September 1944."[43] Here she discussed the youth and adult life of her favorite cousin,

Heinrich von Lehndorff, and concluded with extracts from a letter that he had written "from the bunkers" of Roland Freisler's People's Court: "Christian faith and the belief in a heavenly sphere are the only things that support us in our plight. But the path will probably lead through suffering." Lehndorff then envisioned the future, asserting that "all that is old must first be torn away from us; only then will it be possible to become a new creature. This at least is the faith in which I shall die without fear and angst."

By the autumn of 1946, the first of the more general books and articles on the resistance had begun to appear, among them a piece in *Der Tagesspiegel* by Erik Reger, who had made a name for himself as a critic of German industry at the end of the Weimar Republic. Now he spoke rather disdainfully of the "improvised resistance" of the 20 July plot: the conspirators did not want to root out Hitler but merely tried to preserve what could still be salvaged. In her response of 16 January 1947, Dönhoff vigorously defended Goerdeler, who may have been "romantic or utopian" but was not a "militarist."[44] Rather he had been aiming at "an ethical foundation, equal rights, justice, and freedom of the intellect and conscience, protection against arbitrariness and terror, the recognition of the rights of others, preparedness to achieve concilia- tory compromise [and] restoration of morality." What had been at stake for the Germans was the possibility of regaining their spiritual consciousness, though she also admitted that the failed assassination had been in some ways amateurish.

She then commented on a book by Hans Bernd Gisevius that she deemed "questionable."[45] There were indeed problems with Gisevius's account, but perhaps mainly because he had written about the anti-Nazi resistance very much from the perspective of his own career and peculiar experience, having started his professional life as a high-ranking officer in the Gestapo, where he served until Himmler removed him in 1936.[46] While he maintained some of his earlier and rather dubious connections, for example, with Arthur Nebe and Hjalmar Schacht,[47] he had subsequently joined the military *Abwehr* of Admiral Wilhelm Canaris, an avowed enemy of the Nazi regime, and therefore had some knowledge of the anti-Nazi resistance.[48] Whatever the merits of his book, it no doubt suffered from the fact that information on the German resis- tance movement was still scant in 1946–47. It was Gisevius's lack of informa- tion about 20 July that upset Marion Dönhoff. The men of 20 July, she insisted, wanted to counter the Nazi regime with humanity and the reestablishment of the rule of law. They were a "model" for postwar society. She signed her article very determinedly as "Marion Gräfin Dönhoff."

With her duties as a political editor at *Die Zeit* growing, by the late 1940s her op-ed pieces had turned to more general commentaries on postwar West German politics and European unification. She also proffered her memories of life and landscapes and what had happened in East Prussia in 1945 as the Red Army adopted a merciless campaign of revenge with rapes and murders—a topic that for many women remained too traumatic to discuss in public. These were the years when she met Richard von Weizsäcker, who was assisting in the defense of his father, Ernst, during the trials of Foreign Office diplomats at Nuremberg.[49] Learning about Ernst's role in the Third Reich through the eyes of his son, Marion Dönhoff wrote quite scathingly about the Nuremberg Trials and the judicial decisions of the Western Allies, arguing that they were based on ex post legal norms and that Germans with creditable anti-Nazi records should also have been appointed as justices.[50] By 1950 she was agitating for an end to all war crimes trials and urging US High Commissioner John McCloy to pardon some of the prisoners at Landsberg. It seems that she genuinely held her critical views of Allied policies but also knew that they were shared by many ordinary Germans who resented the de-Nazification procedures.

What was most distressing to Dönhoff, however, was the fact that those same Germans continued to reject the men of 20 July as traitors. Here Goebbels's propaganda was having its long-term impact beyond 1945. As a result, the widows and children of those involved with the 1944 plot were being ostracized, and it took some time for these popular perceptions to change.[51] Marion Dönhoff saw it as her mission for the "Other Germany" to become accepted and to serve as an example of the moral reconstruction that she felt had to be undertaken after the collapse of a totally immoral and corrupt regime that had so blatantly violated all standards of civilization. With this in mind she published, in August 1950, an article on Gerstenmaier, the Protestant minister who, at age 28, had been arrested by the Gestapo in 1934 when he was a student of philosophy at Tübingen University.[52] Subsequently, he finished his doctorate and *Habilitation* thesis at remarkable speed; but when he wanted to teach theology, his *venia legendi*, that is, his right to give lectures, was cancelled in 1937. He was fortunate enough to get a job with the External Affairs Office of the evangelical church that enabled him to travel abroad to promote contacts with Germany's neighbors and also to visit German prisoners. During the war he became a member of Helmut von Moltke's Kreisau Circle, the anti-Nazi resistance group that met at the Moltke estate in Silesia. After describing Gerstenmaier's experiences in prison after the failed coup, Dönhoff concluded her article with a sentence from a letter that had been smuggled to the widow of one of his executed friends. It said that his experiences in the face of death could be summed up by "two insights: first, *Deus est,* and second, *pro vobis.*"

On 23 July 1953 she reviewed a slim volume by Peter Lotar, *Gespräche der letzten Nacht* (Conversations of the final night) that contained renderings of conversations of "the final night" before the execution that she titled "The Image of the Mensch."[53] She added that only "our generation" knew of this unique predicament "between abyss and eternity, filled with deepest skepticism and supreme sovereignty." To her this was the situation in which the "image of the Mensch" was being revealed "beyond the reality of the individuals" who lived through those last hours. Dönhoff wrote in conclusion that "some of these conversations may indeed have occurred." What she was certain about was that from all that had been written about the 20 July plot, its participants should be included in this group. After all, these conversations were the closest "atmospherically to the spirit of the circle of friends around Helmut von Moltke and Peter Yorck."[54]

In 1954 the tenth anniversary of the July Plot was coming up. There had been some movement in West German public opinion, at least as far as attitudes towards the conservative resistance were concerned.[55] This shift included views on the Social Democrat opposition to Hitler—a field in which the SPD and a number of historians had launched their own research projects. Moreover, among the participants in the 20 July coup had been a number of Social Democrat politicians and trade union leaders who were also tried and executed after its failure. Only the Communist resistance against Hitler continued to be a nontopic in the Federal Republic at a time when the Cold War was waged quite fiercely between East and West. While the Communist Party had been outlawed in 1955, Communists had been among the very first actively to resist Hitler until they had been largely wiped out by the Gestapo by 1935. After the war, their widows had great difficulties gaining recognition of their compensation claims in the Federal Republic. Also it took until the 1960s before research projects on local resistance groups began.[56] As to Mannheim, Hitler had never gone to this working-class city to make a speech, knowing that he would be received in icy silence. It took another two decades for scholarly books to appear in the West on the Red Orchestra group that was deemed to have worked with the Soviet Union.[57] This research demonstrated that they had also been in touch with Allied agents in Switzerland. It is to Marion Dönhoff's credit that she began quite early to speak up for recognition of the Communist resistance. After all, she had faced the question of what it took to join the resistance and to risk one's life.

It was in this slowly changing ideological environment that, on 15 July 1954, she wrote an article titled "Das Gewissen steht auf" (The conscience takes a stand) in which she pointed out that "a system that identifies a party with the state and then equates this state with the people is bound to have all those as its opponents who still consider other values more binding or more important."[58] There "are no rules for this conflict," she added: "Everyone must decide for him/herself." Accordingly, it was not surprising to her that, apart from many individual resisters, Hitler also considered the churches as obstacles to his regime. She concluded by quoting in some detail from Pater Delp's letters written when he faced execution. She had taken the title of her article from a book written by Annedore Leber, the widow of Social Democrat Julius Leber, who was hauled before Freisler's People's Court after the failure of the 20 July coup and then murdered.[59] In it Leber had collected some sixty-four biographies of members of the German resistance. Dönhoff concluded her piece by referring to the "chain" of those killed by the Nazis, which had been made up of young apprentices, students, workers, officers, as well as academics. It was her way of demonstrating once more that the Nazi claim that the opponents had merely been a small "clique of traitors" was wrong.

At the same time, she did not forget to make specific mention of the friends she had lost and had first written about as early as 1945, among them three scions of noble families: Helmuth von Moltke, Peter Yorck, and Captain Wilhelm-Ulrich Count Schwerin von Schwanenfeld, who, though he had earlier been active in the ethnic conflicts between Germans and Poles, had been so perturbed when he learned of the mass murder of Poles during the German invasion in September 1939 that he had joined the resistance.[60] Freisler, after a particularly aggressive outburst in his People's Court, sentenced him to death. To stress the importance of this commemoration, *Die Zeit* also published a review, titled "Der 20. Juli" and probably commissioned by Dönhoff, of Eberhard Zeller's recent book *The Spirit of Freedom*.[61]

Realizing how important the young generation was in bringing about a shift in public opinion, she traveled to Flensburg, near the Danish border, to participate in a panel discussion in March 1956. The event had been triggered by a working group of high school seniors who felt that the 20 July plot had been left out of their lesson plan. Responding to this criticism, the school had invited a history professor, together with a theologian and Marion Dönhoff, to discuss the issue.[62] Rather dismayed by the statements of the historian, Dönhoff moved the discussion to the question of the motives of the conspirators and tyrannycide, referring to Trott, Yorck, Leber, Schulenburg, and Stieff.[63]

She confessed that there were moments when "any revenant" might have capitulated and left the meeting in the face of this poorly informed academic, saddened by the sense "that twelve years later no one knows anything about the fire" that these men felt. However, the subsequent discussion turned out to be heated and was concluded by the theologian, who, Dönhoff thought, had been close to the resistance movement. At any rate, this panelist "at the end conjured up something of the spirit" that had driven the men who had given their lives.

Fast-forward to the next major commemoration on the occasion of the twentieth anniversary of the plot in 1964. This time Hans Rothfels was asked to write an article; it was a telling choice.[64] He had started his career as a professor at Königsberg University, where he had promoted the idea of a "Germanization" of the East. Among his followers were Theodor Schieder and Werner Conze, who wrote some very "brown" memoranda on this subject and, together with Hermann Aubin at Breslau, were among the intellectual progenitors of ethnic cleansing.[65] Hailing from a Jewish family, his nationalist reputation saved Rothfels from being forced to leave straightaway in 1933. But by 1936 Nazi anti-Semitism had become so virulent that he had fled to the United States. Brown University in Providence, Rhode Island, first employed him on a temporary basis before he was able to move on to the University of Chicago. When the war had ended, he became one of a small cohort of refugee historians who returned. He accepted a chair at Tübingen University, from which he wielded great influence within the West German historical profession. He was among the founders of the Institut für Zeitgeschichte (Institute for Contemporary History) in Munich and the editor of its influential academic journal, the *Vierteljahrshefte für Zeitgeschichte*. In 1948 Rothfels had published one of the first books in English of the conservative resistance. Titled *The German Opposition to Hitler*, it attempted an "appraisal" of this movement.[66]

Given Rothfels's prestige in the Federal Republic and his refugee credentials, Marion Dönhoff must have been very happy to have recruited him for this article. Rothfels decided to commemorate the work of Adam Trott zu Solz and his attempts to persuade the British government to stop appeasing Hitler.[67] His message: if Chamberlain had confronted Hitler during the Munich crisis of 1938 instead of caving in yet again, Ludwig Beck and Goerdeler might have moved forward with a firm plan to remove Hitler. While the criticism of British policy in 1938 was merely implied, Rothfels examined Trott's ideas on German foreign policy. He argued that they had been thoroughly "Western" and had advocated the preservation of basic values in the face of Hitler's "demonic character."[68] Reinforcing a more generally held view, he advanced the principle of the "freedom and dignity of the Mensch."

Without going into further detail, the Dönhoff Papers contain many more private references to the 20 July plot. It may be that the pain over the loss of her personal friends lessened over the years. But they and the events of 1944 were always on Marion's mind.[69] Among the letters she wrote or received on this subject, there are two that are worth mentioning here. First of all, she had apparently been thinking for some time about writing a dramatization of the 1944 plot for the stage. What led her to this plan was a generational feeling. She believed that it had become difficult to transmit the spirit of the resistance to young West Germans. The way forward seemed to be to write a play. Feeling a strong sense of obligation but not having any experience in this genre of creative writing, she turned to the Swiss dramatist Friedrich Dürrenmatt on the day of the fortieth anniversary of the plot, requesting a conversation on how to conceptualize and structure the project.[70] If the play was never written, it might have something to do with Dürrenmatt's reply, in which he pinpointed the extraordinary challenges of this enterprise.[71] The problem, he wrote, lay in the fact that "opposition inside totalitarian states cannot be judged from the outside." However, the audience would "by force of circumstance stand outside." Furthermore, because the attempt had failed, the conspirators had been "spared from seizing power" in a situation that was quite unpredictable. Dürrenmatt mentioned one of his pieces in which he let "a politician say to a dissident who assumes power: 'Being too menschlich for this world, you will be pushed into inhumanity. And if you do not become inhuman at this point, this land will be even more inhuman.'" In short, there were multiple problems that he would be happy to discuss with her, including the dilemma of "inner emigration" and of what it meant to live under the Nazi dictatorship as an anti-Nazi. It is not clear if this discussion ever took place.

When Marion Dönhoff published another article on the occasion of the fortieth anniversary, it was Gerd Bucerius who wrote to her on the day after 20 July 1984.[72] He observed that the piece contained thoughts "that have tortured me for years." But nothing was more uplifting "than to see one's own disordered ideas in print, and on top of it nicely sorted and splendidly put." That she herself could not let go, either, emerges from a letter she wrote to Pavel Kohut in July 1978:[73] That day "on which I lost all my friends is a very special day full of sorrow and mourning, but also filled with gratitude that I was privileged to be among those who fought for the preservation of law and human dignity."

There can be no doubt that Dönhoff was very serious about such statements. Indeed, her constant struggle with the meaning of her loss raises the question of how millions of Germans or, better still, Europeans, dealt with their bereavement.[74] It is an aspect of the postwar period that has probably been most extensively researched with respect to Jewish survivors, with much work still to be done on what went on in West German families who had lost loves ones.[75] Their situation had been made worse because so many soldiers had died without graves that could be visited. This is why Marion Dönhoff's writings on this subject give us a good impression of how deep the shock was and also of the sense of the gaping holes left in the lives of survivors. At the same time, it never was a purely personal issue for her. From 1945 onward, she had worked indefatigably to get the West German public, but also foreigners with strong anti-German feelings, to accept that there had been "Another Germany" and that the failure to kill Hitler and to topple the Nazi regime must be kept separate from the ethical values that the resistance stood for and hoped to restore to a post-Nazi society.

Since the founding of the Federal Republic in 1949 and the emergence of a free press that was no longer subject to Allied censorship or, since 1949, to judicial review, on grounds of a violation of the Constitution in such cases as those of blatant neo-Nazi propaganda and activism, there had been many articles, pamphlets, and books that condemned the anti-Nazi resistance.[76] This was also the time when World War II veterans and the former members of Waffen-SS units began to organize, among them the Grossdeutschland division. At its 1951 rally, Otto Remer was hailed as the commander of the guard battalion that had been crucial on 20 July 1944 in thwarting the arrest of key Nazis such as Goebbels by the conspirators.[77] When he learned that Hitler had survived the bomb explosion at his Rastenburg headquarters, Remer had stopped the coup in its tracks by countering the orders that were coming out of the Bendlerstrasse to seize the reins of government in Berlin and elsewhere as far away as Paris, where the local top SS brass were temporarily locked up before the failure of the coup in Berlin became known. Writing to Marion Dönhoff about this Waffen-SS rally on 21 May 1951, Axel von dem Bussche, one of the plotters who had survived and now fought for the rehabilitation of his executed comrades, wanted to undermine the claim that Grossdeutschland represented the "opinion of the war generation as such" and to make certain that such meetings did not warp the larger effort of West German democratic reconstruction.[78]

Ten years later, Dönhoff involved herself in another case that she felt ran counter to her quest to make the resistance the lodestar of post-Nazi West

German society. In this case it was more by coincidence that she heard of a plan by the right-wing Seewald Verlag in Stuttgart to publish the reports of the interrogations of the plotters that Ernst Kaltenbrunner, the head of the Reich Security Main Office, had collated for Martin Bormann and his boss, Hitler.[79] Since these documents had not been carefully scrutinized, annotated, and edited by a team of expert historians but were scheduled to appear with only a brief introduction, Dönhoff urged Heinrich Seewald to delay publication until an edition had been prepared that met professional standards. She also mobilized Hans Rothfels and the Munich Institut für Zeitgeschichte. Accordingly, Hermann Graml, one of the historians at the institute, was sent to Stuttgart to convince Seewald that it was in the interest of his firm and its reputation that he should wait. But the latter, thinking that he could land a coup, was either unwilling or for legal reasons unable to heed this advice, published the book, created a stir, and received harsh criticism. Ironically, though, it may have helped the rehabilitation of the men of 20 July.[80] The bias of the reporting, which was designed to confirm Hitler in his views that the plot was a huge "treachery," was just too blatant for even a semi-informed reader. It may be taken as yet another indication of change that Bonn decided in 1963 to fly the Republican flag thenceforth at half-staff on public buildings on 20 July.[81]

It is only against the background of these earlier experiences that we can understand Marion Dönhoff's strong reaction when, in the mid-1960s, two prominent historians, Hans Mommsen and Hermann Graml, began to challenge earlier interpretations of the significance of the 20 July resistance to Hitler.[82] In his conversation with Seewald, Graml had pointed to the serious research that had by then begun at the Munich Institute. One of their tasks had been to look closely at the statements and documents that Goerdeler and others had prepared for the time after a successful coup. Researchers now took the view that the political and constitutional ideas and plans that had been developed in 1944 would not have provided the foundations upon which a parliamentary democratic polity could have been built. The concepts were just too conservative and backward-looking. Ian Kershaw, who was familiar with Mommsen's thoughts on the Nazi regime and its opponents, summarized the critique as follows:[83] "The fateful experience of Nazism confirmed for conservative resistance groups their distrust of mass democracy, since they saw the Third Reich as the logical culmination of the plebiscitary, populist, and demagogic potential of the party-political system."

To be sure, Mommsen and Graml conceded that there were "differences of emphasis" among the plotters, and yet "their political ideas were essentially oligarchic and authoritarian, resting heavily on corporatist and neo-conservative notions advanced in the Weimar Republic." Their visions of the future of Germany within the community of nations did contain a few broad hints concerning the organization of postwar Europe. They envisioned some kind of federation, but on the whole the task they saw in front of them was to restore the territorial national state, and as far as Germany was concerned this meant, for many, a nation within the borders of 1937. It has already been mentioned that members of the resistance such as Adam Trott stood for more progressive political ideas and social reform. But Mommsen probably had a point when he argued that Goerdeler's memoranda were not suited to the formation of the basis upon which a new Germany could have been built.[84]

However, as we have seen, Marion Dönhoff's quest was not primarily concerned with constitutional issues. She believed that Hitler's totally immoral and criminal regime had so radically destroyed all standards of civilization that the Germans had to start to rebuild those standards from scratch. It was this that her friends of the resistance movement had ultimately stood for. It had been their Christian faith, with its ethical axioms, that had given them the strength to act against the Nazi regime and to face death calmly when they were executed under the most sadistic circumstances at Plötzensee prison. Ultimately, it seems, therefore, that Mommsen and Dönhoff looked at the 20 July movement and its lessons on two different levels. In the 1960s and also in later years, this led to debate and some acrimony. But looking at it with be benefit of hindsight from the twenty-first century, it seems that the two camps were both right. To be sure, a democratic order had to be build and made to work properly, but this could be done only on the basis of a new ethical order with a system of deeply embedded values, which would make certain that a relapse into Nazi immorality could never happen again.

As the research and debate on the conservative resistance to Hitler continued into the 1980s, fresh findings moved Dönhoff in at least one respect. She learned that many of the plotters of 1944 had originally welcomed the Nazi seizure of power and, believing that Hitler could be contained or even tamed, had badly underestimated the energy with which the Nazis would pursue their aim of turning the country into a one-party dictatorship. However, she insisted that the context of the time must be considered as well. Thus she took Klemens von Klemperer, a refugee historian from Austria and a professor at Smith College in Massachusetts, to task by telling him, though rather politely, that his approach to the history of the Third Reich was "not quite fair" when he argued from hindsight that Hitler had been a "criminal rather than a savior."[85]

For her it was too much to expect that all Germans should have opposed Hitler "in the first years after 1933." She then added to her typed letter a note in her own hand: after all, Hitler had managed to move "7 million unemployed off the streets in 5 years" so that Germany had full employment by 1938.[86] This background alone, she concluded, explained why Ludwig Beck took the right actions to overthrow Hitler in 1938 but made "naïve statements" in 1933.[87] In a letter of August 1984 to Dolf Sternberger, by then a professor at Heidelberg after an earlier career at the FZ and the FAZ, she evidently had Mommsen and other academic historians in mind when she spoke of "the damned habit of the historians" to measure "past ages with the yardstick of today."[88] This was perfectly in line with the attitude that she had adopted in her 1945 essay and made the theme of a speech forty years later that she had been invited to give in Oxford:[89] "On the Ethos of Resistance."

In light of Marion Dönhoff's tireless preoccupation with the legacy of the participants in the 20 July 1944 coup well into in end of the twentieth century, the conclusions of Eckart Conze in his 2003 "The Uprising of the Prussian Nobility: Marion Countess Dönhoff and the image of the Resistance against National Socialism in the Federal Republic of Germany" deserve serious consideration.[90] As he stressed, he did not wish to criticize her for her effort to give the conservative resistance its proper place in history. Yet this did not prevent him from subjecting the evidence that had been found over the decades to scholarly scrutiny. For Conze it was clear that she had been shaped "by the events surrounding the plot and by the death of a number of her relatives and friends." She had also helped to establish new traditions in the "young Federal Republic" as well as to reconsolidate "the German aristocracy after 1945 and its integration into West German postwar society."

Ultimately, it is indeed difficult to overestimate Dönhoff's experience of a totalitarian dictatorship in which even a slightly critical remark about Nazism could have lethal consequences. Also difficult to overstate is her determination, resulting from those experiences, to reestablish standards of humanity and ethics that she believed the Nazis had totally corrupted and destroyed. Her concern was to restore the country's "moral hygiene."[91] In a letter to Burckhardt of November 1953, she wrote that she always remembered her dead friends, especially on the date that her brother Heinrich had been killed in a plane crash near Kovno in 1942.[92] And she did not stop holding up these men as models for postwar West Germany. The July 1944 attempt on Hitler's life remained a "moral-political deed" that she wanted to see recognized as such by all West Germans without monumentalizing it.[93]

Pondering Her Lost *Heimat* and the
Idea of a Reunified Germany

There is a story related to Dönhoff's mourning that was no less personal to her than her quest for a fundamental renewal of German society: the loss of her *Heimat* (defined later) with the many memories she had of her youth in East Prussia. Even after having established herself quite comfortably in her small house in Hamburg-Blankenese, her longing for the countryside never left her. In September 1988, Kurt Körber, the Hamburgian entrepreneur and philanthropist, remarked in a letter to her that she was "no doubt decisively shaped by your Heimat."[94] It is indeed a notion that she also wrote about a lot, most popularly in the slim volume titled *Namen, die keiner mehr nennt: Ostpreussen* (Names that no one mentions anymore).[95] It was first published in 1962, and its paperback version had reached an imprint of 150,000 copies in the early 1980s. It contains, on the one hand, an account of the tour of Masuria that Dönhoff and Sissi undertook on horseback in September 1941. It also has a chapter on the "economic miracle" of this region two centuries earlier and an essay on the remnants of the "Spirit of the Teutonic Knights," with whom her family had come centuries ago to settle in the East. But at the same time Dönhoff described the "Life and Death of an East Prussian Nobleman," her cousin Heinrich von Lehndorff, and the chaos of the final weeks and days before her own escape on horseback.

So Dönhoff experienced not only mourning for close members of her family and friends but also the loss of all that Friedrichstein represented. When the Russians arrived, the schloss first went up in flames and was later razed to the ground. Invaluable collections, photos, and documents were destroyed that would have reminded her of the happy days she had spent on the Dönhoff estates. This was her *Heimat*—a term that is very difficult to translate and that the American historian Celia Applegate has written about.[96] It is not a rational concept but one that stirs up emotions. It reflects an irrational attachment to a place and its cultural traditions that no longer existed in Dönhoff's postwar life. Later she admitted that it had taken "decades until I was able to accept" what the loss of *Heimat* meant to her:[97] She "was missing the landscape, Nature, the animals of that disappeared world." There were also those thousandfold sounds that had become forever "encased" in her mind. For a long time, she added, she had been hoping against all hope that "some miracle would happen." There was the consciousness of her earlier life during the day, but also "the nocturnal dreams" that her *Heimat* would be restored.

However, those dreams could not be separated from the political realities that had come to exist in Central Europe after 1945. Millions of refugees and expellees had fled to western Germany.[98] By the late 1940s they had begun to organize to demand the restoration of former German territories in the East within the borders of 1937. Some of them hoped to achieve this by peaceful negotiation with the Soviet Bloc countries. Others were much more militant and set their hopes on the United States, many of whose politicians had adopted a radical Cold War rhetoric in the East-West conflict. President Dwight D. Eisenhower's secretary of state, John Foster Dulles, was not the only one talking about rolling the Soviets back behind their prewar borders and of liberating its satellites from Stalinist rule.[99] It seems that Dönhoff also harbored revisionist thoughts of this kind, even if they lacked a military dimension and looked for a negotiated settlement of border problems.

Such an opportunity seemed to have come when in the spring of 1952 Stalin offered the reunification of a neutralized Germany. This, as we have seen in chapter 1, unleashed a huge debate in West Germany and also among the Western Allies on whether to accept this offer and enter into Four-Power discussions or to reject it out of hand as a Soviet ploy to prevent the Federal Republic from making a military contribution to NATO.[100] While Paul Sethe, Rudolf Augstein, and other journalists favored exploring Stalin's offer, Chancellor Konrad Adenauer firmly rejected it. Dönhoff took a middle position. In an article titled "Five Minutes to Twelve" she declared the issue to be a question of conscience.[101] She felt that an attempt had to be made to explore Stalin's offer. The initiative went nowhere, and within a year Stalin was dead, unleashing a power struggle in Moscow from which Nikita Khrushchev eventually emerged as the victor. Next there was the June 1953 uprising in East Germany that showed the fragility of communist rule but also that the Kremlin would not abandon its Western possessions.[102] It also became clear that, their Cold War rhetoric notwithstanding, the Americans would not come to the rescue of the East Germans in 1953 or to that of the Hungarians and Poles in 1956, realizing that this would lead to a nuclear confrontation.

Even before these developments, there had been voices in the United States who wanted to replace the increasingly empty rollback propaganda with a policy of de-escalating the Cold War.[103] They were strengthened by the observation that the Soviet Union was undergoing a transformation under its post-Stalinist leadership, culminating in Khrushchev's "thaw" speech before the Twentieth Congress of the Soviet Communist Party in February 1956. As far as West Germany was concerned, these shifts appeared to be genuine when

Adenauer was invited to come to Moscow and returned with a success that was very popular at home: the repatriation of the thousands of German POWs who had been held in camps under extremely harsh conditions since the war. In return, the chancellor had agreed to establish diplomatic relations.[104] Dönhoff did not approve of Adenauer's trip and joined the chorus of critics.[105] She suspected the Kremlin of pursuing a dual-track policy reminiscent of that in place before the conclusion of the Nazi-Soviet Pact in August 1939. Favoring trade with the East but no more, she argued that economic policy could be conducted without ambassadors in Bonn and Moscow. What was required was a "firm timetable for the reunification" of Germany.

By October 1955 she spoke in favor of détente. Her article of 27 October took up a question that the London *Times* had asked, whether Cold War pressures on the Soviet Union should be continued or whether a relaxation of tensions should be pursued.[106] Recalling the Stalin offer of 1952, she wrote that the "path [to be taken] is clear to us. Détente can only mean stepping back from [the use of] violence [but] not capitulation." She signed off with "Marion Countess Dönhoff," presumably to make a revisionist point. However, with the two superpowers quietly recognizing the spheres of influence that had been established in 1945 and confirmed in 1953 and definitely during the Hungarian revolution of 1956, it slowly dawned on her that reunification meant, if anything, no more than a merger of East and West Germany and not the reconstitution of the German territorial bloc of 1937, which would have included East Prussia.

In any case, for her this was certainly the moment when West German foreign policy had to become more proactive. Since the European policies of the Kremlin were still opaque, she now wanted Bonn to operate on two tracks: to complete the rearmament of the Federal Republic within NATO and to come out of its "position of perennial defense" politically.[107] The path toward diplomatic relations could be paved by establishing trade delegations in Warsaw, Budapest, and Prague as a first step. Otherwise Germany would merely lend support to the theory that all paths lead through Moscow alone. On 27 September 1956, Dönhoff raised the question of whether a delegation of parliamentary deputies should accept an invitation to Moscow.[108] She thought the time was ripe, since being a traveler to the East did not mean being unpatriotic, just as being reluctant to go was not treasonous. Looking at the pros and cons of such a visit, she introduced a noneconomic consideration: with the decline of Stalinism in the East there was an increased opportunity to compete intellectually and politically by being hosted by those "who prevent our brothers' self-determination."

With national elections coming up in the autumn of 1957, Marion Dönhoff drew attention in January of that year to the major problems that the
West Germans were facing, that is, the shaping of Ostpolitik, the question
of the Oder-Neisse Line, and the acceptance of rearmament while at the
same time pondering the larger problem of disarmament between the two
blocs, all of which required sober discussion.[109] She saw the urgent need to
reduce nuclear armaments, all the more so after the fission bomb had been
complemented by the vastly more destructive hydrogen bomb. Appreciat-
ing the awesome power of nuclear weapons and the need to prevent a third
world war, she sympathized with physicist Otto Hahn and other academic
opponents of NATO's atomic policies. A few months later, on 6 June 1957,
she wrote that she believed the West should make the Soviets a disarmament
offer but "simultaneously" put German reunification on the agenda.[110] In an
article under the title "Talking and Rearming," she came back to this theme
on 26 October, soon after the national elections at which Adenauer's CDU
and its Bavarian sister, the CSU, won the absolute majority, stating that the
chancellor's prestige in Europe had never been greater.[111] Even if Khrushchev's recent speeches had not been helpful, an attempt at negotiation should
nonetheless be made; in this opinion she was invoking the thoughts of her
friend George F. Kennan who favored reducing the military threat by trying
to forge compromises with the Soviets. On 9 January 1958, she railed at the
"eternal chit-chat" that whoever traveled to Moscow was a communist.[112] If
the world perished, it would not be because of the "malice of the bad people"
but because of the "weakness of the good ones."

Her articles in *Die Zeit* in this period certainly fit in with what was written
in other West German newspapers, especially *Die Welt*, which I will discuss in
chapter 3.[113] What is important here are the implications of her shifting arguments for her own politics. As Haug von Kuenheim put it in his study, Marion
Dönhoff finally and after a long inner struggle had come to accept that the territories east of the Oder-Neisse Line had been lost. Further resistance to the
new realities was tantamount "only to retribution and hatred."[114] He quoted
her as saying that she could not imagine that "the greatest love for the *Heimat*
could be documented" by hating those who now lived in this territory. Nor
was it right to denounce those "who agree to reconciliation." When she was
thinking of "the woods and lakes of East Prussia, of the expansive meadows
and the ancient tree-lined roads," she was "certain that they are still as incom-
parably beautiful as they were at the time when they were still my *Heimat*.
Perhaps the highest degree of love is to love without possessing."

However, it would be a mistake to think that the road to the treaties of the early 1970s was smooth. To begin with, Willy Brandt, from whose name West Germany's reconciliation with the East is inseparable, was himself merely at the very beginning of the initiatives he had launched as governing mayor of West Berlin.[115] While the building of the Wall in August 1961 was a great shock at first, in the long run it actually facilitated his policies. As the Wall had been erected to stop the flood of refugees from East Germany to the West, it had had a stabilizing effect on the Ulbricht regime that enabled Bonn's Foreign Office to put out feelers to other East European governments. While these feelers revealed that none of them could succeed without Moscow's involvement and approval, Brandt, again with nods from the Kremlin, began to negotiate an agreement with East Berlin that allowed West Berliners to visit their families in the East. There is no space here to trace the subsequent stages of this rapprochement, which received a great boost when in 1967 the CDU/CSU and SPD formed the Grand Coalition and Brandt became vice chancellor and foreign minister. In 1969 the FDP signaled its willingness to join a coalition with the SPD, whereupon Brandt dissolved the coalition with the CDU and was elected chancellor himself.[116] Under the Basic Law he was now in a position to determine the guidelines of West German foreign policy, which in this case meant entering into serious negotiations with the East. Eventually the texts of the Eastern treaties were initialed and sent to the Federal Parliament, which finally approved them in 1972 under dramatic circumstances.

Marion Dönhoff supported Brandt in his efforts, but it was a step-by-step process by which she became an advocate of the treaties. The reason for this was that West Germany's politicians and public opinion, still under the influence of the refugee organizations, moved even more glacially. The main stumbling block was and remained the recognition of the current borders as final. Therfore, on 17 April 1959 she reported that the Federal Parliament had unanimously resolved that all border questions would have to be settled in a peace treaty, the signing of which the Cold War had prevented so far.[117] This applied in particular to the Oder-Neisse Line and the settlement with Poland. To her, there were two extreme and unacceptable solutions. On the one hand, some people had "written off" this question altogether; on the other, the SPD wanted to recognize the border, but without any compensation, which made no sense to Dönhoff, either. She criticized the government, believing that much would have gone differently if Bonn had acted much sooner. But now the question that had been taboo for years had at last been taken up. The task was therefore to define the framework "within which the discussions reasonably ought to be moving, since this will destroy illusions on all sides."

On 5 October 1962, Marion Dönhoff reiterated that a renewed expulsion of the Poles from the "ancient German eastern territories" was unthinkable.[118] The only way forward was to establish diplomatic relations with Poland, and although opportunities had been missed, it was not too late to seize the initiative. On 4 September 1964 she came back to her earlier theme of reconciliation, but without giving up the territories east of the Oder-Neisse Line.[119] The occasion of her article was the celebration of *Heimat* Day in the Federal Republic on 13 September. She continued that it was possible to accept losses and also to abandon economic assets. However, "no one who hails from the East will give up land." If this were done, it would be equivalent demanding them "to betray their dead." Moreover, how could the Poles believe that "one simply abandons 700 years of history." The promise not to resort to violence had been made and was firm; now serious consideration should be given in the West to buttressing this promise with a formal guarantee.

Although Dönhoff had been skeptical from the start of Gaullism and de Gaulle's covertly anti-American vision of a Europe up to the Urals and had said so in two articles of 1 and 15 February 1963,[120] in a later piece of 3 December 1965 she thought that French ideas to develop a more active foreign policy toward the Soviet Union opened up fresh possibilities.[121] In April 1967 she discussed a government declaration by the CDU/CSU–SPD Grand Coalition.[122] The document contained the affirmation that West Germany would not try to acquire nuclear weapons. Also significant, it declared that the 1938 Munich Agreement was null and void. Although Chancellor Kurt-Georg Kiesinger sympathized with Poland's desire to have a secure western border, he insisted that the Oder-Neisse Line could be recognized only once Germany was reunified. Given all these momentous changes, Dönhoff warned in the end against hectic decision-making now that the ground had been prepared for the 1970s. After all, sometimes "being able to wait" was "the most important thing in politics." In the end, it took another four years for the treaties with Germany's Eastern European neighbors and the Soviet Union to be signed and ratified, but Brandt had achieved the breakthrough, and *Die Zeit* had made a significant contribution to these momentous developments.

Brandt had personally written to Dönhoff as early as 6 March 1958 when he was taking the first steps toward Ostpolitik as governing mayor of West Berlin.[123] In his letter he had said that he would be glad "if you would continue to support our efforts to move Berlin to the center of the struggle for the whole of Germany." During the following years, Marion Dönhoff did indeed use her influence to promote Brandt's policy toward the East, and in a letter that she sent him in January 1967, she thanked him for the insights that he had given her into his thinking.[124] She added that they both knew that opportunities had been missed after Stalin's death and praised him for his foresight and also for his noblesse in the treatment of his opponents, such as Adenauer, his antipodes, such as de Gaulle, and also his friends. When, a few years later, the treaty with Poland had been drawn up, the chancellor invited her on 28 November 1970 to accompany him on his trip to Warsaw for the signing of the document. She declined, feeling it would be too painful for her, however much she approved of the treaty from a moral and rational point of view. And on 28 February 1973, when everything had been ratified, Walter Scheel, then foreign minister in the Brandt Cabinet, praised Dönhoff for her role in drawing both the domestic and the foreign policy outlines of the Federal Republic.[125] By being an early protagonist of Ostpolitik she had facilitated the turn from an illusory policy to one of realism.[126]

Accordingly, she continued to defend Brandt's policies, as can also be seen in the intriguing correspondence she had in 1979 with her cousin "Pucky" zu Ysenburg und Büdingen, which was mentioned earlier in the context of their exchange on the pro-Nazi attitudes of some members of their families.[127] Pucky had sharply criticized her for her support of Brandt, who, he alleged, was aiming to convert West Germany into a socialist country. Pulling no punches, Dönhoff firmly defended Brandt's policies and said she wondered if Pucky was a supporter of the neo-Nazi NPD, whose members had learned nothing from the past. After he refuted this criticism and insisted on his conservative views on the parlous state of German domestic and foreign policy under the Social Democrats, in the end they agreed to disagree, but not to allow their political differences to disrupt their ancient family ties.

However, the establishment of Eastern treaties with the Soviet Bloc also presented a moment of sadness, leading Dönhoff to title the essay that she published just before the signing of the treaty in Warsaw "A Cross on Prussia's Tomb."[128] She knew, she wrote, that if she went back to the places of her youth in East Prussia, she would do so as a tourist. However, on another occasion she was invited to attend, as the person of honor, the reinstallation of Kant's statue in Kaliningrad, the former Königsberg.

Marion Dönhoff's Atlanticism and Its Networks

However, it would be very misleading to assume that the difficult decisions Marion made about her *Heimat* and the backing she gave to Brandt's government (and had forcefully reaffirmed in 1979 in her correspondence with her cousin Fürst Ysenburg Büdingen) caused her to neglect her Atlanticism. True, she had had critical things to say about the de-Nazification and occupation policies of Britain and the United States, but she always knew that the moral, but also the political and socioeconomic, reconstruction of West Germany would not have been possible without the support of Washington and London and the military security it offered against the Soviet Bloc under the umbrella of NATO.

In the early postwar years, her contacts may have been closer with Britain. After all, Hamburg had been the most English city in Germany for many decades before World War II, and ancient commercial and cultural ties were reestablished once the restrictions of the early occupation had been removed. It was also easier to travel across the Channel than to fly across the Atlantic. It is therefore hardly a coincidence that Marion Dönhoff went to join David Astor's *Observer* in 1953 when she disagreed with Tüngel's decision to open the pages of *Die Zeit* to Carl Schmitt, who had provided the legal-theoretical backing to Hitler's rule. Later she frequently traveled across the Atlantic to inform herself about American foreign and domestic policy. She regularly visited key people of the East Coast Establishment. Her papers contain much correspondence not only with David Astor and Alan Bullock on the British side but also with Kennan, Hamilton Fish Armstrong, Zbigniev Brzesinski, John McCloy, and Shepard Stone in the United States.[129]

The latter two men had gained a better understanding of the "good Germans" at a time when the High Commission and also the British continued to be concerned about whether West German society was making a steady transition to a stable democracy. Their worries were reflected in the constant monitoring of public opinion during the early 1950s. They were concerned not just about the negative attitudes toward the alleged "traitors" of July 1944, but also about the persistence of remnants of Nazism.[130] When, with the founding of the Federal Republic in 1949, Allied licensing of political parties ended, a number of radical parties as well as neo-Nazi associations cropped up in various parts of the country, especially in regions where the NSDAP had once been strong.[131] On the extreme left, there was the Communist Party, and with the Cold War escalating, political opinion in favor of proscribing the KPD had become so strong that the Adenauer government asked the Constitutional Court to outlaw it.[132] In 1955 the judges finally ruled in favor of the government.

However, radical parties were also being founded on the extreme right. We will see in chapter 3 how a Conservative Party emerged on the initiative of the former Reichstag deputy of Hugenberg's German National People's Party (DNVP), Otto Schmidt-Hannover.[133] By 1950 an unreconstructed neo-Nazi movement that brought into being the Socialist Reich Party (SRP) garnered considerable support in the eastern parts of Lower Saxony around Wolfsburg.[134] In 1952 their agitation had become so extreme that the Constitutional Court intervened to ban it. Shortly thereafter, the British High Commission became convinced that former Nazis had been infiltrating the North-Rhine-Westphalian Free Democrats. Using Allied residual rights, they put a stop to these tendencies.[135] It goes without saying that Marion Dönhoff was totally opposed to these stirrings. Returning to the FDP scandal on 1 December 1955, she compared the party's liberal manifesto of 1952, on the one hand, with its acceptance of former SS officers and high-ranking Nazis from the Goebbels ministry, such as Werner Naumann, on the other.[136] To her it was an amazing "confusion of the minds" that the FDP had gotten itself into. To be sure, she had been more lenient toward Ernst von Weizsäcker when he, defended by his son during the Nuremberg Trials of former Foreign Office personnel, was sentenced to imprisonment. She had also demanded an end to the Nuremberg proceedings after the major war criminals had been tried and executed in 1946. But although she was inclined toward leniency with respect to de-Nazification, her opposition to all neo-Nazi organizations was categorical. Accordingly, her article of 17 May 1951 commented with alarm on the outcome of the elections in Lower Saxony, the rise of the SRP, and what she thought was a "disintegration of the bourgeois center."[137]

In December 1952 she took up her pen again, this time commenting on the welter of right-wing refugee and expellee parties, including the Bund Heimatvertriebener und Entrechteter (BHE), the party that Adenauer had included in his coalition of 1949 in order to secure a slim parliamentary majority for his government.[138] She charged BHE leaders and members with not having learned a thing from the past despite the death, devastation, and *Heimatlosigkeit* (having to live without a *Heimat*) that the Hitler dictatorship had caused. Looking back on the 1950s in February 1959, she averred that *Die Zeit* had never tired of confronting the activities of right-wing movements or individuals with an unacceptable Nazi record.[139] Looking beyond the borders of the Federal Republic, she admitted that the economic and political resurgence of West Germany had generated anger and fears among her neighbors, especially when "anti-Semitic and other incidents" kept hitting the headlines. Nor did she show leniency when it came to the trials of camp guards or other outright Nazi criminals. As early as July 1954, she had written on the trial of six concentration camp leaders, who had been condemned to death by a French court.[140] Of course, she reported, they had invoked the usual defense that they had been forced to follow orders from above. Having described the camp conditions as presented at the trial, Marion Dönhoff ended with a crucial question: whether refusing to participate in the torture and killing of inmates and being sent to Stalingrad in consequence was really an impossible choice. It was a choice between falling in action as a soldier rather than becoming a killer in a camp. All defendants, she concluded, presumably could differentiate between "good and evil."

Conversely, when Kurt Ziesel, a former Nazi journalist and author of several right-wing books, accused her of being seen in a 1933 photo at a parade of the Nazi Automobile Corps in the company of Wolf Heinrich Count von Helldorf, an SA leader and chief of the Berlin police after the Nazi seizure of power who later joined the anti-Nazi resistance, she dismissed the accusation as "totally irrelevant."[141] Instead she mentioned her Nazi relative Bogislav Dönhoff, who in 1944 had betrayed her to Gauleiter Erich Koch, Ziesel's employer at the time.

While there is thus little doubt that Dönhoff, MCloy, and Stone were on the same page about whom to promote and whom to watch, there was also the larger context of her involvement in a very different cluster of associations that promoted relations with Britain and the United States. Thus she attended the Anglo-German conferences held regularly at Königswinter, near Bonn. In Hamburg there were the events of the British-German Brücke association and also those of organizations that promoted political and cultural dialog between Germany and the United States. In June of 1955, Carlo Schmid, SPD leader and a prominent protagonist of the Congress for Cultural Freedom (CCF), wrote to her urging her to attend a major CCF conference in Milan at which many prominent European and American intellectuals were scheduled to present papers.[142] Apparently she did not go. However, in 1960 she wrote a longer article on the work of this Association.[143] She began by looking back to its founding rally in Berlin in 1950 and recounted its panel discussions with their illustrious participants. She concluded that the CCF had been a worthwhile experiment but added that if there had been a problem it was the tension between, on the one hand, the agendas of the Europeans, who were debating Europe's past sins and, on the other, those of the Asians and Africans, who were demanding practical advice and aid with respect to the problems of the Third World.

In the 1950s Stone had not been a member of the CCF, but, together with McCloy—a trustee of the Ford Foundation—he funded its manifold activities until it was found that the US Central Intelligence Agency had also financed it.[144] Out of the resulting scandal, which alienated many of its members who had attended CCF congresses and contributed articles to the "family" of

CCF magazines (which included *Encounter, Der Monat,* and *Preuves*), there emerged the International Association for Cultural Freedom. Stone became its president in 1967. But with the new association having lost its luster and the Ford Foundation retreating as a funder, he could not find European foundations that would step into the breach. When Stone's unhappiness over these developments became known to Willy Brandt, the latter developed a plan to establish, together with his mayoral successor in West Berlin, a branch of the Colorado Aspen Institute in West Berlin. They would appoint Stone as its director. Next to Richard von Weizsäcker, it was Marion Dönhoff who made this idea her own.[145] With the support of the city of West Berlin, "Aspen Berlin" flourished under the leadership of Stone, who knew Berlin well from his student days before 1933 and who had visited the divided city as public affairs director at the US High Commission in the 1950s. No less important, Brandt saw Stone as a mediator between the West German and American policy establishment at a time when Henry Kissinger and others were quite suspicious of Ostpolitik. This story shows the continuities of Dönhoff's connections with the United States both during the Cold War and beyond. There is no space here to examine how she complemented her travels to the United States by visits to virtually all other regions of the globe. These visits and the many reports she wrote on her impressions of Africa, Latin America, and Asia were another indispensable part of her quest to internationalize German politics and to reintegrate post-Nazi society into the community of nations.

Among the many issues and people that Dönhoff remained close to, there was one domestic topic, the Spiegel Affair, which we will pass over for now but will discuss in chapter 4 in the context of interpersonal relations and media politics in Hamburg during the two decades after 1945.[146] This leaves two themes I wish to explore here relating to Marion Dönhoff as a member of the Generation of '32 and her experiences, which constitute my concluding thoughts on her life and work.

Her "Prussian" Values and Critique of the Evolution of Capitalism

The first theme relates to Marion's deep roots in Prussia.[147] Her father and grandfather were not only Prussian landowners of ancient stock but had also been active in government service and high politics. Her father's membership in the agrarian German Conservative Party and later his support of the

Fatherland Party in World War I indicate that he belonged to the reactionary wing of Prussian agrarianism and apparently remained a loyal adherent to
the Hohenzollern monarchy, notwithstanding occasional criticisms of "his"
king, Wilhelm, who was also emperor. His daughter Marion was also a staunch
Prussian, but hers was not the Prussia of the Wilhelmine period or of World
War I. Her affinities went back to the eighteenth and early nineteenth centuries. When she had researched the history of Friedrichstein in the early 1930s
for her doctoral dissertation, she had studied the economic history of East
Prussia as far back as the Middle Ages and had cast the rule of the Teutonic
Knights in a positive light. As for the sixteenth and seventeenth centuries, she
described the "extraordinarily liberal conditions" of the kingdom under Frederick Wilhelm I and later under Frederick II, or "Frederick the Great," as she
called him. Overall, what Prussia had experienced two hundred years earlier
amounted, she wrote, to an "economic miracle."

She also looked at Prussia's political and cultural development. Thus, in
January 1962 she published a longer analysis on the occasion of the 250th
birthday of Frederick II. It was billed as a "memory of the monarch who
shaped a state."[148] Among his achievements she pointed to his policies of religious toleration and to Prussia's nonpartisan judiciary, which would mete out
justice without consideration of an individual's social origins or status. She
also mentioned that criminal law could not be applied ex post, unlike—as
she added slightly sarcastically—the justice that the Allies had rendered in
the Nuremberg Trials. Moving forward into the post-Frederickian era, she
referred to the administrative reforms and reconstitution of the Prussian
army under Scharnhorst. Finally, she listed the emancipation of the serfs as
another achievement in the era of reform. Extending her discussion to the
postwar period, she commented on the dissolution of Prussia by the Allies
after World War II: "It is of course possible to dissolve administrative units,"
she wrote; the Allies could also extirpate Hitler's state ("which had nothing in common with that of Frederick II"). But, she concluded, "one cannot
proscribe with any law the true Prussian spirit and the style that comes with
it. The fate of our Volk as a nation will depend on the question of whether
this spirit survives."

The defeat of the French in Indochina at Dien Bien Phu and the memory of
Stalingrad stimulated Dönhoff in May 1954 to raise the question of bravery and
rational restraint in connection with the siege of Kolberg during the Napoleonic Wars.[149] As she put it: "When Prussia collapsed on the battlefield of Jena
and Auerstädt in 1806 and only Gneisenau held out in the fortress of Kolberg,

nobody knew that this deed would one day become the precondition for the regeneration of a broken state and the point of departure of a new state."

However, Dönhoff's most explicit identification with Prussia came in February 1967 on the occasion of the twentieth anniversary of the abolition of Prussia by the Allied Control Council.[150] This Allied law, she began, had been based on two errors: that Hitler had been a Prussian and that his system of terror had been the final link in a chain of traditions that were rooted in Prussia. Having refuted both arguments, she returned to the Allgemeine Landrecht, the Prussian Civil Code, with its principles of "secularization, humanization and demythologization." This code, she wrote, became "the most progressive and liberal" law of "contemporary Europe." Torture had been outlawed as early as 1740. Hitler, she added, had been the antithesis to the Edict of Toleration that the Great Elector had promulgated in 1687. She then asked if anything could still be learned from Prussia in the age of "industrial society and space research." Thinking of the "Public Relations Society" in which the West Germans lived, she believed that Prussia could indeed teach "a bit more inner independence," more engagement with issues for their own sake that "does not ask what utility something might have for oneself" and that is not immediately concerned with one's public image. In other words, "today we could use quite well a bit more Prussian restraint and Prussian strictness and Prussian modesty." Finally, she came back to what was probably the ultimate purpose of her plea for a revival of Prussian values: to promote the idea that the forces of state formation had once emanated from Prussia. The state had disappeared by Allied fiat, but Prussia had not. That is why she wished to uphold "the hope for a genuine state that one day would replace the two partial states" of East and West Germany.

Marion Dönhoff lived to see the reunification of Germany in 1989-90. While she welcomed the revolutionary developments that ended the Cold War, the last question to be raised here is how happy she was with the socioeconomic evolution of the New Germany during the 1990s. This was not merely a question of her politics but one that is crucial for an understanding of her life and work. It is concerned with the deeper layers of her consciousness and identity, which can be traced back to her upbringing as a Prussian noblewoman and the experiences that shaped her up to 1945. These resurfaced toward the end of her long life.

To clarify this point it seems best to start in 1989 just before the reunification of Germany. It was in May 1989 that Marion discussed a number of corruption scandals and bankruptcies in Europe, Japan, and the United States.[151] Hers was a very critical analysis as reflected in its title: "The Money Comes First and Morals Thereafter." Asking how these scandals were possible, she averred that many people had but *one* interest: to maximize their income." In other words, what counted was not "the being (*Sein*) but only the having (*Haben*)." In the past there had always been "authorities that restricted such actions and intentions," or there were at least "morals and conventions," accompanied by outrage, "if they were not maintained." For the first time, she concluded, none of these morals still existed. There was just "limitless freedom, as if this was the essence of democracy." However, if there were no higher goals than the achievement of a high living standard, if there was no other "yardstick than income for measuring achievement, prestige [and] well-being," all that was left was God's mercy for the survival of "our democratic form of life."

Marion Dönhoff's next stern admonition appeared in *Die Zeit* of 2 March 1993 and was titled "A Society without Moral Yardsticks Lapses into a Danger Zone."[152] This time her main theme was the brutalization of life and the uninhibited display in the media of, for example, a seriously injured person or of someone in his or her death throes. She also railed at "voyeurism as practiced by Reality TV" and at the lyrics of rap and pop. And worse: "In this late phase of positivistic-materialistic notions, the intellectual poverty of an epoch becomes very clear that thinks only in categories of power and success." Yet the Mensch cannot live "without a metaphysical relationship and will lack orientation if there is no higher authority. He will merely deem himself omnipotent." All this, she continued, had become all too evident under National Socialism and Stalinism. It had been the negation of the metaphysical that had facilitated the subjugation of the individual to a totalitarian power. But the great scientific and technological breakthroughs being made, with their possibilities of communication that no one ever dreamed of, had not made the Menschen more humane. Dönhoff then insisted that there had to be a fundamental change. Referring to the younger generation, without jobs or youth clubs, she proposed the creation of social and community service. The fact that Hitler allegedly invented the Labor Service did not constitute a reason to distance oneself from the one that had existed prior to 1933. The original idea had been to unite workers, peasants, and students in educational camps. This type of labor service had had some 100,000 members during Brüning's chancelloship. The objective was to rehumanize society, to replace egocentrism and *Anspruchsdenken* (an entitlement mentality) with a sense of the general public good of social solidarity and transform disillusionment with politics into active participation in it. This, to her, was the only way to strengthen "our democracy again that is being endangered today."

Dönhoff's next move in her criticism of West German society came in 1996 on the occasion of her being awarded a prize in Dresden, given in memory of the leftist writer Erich Kästner.[153] This time she formulated her acceptance speech as a demand and exhortation to "Civilize Capitalism," as its title shows. By November 1995 she had expanded and deepened her critique of German society and its economic system when she spoke at a symposium at Hambach Castle. By this time her views of the future had congealed into a speech titled "Twelve Hypotheses against Extravagance," which represented a digest of her value system and moral compass.[154] As she put it:

1. No community can exist without modesty and self-discipline, while unlimited liberalization led to chaos and ultimately to its antithesis, autocracy. All societies, therefore, needed a minimal ethical consensus or they would disintegrate.

2. The push for progress, more freedom, and the satisfaction of constantly rising expectations was destroying society and would ultimately lead to anarchic conditions.

3. Competition was the essence of a market economy, but the pressure to maximize gain was destructive of solidarity and prevented the emergence of a sense of responsibility.

4. An overemphasis on achievement and on making money marginalized the spiritual, the humane, and the artistic.

5. At a time of many temptations and titillating offers, the quest for a moral orientation and a binding system of values was growing.

6. Freedom without limits automatically ended in an authoritarian regime, while violence, sex, and crime in the media were popular and guaranteed the highest material returns.

7. Ruthless economic extravagance and the stress of constant growth had adverse environmental consequences. The capital of future generations was being used up, and growing debt diminished future consumption. At the same time there was the question of whether social welfare could be increased to a level at which many countries and communities faced collapse.

8. Visions of the future were lacking, and intellectual life was characterized by helplessness and an anguished emptiness.

9. With participation in politics declining, democracy was not endangered by right-wing radical groups, and if the earlier mentioned developments continued, capitalism would collapse just as Marxism had done.

10. What was needed was a transformation of humanity due to a more sensitive legal consciousness.

11. Liberalization was going too far, and decision-makers were losing their sense of justice, while economic corruption and tax evasion were increasing.

12. The rule of law (*Rechtsstaat*) created the preconditions and the framework for a civil society within which the ethos and comportment of the *Menschen* that a secularized world did not have would be encouraged.

It must be possible, she concluded, for capitalist structures to be complemented in such a way that humans might be encouraged to act humanely rather than making egotistical demands.

Ultimately, it seems, Marion Dönhoff's criticism was directed not merely at West Germany's politics and society and its economic system but also at those of America. It had been under Ronald Reagan that the United States had taken the turn toward neoliberalism with its push for privatization and deregulation.[155] In a letter to Helmut Schmidt of 27 August 1982, Dönhoff had still spoken of an equilibrium between those who complained about Germany's market economy and those who criticized the social welfare state.[156] By the late 1980s, neoliberalism had been introduced full steam in Margaret Thatcher's Britain and was beginning to spill over into Continental Europe. It is against this background that Marion Dönhoff had written an article "condemning" American capitalism, as her friend Shepard Stone put it in his letter to her of 27 September 1989.[157] He agreed that many of the facts that she had enumerated were "shameful" for the United States, but he then insisted that, "all in all," American characteristics and institutions were as attractive as they had been in the early postwar decades.

Stone's epistle takes me back to his first encounter with Dönhoff some forty years earlier, when he had returned to West Germany as the public relations director under US High Commissioner John McCloy. At that time they had not yet formed the close friendship founded on an elective affinity and a convergence of views that also marked her relationship with the Columbia University historian and Jewish refugee from Breslau, Fritz Stern. In fact, as she recalled, Stone had treated her rather gruffly.[158] Was this due to Stone's reservations about her and her Prussian nobility? After all, it was not just that she had written articles in *Die Zeit* that were critical of Allied policies of de-Nazification, justice, and industrial de-concentration. Having studied German history and obtained a doctorate in this discipline at Berlin University in 1932, Stone was also familiar with the negative influence that the Prussian aristocracy and the German Nationalist People's Party had had on the demise of the Weimar Republic. He probably also associated Prussian agrarianism with an opposition to industrial capitalism and an anti-Americanism that was widespread in conservative circles throughout the interwar years. It is not clear how much Stone knew at this point about Marion Dönhoff's family and the families of the friends she had lost as members of the anti-Nazi resistance. Whatever briefings he had received before her visit, he was certainly right in believing that a young countess had come to his office who was marked by her upbringing and beliefs in the continued validity of Prussian values. Christoph Bertram, who knew her well at *Die Zeit*, was probably right when, in a letter to her of 2 December 1998, he praised not only her openness and adherence to principles but also her somewhat "old-fashioned virtues."[159] During his time at the High Commission and at the Ford Foundation, Stone seems to have found it easier to connect with Inge Scholl, the surviving sister of Sophie and Hans and their struggle against Nazism and was therefore happy to give his support to Inge's efforts to build up the High School of Design at Ulm. But what was he to make of this young journalist from Hamburg whose weekly was not doing well?

By the 1950s, Dönhoff had moderated his criticism of the Allies and had become an avowed Atlanticist who knew how indispensable the United States was to West Germany's economic prosperity and military security. Yet, as happens quite often with age, she had begun to see the world increasingly in terms of the ethos of Prussia, whose principles she had summarized so well in her "Twelve Hypotheses against Extravagance" in November 1995, all of which sounded as if it had been taken quite straightforwardly from the history of the world she grew up in and had imbibed either from her teachers or from the culture of aristocratic Germany, complemented by liberal elements that had turned her against the Nazis and Hitler.

Marion nevertheless had a curious ambivalence toward those members of the aristocracy who did not share her views. As we have seen, some became outright Nazis. She argued with them, but, with a few exceptions, maintained contact with them afterward if, like her brother Christoph, they were members of her family.[160] This leniency also extended to those who initially thought that the Nazi seizure of power in January 1933 would facilitate a new, though authoritarian and anti-democratic, beginning. To be sure, as she stressed in her verdict on Ludwig Beck, they were "naïve" and hopelessly underestimated the criminal energy of Hitler and his entourage. But it seems that these men deserve a more critical assessment. Mommsen and others, in scrutinizing the constitutional and political precepts of Goerdeler and the men of 20 July, argued on a more purely political plane than the one on which Marion Dönhoff operated. Her level of argumentation was more basic when she highlighted the ethical impetus behind the 1944 attempt on Hitler's life and its significance for the moral reconstruction of a demoralized West German society that, as she wrote on 6 July 1960 with reference to two world wars, had twice been put "through the meat grinder" of a violent history.[161]

But not only were there millions of Germans who had seen through the lies of the Nazis' propaganda and opposed them before 1933. After Hitler's seizure of power, some of them went underground and resisted with often very primitive means until they were caught, tried, and in many cases executed. By contrast, the trouble with the men who elevated Hitler into the chancellorship was that they were so blinkered by their ideology and misperceptions of the true character of Nazism that they acted irresponsibly.[162] It is on this issue that Marion Dönhoff remained ambivalent, arguing rightly that they did not know the future. She had disagreed with her brothers over their attitude toward Nazism, but never to the point of severing relations with them.[163] Her position in the 1930s can rightly be defined as "inner emigration." She first went to Switzerland for her doctorate, but then went back to Friedrichstein to do research for her dissertation and then stayed to help manage the family estate. Apart from her anti-Nazi brother Heinrich, she kept meeting other opponents of the regime and, as the war unfolded, moved more closely toward a position of active resistance, working as a messenger between men who were involved in the 1944 attempt to kill Hitler. After the failure of the coup, she was interrogated by the Gestapo but let go.

This record is important, as West German society slowly came to recognize that the anti-Nazi Germans offered foundations on which to build the Federal Republic. However, it was not just her advocacy for the "Other Germany" but also the articles on the political and moral reconstruction of the country that she regularly wrote in Die Zeit that earned her recognition and admiration. Dönhoff made a relentless effort to nudge the West Germans to support once again the ethical and humanistic principles enshrined in the Basic Law and to work not only for the country's integration into the European community of nations but also for reconciliation with their eastern European neighbors.

If the members of the resistance but also those who experienced inner emigration were important as beacons during the years of criminal Nazi rule, Dönhoff also belonged to those journalists who fought for a society and a political system that would never again produce a totalitarian or even an autocratic regime. Like Sethe, she therefore fought for civil liberties and in particular the freedom of the press when it was threatened in the 1950s and beyond. While she stood for firm constitutional principles in domestic affairs, she had greater difficulties adapting to the changing international situation of the postwar world. She favored the integration of Western Europe and the Atlantic partnership with the United States, but it took her longer to reconcile her rootedness in East Prussia with the loss of those territories and to work for Brandt's Ostpolitik. When it came to her attitudes toward the development of Western capitalism, she supported the creation of a welfare-statist market economy. But she never took the turn into neoliberalism and by the 1990s was deeply worried about its promotion of selfishness and about the rapidly declining sense of social solidarity and responsibility toward the weaker strata of society. In the end, her criticism of neoliberalism went so far as to demand that this peculiar variant of capitalism be "civilized."

The next chapter examines how another inner emigrant responded to both Nazism and its fallout in the post-1945 decades.

3

Hans Zehrer's Intellectual Journey from Weimar Berlin to Postwar Hamburg

STRUGGLING WITH PAST AND PRESENT, 1923–1966

The Larger Setting of Weimar Politics

Only a few weeks after its birth, the Weimar Republic and the Constitution that had been adopted by the National Assembly in January 1919 had to struggle with unprecedented challenges to their survival. In the elections for the National Assembly some 76 percent of the voters had cast their ballot for the parties that supported the new constitutional order, the Social Democrats (SPD), the Catholic Center Party, and the left-liberal German Democratic Party (DDP). But only a year later, this impressive victory had been lost to political forces on the anti-Republican Right and the extreme Left, which irreconcilably refused to accept the new parliamentary-democratic Republic. Between 1924 and 1929, it is true, there followed a period that produced functioning party coalitions that were joined from time to time by the German Nationalist People's Party (DNVP), anxious to participate in government. This was a purely tactical rapprochement in order to get legislation passed in the Reichstag that favored the interests of their still anti-Republican voters. As one of the leaders, Hans-Erdmann von Lindeiner-Wildau, put it in 1924:[1] "The Republic is beginning to stabilize itself and the German people is becoming reconciled to the status quo. . . . If we wish to retain and reinforce the DNVP as an influential and powerful movement of the Right, we must move to share

Hans Zehrer, 1899–1966.
Photograph courtesy of Antje and Angelika Brammer.

power in the State." The stabilization of the economy that was achieved in 1924 with the help of the Dawes Plan, which settled, at least for the time being, the thorny question of German reparations payments and facilitated the flow of American loans and direct investments to German industry. Similarly, the conclusion of the Locarno Pact of 1925, which secured recognition of the territorial status between France, Belgium, and Germany in the West, had a calming effect on Weimar foreign policy.[2]

But parliamentary government did not last, and the 1929 worldwide depression destabilized the Weimar Republic once more. The American loans were withdrawn, bankruptcies spread, and unemployment increased rapidly. In the national elections of 1930 the anti-Republicans of the extreme Right and Left gained the upper hand, so majorities prepared to support parliamentary government could no longer be found. It was replaced by Reich president

Paul von Hindenburg's autocratic rule with the help of Article 48 of the Constitution. Reichstag legislation was substituted by decrees drawn up by Reich Chancellor Heinrich Brüning and signed into law by Hindenburg. Even more alarming, as the Great Depression began to bite, Adolf Hitler's National Socialist German Workers Party (NSDAP) won a stunning victory at the ballot box in September of that year, garnering 4.6 million votes. The Nazis now moved into the Reichstag with 107 deputies determined to prevent a revival of parliamentary government. Bent on destroying the Weimar Republic, they aimed at a one-party dictatorship with Hitler at the helm.[3] The Communists, following orders from Moscow, also worked for the demise of the Republic.[4]

The Republic had reached its crunch point, as no parliamentary-democratic system can survive a lengthy crisis period of this kind if a growing percentage of its citizens, exercising their constitutional right to vote for the party of their choice, including those who advocated the destruction of that system, want to live under an alternative political order.[5] They disagreed and fought over those alternatives, but the persistent negative consensus to abolish what had emerged from the defeat of the Hohenzollern monarchy and the revolutionary upheavals of November 1918 was sooner or later bound to lead to a new power structure.[6] After 1930 it took three more years of agony and helpless maneuvering to find a way out of the crisis, until the Nazis, flanked by the DNVP and other anti-Republican forces, finally defeated the Weimar order. At the end of January 1933, Hindenburg dismissed Kurt von Schleicher, the last Weimar chancellor, and replaced him with Hitler, who, within less than a year, transformed the political system into a brutal dictatorship.[7]

As the Nazis were developing their strategy of anti-democratic conquest, some influential conservatives and also Reichswehr officers were contemplating other ways of transitioning from a parliamentary democracy to a more permanent authoritarian regime based on the constitutional emergency powers of the Reich president.[8] This "presidential solution" became more and more influential in the early 1930s.[9] With the Nazis having gained 107 seats in the Reichstag, flanked on the extreme Left by 77 no less radically anti-Republican Communist deputies, the Social Democrats could not be brought together in a coalition with the Catholic Center Party and a welter of shrinking middle-class parties to uphold parliamentary government. Instead Hindenburg stepped in to rule with the emergency "dictatorship" provided for in Article 48 of the Weimar Constitution.[10] This allowed him to nominate the Reich chancellor and ministers without the consent of the Reichstag and to sign executive legislation into law as constitutionally binding decrees that "his" Reich chancellor had drawn up for him. Article 48 could lapse only if the parties of the middle succeeded in forming a coalition that reestablished a parliamentary majority and was prepared to elect a new cabinet independent of Hindenburg's presidential emergency powers.[11]

Hitler, as we will see in a moment, found such a majority after the March elections of 1933. After further cunning manipulations of the Weimar Constitution, this made it possible for him, a few weeks later, to get the Enabling Act passed, by which the Reichstag rather than Hindenburg gave Hitler full executive powers for the next four years. In other words, with Hindenburg having lost his powers under Article 48, Hitler did not have to go to Parliament for approval of his own executive decrees. Exploiting these powers to the full, from April 1933 onward Hitler established Nazi rule at breathtaking speed. I shall come back to how this was done later, as it is quite relevant to the biography and intellectual journey of Hans Zehrer, a prominent journalist and intellectual during the final phase of the Weimar Republic, whose life and career are at the center in this chapter.

Family Background and Early Career

Zehrer was born on 22 June 1899 into a middle-class family in Berlin, the son of a senior post office inspector (*Postoberinspektor*).[12] Although it is difficult to reconstruct his early life, it seems that he took his father as a role model, whereas his attitudes toward his mother vacillated between love and alienation. Pensive and at times even depressed, as a teenager he may have been captivated by the Youth Movement and its romantic ideology before signing up for the German Army at the very end of World War I, after finishing his *Abitur* at the Royal Prinz-Heinrich-Gymnasium in Berlin. He was wounded several times and awarded the Iron Cross. Although he saw himself as a member of a generation that was believed to have experienced the allegedly egalitarian atmosphere of the trenches, he was an anti-Communist of the first hour and signed up for one of the Free Corps units that were constituted by the Ebert government in 1918. Their mission was to defeat Germany's Bolsheviks, who, in January 1919, took up arms to establish a revolutionary Leninist regime.

Zehrer's last military engagement was after the failure of the Kapp Putsch in March 1920, when demobilized Free Corps units tried to overthrow the Republican government in Berlin but failed. This, in turn, unleashed another wave of radical left-wing uprisings in various working-class neighborhoods, especially in the Ruhr industrial region. Again Zehrer served in order to quell

Communist uprisings in a unit of volunteers in Berlin that, according to one of its members, suffered very heavy losses.[13] It seems that this experience convinced Zehrer that it was time to return to civilian life. Registering at Berlin's Humboldt University, he first thought of studying medicine and psychology but then attended the lectures of two eminent theologians, Ernst Troeltsch and Adolf von Harnack, as well as the economist Werner Sombart.

Intelligent and upwardly mobile, Zehrer became interested in journalism and in October 1923 was hired as an intern (*Volontär*) by the liberal *Vossische Zeitung*, which belonged to the German-Jewish Ullstein publishing house. An admirer of Georg Bernhard, the paper's legendary editor in chief, he wrote his first op-ed piece on the "crisis of parliament" in October of that year. His moves in the midtwenties are difficult to reconstruct. It seems that he left *Vossische* for a while to continue his studies at Heidelberg University, where he attended the lectures and seminars of the sociologists Alfred Weber and Karl Mannheim. The latter was then making a name for himself as an analyst of the role of intellectuals in modern society. Mannheim's approach to generational change, discussed in the introduction, apparently appealed to Zehrer, who saw himself as a member of the "front generation" of World War I.[14] Next to Alfred Weber's sociology, Zehrer was also introduced to the ideas of the Italian social scientist Vilfredo Pareto and his model of how people rose from the "masses" to become a particular country's elites.[15] Rejecting Karl Marx's interpretation of socioeconomic change through class struggle, Pareto had postulated that gifted individuals rather than entire groups and classes could gain access to elites thanks to superior intelligence and guile. Conversely, he warned that elites would become calcified unless they refreshed themselves by integrating smart and dynamic individuals from below. Indeed, elites who did not provide such openings would end up in the graveyards of history. According to Pareto, these were filled with elite groups who shut out the upwardly mobile, causing their own decline and ultimate downfall.

It is perhaps not surprising that Zehrer, the young man of middle-class background and a former soldier, should be intrigued by Mannheim's and Pareto's ideas. He was an ambitious intellectual who wanted to transcend the staid bourgeois life of his family. He may also have viewed himself as a member of Mannheim's "free-floating intelligentsia." He most certainly was critical of the many conservative and reactionary positions of the generation before him, who had looked back to the golden age of the Wilhelmine monarchy. When he left Heidelberg without taking a final exam and returned to the *Vossische*, there appear to have been intergenerational affinities between his political attitudes and those of Georg Bernhard, the paper's senior editor. After all, Bernhard was not a liberal Republican like his rival Theodor Wolff at the *Berliner Tageblatt*, against whom he leveled some sharp criticisms. Instead he veered more toward corporatist ideas. Though a patriot, he favored reconciliation with France but had reservations about Britain and the United States, all of which may have contributed to the rapport that Zehrer, writing a regular column on foreign policy questions, developed with Bernhard.[16] However, the budding young journalist was no longer attracted by the radical anti-Republican Right and explicitly rejected its anti-Semitism. In fact, in 1923 or 1924 he married Margot Mosse-Sussmann, who was related to the famous Jewish Mosse publishing family. Later in this chapter I shall examine how she survived Nazi persecution with her husband's help.

What apparently shattered Zehrer's relatively moderate political views was the shock of the Great Slump of 1929, which was followed a year later by the ascendancy of Hitler's Nazi Party. He continued his work for the *Vossische* during this time of mass unemployment, but, together with a few journalist friends, also began to write for Eugen Diederich's *Die Tat*, a more right-wing intellectual monthly.[17] This journal did not sell more than eight hundred copies in 1929/30, but in 1931 it came under the influence of Zehrer's group, known as the *Tat Circle*. Losing hope in parliamentary democracy, they began to advocate authoritarian solutions to Weimar's economic and political crisis. Zehrer's position on the staff of the *Vossische* became untenable when his illiberal essays appeared in *Die Tat*. He finally left the daily and on 31 October 1931 became editor in chief of the monthly.[18] Thenceforth he and his friends devoted themselves energetically to boosting the circulation and influence of *Die Tat* while denying that he had any connection to radical right-wing circles, especially not to the Black Front of Otto Strasser, who represented the revolutionary "left" wing of the Nazi movement. On the other hand there was Strasser's brother Gregor, who had become the key figure in organizing and mobilizing the NSDAP's membership. Gregor was a very powerful man and a rival to Hitler, and I shall return to him after the following, more detailed, analysis of Zehrer's articles in *Die Tat*.

Shaping *Die Tat* into a Major Voice
of the Authoritarian Anti-Nazi Right

Zehrer's first piece as editor in chief appeared in the November 1931 issue of the journal. It was a short comment (*Glosse*) in which he asserted that the

world depression and the crisis in Germany offered an opportunity to rebuild
the state, revitalize the economy, and regain freedom from the restrictions
of the Versailles Treaty.[19] But, he continued, the opportunity had come too
soon. What Hindenburg's presidential regime under Article 48 and Heinrich
Brüning as Reich chancellor could hope to achieve was at best to lead the
country to a point at which the terrain was open for casting off the "chains"
of Versailles and for revamping of the economy and politics. In his view, the
right-wing opposition was not ready to take over, either. If this opposition—
and he evidently had the Nazi Party in mind—could launch a "total [and]
new program" in time and also train its leaders for its implementation, change
might come without major frictions. However, if this opposition gained power
before all this had been put in place, it would trigger an "unspeakable catastrophe." Consequently, the next months required an intensification of Nazi
self-preparation in cooperation with other groups. Zehrer's recommendations
of November may have to be seen in the context of the "front" that the DNVP
and the Stahlhelm veterans' association had formed with Hitler in the fall of
1931 in the provincial town of Bad Harzburg, in the foothills of the Harz Mountains south of Braunschweig. However, the coalition had very quickly fallen
apart due to Hitler's recalcitrance and claims to leadership.[20] It seems that
Zehrer viewed this behavior was as a sign of Nazi immaturity that training in
political responsibility could resolve. He also thought it was a sign of a lack of
preparedness for assuming political power that Hitler, buoyed by his electoral
success in 1930, continued to pursue as a strategy of gaining a majority in the
next national elections. Accordingly, the Nazi leader had refused to join an
expansion of Hindenburg's authoritarian presidential regime under Article
48. He wanted nothing less than to claim the Reich chancellorship for himself.

If Zehrer had become a supporter of Hindenburg by the winter of 1931, he
also began to sympathize with conservatives and officers in the president's
entourage who contemplated a more permanent transformation of the Constitution. He shared their view of a presidential regime that offered not merely
a temporary solution of the economic and political crisis, to be reversed once
the emergency was over and a majority could be found again among the pro-
Republican parties to elect a Reich cabinet led by a chancellor who enjoyed
the confidence of that majority. Instead he envisioned the regime being continued and replacing the parliamentary-democratic Weimar Constitution.
With Reich Chancellor Brüning having no more popular support than that
from the voters of his Catholic Center Party, Zehrer also began to hope that
Hindenburg would dismiss Brüning and appoint a new Reich chancellor who

would succeed in getting Hitler to join a presidential cabinet and thus obtain the political mass base that Brüning so patently lacked. At the same time, he was sufficiently suspicious of Hitler and his inflexible electoral strategy to believe, as before, that the NSDAP was not yet ready to join a presidential authoritarian government.

The editorial that Zehrer published in the January 1932 issue of *Die Tat* represents a more detailed digest of his thinking during that winter.[21] The coming year, he wrote, would be fateful for the country. The existing "state" was about to give up its foundations while still adhering to the illusion that it could hold onto the political status quo. Similarly, private industry and commerce worked with a notion of free enterprise that no longer existed. It was against this background that political leaders and their followers had become increasingly fatalistic, maneuvering helplessly in the face of two problems: the insurgency of the "masses" and the absence of a stratum of determined leaders. Like so many other right-wingers at this time, Zehrer invoked the Spanish philosopher José Ortega y Gasset, who had published a bestseller titled *The Revolt of the Masses*. The editor in chief of *Die Tat* had meanwhile come to believe that the German masses had seized power and were preventing the formation of an elite capable of assuming national leadership. Worse, these masses were systematically trying to level socioeconomic differences and were now set to conquer the last bastion of liberty: money [that is, wealth], thereby pushing the propertied classes to look for an exit strategy.

The old elites of the Wilhelmine period, Zehrer continued, had disappeared in November 1918. But—and here Pareto may have been at the back of his mind—there was a new elite of "qualified individuals" waiting in the wings. The trouble was that they lacked experience. Moreover, their advance was blocked by the old bureaucracy. Furthermore, the problem of the masses was exacerbated by the "fiery steamroller of National Socialism." Ever since the elections of September 1930, Germany had witnessed the rise of a "National Socialist flood" that had proved unstoppable. Notwithstanding this menace, Zehrer had not changed his mind about Nazism and argued that it was too soon for the NSDAP to enter a presidential cabinet. While this would clearly broaden Brüning's popular base, the Nazis would nonetheless never gain more than 40 percent of the vote. In other words, Hitler had no chance of conquering a Reichstag majority, which the Nazi leader was agitating for. In this situation, the editor of *Die Tat* saw three other power factors that might become partners in a presidential regime: the Army (*Reichswehr*), industry, and the Center Party.

Meanwhile, Hitler continued to ignore calls for cooperation, claiming nothing less than the chancellorship for himself. After the failure of the Harzburg Front, the next blow to Zehrer's strategy came in the spring of 1932, when Hindenburg's seven-year term was up and a successor had to be elected by popular vote.[22] Nudged by Brüning and the dwindling number of deputies from among the middle-class parties, Hindenburg, by then aged 84, agreed to enter the race for another seven-year term, whereupon Hitler announced his own candidacy. Not to be left behind, the remnants of the Harzburg Front, led by the DNVP's Alfred Hugenberg, nominated Theodor Duesterberg, the second *Bundesführer* of the Stahlhelm association of conservative veterans, with Thaelmann again standing for the Communists. When Hindenburg barely missed being elected, gathering 49.7 percent of the vote against Hitler's 30.2 percent, the runoff elections in April 1932 were finally won by Hindenburg. He received 53 percent (19.36 million), not least because the Social Democrats had supported him. Thaelmann fell back from 13.2 percent in the first round to 10.2 percent. However, even if he lost the race, Hitler's position should not be underestimated. To begin with, his entry into the race reflected his undiminished determination to seize power by "legal" means. After Hindenburg refused to give him the chancellorship, trying to gain the presidency was even more alluring and would have enabled him to govern with the presidential rule by decree offered by Article 48 of the Constitution. In the end, the Nazis garnered 13.4 million votes and 36.8 percent of the total.[23]

Following the upheaval of the presidential elections, the Hindenburg regime continued. But after two years of ruling by decree with no more than a few signs of economic improvement, Brüning had become increasingly weakened. He could be dismissed by the president at any time, and Hindenburg's entourage was urging him to find a replacement and to call national elections. These took place on 31 July and resulted in another remarkable success for Hitler's party. The NSDAP attracted 13.8 million votes and now had 230 seats in the Reichstag. Brüning was dismissed, and the position of Reich chancellor was filled by Franz von Papen—an untrustworthy Catholic politician who did not even have his own Center Party behind him. However, General Kurt von Schleicher had entered the Cabinet as war minister and became the power behind Papen's throne. His plan was to strengthen the presidential regime with the appointment of nonparty "expert" ministers and to try to lure the Nazis into the government to provide Hindenburg with a popular base. It is against this background that the forcible removal of the Social Democrat government in Prussia, by far the largest federal state in Germany and a thorn in the flesh of the authoritarians in the Reich, through an illegal coup has to be seen. And then there were the endless debates on how to "tame" the Nazis by bringing them into the government. With Hitler still insisting on being given the chancellorship and Hindenburg refusing to hand it to "the Bohemian lance corporal," Papen and Schleicher spent the summer and autumn 1932 trying to find a way out. This, in turn, provided Zehrer and his circle with an opportunity to develop proposals as to how to get the country out of the impasse.[24]

To grasp the evolution of Zehrer's thinking, it is necessary to go back to the article he published in the March issue of *Die Tat*.[25] In it he had postulated the unification of what he called the national and social wings of Weimar's political spectrum. More specifically, he envisioned a coalition of Nazis with the socialist and the Christian trade unions, with Hindenburg at the top, using his powers and influence to facilitate a grand bridge-building operation between the Right and the noncommunist Left, into which religious, corporatist (*ständische*), regional (*landschaftliche*), and *bündische* groups were also to be drawn. In other words, the common bond of this "axis" would be that it was formed from organizations that were not part of the traditional Weimar parliamentary parties. Hindenburg, Zehrer added, would provide the necessary *auctoritas* for this process, supported by the *potestas* of the Army, the Reich bureaucracy, and the representatives of the Reich Economic Council (*Reichswirtschaftsrat*).

Zehrer's logical next steps appeared in the April and May issues of his journal.[26] Here he bluntly criticized Hitler's strategy of trying to seize power through the ballot box. Perhaps with the results of the presidential elections in mind, he argued that the Hitler "myth" had failed to perpetuate itself. The "*Führer*" was no more than a populist "drummer" who lacked the steady hand and calm self-assurance of an army general. Thanks to Hindenburg's victory, an "immature revolution" had been thwarted. According to Zehrer, the NSDAP was at a crossroads. It could either move in an authoritarian direction in cooperation with other forces or it could continue with its "liberalistic" methods of using the ballot box. The editor of *Die Tat* urged the Nazis to free themselves from the stranglehold of its bureaucracy at Hitler's Munich headquarters and to commit themselves to building an autocratic presidential regime under Hindenburg, whose administration would remain decentralized in the different regions of the Reich. The system would also rely on the extra-parliamentary associations, including the socialist and Christian trade unions.

Zehrer expanded on his critique of Hitler's dogmatism in the May issue, asserting that neither a Bolshevik nor a Fascist dictatorship was suitable for Germany. Further elections would produce no more than soap bubbles. The constant agitation of the masses should be abandoned and central authority be strengthened instead. The demands for a military or a Hitler dictatorship would merely lead the country into a cul-de-sac. With Hindenburg's reelection, Zehrer wrote, the path had been cleared for the creation of a third front based on presidential authority. A *Glosse* at the end of the May issue was not signed but was in agreement with Zehrer's published views.[27] Hitler's situation was judged to be "not rosy." The Nazi Party would begin to decline if it merely went on rolling the drums for more elections. In June 1932, Zehrer had deemed Brüning's dismissal necessary, even if it gave him no joy. He praised the Reich chancellor's integrity, sobriety, and religiosity but urged Hindenburg to create a broad front that relied on the ministerial bureaucracy and the Reichswehr but also on the estates, the Reichswirtschaftsrat, the associations, and the youth organizations.

In light of this analysis of political conditions in the late spring of 1932, Zehrer must have been dismayed that Hitler attracted close to 14 million voters in the July Reichstag elections. Although he was still convinced that the Nazis would never gain a majority of the votes, it was evident that his exhortations in an intellectual journal to form an extraparliamentary front as an alternative to Hitler's ballot-box strategy needed to be complemented by an activist approach of an editor in chief who would try to mediate the formation of a Third Front. Zehrer seems to have taken some encouragement from the observation that various factions were indeed beginning to talk to each other outside the Reichstag. In June he noted that the Social Democrats and the Communists were discussing cooperating on vital social policy questions.[28] Then there was a speech by Gregor Strasser, the leader of the Nazi trade union, whose tireless organizational efforts had turned the Party and its affiliates into a powerful political instrument. Zehrer, in pursuit of his aim to unite Hindenburg's *auctoritas* with the military-administrative *postestas* as well as with the "will of the people," asserted that, while the president's authority was intact, *postestas* was in a shambles, except for the Reichswehr. Meanwhile the "will of the people" was waiting to be unified, the more so since this idea was widely known to be close to the president's heart. Zehrer's article in the August issue of *Die Tat* merely reiterated that this unification could be brought about if the religious, national, and social movements could be made to cooperate and to abandon their affiliations with party organizations and rely on the Christian and Social Democrat trade unions instead.[29]

From all that has emerged about Schleicher's calculations, the general and war minister in the Papen Cabinet was also concerned about Hitler's totalitarian claims and electoral strategy and had begun to be interested in the solutions that Zehrer's magazine was ventilating. Although its circulation had increased to 20,000 and it was apparently read by a much larger circle of intellectuals and educated people on the Right, the turnout at elections of around 80 percent of the population indicated a degree of mobilization of the masses so high that the *Tat* Circle began to look around for a daily to reach a wider readership with its ideas. Accordingly, *Die Tat* reported in September that the Circle had acquired the *Tägliche Rundschau,* with Zehrer as the publisher and Ferdinand Friedrich Zimmermann (pen name Ferdinand Fried), Giselher Wirsing, E. W. Eschmann, Hellmuth Erbrechter, and F. W. von Oertzen on the editorial board, all of them also regular contributors to the journal.[30] Its mission was to promote collaboration among the Protestant movement and the associations of civil service workers and other employees whose political and ideological positions were in line with those advanced in *Die Tat.* The announcement stressed that the money to purchase the newspaper had come exclusively from the *Tat* Circle. However, rumors quickly began to circulate that Schleicher had been one of the investors. While it is unlikely that firm evidence of subsidies coming from the latter as head of the Reichswehr ministry will ever be found, it is quite certain that the general had become interested in Zehrer's ideas and that there had been conversations between him or his envoys and members of the *Tat* Circle. The important point is that Zehrer had decided not merely to write articles but also to offer the ideas expressed in them directly to people in power.

While Zehrer had welcomed Brüning's dismissal and had a low opinion of the new chancellor, Franz von Papen, it was generally known that Schleicher had become a trusted advisor of the president. In the summer of 1932 and especially after the Reichstag elections that had made the NSDAP the largest party, Schleicher toyed with two plans. The first one might be called the Hitler Solution, the second the Anti-Hitler Solution. The general knew that Hindenburg was dreaming of presiding over a broadly based coalition government that united all right-wing parties as well as the Catholic Center but excluded the Social Democrats and, of course, also the Communists. Accordingly, Schleicher began to talk to Hitler and the Catholics, as well as Hugenberg's DNVP and the German People's Party (DVP), now led by Eduard Dingeldey. The Catholics, among whom Brüning continued to have considerable influence, refused to enter into a coalition with the Nazis. But by early August negotiations with Hitler had reached a point at which a meeting with Hindenburg was arranged. However, this meeting did not go well because Hitler, rather than gaining a number of ministerial posts in a presidential cabinet, demanded nothing less than the chancellorship for himself. Hindenburg, weary of Hitler's abusing his powers to sideline Hindenburg and establish a Nazi dictatorship, refused to make him chancellor.

After this setback for both Hindenburg and Hitler, the autumn saw an incredible amount of maneuvering among all parties, especially in the NSDAP. Hitler still believed he could win a majority in the Reichstag, which would increase his leverage with the president to give him the chancellorship. What raised his hopes were further electoral successes in regional elections and the news that Hindenburg had handed Papen a decree to dissolve Parliament, which, after tumultuous scenes in the Reichstag, was finally tabled on 12 September 1932. However, Hitler's calculations proved wrong. In the national elections that were finally held on 6 November, the NSDAP lost some two million votes and the number of its seats shrank from 230 to 197. When this unleashed a crisis within the Nazi leadership, Schleicher, with Hindenburg's approval, initiated another round of negotiations with Hitler in the expectation that the latter would at last drop his claim to the chancellorship and be satisfied with several ministerial posts in a presidential coalition cabinet. After Schleicher had paved the way, Hitler was received by the president on 21 November. With Hindenburg still not prepared to hand Hitler the chancellorship that the Nazi leader insisted on gaining, the Hitler Solution once more came to naught. But it had the advantage that it nudged the president to give Schleicher a chance to pursue what I have called the Anti-Hitler Solution.

In an effort to bolster his position with Hindenburg, Papen in July 1932 had resorted to a move that was in fact a breach of the Constitution but had the advantage of tightening Hindenburg's autocratic regime: the removal of the Social Democrat government in Prussia. As this state represented two-thirds of Germany's territory, it had remained a bastion of left-wing Republicanism opposed to the political maneuvering at the Reich level and the attempts to transform the Constitution so radically as to turn the country into a permanent authoritarian regime. Papen's "coup" succeeded to the extent that a Reich commissar was appointed by an emergency degree to take the reins, making Prussia part of the presidential sphere. The Prussian government challenged the move in the Staatsgerichtshof, which, sympathetic to Hindenburg, refused in its opinion of 23 October to undo the fait accompli, though it rejected the argument with which the president had justified his decree: that the Prussian government had violated its duties. This qualification of the verdict had the odd result that the Social Democrat ministers were able to stay in charge of Prussia.[31]

Also over the summer, Hindenburg's entourage, again with the aim of strengthening his autocratic position in the face of the onslaught of populist politics and Hitler's pseudo-democratic electoral strategy, was pondering whether it would be possible to dissolve the Reichstag but postpone the elections (which, under the law, were supposed to be held within sixty days of the dissolution) until much later and to rule by presidential emergency degree in the meantime. A number of constitutional lawyers, including Carl Schmitt and his former student Horst Michael, considered such a move justified in light of the extreme emergency situation in which the Weimar state found itself.[32] Without going into the intricacies of this particular legal debate, the crucial point was that Schleicher was once more a key player. Even more important, he—who was by this time reading Zehrer's articles if not talking to the editor of *Die Tat*—became more interested in the Anti-Hitler Solution that Zehrer had developed.

Furthermore, if Hitler remained so stubborn, were there perhaps forces inside the Nazi movement that were prepared to join a coalition of religious, "social," and "national" groups; trade unions; and regional organizations? The man who was thought to be amenable to such a solution was Gregor Strasser, the head of the Nazi trade union.[33] It was known that Strasser was critical of Hitler's electoral strategy and familiar, as so many intellectuals and politicians were by the autumn of 1932, with Zehrer's "axis" proposals to break the impasse between Hindenburg and Hitler. On 4 September Strasser had made a speech in which he called for a "Front of Work Creation," knowing that the Social Democrat trade unions (ADGB) also saw unemployment as the most serious domestic problem. Ten days later, Theodor Leipart, the ADGB leader, indicated in a speech that he was prepared to enter into talks.

After the collapse of the Hindenburg-Hitler negotiations in August, Schleicher had put out feelers to the leader of the National Socialist Factory Cell Organization. The idea was to create, as Zehrer had envisioned, a *Verbändeachse* (axis of associations outside the party system) instead of trying to cobble together a party coalition.[34] It is not surprising that this plan found sympathy among other authoritarians around the president because of its antiparliamentary design. Rumors about Strasser joining a presidential cabinet without Hitler were fueled by a speech the former had made on 14 November titled "The Commandment of the Hour" in which he had argued that the time had come for the NSDAP to enter the government. Not surprisingly, Hitler had by now become extremely suspicious of Strasser. Major rows ensued within the NSDAP in which Hermann Goering, Joseph Goebbels, Heinrich

Himmler, and Ernst Röhm sided with Hitler. Strasser, who had been making scathing remarks about Hitler's cronies, remained uncertain about how much support he would have if it came to a revolt that would split the Party.

Put on the spot by Hitler after the November elections, Strasser suddenly admitted defeat and on 8 December sent Hitler a letter in which he resigned from his positions in the Nazi movement. After this, Schleicher's conversations, if they ever had a chance of success, went nowhere. December and January were full of intrigues and back-door talks directed against Schleicher's Anti-Hitler Solution. To prepare the ground for this solution, the general had persuaded the president to dismiss Reich Chancellor Papen and to make him his successor. This would enable Schleicher to present Hindenburg with a cabinet that would continue his authoritarian regime but would also make it possible to claim that his government had broad popular support on the Right and the Left through the much-vaunted *Verbändeachse* as an alternative to Hitler's "parliamentary" mass party.[35] The crucial point is that Papen, seeking revenge against Schleicher for having engineered his dismissal, now used his contacts to pave the way for a Hitler Solution. Hearing of this, Schleicher tried to convince Hindenburg to dissolve the Reichstag and call fresh elections, but postpone the date of holding them beyond the required sixty-day limit. In other words, the president was asked to breach the Constitution and to rule without the broad "axis" that the general had failed to procure when Strasser dropped out. Unwilling to accept this, Hindenburg began to veer toward Papen, who proffered him a cabinet with Hitler as chancellor. But he would be surrounded by conservative ministers who would contain the Nazi leader. Faced with these two choices, Hindenburg rejected Schleicher's strategy, dismissed him, and, on 30 January 1933, nominated Hitler as Reich chancellor. What may have accelerated this shift were rumors that the Reichswehr might intervene to install a military regime.

The Establishment of the Hitler Regime

What facilitated the Hitler Solution was that Hindenburg, who had turned 85 in October, thought that he had secured the broad national front while at the same time having buttressed his presidential regime under Article 48. Moreover, the Nazi ministers were in a clear minority and "framed" by conservative authoritarians like Reichswehr minister Werner von Blomberg and economics minister Hugenberg. They would surely alert Hindenburg should Hitler make moves toward establishing dictatorial powers of his own without the president's backing. Under Article 48 he could have dismissed Hitler at any time, as he had done quite unsentimentally with Brüning and Papen in 1932 and with Schleicher in January 1933. After January 1933, there were two ways for Hitler to avoid such a backlash against himself and his party. On the one hand, the death of the octogenarian field marshal could be expected any day, in which case the Reich chancellor could step into his shoes with extensive powers. The alternative was for Hitler to free himself from the constraints that the presidential regime imposed on him due to the constant threat of an early dismissal by Hindenburg.

Hitler could remove this threat by reviving the parliamentary pillar of the Weimar Constitution, which had been dysfunctional since 1930. He would have to persuade the president to dissolve the Reichstag and trigger yet another national election. With the Nazis having a well-oiled campaign propaganda machine in place but now also commanding the public relations apparatus of the state through Joseph Goebbels's appointment to a new Ministry of Propaganda and Popular Enlightenment, they could hope to increase their vote again and then persuade Hugenberg to add his DNVP's seats in the Reichstag to form a parliamentary majority. It was this coalition that would then elect a new government with Hitler as chancellor. Having emancipated himself from the grip of Article 48 in this way, Hitler's next step would be to introduce an Enabling Act through which the Reichstag would surrender its legislative powers to the chancellor for a longer period. With Hindenburg having been sidelined, Hitler could use these powers to suppress all opposition and install a one-party dictatorship, which is what Hitler did within less than a year.[36]

As late as 30 January, Hugenberg had opposed early elections, preferring the continuation of Hindenburg's autocracy. In a dramatic scene outside the president's office where Hitler and his ministers had assembled to be sworn in, Hitler had a furious argument with Hugenberg until the latter fell silent, partly because Hindenburg's secretary of state appeared, announcing that the field marshal could not be kept waiting any longer, and ushered them into Hindenburg's office. In a book about this scene and the final hectic weeks of intrigues and last-minute deals, the American historian Henry A. Turner has challenged structuralist interpretations of the Nazi seizure of power and its seeming inevitability by reviving the notion of contingency, even for an event as momentous for the subsequent course of world history as Hitler's appointment as chancellor.[37] Ultimately, it seems to me that both "structure" and "agency" produced this outcome. In studying the strategizing that Hitler, but also Hindenburg and Schleicher, constantly engaged in during the months before January 1933, there was, if nothing else, a certain logic to the victory of Hitler and his mass movement and the defeat of Schleicher and Zehrer with their Anti-Hitler Solution.

It was not unknown what Hitler would do after being appointed to the Reich chancellorship. To hold early elections and revive a parliamentary government sidelining Hindenburg's powers had been a central plank of Hitler's insistence on being given the chancellorship after his failure to gain the presidency in 1932. After all, he was now the leader of the largest party, which had gained 17.3 million votes (43.9 percent) and 288 seats in the March 1933 elections. Hugenberg's DNVP had garnered 3.1 million votes (8 percent) and 52 seats, just enough to give a Hitler-Hugenberg coalition a bare majority. His Enabling Act required a two-thirds majority, though. This he received on 23 March, when the remaining bourgeois splinters and the Catholics voted to give Hitler full executive powers for the next four years. The Communists had meanwhile been banned in the wake of the Reichstag fire, for which they had been promptly blamed. With many Communists already arrested and interned, KPD deputies were prevented from voting. Only the Social Democrats defied widespread Nazi intimidation and rejected the Enabling Act. Since Hindenburg and his advisors were aware and afraid of the dictatorial possibilities of Hitler's chancellorship, their worries explain why they had been casting around for other solutions for so long.

Zehrer had been, of course, a witness and, more marginally, an actor in these developments since the summer of 1932. He had opposed a Hitler Solution and had nudged Schleicher to explore the extraparliamentary alternative by drawing in Strasser and those other political forces that he had discussed in his articles since the spring. In December 1932, he had raised a worrying question relating to the age of Hindenburg, now 85, and what would happen if he suddenly died.[38] According to the rules of succession, the Reich chancellor would have stepped into his shoes, and to the president this was another reason that he did not want to see Hitler appointed as chancellor for so long. When the Enabling Act was passed, he must not only have realized that Hitler's maneuvers had not only sidelined Hindenburg, leaving him without his previous powers under Article 48, but also that the authoritarian solution that *Die Tat* had been rooting for since 1931 and that Schleicher had been pondering was also off the table. In May 1933, the police president of Berlin temporarily banned *Tägliche Rundschau*. The ban was renewed on 8 July, whereupon the paper folded completely. Zehrer also knew that the Nazi seizure of power had been accompanied by an unprecedented wave of physical violence unleashed

by the Nazi Brownshirts against Communists, Social Democrats, trade unionists, and supporters of the Republic inside and outside the bureaucracy, as
well as against Germany's Jews. After January 1933, people were beaten up,
arbitrarily incarcerated, tortured, and murdered with impunity. In short, he
could see the writing on the wall.

With his vision for a New Germany defeated, Zehrer now went into "inner
emigration." He sold his house in Berlin and, taking the name of "Lehmann,"
moved to Kiel until friends offered him and his wife a furnished studio in
Hamburg-Blankenese, where he stayed well into 1934. No doubt rattled by the
Night of the long Knives on 30 June 1934, when Schleicher was murdered, he
retreated to the island of Sylt in the North Sea near the Danish border. He lived
there until the end of the war, when he turned up in Hamburg in the hope of
resuming work as a journalist. His Jewish wife, hearing and reading about the
escalating persecution of Germany's Jews, became more and more desperate.
She wanted to escape to Britain and apparently tried hard to persuade her husband to join her. Not surprisingly, their marriage, which had been under stress
even before 1933, had began to break down. But Zehrer refused to divorce his
wife, knowing that her marriage to him protected her, at least for the time
being. But this, in turn, put him under a cloud with the regime. While he
encouraged her to go, he could not bring himself to leave the country. From
the summer of 1933 he merely stopped writing on politics and, after the ban on
Tägliche Rundschau, was also forced out of *Die Tat*.[39] Still, there is a problem
with Zehrer's inner emigration that shows how difficult it has become to make
sense of his life and attitudes in the spring and summer of 1933. He continued
to publish a few articles that seem to reflect his agonies. They raise the question
of whether he was nostalgically looking back to the failed anti-Hitler Solution
or whether he was trying to appease the "Führer" and buy into the new regime.
What did he write about in some of the pieces he published up to the summer
of 1933, some of which appeared under a pseudonym?

The first one was published in the March 1933 issue of *Die Tat* under the
title "The Tasks of the Army" and exhorted soldiers, especially the younger
officer corps, to work closely with all parts of the population to fulfill their
basic military mission.[40] The army was deemed to be the bearer of the synthesis between the nationalist and socialist forces in society and thus between
Right and Left. The same issue also contained a *Glosse* that was signed by "a"
and titled "Schleicher and Strasser."[41] Both men, the author averred, had been
personalities who seemed to have a great future ahead of them. But then they
had been "quietly and rather unexpectedly" pushed aside. At the same time,

their exit had been "unnatural" because their positions and personalities had been too strong to have allowed them to be dumped like that forever. Their stepping aside was merely temporary, relegating them for the time being to the "leadership reserve."

There had been, the author continued, many points of contact between the two men. Schleicher had been working for a synthesis within an authoritarian state and had built bridges between Right and Left. Strasser had tried to do the same by appealing to the trade unions. Both of them had failed "because today this bridge cannot be built yet." Instead Papen had succeeded in integrating the NSDAP into the state. The *Glosse* bemoaned the tragic fate of Schleicher and Strasser, whose policies had been motivated by their desire to unite the country, as both had rejected the overt struggle between Right and Left. Toward the end, the article reported somewhat coyly that it was not clear to what extent there had been a "certain cooperation" between the two men and hence whether there was truth in the notion of "a vice-chancellorship of Strasser," which had been rumored for a while. For the moment it was important that the policies of the two should not be forgotten. They had been excluded by the actual developments since January, and only history would be able to provide a justification for their activities. What needed highlighting was Schleicher's and Strasser's character. If, on the other hand, history did not justify the current developments, the "call of fate" might well reach them in their retreat. The *Glosse* therefore seems to reflect a more widespread assumption that was floating around in conservative circles at this time that Hitler would not last for long. They were all wrong, and for Zehrer to write about Schleicher and Strasser in this tone is bound to have irritated the new Nazi leadership.

In the *Glosse*, "a" then came back to the question of Hindenburg's successor, which he had raised in December 1932. Of course in March 1933 Hitler was no longer kept waiting outside the door.[42] Hindenburg had at last handed him the Reich chancellorship. This was therefore not the time to investigate the details of the shift from the Schleicher to Hitler. Instead "a" commented on the strange coalitions that had been formed and, in a half-sentence, alluded to the violence surrounding the Nazi seizure of power, when "gunshots are whizzing through the streets and cause ever more numerous victims." Still, parliamentarism and capitalism, the author added, must be liquidated and an authoritarian state built on the basis of a German socialism. Schleicher had tried to restore the balance between authority and socialism. Zehrer now saw Hitler's nomination to the chancellorship as a rupture of previous developments. However "sensational" this shift might have been, it was full of tensions

(*Gegensätzlichkeiten*). In a covert criticism of Hitler, he pointed to the "victory of parliamentarism" and the "momentary [!] liquidation of the authoritarian form of government." He continued that the election campaign would once more politicize the police and the civil service and asserted that "there is no German fascism," as this would mean that one party would take all power in the state via a parliamentary majority. Although this was Mussolini's path to power, Zehrer, in a fit of cognitive dissonance, believed that it could not happen in Germany. With many others, he was wrong again, and so were the predictions he made for the outcome of the March elections.

A third article, which appeared in the August 1933 issue of *Die Tat*, may be taken as a farewell note.[43] It was written under his pen name, "Hans Thomas," and was also the last one Zehrer composed as editor in chief. Disillusioned, he now offered a historical retrospective. Covering several centuries, he discussed how the world had become oriented more and more toward the here and now (*Verdiesseitigung*). After the Middle Ages, the Enlightenment and economic change had unleashed the masses, which now raised the question of the meaning of Progress. Once again the author postulated the victory of a religion of Progress that had become the religion of the masses, leading to a rupture between the intellectuals, the state, and the masses until the religion of Progress among the masses lapsed into a crisis. Other possibilities had been lost in the process. Doubts about the existing system began to grow and, whatever moves man made to avoid stagnation, none of his attempts would protect him against himself and the fact that "faith in the *Diesseits* (this world) has failed." It looks, therefore, as if "Hans Thomas" took refuge in religion and the *Jenseits* (the transcendental).

But before he reached that point in August 1933, he published a signed article in the April issue of *Die Tat* that we must consider.[44] Here, shortly after the passage of the Enabling Act, he averred that the Hitler government was now in a position to do positive work. Left and Right had ceased to exist, and the erstwhile polarization had disappeared. Zehrer next talked about the greats tasks that the Catholics and Protestants had lying ahead of them. There was furthermore a need for a decentralization of the regions and corporatist associations. But these familiar demands of Zehrer's were followed by more vexing statements. It was the task of the authoritarian forces to "exterminate" the rudiments of liberalism. He approvingly referred to the "cleansing actions" among the bureaucracy and the police and advocated the "depoliticization" of the "masses" to enable them to cooperate in a *sachliche* (matter-of-fact) fashion. Where it was impossible to dissolve associations, they should be put under the supervision of the state. And finally there was a total cop-out: "Little can be said so far about the actual tasks of the revolution."

Was Zehrer's article of April 1933 his way of making his peace with Hitler and his regime? Was this what his intellectual journey had now come to? It was such statements that many who remembered his journalism and activities in 1931–32 reproached him for later. They viewed it as his moral failure in the face of Nazi violence and dictatorial rule at this time and therefore dubbed him a precursor of the Hitler regime. After all, he knew, as he had put it himself in the March issue of *Die Tat*, that shots were ringing through the streets, killing numerous opponents of the Nazi regime, while others were being maltreated in the early concentration camps.

Surviving the Hitler Dictatorship on the North Sea Island of Sylt

However, the story seems to be more complicated. In light of Zehrer's past criticism of Hitler and the Nazi movement, posing as an open opponent of the regime in the spring of 1933 would have been very dangerous. Instead of falling silent altogether, in the early phase of the Nazi dictatorship he wrote things that were probably also a form of self-protection. Zehrer rightly feared that he had been blacklisted and might either be arrested to be sent to a concentration camp or, worse, murdered. Later he recalled a strange, unannounced visit in the autumn of 1932 by no lesser Nazi than Heinrich Himmler, accompanied by Wilhelm Keppler, Hitler's economic adviser, and the latter's nephew, Fritz Kranefuss. It is not clear why they turned up. It could be that they wanted to talk to Zehrer about *Tägliche Rundschau* and that they had been in touch with Wirsing. The latter was on the editorial board of the paper and since the summer of 1932 had been in frequent contact with Himmler and soon made his peace with the SS. By 1938 Wirsing had risen to the rank of SS-Hauptsturmführer (captain), just as Fried became Obersturmbannführer (lieutenant colonel) after 1933 and worked in the Rasse- und Siedlungs-Hauptamt on Himmler's massive resettlement and deportation programs. In 1932 the three prominent Nazis did not get very far, as Ursula Bier, Zehrer's private secretary, told them that he was not available and showed them the door. Clearly angry, they left with the words that she would be held accountable for her actions.[45]

Several weeks later, Himmler made another attempt to see Zehrer. Again Bier—as she wrote later—put Himmler "on ice" in the waiting room and then told the Reichführer SS that Zehrer had not expected him. Recalling the scene in 1965, Bier thought that they had had a good deal of fun in the office after Himmler's departure. But she was astute enough to realize that in 1933 things were no longer so funny. Indeed she feared, probably with good reason, that Himmler might make good on his threat of the autumn 1932. In the spring of 1933, Bier, who was Jewish, decided to leave her job in light of the changed political conditions. She escaped to the United States, where she married the well-known German writer Heinrich Hauser. As Zehrer put it in a retrospective statement, "Ms. Bier would have [had] to reckon with reprisals, if she [had] decided to stay."[46]

It seems that Zehrer began to harbor similar fears. He was derogatorily dubbed a "*Literat*" in the SS paper *Das Schwarze Korps* and subsequently thought it wise to disappear from Berlin. He moved first to Kiel and Hamburg and later to Sylt, where he lived in a one-room railroad guard's cottage in Kampen, out of the immediate reach of the Gestapo. If he had stayed in Berlin, it might well be that he would have become a victim of the purge by the Storm Troopers. On that terrible Night of the Long Knives on 30 June 1934, Ernst Roehm, the leader of the SA, and a number of top SA brass were unceremoniously shot without trial. To be sure, there had been massive criminal behavior by the Nazis throughout the previous year, but it was in June 1934 that Hitler and his cronies showed their preparedness to murder in the most blatant fashion. A number of non-Nazis against whom Hitler bore an enormous grudge were liquidated, among them Schleicher, Strasser, and Edgar Jung.[47] After Himmler's two visits, Zehrer must have wondered if he, too, had been earmarked for "reprisals," and it seems that the "fellow-traveling" articles he had written during the first six months after the Nazi seizure of power must be seen in this context, after which he absconded to far-away Sylt.

The next big question is what transformations, if any, did he undergo in his cottage up to the end of the war in 1945? The sources available to answer this question are frustratingly thin for gauging Zehrer's attitudes and actions. But there is at least some evidence for the 1930s. The murders of 30 June 1934 likely confirmed him in his belief that it was wise to stay out of the immediate reach of the Gestapo and the SS. To be sure, it did not take Himmler's henchmen long to find out where he was, and his knowledge of the increasing repressiveness of the regime may have contributed to his lapsing into a depression. He had guilt feelings about his past activism and feared that Germany was headed toward an apocalypse. There was also the matter of his anxious Jewish wife. For a while he seems to have supplemented his meagre income by working at a local riding stable in Kampen, where wealthy Hamburgians had their second homes and went out to ride among the dunes and along the beaches of the island.[48]

Zehrer began to read and continued a contemplative life in subsequent years in preparation of his book *Man in this World*. The books he read were heavy fare in conservative modern philosophy, among them those of Augustine, de Maistre, and Ortega y Gasset. But he also immersed himself in the writings of Soeren Kierkegaard and C. G. Jung and, having rediscovered religion, in the Bible. And yet he remained a journalist at heart. The regime had not officially banned him from writing, and in a moment of deep pessimism over his fate and his financial plight, he decided to write a novel conceived, as he put it to a visitor, "in the bathtub."[49] Titled *Percy auf Abwegen* and published using his old pen name of Hans Thomas, it was a light-hearted story about a wealthy Englishman who, bored with high society, decided to live among ordinary folk as he traveled around Europe. The book sold well, and parts of it were serialized in a ladies' magazine. The publisher, Henry Goverts, who had a house in Kampen, helped him to get a contract to translate one of Howard Spring's novels. Since his English was rather poor, his wife prepared a first draft. The payment for this job and the *Percy* royalties were apparently great enough to improve Zehrer's economic situation. His name was added to the membership list of the Reich Association of the German Press, and the book was translated into several foreign languages.[50]

Zehrer's novel was even scripted for a movie that was never completed. Looking back on the affair in 1950, Zehrer wrote that he withdrew his participation in the scripting after a mere four weeks because the filmmaker, with Hans Albers in the main role, was planning to turn it into a cheap *"Klamauk"* (hilarious) or *"Reisser"* (nail-biting) movie. When the war broke out, Goebbels's censors intervened. After Britain had joined the war against Germany, it had become impossible to have an Englishman as the protagonist in a movie to be screened to German audiences. The rights—as Zehrer later recalled—were bought up by the Tobias Film Company for 8,000 marks.[51] The book fared no better after the beginning of the war. In February 1940, C. Soschka, the editor, informed Zehrer, "extremely cold-heartedly," that his publishing house was no longer interested in further impressions.[52] Zehrer felt particularly bitter about having been abandoned in this way. Soschka knew that, because of his by then Jewish ex-wife, his predicament was, "to put it mildly, precarious." Since he had not been offered advances or other employment opportunities, as all better houses tended to do, the matter rested until the end of the war, leaving Zehrer to fend for himself in Kampen. The case was reopened after 1945 with no less acrimony, as will be seen later in this chapter.

Things began to improve beginning in 1936, and it was also a relief that his wife finally got permission to enter Britain, from where she later moved to Montreal. Their divorce was officially recorded in November 1939. In 1938, another opportunity arose to boost his income: Heinrich Stalling, perhaps after hearing of his plight, approached Zehrer to employ him as an editor at his fairly reputable Stalling publishing house.[53] At first the functionaries of the Schrifttumskammer (Chamber of Writers) objected. But Stalling finally prevailed. On a provisional basis and with the stipulation that the permission could be revoked at any time, Zehrer could become a member of the *Fachschaft Verlag* (Nazi Publishers' Guild), provided he did not work as a publisher himself. This rule changed in 1942 when Stalling, just before his death, made Zehrer chairman of the Stalling management board until the end of the war. Under his aegis, the house continued to publish the writings of men such as Ernst Forsthoff, Helmut Rössler, and Michael Freund, who had bought into the regime. But there were also the non-Nazi historian Franz Schnabel and the Catholic corporatist Joseph Winschuh. Stalling also continued to pay royalties to Dr. Erwin Reisner, a pastor and member of the anti-Nazi Confessing Church, and Dr. Maximilian Müller-Jabusch of the former *Berliner Tageblatt*. Hans Herzfeld, a Jewish historian whose wife was a Christian and who was able to avoid deportation, and Max Bildner, the cellist of the former Klingler Quartet, were also supported. For reasons that again are obscure, but possibly for self-protection, Zehrer, the veteran of World War I, joined the Luftwaffe in 1943 but was apparently never deployed to the front.

Zehrer's salary and also the royalties from his novel, while flowing more irregularly, gave him enough time in his cottage to devote himself to a more serious book than *Percy auf Abwegen*. After his wife's emigration he had still wondered about going abroad himself. As he wrote to her in October 1938, he would have left five years earlier if he had been Jewish.[54] But he wasn't, and he believed that living in Germany gave him strength. Apparently still expecting the regime to collapse sometime soon, he decided to wait. Emigration was an option, but not at this point, and he seriously considered it only once he was forced to conclude that the Hitler dictatorship that he despised had become stabilized. The regime did so, in the sense that it embarked upon a war of conquest and exploitation to realize its imperialist ambitions and to tighten its grip over the German population. Once the war had begun, emigration became impossible. Zehrer was now confined to his cottage on Sylt, with plenty of time on his hands to look back and also to begin to imagine the future. Still very much the Central European intellectual interested in ideas, he expanded his knowledge of philosophy and religion, which he had first acquired as a student at Berlin and Heidelberg, to produce something like a stock-taking of his life, of modern history, and of what, he believed, had gone wrong. He also wanted to include a look into a postwar future that, he decided, must be based on a Christian morality and religiosity that the Nazis had so completely corrupted and destroyed. It seems that he had mellowed a lot from his activist Weimar days. If Sofia Schleehahn, whom Zehrer employed after her flight from Dresden with her three children, is to be believed, he had become considerate, a "*guter Mensch.*"[55]

Given the scope of his project, the manuscript took some time after the war to be published. When it finally appeared in 1948, it was introduced by the Protestant bishop Hanns Lilje of Hanover, who invited readers to send any comments to the Research Department of the Evangelical Academy at Hermannsburg in Lower Saxony.[56] Lilje was full of praise that the author had raised, "albeit in a most individual manner, the questions of existence affecting our Christian faith."[57] To the Bishop the book was forward-looking and did not merely dissect the past but also dealt with humanity's future. The volume was also translated into English, and no lesser person than the well-known American journalist Dorothy Thompson helped him find an American publisher.[58] The book was finally published by the New York University Press in 1955, and although it is a difficult read, the translation was excellent. This is why a summary of its contents has been included here.

Zehrer arrived at the ultimate goal of his book only after several detours into European history all the way back to the Middles Ages.[59] This, he postulated, had been the period when the Christian God was still a living reality and the faithful were conscious of their guilt. Moving swiftly through the Thirty Years' War, Zehrer then discussed the Renaissance and the rise of science. This, in turn, led him through the French and Industrial Revolutions into the intellectual history of the nineteenth century and his most important figures, Karl Marx and Auguste Comte.

Given Zehrer's background in Weimar journalism,[60] it is not surprising that he offered a critique of industrial capitalism as well as socialism and Bolshevism before lapsing into a familiar deep cultural pessimism. He saw the erosion of traditional values and family structures as part of a process of democratization and the conflict-ridden interaction between elites and the "masses," which threatened to demolish received authority systems, including the authority derived from wealth. After a detour into gender relations and the rise of homosexuality, Zehrer discussed Man's restless activism and his inability to blame himself for developments that have produced toughness and the acceptance of cruelty and even torture. Moreover, with the advent of the twentieth century, the "masses," he continued, began to align themselves with the bureaucracy, pushing society and the state into the adoption of an ever more extreme nationalism and ultimately imperialism. World War I was to Zehrer about the seizure and redistribution of territory. Accordingly, he had little time for institutions and policies, such as the League of Nations and the Peace Treaties of 1919 and their attempt to bring stability to the chaos left by total war. Leaping to World War II and its outcome, he concluded that it sealed the fate of Germany as a nation-state and of Europe as the erstwhile center of political power. Instead it confirmed the United States and Russia as the new world powers, locked into an ideological and geopolitical conflict.

But where in this world did Zehrer place Man? To Zehrer, Man was destitute, sitting in a hut, almost reminiscent of Heidegger's, except that it was located on the "abyss of nothingness." And yet Man's position was not hopeless, provided he rediscovered his Christian faith and his belief that God could make his existence secure again. What is one to make of this book with its ambitious scope and its many detours, evidently designed to demonstrate Zehrer's no doubt impressive *Bildung* as well as the lessons that he felt he had learned from the Weimar and Nazi periods? The book is marked by a continued disdain of the masses and the leveling impact that they supposedly had on German society. It is also pervaded by a distinct elitism. His rejection of communism is palpable, while his references to fascism are vague. There is no direct mention of the fate of Europe's Jews. Nor does he allude to what he must have known about Nazi policies, if only because he was married to a Jewish woman who fled to Britain while he stayed behind. His silences are therefore more surprising than those of many other Germans, who were busy in the early postwar years trying to sweep Nazi crimes and their involvement in the regime under the rug. If he had felt any optimism before 1933, now there was a sense that everything had been destroyed. There was no hope in the future unless Man returned to his Christian faith.

While Zehrer's turn to hope and consolation in religion is no doubt a personal response to what he had experienced under Nazism, there is also the larger context to be considered. Many other Germans had also rediscovered their *Christian* God. Thus the Rhineland and Bavaria experienced a revival of Catholicism that many, especially older people, had continued to adhere to privately. In the Southwest and the North, Protestantism began to flourish in its various guises. This shift was not surprising in the sense that an increase in religiosity can also be found in other societies that have undergone a catastrophic material and moral collapse. It did not matter to them that both churches had made their peace with the Hitler dictatorship. To be sure, there had been individual and sometimes even collective resistance against the totalitarian claims of the Nazi regime. The example of Clemens von Galen, the bishop of Münster, comes to mind. He protested against the murder of tens of thousands of people with disabilities in the mental hospitals of the Third Reich,[61] but the Vatican never explicitly condemned these crimes or the extermination of the Jewish populations of Europe.[62] As to the Protestants, there were the members of the Confessing Church[63] who refused to join the Nazified "German Christians."[64] However, in coping with the pressures of Allied de-Nazification procedures, there was also a heavy dose of opportunism involved when it came to obtaining *Persilscheine* (whitewash certificates) to show that they had been opposed to the regime.[65] Catholics could also find comfort when, after confessing their sins in the confessional, their church had the power to forgive them. Meanwhile, the Protestant clergy tended to be a bit harder on those who had joined the "German Christians." But ultimately the West German evangelical church also offered forgiveness.[66]

Zehrer's Search for a Postwar Career and Return to *Die Welt*

It is against this background of his life since 1933 that we look at Zehrer's travel to Hamburg soon after the end of the war. He learned that the British occupation authorities were planning to establish a daily newspaper, and he could point to his time with the *Vossische Zeitung* during the 1920s, his opposition to the Hitler Solution in 1932, his dismissal from the pro-Schleicher *Tägliche Rundschau*, and his retreat to Sylt in fear of Nazi persecution. He could also refer to his Jewish former wife and his Jewish personal assistant in the office of *Die Tat*.[67] Not knowing anything about the role of Zehrer's journal in 1932, Henry B. Garland, a scholar of German literature and now the press officer in Hamburg in charge of media appointments, asked Zehrer to develop a plan for the founding of a daily to be financed by the British.[68] The latter went to work without delay and designed the first issue of a paper that he proposed to title *Die Welt*. It was only when Social Democrats in Hamburg, with a good memory of the Weimar period, claimed—not quite accurately—that Zehrer had been a stirrup holder of the Hitler regime.[69] He was unceremoniously dismissed in March 1946; however, what he had set up technically reestablished his reputation as a dynamic journalist. He caught the attention of Lilje, who promptly appointed him the editor in chief of his *Allgemeines Sonntagsblatt* at a rather meagre salary.

This is also when Ernst Ledig-Rowohlt gave Zehrer a contract for *Der Mensch in dieser Welt*, a book quite different from his novel *Percy auf Abwegen*, heavy stuff that could not be expected to become a bestseller. The manuscript was to be delivered on 1 September 1947 and was due to be published a year later.[70] Zehrer and Rowohlt had been friends since the mid-twenties, when the elder Rowohlt had once teased Zehrer about being "too young" and, at age 26, prone to churning out endless "declamatory slogans" that might be acceptable till age 20.[71] They had kept in touch during the war, when they were part of a small social circle of Kampen neighbors, among them the Underbergs of the cordial distilling family, the von Opels of Opel Cars, and, until his arrest and execution in 1942, Harro Schulze-Boysen, a key member of the Red Orchestra resistance group. Although not active resisters themselves, Zehrer and Rowohlt were united in their opposition to Hitler. However, they disagreed over the implications of the failed attempt on Hitler's life in July 1944, with Zehrer expecting an early end to the war, whereas Rowohlt believed that the regime would hold out and fight to the last bullet.[72] Their differences of opinion continued into the postwar period. Therefore, in February 1948 Zehrer's "paternal" friend rejected his increasing pessimism, announcing that he saw ahead a "rosy future" and was looking forward to having a bottle of schnapps with him on the publication of *Mensch in dieser Welt*.[73]

Without savings or a pension, Zehrer, anxious to obtain some withheld royalties for *Percy auf Abwegen*, also contacted Soschka, now in charge of Deutsches Druckhaus Tempelhof, which the Ullsteins had owned until their press empire was "Aryanized" by the Hitler regime. The Druckhaus had been printing various Nazi papers, and there was hence some confusion over its ownership after 1945. This is probably why Zehrer first thought that the rights to his book had fallen back to him.[74] When Soschka corrected him, saying that the rights were with Deutsches Druckhaus Tempelhof and that they wanted to republish the novel, Zehrer found more bitter words for Soschka, reminding him of the "amoral" behavior of the predecessor company and claiming that Ullstein had "de facto" abandoned the rights in 1940, when publication of the book had ceased.[75] When it became clear that this did not give him a legal claim, he relented and asked for royalty payments, which were subsequently, though irregularly, transferred into his account. On 2 January 1952, apparently soon after the Druckhaus had been returned to the Ullstein family, Soschka had good news for him: Rowohlt wanted to print a pocket book version of 50,000 copies at a license payment of 25,000 marks.[76] Zehrer was delighted and wrote back on 24 January 1952: "What would the situation be if I did not have my 'Percy'! Send me my royalties income with you to Hamburg [where] I can make good use of it."[77] In 1959, when his financial situation was again very comfortable because of his work for *Die Welt*, he was approached by West German film companies about a rescripting of the film version of his novel with the well-known actor O. W. Fischer as Percy. In 1964 Ullstein inquired if Zehrer would agree to rework the novel into an operetta or musical.[78]

Rowohlt also printed the articles that Zehrer had published in *Allgemeines Sonntagsblatt*, which he gave the telling title *Stille vor dem Sturm*.[79] If his two earlier books were products of the pre-1945 years, this one, though taking up various themes of *Der Mensch in dieser Zeit*, reflected his thinking of the early postwar years and will therefore be analyzed en bloc later in this chapter in the context of the pieces that he wrote in *Die Welt* during the 1950s and 1960s. In addition, there were also the short commentaries that he had published until 1961 under the pseudonym "Hans im Bild" in the mass-circulation *Bild-Zeitung*, which made Springer—hitherto the publisher of the local *Hamburger Abendblatt*, the women's magazine *Constanze*, and the very successful *HÖR-ZU!* (a weekly radio programming magazine; the exclamation mark was later dropped)—into a major power in the West German press landscape.

It is therefore safe to say that by the mid-fifties Zehrer's financial woes were a thing of the past. When in 1946 Zehrer was forced to resign as editor in chief of *Die Welt*, his successor, Rudolf Küstermeier—a man who had survived twelve years of internment in Nazi concentration camps and a socialist with a strong religious commitment—had increased the circulation from 160,000 to 600,000 in 1947. The decision to publish in all three Western zones pushed circulation up to one million by February 1949. With the founding of the Federal Republic, competition from other newspapers became very stiff, and the British began to lose interest in maintaining the paper. Nor did they have a stomach for editorial conflicts with Küstermeier. The latter was replaced by Bernhard Menne, a former Communist who had fled to Prague and later to London, where he, politically by then a socialist, held a teaching position at Wilton Park. After him came Paul Bourdin, who had been brought to Hamburg from the *Kurier* in West Berlin. Following a rebellion among the editorial staff, he was replaced by a triumvirate and in January 1952 by another single editor in chief. Given all these difficulties, it is not surprising that the British decided to sell *Die Welt*. With more and more German-owned papers coming onto the market, circulation had begun to decline. There was some fierce bidding for *Die Welt* and also some string-pulling, with chancellor Konrad Adenauer putting in a good word for Axel Springer. The latter finally purchased the paper in September 1953.[80]

The new owner, by now in charge of a large press empire with a lot of very successful newspapers and magazines, did not have to look for a new editor in chief of this paper that he hoped to turn into a major voice in the Federal Republic, competing with the FAZ for national and international prestige. It so happened that Springer had met the older and much more experienced Zehrer during the war in Kampen, where the Springers had a vacation home. They had taken long walks among the dunes and beaches talking about politics and the future of Germany's media landscape, with Zehrer acting as a mentor, strategist, and business adviser to Springer.[81] As in 1946, there were some critical voices about the proposed appointment of Zehrer, among them that of Fritz Saenger, once attached to the Nazi DNB and now in charge of the *Deutsche Presseagentur*. But with the British having lost their earlier influence as an occupation power, Springer, as the owner and publisher of *Die Welt*, had the exclusive right to choose his favorite journalist to shape the new flagship paper.

In a first *Glosse* of 26 September 1953, titled "Damals," Zehrer stressed the endless individual variety of experiences, with every German carrying the burden of his own past.[82] In these circumstances, he continued, there was no better way forward for those individuals as well as for the Germans as a whole than "to unearth, lay bare, deactivate and then to go forward into the future several hundred-weight lighter." Along with writing his first *Glosse*, Zehrer's other important task was to weld a team together that would raise the profile and increase the circulation of the paper. Not all editors welcomed him with open arms, but soon they began to appreciate Zehrer's authority and experience as a journalist. Compared to the Weimar days, he had become more philosophical and had lost his former activist energy. But he was ambitious and keen to turn *Die Welt* into an organ that fit well into the liberal conservatism of Hanseatic Hamburg with its Protestant-Republican traditions. Apart from his memories of the *Vossische Zeitung* under Julius Elbau and Georg Bernhard, he also hoped to use the London *Times* as his lodestar. Looking at the key people who were recruited to the different departments, it is difficult to discern a clear strategy.[83] Some of them Zehrer brought along from *Allgemeines Sonntagsblatt*,

such as the economist Ferdinand Friedrich Zimmermann (Ferdinand Fried),
who had been the economics editor of *Die Tat* before joining the Race and
Settlement Main Office of the SS. In 1937 he had published an anti-Semitic
book titled *Der Aufstieg der Juden*. He was therefore a very controversial figure
among his new colleagues, even if he kept reproaching himself very severely
for his shameful Nazi writings.

Konrad Ahlers joined *Die Welt* as Zehrer's "young man" from Lilje's paper.
Among the experienced newspapermen in the political department was Wolf-
gang Höpker, the editor in chief of the Southwest German weekly *Christ &
Welt*. Foreign policy was covered by Alfred Hildebrand, complemented by
Herbert von Borch, until he became the correspondent of the FAZ for North
America. Also lured away from the FAZ was its London correspondent, Peter
Grubbe, who was reputed to be a moderate liberal but, like Fried, had badly
compromised himself during the Nazi period. Another recruit, Heinz Pentzlin, might be considered a conservative counterweight. He had written on
North German issues in *Deutsche Zeitung und Wirtschaftszeitung*. Before 1945
had been on the staff of the right-wing *Deutsche Allgemeine Zeitung* and had
also contributed to Goebbels's *Das Reich*. Zehrer also thought of bringing in
Giselher Wirsing, his former close colleague at *Die Tat*, who had succeeded
him at the journal in 1933.[84] Having joined the SS, his journalism had enjoyed
the protection of Himmler. To top off his career as a high-ranking SS officer
and Nazi journalist, he had published a virulently anti-American book titled
Der masslose Kontinent in 1941. In the end, the plan did not come to fruition,
and Wirsing became editor in chief of *Christ & Welt*, founded in the Southwest
by Eugen Gerstenmaier, who had been involved in the July 1944 plot. This was
perhaps another example of the strange alliances that formed in the media.
However, Wirsing, who may have used his SS rank to protect Zehrer after 1933
against Himmler's animus over the earlier curt treatment by Zehrer's Jewish
secretary, stayed in touch with him, especially when Wirsing's weekly ran into
financial troubles in the 1960s.[85]

Like so many other members of West Germany's elite, Zehrer relied on his
networks—or, to use the perhaps better but untranslatable term *Seilschaften*
(a mountaineering term referring to how a team of climbers were roped to
each other, with the person at the top helping the others down below). In
line with Zehrer's outlook on the world, as articulated in his books, his team
at *Die Welt* was tilted toward conservative positions as far as the political and
economic pages were concerned. At the same time, the cultural sections were
decidedly more liberal. To begin with, there was Willy Haas, supported by

Friedrich Luft as theater critic and Georg Ramseger. Haas's fame dated back to the Weimar days, when he had edited the highbrow *Die Welt der Literatur*. Perhaps the most striking case, at least in this early phase, of Zehrer's quest to be pluralistic, was his hiring of Erich Kuby, although he arrived somewhat later and did not stay for long. Decidedly leftist and anti-military, Kuby may be seen as an early representative of West German investigative journalism. His conservative counterpart was Walter Görlitz, the guardian of Prussian military values, who was put in charge of the review section for political and historical books and features.

A major acquisition was Paul Sethe, who had been one of the publisher-editors of FAZ until he fell out with his colleagues in 1955, when he insisted on his right to criticize Adenauer's foreign policy as being too exclusively wedded to *Westbindung* and the United States, as we saw in chapter 1.[86] His move reinforced the positions that Zehrer himself believed in with respect to German reunification, so Sethe helped shape *Die Welt*—as did Marion Dönhoff at *Die Zeit*, Rudolf Augstein at *Der Spiegel*, and Henri Nannen at *Der Stern*—into something like a North German Protestant phalanx against the Catholic press, as represented by *Rheinischer Merkur*, and the elite groups around Adenauer, who had long been deemed a dyed-in-the-wool Rhenish politician, highly suspicious of all traces of Prussianism and contacts with the countries of the Soviet Bloc.

So, even if it took a while, by 1955 Zehrer had put together a team with which he hoped to boost the circulation of *Die Welt*, and this proved to be an arduous task. Instead of showing an immediate uptick, circulation continued to drop from one million copies in February 1949 to a paltry 187,000 and finally to 162,300 toward the end of 1955.[87] If it improved thereafter, this may have been at least in part because the editor in chief and his publisher abandoned their moderate line and turned to a political activism toward the East until circulation again began to decline in the mid-1960s, when, after Zehrer's death, the Springer press got into the firing-line of a rebellious student generation.

But Zehrer enjoyed considerable authority among his colleagues by virtue not only of his experience as a journalist and editor but also of his style of leadership. Inevitably there were heated debates over particular reports or editorials. But Zehrer usually succeeded in calming the waves and fostering a spirit of cooperation. His relationship with Axel Springer was close. They often called each other early in the morning, as the publisher and owner presided over an expanding and increasingly powerful press empire. It was now openly their ambition to establish *Die Welt* as a national paper in competition with the FAZ, even if for the moment its reach remained limited to North Germany and the northern parts of the Rhineland. Apart from Hamburg, it was printed on modern presses in Essen and Berlin. Whatever plans may have existed to expand the paper into southern Germany, the idea of challenging *Süddeutsche Zeitung*'s regional hegemony never got beyond the drawing board. The only paper that became available all over West Germany was Springer's mass-circulation *Bild-Zeitung* at an initial street price of 10 pfennigs.

The Springer-Zehrer Interventions in International Politics

As to Zehrer's larger vision of the role of *Die Welt*, it seems best to differentiate between the editorial lines that he pursued with respect to more tangible issues of contemporary politics in the mid-1950s and the broader conceptions of modern society and international relations that he also developed. His thoughts and attitudes on the latter themes will be discussed at the end of this chapter.[88] My concern at this point is to focus on topical questions of the day, not least because they also relate to changes in the relationship between Zehrer and Springer and to the position of *Die Welt* within the power structure of the corporation.

First of all, there were the interactions between the United States and the Soviet Union as the two nuclear superpowers locked in a dangerous and escalating arms race. After the death of Stalin in 1953, his heirs in the Kremlin seemed to be steering toward a more conciliatory course. Meanwhile, on the American side there were many who advocated a de-escalation of the Cold War before it threatened to turn into a hot one and a nuclear catastrophe.[89] It is against this background that a Four-Power conference was organized in Switzerland in 1955, and the new "spirit of Geneva" seemed to open up possibilities of détente and negotiation to settle at least some of the many unresolved issues of the early postwar period. Not surprisingly, West Germany's political and economic elites felt that this might open up opportunities not only for trade but also for discussions to end the division of the country. These hopes were reinforced when the new Russian leadership invited Adenauer to Moscow from September ninth through the fifteenth.[90] The trip was doubly encouraging to the West Germans. The chancellor not only accepted the Soviet offer to establish diplomatic relations but also came home with Moscow's promise to release the last 9,262 German POWs still held in camps as forced laborers in

Siberia and elsewhere. These developments encouraged Zehrer to hope that it would be possible to begin talks with the Kremlin with a view to gaining concessions on the status of Berlin and the question of German reunification. To inform himself on what was going on in Moscow, he undertook a trip in 1955, after which he professed to have become a proponent of coexistence.[91]

By 1956, influential members of the West German Foreign Office had also begun to wonder if the time had come to strengthen the dialog with Moscow, especially after Nikita Khrushchev had condemned the Stalinist purges in his speech before the Twenty-first Congress of the Communist Party of the Soviet Union in February. In the West, experts had the impression that a "thaw" was setting into East-West relations. However, in the fall of 1956 the Hungarian revolution broke out, along with unrest in Poland that demonstrated how thin the ice still was on which détente was being explored. Still, the nonintervention of the West in Soviet Bloc affairs in 1956 implied that the two sides had tacitly agreed to respect the spheres of influence that had emerged after the end of World War II. Consequently, by 1957 it was not only diplomats but also West German newspapers that advocated testing whether the Soviet leadership might be agreeable to the reunification of the two halves of Germany. Since Zehrer had never abandoned his quest to do everything in his power to pave the way toward this goal, he used *Die Welt* as his mouthpiece, knowing that his boss and friend Axel Springer was generally happy with a policy that tried to nudge Adenauer away from his strict course of *Westbindung*.[92] In one of his articles in *Die Welt* of 3 November 1956, Zehrer even dared to predict that in two years Berlin would again be the metropolis of an all-German state. Consequently, the editor in chief was not discouraged when in May 1957 he learned that Herbert Blankenhorn, the high official in the West German Foreign Office who had become an advocate of talking to the Soviets, failed to move Adenauer.[93]

Unwilling to give up, Zehrer found that it had by then become a relatively small step for him to move from thinking and writing about German unity to attempting to engineer it directly by persuading Khrushchev that it was the right moment for the Kremlin to seize the initiative. This, at least, is the background to the no doubt very unusual decision by Zehrer and Springer to arrange a visit to Moscow to convince the Soviet leadership that it was in its interest and that of détente between East and West, as well as world peace more generally, to open the door to negotiations. However, Khrushchev had meanwhile changed his position and adopted a new strategy. Partly buoyed by the sensational launching of *Sputnik* but also worried by the precarious state of the Soviet Union's East German satellite, he had decided to stabilize the Ulbricht regime in East Berlin by putting pressure on the United States, Britain, and France and their foothold in Berlin's three Western sectors.[94] When, after several delays and hesitations, Springer and Zehrer finally landed in Moscow in January 1958, Khrushchev was not at all welcoming.[95] He kept the two men and their entourage waiting in their hotel for more than two weeks. And when they finally got their appointment, the Soviet leader treated them as if they were journalists rather than high-level diplomatic emissaries. Springer and Zehrer were, not surprisingly, very disgruntled by this treatment but tried to play down that they had in fact returned home empty-handed.

It is against the background of this experience that Springer now implemented several changes to the role that he had been playing in his press empire. After purchasing Die Welt, he had continued to be a relatively "apolitical" owner and chief executive who was mainly interested in the prosperity of his capitalist enterprise. Having come under the spell of détente and the idea of negotiating the reunification of Germany in 1955, he decided to wield more influence on the positions that both Bild-Zeitung and Die Welt were taking up with respect to West German foreign policy and national unity. From 1958, after he had been rejected and humiliated by the Soviets, he—always a strong opponent of communism as an ideology and regime—not only countered the Kremlin's policies head-on but also worked to undermine the always dodgy stability of the Ulbricht regime in East Berlin.[96] If Khrushchev's Berlin ultimatum of 1958 had been designed to elbow the Western allies out of the city, Springer now used his papers to weaken East Germany. Although there are several reasons for the increase in the number of East Germans who in 1959 and 1960 decided to leave all their belongings behind and escape via East Berlin to the still open Western parts of the city, the steady drumroll of his papers to abandon the dreary economic and repressive political conditions of the German Democratic Republic for the prosperous Federal Republic no doubt contributed to the decision of the Ulbricht regime to build the Berlin Wall and to stop the drain of often highly qualified industrial workers and white-collar managers and employees in August 1961. And in order to demonstrate that he was not afraid of the Soviets' holding the West Berliners hostage, Springer responded by deciding to move parts of his offices to the city and, to make the provocation complete, to erect an imposing high-rise building in Kochstrasse right next to the border with East Berlin.[97]

Springer's political activism also made him realize that, if he wanted to be the top executive of a sprawling media empire and influence German and international politics, he needed an organizational infrastructure and a devoted team of managers to implement his decisions and secure the adherence of his editors to the guidelines that he set. This policy was bound to lead to tensions with those who were charged with the daily editing of his papers. Some of them remembered the unfree conditions of journalism under the Nazis and therefore wanted to make doubly certain that the freedom of opinion and the press, enshrined in the Basic Law of the Federal Republic, were not eroded. The trouble was that this freedom ultimately did not lie with the editors but with the publisher and owner. Springer had the power to dismiss not only incompetent staff but also journalists who opposed the publisher's guidelines. This applied very crucially to *Die Welt*, conceived of not as a vehicle of light entertainment but of serious information and influential editorial comment. All was well as long as Springer, in his "apolitical" phase of 1953, let his friend and mentor Zehrer mold his quality newspaper. The latter's position as editor in chief did not come into question when Springer morphed into a more political publisher, as the two men began to root for German reunification, culminating in their trip to Moscow. The treatment by Khrushchev had been no less embittering to Zehrer than it had been to Springer. He, too, became an advocate of moving *Die Welt* to Berlin, although in his case a heavy dose of nostalgia was added to the mix. After all, almost opposite the site of the Springer building in Kochstrasse had once been the offices of *Vossische Zeitung*, where he had begun his journalistic career in the 1920s.[98] Unlike the Hamburgian Springer, Zehrer felt a strong attachment to Berlin as a place of intellectual and cultural life that he remembered nostalgically from his Weimar days.

The foundation stone of the building in Kochstrasse was laid on 25 May 1959 in the presence of Willy Brandt, the governing mayor of Berlin, and Ernst Lemmer, federal minister for All-German Questions. The turmoil over the building of the Berlin Wall in August 1961 and other problems delayed the *Richtfest* until 7 July 1965. But this did not prevent Zehrer from moving to Berlin. As early as May 1960, he had raised with Springer some organizational questions that he felt could be more definitively resolved only once the move to Berlin had been completed. Interestingly enough, he also thanked Springer on this occasion for allowing him to stay at Springer's spacious house on Sylt.[99] It had been only in 1958, he confessed, that he had overcome his bad memories of the island where he had lived in cramped conditions and fearful of the Nazis. This time he had enjoyed his stay without the "ballast" of the past.

Zehrer was therefore very happy with the plan to move. It was not only that he would live again in the city in which he had been born and to which he felt a strong attachment both in light of his memories of it as a vibrant cultural metropolis before 1933 and as the symbol of Germany's postwar division, which he wanted so fervently to overcome; rather he was also looking for relief from the stresses and strains of running a national daily. After all, editing one involved routine and, over time, also boredom. He had turned 60 in 1959, and time was passing ever more quickly. Consequently, when the tenth anniversary of his editorship of Die Welt had gone by, he informed Springer on 17 October 1963 that he was anxious to retreat from his daily chores.[100] He added that he wanted to ponder the larger political questions of the time and suggested that an executive editor be appointed to be responsible for the day-to-day operations of the paper. For this position he had a candidate: Hans Wallenberg, whom he had known professionally for more than thirty years, along with his father. Both were Jewish refugees from Nazism. Hans Meidinger was to be the deputy editor in chief. With Zehrer in Berlin, it was finally agreed in October 1964 that Wallenberg and Meidinger would be in charge of operations in Hamburg.[101]

Zehrer's Slow Demise within the Springer Media Empire

It is not quite clear to what extent Zehrer was pushed into these changes in the face of a larger structural reorganization of the corporation in the wake of the death of Heinrich Schulte, the executive director of the paper from its first hour and a loyal protector of Die Welt.[102] While Zehrer was keen to live in Berlin and reluctant to travel to Hamburg all the time, tensions quickly mounted over editorial policy. For example, he had asked that a recent book on Prussia by the conservative historian Hans-Joachim Schoeps be reviewed. When his colleagues in Hamburg failed to commission this review, Zehrer exploded.[103] Saying that this refusal to follow the directions of the editor in chief, who he, after all, still was, constituted a link in a much longer chain of lapses, he demanded to be fully kept in the loop, and also informed about changes in the titles of any editorials that he continued to send in. The trouble was that Springer, while himself failing to provide clear lines of authority within the corporation, had also begun to distance himself from Zehrer, his friend and mentor since their days on Sylt during the war. Worse, he had felt that Die Welt was losing ground under Zehrer's increasingly remote leadership.[104] This was the background to the emergence of Hans Wallenberg, the former editor in chief of Die Neue Zeitung (NZ), who was supposedly hired to take charge of all personnel matters at Die Welt and to give directions to the paper's departmental heads, all of whom were based in Hamburg.

Tensions soon also arose between Zehrer and Wallenberg over the way the new man saw his role as executive editor. As part of the reorganization, the rights and duties of the person in the new position had been laid down in a document, stipulating that as of October 1964 Wallenberg should be involved in all editorial decisions made by the editor in chief. Springer had informed Zehrer of these new rules in a letter to which the latter had not replied but had also voiced no objection.[105] There is some evidence that Zehrer had reservations after all. For it was during that same month that a graphologist was asked to submit an assessment of Wallenberg's character.[106] Though positive overall, the report came to the conclusion that Wallenberg was not "particularly adaptable." He was said to lack the psychological capacity to guide staff in a fair and smooth manner. It is unlikely that, even if Zehrer did not commission this assessment, he did not know about it. It was filed away among his personal papers. Moreover it is likely that he learned of Wallenberg's leadership style through other sources. With Wallenberg arriving under a graphological cloud, trouble was not long in coming.

Apart from having recommended Schoeps's book for review, Zehrer had asked no lesser person than Willy Brandt to write an article on the occasion of the 150th anniversary of Reich Chancellor Otto von Bismarck's birthday.[107] Sensing that this might not go down well among the conservatives around Springer, Zehrer suggested that the CDU's Eugen Gerstenmaier be asked to provide a "counterweight."[108] When Brandt agreed to make a contribution, it turned out that Zehrer had not informed the executive editor in Hamburg. So the question arose once more of who was in charge of making such decisions and who had the right to accept or to reject Brandt's article when it came in. One might have expected that Zehrer and Wallenberg would try to settle the matter quietly between themselves. But this is not how things worked anymore in the Springer empire. Instead the question reached the desk of Ernst Cramer, the publisher's trusted new man in Hamburg, who was charged, inter alia, with corporate coordination.

On 28 January 1965, Zehrer received a stern letter from Cramer reminding him of the new management structure.[109] He added that the legal position was not as important as the functioning of the paper's editorial decision-making process. If the executive editor, Cramer continued, was simply bypassed, this new arrangement was being endangered and the entire "command structure" would be affected. He saw only two alternatives: either the agreed structure would remain or Zehrer would have to resume all his former duties again in Hamburg. Cramer, anxious to settle the case, then made a proposal. The question of Brandt's article would be swept under the rug. No further discussion was needed, and Zehrer's silence would be taken as his renewed agreement to the decision-making structure. If he did not agree, it would be necessary to have a more fundamental conversation with all members of the executive editorial board, as well as with Springer and the commercial leadership of Die Welt. Cramer concluded that he did not expect such a meeting to be necessary and signed off "With cordial greetings." Zehrer, though livid, demurred. In a letter to his "Dear Axel," he wrote a day later that Cramer was right from a legal point of view.[110] But it had been "unwise" to play up the Brandt issue once more, and from a human point of view he found that Cramer's "*Ladenschwengel-Arroganz*" (loutish arrogance) was "simply making me want to throw up." He signed the letter "Cordially, Hans." The Brandt affair was not the only source of trouble. Just a few weeks earlier, Cramer, probably on the orders of the Hamburg headquarters, had rapped Heinz Barth, the Paris correspondent of Die Welt, over the knuckles for publishing an op-ed piece in the paper. It was his task, Cramer wrote to Barth on 8 December 1964, to make certain that "we get from the correspondents exactly what we want."[111] It was not possible for Barth to decide for himself whether a report filed by him was to be cast as an opinion piece. Should he wish to write op-eds in the future, this would have to be agreed to in advance with the editorial board. Several months later, another quarrel erupted over an article that the highly regarded Kurt Becker had written. This time Zehrer and Cramer met over dinner, at the end of which Cramer asked if Zehrer wanted to return to Hamburg to resume his rights and duties as editor in chief.[112] The latter was unenthusiastic and told Springer that Die Welt was racked by a "struggle of the little people." The conflicts reminded him of the "uprising of the kitchen personnel after the lord's family" had gone away. The air, he added, was polluted and poisoned. Relations with the editor in chief merely made the internal crisis more acute. If he did not feel a bond of friendship with Springer, he would ask him to let him go today. At most he would stay for another two years and in the meantime pave the way for his successor, as the burdens of the job were undermining the joy that he had been bringing to it.

As tends to happen in a crisis like this, other problems sapped Zehrer's energy and motivation as well. While he enjoyed Berlin, where he had bought an attractive villa in Dahlem, he agonized over signs of serious illness. He felt tired and also found it more and more difficult to write. When Springer encouraged him to focus on short *Glossen*, even this was drudgery.[113] With Wallenberg apparently never quite having settled into his job, Springer kicked him upstairs in May 1965 to head the Ullstein publishing house that the mogul, after much toing and froing, had finally succeeded in acquiring. Zehrer now suspected that Cramer, himself a seasoned journalist from his days at NZ, wanted to steal his clothes.[114] As he was thinking of his retirement, there was the question of his pension entitlements. In 1964 he first began to draw comparisons with his predicament in 1933.[115] His material position was no doubt better now than it had been when Hitler came to power. He owned a home, had some 250,000 marks in the bank, and expected Springer to be generous with his pension.[116] But he felt a similar restlessness as in the 1930s, perhaps exacerbated by his fear of the Soviets and the East German regime just across the Wall, where the new office building was going up.[117]

With all these changes, rumors were bound to spread that *Die Welt* was in trouble. Its circulation had dropped below that of the FAZ and key journalists were leaving, among them Georg Ramseger and Kurt Becker.[118] In deploying his papers for the promotion of his ideological agenda, Springer had made himself increasingly unpopular among virtually all political parties. Meanwhile, Zehrer continued to flounder personally and professionally. At one point he was wondering if he should just join the editorial advisory council and write lead articles.[119] At another point, realizing that his friend Springer was searching for solutions to the management of his huge press empire, he was hoping for a comeback.[120] The autumn of 1965 was a period of uncertainty, as Springer was vacillating. For a while it looked as if Cramer was being promoted by the publisher. But by the end of September Springer seems to have realized not only how much he owed to Zehrer but also that Zehrer would continue to lend prestige to *Die Welt*. So, Cramer lost out, although Springer was anxious to keep him to help manage his empire, and so he stayed on for many more years as an advisor. Zehrer was pleased. His contract ran until 1967, and he thought that then would be a good moment for him to retire. One of his troubles was that he struggled with writing editorials and short comments. Putting pen to paper had become an ordeal. He slept poorly. Worse, his health rapidly deteriorated. At first it was stomach and gallbladder problems, soon exacerbated by malfunctions of his liver. He suffered from constant fatigue. In January 1966 he had a gallbladder operation, followed by liver surgery.

When, after a longer rehabilitation period, Zehrer tried to return to the paper in the spring, it quickly became clear that he no longer had the energy to run a complex operation from Berlin, with much of the editorial work and administration continuing out of the Hamburg headquarters. On 24 May 1966, he asked Springer to be relieved of his duties, perhaps knowing that he might not live much longer.[121] He died on 24 August 1966.

Up to now, I have spent some time discussing Zehrer's life and work as editor in chief of *Die Welt*. Insofar as this work touched upon his political views, the focus has been very much on his immediate concerns and attitudes toward the burning issues of the day during the 1950s and 1960s. This is the point at which to broaden the scope of my analysis and to look at the broader beliefs and perceptions of the world that Zehrer adhered to in those years, to survey the continuities and discontinuities in his life and to assess what, if any, learning curves he negotiated during a period that had undergone some extremely radical changes. This means that I shall evaluate his early postwar writings before I return to the historian Ebbo Demant, whose book contains a detailed analysis of Zehrer's pieces in *Die Welt* and *Bild-Zeitung* from the 1950s up to the mid-1960s.[122]

However, it should also be mentioned at this point that Demant arrived at a rather critical assessment of Zehrer as a journalist and public intellectual in the Federal Republic. To him Zehrer represented "without doubt the outstanding figure in the sphere of antidemocratic thinking in journalism from Weimar to Bonn." It is the "continuity of a mode of thought that united irrationalism and cultural pessimism, elite theory and disdain for the masses, striving for authority and anti-pluralism, nationalism and conservatism, romanticism and destruction, chaos and crisis, vision and prophecy." Zehrer, Demant continued, thus invaded the public consciousness of the emerging Federal Republic with "almost the same formulas upon which he had relied" before 1933. He was, the author concluded, the "most significant [member] of a journalistic-ideological school that continues to exist." The democratic state and society would have to deal with it. Both of them, Demant wrote, must remain conscious of the fact that it is not just groups that remain outside the democratic-constitutional order that threaten to do damage to democracy. A rightist German spirit of yesterday could also destroy a democracy, as had been the fate of the Weimar Republic.

There is much in this verdict that deserved serious consideration. And yet there is also the question of whether the path of Zehrer's intellectual journey was more twisted than Demant had made out. This is why I would now like to spend some time discussing a volume of shorter pieces that appeared in 1949, one year after the publication of his tract *Der Mensch in dieser Zeit*, which has been examined earlier. While the latter book was conceived and written in Kampen on Sylt during the dark days of the Nazi period, the collection *Stille vor dem Sturm* dates from the post-1945 years.[123] The origin of this book is not quite clear. It appears that some of the articles in the 1949 volume were reprints of op-ed pieces that Zehrer published while he was editing Lilje's *Allgemeines Sonntagsblatt*. But others seem to have been written separately, although the circumstances of his writings at this time remain obscure. All we know is that his income even as editor in chief of this paper remained low and that he was still fighting over royalties for his novel *Percy auf Abwegen*. This is why the focus here is on *Stille vor dem Sturm* as the more detailed and accessible source.

Stille vor dem Sturm as the Sum Total of Zehrer's Weltanschauung

Featuring no fewer than forty-four articles, *Stille vor dem Sturm* (The calm before the gale) is an odd volume in that it contains contributions that raise major philosophical and political problems of the kind that Zehrer had first wrestled with in his *Der Mensch in dieser Zeit*.[124] But the last two sections cover topics that are much more down-to-earth and concerned with issues of contemporary politics and society in the early years of West German reconstruction. Thus there are continuities in his thought and attitudes that go back to his wartime cogitations about humanity and the world, on the one hand, but, on the other hand, there are articles that seem to point, if not to straight ruptures in his thinking, at least to transformations of thought that make it more difficult to view him as an unreconstructed intellectual of the Right who remained steeped in his prewar ideological positions and attitudes.

However, this more differentiated view of Zehrer seems to be undermined by the fact that in the years immediately after the end of the war, while still living on Sylt, he was in touch with Otto Schmidt-Hannover, who had also retired to the island after the establishment of the Hitler dictatorship. Schmidt-Hannover, a Reichstag deputy of the DNVP, had sided with Hugenberg's radically anti-Republican strategy in 1928. While supporting Hugenberg at the time of the Harzburg Front, by the summer of 1932 he had become increasingly skeptical of his leader's policies and his own ability as leader of the party's Reichstag faction to keep it together.[125] He did not support Schleicher's chancellorship directly but was prepared to give him more time to implement his anti-Hitler stabilization concept. When both Hindenburg and Hugenberg opted for the Hitler Solution on 30 January 1933, Schmidt-Hannover was disappointed and, witnessing the brutal methods of the Nazis' seizure of power,

spoke up for the maintenance of the rule of law. With the DNVP slowly disintegrating, he seems to have made a "sharp Anti-Nazi speech" in May 1933
that lost him support among his peers in the DNVP Reichstag faction, some
of whom were by then toying with the idea of joining the NSDAP. All of this
was accompanied by overwork, mental exhaustion, and poor health, which
subsequently forced him to resign his positions in the DNVP and to take an
extended cure at Marienbad. By October he announced that he would retire
from politics, but after his return from the spa he continued to stay in Berlin. He apparently looked for an advisory position in the food industry. But
then the Night of the Long Knives intervened and, while it is not clear if he
appeared on the lists of those to be murdered or was merely to be put in custody during those dramatic days, he went into hiding for a few days in the
home of an old wartime friend and re-emerged when the danger had subsided.

Drawing a pension as a World War I officer and another one as a former
Reichstag deputy, Schmidt-Hannover stayed in Berlin until 1941, when he
moved to Sylt. He stayed there unharmed until the end of the war. At age 57,
he apparently felt too young to stay away from postwar politics. With the British occupation authorities licensing political parties, he was convinced that a
conservative party was needed. By January 1947 he had drafted a "Conservative Manifesto" that proclaimed the obvious: that the population was totally
exhausted and social structures were in a state of dissolution. It postulated
that all "power groups and leadership strata" had failed. All of them had erred
and had been both duped and disappointed. The task was now to save "the
German Mensch, German soil, and the spiritual values of the Occident."[126]
The manifesto appealed to the Ten Commandments and the need to protect
the rights of the weak. The family was to be restored as the "germ cell of all
communal life," and "mass thinking bereft of God" was to be abolished. The
thinking in totalities that had marked fascism, nationalism, and communism
was to be replaced by a federal system, a return to the rule of law, an independent judiciary, and an incorruptible civil service. Finally, there was one
striking programmatic demand: postwar Germany's political framework was
to be a "constitutional social monarchy," apparently modeled on the British
parliamentary system. Without going into the details of the manifesto, I just
want to point out that one of Schmidt's neighbors, Hans Zehrer, helped him
draft this document.[127]

It is not clear whether Zehrer participated in Schmidt's political activism before or after his attempt to found, with the support of the occupation authorities, a British-financed daily, *Die Welt*, which ended in Zehrer's

dismissal in 1946 as editor in chief when his earlier work for *Die Tat* became known to the British.[128] Nor is it possible to reconstruct what his specific input into Schmidt's manifesto was. What is certain is that he did not engage in any of the subsequent efforts of the party that the former DNVP politician and his associates finally founded in June 1947. His *Stille vor dem Sturm* therefore seems to be a better window into Zehrer's thinking in the late 1940s. Some of the essays, as he mentioned in the preface, appeared in *Sonntagsblatt*, and in looking more closely at them, I begin with the more topical and sober issues that he raised in the later chapters of his book.

In his final essay Zehrer asked what had changed in Germany since 1945.[129] Of course everyone knew about the war, the destruction, and the occupation, but there was the more important question of what had been the meaning of it all and what was now different from before. The lives of the fathers and grandfathers had still been well ordered and unshaken. But were they now still secure "without the German Reich, without the nationalist, capitalist, and socialist promises of the future," without family, profession, and property? In 1914, Zehrer continued, a development had set in that had not yet come to an end. Not only had much happened during the past thirty-five years that had cost the Germans dearly. There had been enormous upheavals, while people had sought shelter in collectives. But things were different now, and there prevailed an "inner gaiety" that is "smoldering inside us today and can become a fire tomorrow that is not only burning, but also bright and warming." This did not mean that all was rosy, but at least it was again possible to think freely and to begin to put order into one's inner life. The Western world in particular had provided the Germans with many new ideas that Zehrer wrote "we have avidly worked through." Many of them, he argued, evidently referring to his vigorous anti-communism, lacked the strength to face the dark forces that had been unleashed and were now at work in the world.

To be sure, there was East Germany, where people were not free to rethink their lives and existed under dire economic conditions. To him the important question was what would happen to those 25 million Germans on the other side of the Iron Curtain, "while we can enjoy the luxury of thinking and even speaking." If the West Germans harbored thoughts that were different from those in London and New York, they did not lie in "nationalism, National Socialism, National Bolshevism nor anywhere else," as many outside the country suspected. Even though the West Germans were now well fed and keeping warm, they lacked a lasting sense of security. It could be that an era of peace and prosperity, of freedom and equality, had begun. But what if it was no more than time for short breather, similar to the period of stabilization during the Rentenmark years in the mid-1920s? In short, those who feel secure today, might be hit much harder tomorrow.

With this being the spiritual situation of the West Germans, according to Zehrer, he returned to his old assertion that whoever wanted to live in freedom and without anxiety could do so only within the framework of Christianity. Beyond this, the reality that was taking shape in West Germany at this time required an enormous sobriety that could not be found outside the Christian faith. In an earlier essay Zehrer had tried to define more specifically what it meant to live in Germany.[130] Europe, he argued, had been in crisis for the past thirty-four years, but it was also in a period of transformation. The freedom that had been gained had been full of pain and misery so long as memory had been alive.

Living in no-man's land between the two fronts was dangerous but did not frighten Zehrer. On the contrary, he wrote, "there is no country in the world where one can live more humanely than in Germany, if only because the Yesterday" was already lying in ruins. At the same time, the humanist concept of Europe had lost its magnetic power. Instead the contours of the "*Abendland*" (Occident) had appeared on the horizon. This occidental world would provide the seeds of the spirit that would open up when "a unified world culture" took shape—a process, to be completed in the twentieth century, that would result in "emptiness and boredom." It seems that Zehrer evidently continued to harbor his earlier reservations about the Anglo-American world, which he juxtaposed with visions of a Western European *Abendland* as the cultural center of the West in its struggle against the communist East. Here a connection has to be made with another essay and Zehrer's conception of the German Volk.[131] Germans, he argued, no longer talked of the German nation or of the German Reich. Even if they used the term "Germany," they were more likely to mean "*Heimat*." Indeed, *Heimat* was all the more central to them after millions of refugees, expellees, and returnees had lost it. Finally, there was the notion of "Volk" as the only one that could overcome all differences, not merely those between East and West. At the same time there were nevertheless two Germanys based on divergent political and socioeconomic systems. Divided into two increasingly antagonistic halves and lacking a nation-state, the Germans would have to make do with the concept of Volk.

Zehrer had long perceived the world in generational terms.[132] There had been, he argued, a young generation that was around 50 today; but it no longer constituted a generational community. It was followed by a generation without

hope and of those who had been cast aside; they did not even see themselves
as a generation and thus lacked a decisive precondition of generational cohesion. It had been different at the end of the nineteenth century, Zehrer added,
when an older generation had been in conflict with a younger one. But instead
of reaching maturity, this younger generation had been thrown into the catastrophe of 1914, which had still not come to an end. Hitler's Third Reich, then,
had brought the defeat and the end of the "young generation." National Socialism had torn it apart and left behind a scene of devastation that had turned
them all into individuals that encountered others "like atoms. For them to
come together again as a generation could occur only within the religious
sphere, and any future word of this generation would have to rest on a lively
interpretation of Scripture. Zehrer's continuing concern with religion implied
that there was still a factor that individuals could not do without: God. To
initiate the young generation into the transcendental was thus another task
that he saw ahead, presumably led by an older generation of intellectuals, the
"Generation of '32," which was guided by their experience of the first half of
the twentieth century.

Zehrer's essay "*Die grosse Mühle*" elaborated on this latter experience with
its slogans and insecurities.[133] With everything in ruins, it was vital to help,
above all, those who could not help themselves. In his view, the crisis of the
late 1940s was so great that new categories of thought were required, and in
order to master it, men had to enter the sphere of religion. Pondering how
one should thenceforth lead one's life, in the next article he harkened back to
the dark days of dictatorship but spoke of the currency reform of 20 June 1948
as an important turning point.[134] For it was on this day that West Germans
had been given back, in the form of "a colorful scrap of paper," what Hitler
had taken away from them: their responsibility for themselves. This, Zehrer
added, was what defined a human being's dignity and also his special place in
the rest of the world. Of course freedom was always accompanied by fear and
worries, and there was hence no need "to read Heidegger to experience this."

Leading one's life also produced a responsibility for one's neighbor and thus
for the care of the whole—"a democracy that did not exist in Germany before
because the preconditions for it did not exist." According to Zehrer, genuine democracy cannot be created merely through education, enlightenment,
and programs but must grow from within democratic men who would never
abandon responsibility to some "*Führer*" as the "hallmark of the totalitarian."

Of course, he wrote, to be thrown into the cold waters of freedom could
result in tangible hardships. But this, too, was part of the learning process of

"leading" one's life. And this is why humans needed some higher force, quite different from former leaders and collectives. In short, Zehrer came back once again to his postulate of "a religious contemplation of the world and of man." This placed him "immediately before God" rather than before a leader or the totality of a bureaucratic apparatus. Meanwhile, the churches, as conservative institutions, had to watch over the preservation of "living values." And since they were also a social power, they had to make certain that the commandment to give neighborly love was not being violated ever again. In this sense, the churches were for Zehrer all in one: "conservative, liberal and social."

If Zehrer's argument about how to lead one's life revolved around the individual in a democratic polity that was nevertheless connected to a transcendental authority, the next essay turned to the question of socioeconomic and professional stratification.[135] Here he thought he was a witness to a process of differentiation. To him it was futile to ask why some humans were more achievement-oriented than others. With the boom of the early 1950s in mind, it was simply self-evident to Zehrer that there was a small elite that was scattered throughout public life and constituted "the sourdough of the whole." At the same time, in his view men did not work less than in earlier times, but the center of gravity of their efforts had shifted. In the past, the military and the national orientation had been central until these had been replaced by the "political," as embodied by National Socialism. Zehrer saw the technical civilization as a necessary evil, to be reduced to a minimum so as to gain time for more attractive pursuits, though there were limits to reshaping work in such a way as to make it rewarding again. The shift from work to other occupations was seen by Zehrer as "justified and healthy" because it reflected a person's will to do his own thing. To him the effort of work was necessary to enable a person to engage in more rewarding pursuits. Whoever was not prepared to join this quest would not be able to afford a home or a boat. The impetus for this had to come from one's inner self rather from the "outside."

The articles that have been examined so far were largely concerned with the practical aspects of life and seem to reflect a certain adaptability to the conditions of the post-1945 world and the reconstruction of West German society. They were preceded by a number of pieces that were suffused by a cultural pessimism and critique of modern society that confronted me with the difficulty of understanding Zehrer's world of ideas and what was ultimately going on in his mind. But before trying to draw a balance sheet on *Stille vor dem Sturm* I will try to summarize those preceding expectorations. The title of the book provides a pointer. Although the Third Reich and the Second World

War had just ended, Zehrer did not call it the "Calm *after* the Storm." Indeed, in his view the storm was still coming. As he put it quite bluntly in the preface, he saw two possibilities, one that was compassionate and the other without pity.[136] The former, however, was a lie because it assumed that the storm had subsided and that humankind had once again survived. By contrast, and according to the second possibility, amounting to pitiless reality, it was only the second storm that humanity had survived, and it was now living through the calm prior to the third storm. All humans were living in the intermediate phase right now; but it affected the Germans most directly and consciously because they found themselves in a no-man's land between fronts and had become the object of larger postwar developments. For the "60-hour world in which we live," Zehrer wrote, "is undergoing the labor pains of its unification." At first this unity would no longer be like a shell, without spiritual substance.

In light of this, the unification of the world would not be something that one could feel enthusiastic about. The individual had begun to experience an enormous upheaval of the world. But, Zehrer asked, was the only choice between a compassionate lie and pitiless reality? Basically, humankind had always been confronted with those two possibilities. Yet there was something new in the current situation in that man was constantly forced to face the memory of old truths and to remain upright in facing them. It was also new that inner and outer realities were throwing man into a situation in which there was no way out. All that was left was to search for another reality that would make him free and independent, a reality in which he could see the impending storm without living in fear of it.

Even if there was no way out, humans still could not expect anything for themselves. However, the calm both after the last storm and before the next one provided humans with a brief moment to speak up, to listen, and to ponder. And so Zehrer turned to an essay titled "Interpreters of the Future" in which he mapped out three possibilities. First came hopes vested in the United Nations, which he dismissed, like the League of Nations, for weaknesses that indicated to him that the future government of the world would not be a "world democracy." The second was the East-West conflict between "freedom and compulsion, individualism and collectivism, democracy and totality." The third alternative was that the dualism was in essence a polarity that carried within it a tendency toward unity. However, this unity would not come about peacefully. On the contrary, Zehrer opted for the worst-case scenario, adding, in a mood of deep pessimism, that "it is always better to reckon with the worst than to abandon oneself to a shallow optimism." This meant that the unity of humankind would be achieved only after an "epoch of cruel civil wars." This view may have anticipated Samuel Huntington's "Clash of Civilizations."[137] Zehrer certainly assumed that humanism would fall by the wayside.

Accordingly, he also expected, as he put it in his next essay, the "Extinction of Progress."[138] Referring to Sorel and Pareto, he argued that modern psychology had shattered the foundations of rationalism and the belief in the "autonomy of reason." The self-image that humanity's grandfathers had of themselves before 1914 had vanished. Their grandchildren looked apprehensively into a future at the dawn of the atomic age. Nationalism, capitalism, and socialism lay in ruins. This to Zehrer explained the change in the image that they had of themselves. What they were dreaming of was perhaps not Zehrer's Heideggerian hut, which he had inhabited at the beginning of his wartime book *Der Mensch in dieser Zeit*.[139] Rather it was an idyll that has already been mentioned: "A small house in the countryside, two trees in front, a garden and a plot of land, a few animals as well as quiet and calm, plenty of quiet and calm."

It was but a small step from there to proclaim in the next essay "The End of History," but the end Zehrer foresaw was of a very different kind from that Francis Fukuyama deployed in the 1990s.[140] The twentieth century had produced the outbreak of global civil wars and with it the rise of cesaristic leaders. Yet ultimately the end of history was tantamount to the end of a life directed toward the outside, with humankind turning toward the inside, ushering it into a space without history in which eternity has its home. Zehrer then became more concrete and focused on "Europe and the Occident."[141] Tracing the latter concept through the centuries and having discussed Oswald Spengler's *The Decline of the West*, he concluded that the situation of post-1945 Europe was still precarious, not least because it had become an object of the East-West conflict. Still, the re-emergence of the concept of *Abendland* indicated a shift in which its Christian foundations were beginning to surface. Beyond humanism, the issue was not the restoration of medieval ideas but of the preparation of a Christian *renovatio*. Linking this idea in his next essay to the East-West conflict, Zehrer envisaged an alliance not only between the leading European powers but also with an extra-European, though not extra-Occidental, power, the United States of America. The task of this alliance was to contain the revolution that was blowing from across the steppes of Asia and to extinguish the fires that the Eastern winds had lit.

The question was whether God himself had become transparent behind these events and how far the response of the people involved an admission of a personal guilt. Again, Zehrer added, the question had been put to Christianity and its churches as to where they stood at a moment in history when two blocs were beginning to form. This is why the choice was not between revolution and restoration; it was about a renovation of man in a world based on the Christian faith. At the same time, this renovation is closely tied to the cognition and admission of one's own guilt. In this sense, Zehrer insisted, the churches had the mission not only to reveal man's guilt but also to spread the word of forgiveness.

In "The Struggle for a Third Position" he argued that the East-West conflict contained a third one from which a new whole would emerge.[142] To be sure, there were tensions between Washington and Moscow and between capitalism and bolshevism. But if there was an independent West German foreign policy, it would probably be based on the idea of mediation between the two blocs. In this sense, Zehrer asserted, the Germans were ahead of the other countries of the Occident by several lengths. However, before Germany could play a mediating role, before an attempt could be made to present it as a model to the rest of the world, it had to pave a third way for itself. Both Russia and America represented the extreme wings of the East-West polarity, whereas Occidental man, already captured by both worlds, found himself in the middle of this force field. The question was whether this figure would be able to transform the world or merely offer his ideas to those who would mold a new reality using their own resources.

In his "Three Concepts of the World" Zehrer saw global politics in terms of the conflict between three ideas in a world that was moving toward unity.[143] All three were interrelated but had developed sequentially so that socialism and existentialism were gradually overtaken by Christianity. Even if the former two vigorously fought the latter, Zehrer believed that ultimate victory against the other two movements belonged to Christianity, which was now returning to its beginnings and was absorbed by its own renovation. As he postulated in his next essay, there was only one "revolution." namely that of the *Abendland*,[144] and this Occidental revolution was unthinkable without Christianity. The goal of this revolution was "the implementation and completion of Christian hopes and expectations by humankind" within this world.

It is against this background that another article, titled "Liberty, Equality, Fraternity," must be seen.[145] Starting from the eighteenth-century notion that humans possess reason, liberty became closely tied to the idea of equality. But in order to secure liberty in the spheres of the intellect and the economy, inequality was preserved by reference to the "notion of genius," "the rights of the strong," and the "struggle for survival." Consequently, the nineteenth century became the epoch of freedom, whereas the twentieth "appears to become the century of equality." But, Zehrer asked, what was the way out of the vicious circle that had arisen? To him, liberty, equality, and fraternity were ideas that the French Revolution had leased from the Christian faith. It was the religion of freedom but also of equality and fraternity among all humans. However, it could not make "loans" to movements on the Right or on the Left. Instead it would ultimately prevail over all of them.

This led Zehrer to focus on the "planners" of the future in this world.[146] What had been learned in the first half of the twentieth century was that rationality did not exist in all humans in the same way. Rather experience had shown that the masses were irrational and that a majority might elect a planner who would lead them into catastrophe. After all, Germany was a good example. It had had a "psychopath as its manager who had a corresponding programmatic plan." Zehrer then asked "who is planning the planners" and referred once again to his teacher Karl Mannheim, who had doubted that it was possible to plan everything to the last detail. In other words, "where do the human Gods come from who will direct an artificial world of humans and machines sensibly and fairly"? He thought that these individuals were bound to reach their limits, at which point the question of planning would tip over into the religious sphere and force the Christian churches to respond. They would have to assume the guardianship and see to it that man's path to God remained open and contained the excessive power of the planners. As before, Christianity was in Zehrer's view the "religion of freedom" because it was only through this "freedom that man's path will ultimately lead to God."

Having referred once more to the gullibility of the "masses" and made them responsible, or at least co-responsible, for the rise of a "psychopath," it was not surprising that he should claim that "the fate of the *Abendland* is determined by the fate of its leading strata."[147] But, he added, these strata no longer existed, at least not those that were capable of offering a "living model" to the "broad masses." Elites had not only been removed from below but had also destroyed themselves. There had been a levelling that had been very dangerous for its culture. On the one hand, there was the threat that this culture would veer toward cesarism or, on the other, that the determination to lead would weaken and that the culture would be slowly transformed into a primitive state. In the end, the fate of the Occident, Zehrer asserted, depended on whether some succeeded in setting themselves apart from the shapeless "mush," which had neither shape nor style, to become models that others could use as their orientation points and that they would find it rewarding to follow.

Placing developments into a global framework and elaborating on his views on the rise of the state machinery and the collective,[148] for Zehrer there was always also the "Shadow of the Past."[149] And yet, Zehrer continued, this was an age in which there were no feelings of guilt and remorse, of atonement and confronting the past. Consequently, it was useless to institute, along this path, tribunals and questionnaires that, instead of shattering the past, would merely result in putting up barricades of resentment.

Accordingly, Zehrer next examined "frozen *Menschen*," men who were paralyzed, even if they merely appeared to be petrified.[150] There were still energies inside the *Mensch*, and the question was from whence he took the strength to cope with his own guilt after he had learned to search for it inside himself. After all, in sight of the piles of rubble and ruins before him, he could not say that these had been produced by the Nazis or the British, the Russians or anyone else. Rather it was he who had done it all. Zehrer portrayed Man as Prometheus, who was tirelessly laboring and yet tied up in great pain by the "apparatus."[151] He could not change it, but there might be a point when this slavery would become unbearable. Yet even when he broke his chains, all he would have achieved would have been to gain an outer freedom, while his inner freedom would be given only if he accepted a superior transcendental power

On subsequent pages Zehrer broached even larger questions of decline, morality, and death, including an essay on his newfound belief that it is possible to talk about God again.[152] Overall, these passages from *Stille vor dem Sturm* provide a broad impression of Zehrer's thoughts in the late 1940s, most of them philosophical and ultimately transcendental but also pragmatic and related to the actual situation of West Germany within the international system. There are discussions, often put in historical perspective, of the predicament of the "masses," of elites, and of unspecified individuals. Only in one essay does Zehrer talk about his own profession.[153] In this essay, titled the "Crisis of Journalism," he began by praising the high quality of the writings of Maximilian Harden and Theodor Wolff. They had still concentrated on what was real, whereas current journalism was preoccupied with the unreal, although the most real and most effective approach was to tell the truth, to say what is. If writing about foreign policy was perfectly possible on the basis of large numbers of books, the building stones of logical thought had become more obscure and mysterious. Consequently, journalism had become more unfinished and its influence on political developments more uncertain. Worse, there was the question of who was a *Mensch* and what was truth. Having to answer these questions as a journalist, Zehrer wrote, would amount to the end of the profession and hence of journalism. To be sure, he could be a "specialist" doing a particular job.

But to ask fundamental questions of truth and reality could, Zehrer maintained, be done only if it was acknowledged that this could no longer be achieved on the firm basis of the Renaissance and humanism. At the same time, the journalist was afraid to take the "'leap' into faith, as Kierkegaard called it." This leap was not identical with a commitment to the Christian churches, as they, too, continued to carry the burdens of the past. However, there was hope for them, as there was hope for all who were prepared to turn to Christianity. Accordingly, the remaining articles are also devoted to Man's desperate predicament, his fears and insecurities, his withdrawal to his *Heimat*, family, profession, and property.[154] In these circumstances, the spiritual development of mankind would be determined by a small intelligentsia standing apart from the imaginations and expectations of the collective. And this intelligentsia was now turning toward a religious bond. Quoting Ortega y Gasset, Zehrer insisted that man was in need of a "new revelation,"[155] the note on which he ended virtually all his more philosophical pieces of this intriguing volume.

The challenge is now to link these essays with Zehrer's articles in *Die Welt* of the late 1950s and 1960s that Ebbo Demant has analyzed. Here the editor in chief of Springer's flagship paper emerges as a deep pessimist who, after the building of the Berlin Wall, asked if the Bonn Republic was about to repeat the experience of its Weimar predecessor. He feared a relapse into totalitarianism, which he believed could be avoided only if freedom and independence were paid for with a restriction of personal needs and desires, or at least a preparedness to limit them. Demant also highlights Zehrer's criticsm of "mass democracy," which existed in "the glass house of prosperity" and the "ivory tower of security."[156] He also finds Zehrer appealing to us to think of "the whole" and of German unity. Demant's book, therefore, emphasizes the continuities in Zehrer's thoughts. He sees the old links between his cultural pessimism and "irrationalism," his elitism and "disdain for the masses," his "striving for authority and "anti-pluralism," his nationalism and conservatism.

Having examined Zehrer's life both before 1933, under Nazism, and after 1945, as well as his writings in greater detail, I wonder if he was not a more interesting and complex intellectual than earlier scholarship has made him out to be. Of course there are continuities, but there are also transformations. He was clearly deeply marked by his direct encounter with the Hitler dictatorship, during which he went into "inner emigration" and accepted a life under difficult economic circumstances and, though he did not involve himself in any resistance movement, in fear of becoming again a target of Nazi persecution. Although he came from a Catholic family, he may not have been a particularly religious person during the Weimar years. But he did become one in subsequent years. In this respect he joined many other German intellectuals who (re)discovered their faith by the end of the war and in the years of upheaval thereafter. What made him stand out was that, instead of merely going to church, he thought intensely about how religion could and must be related to postwar West German society and politics.

The evolution of his thoughts can be traced from his wartime book *Der Mensch in dieser Zeit* through his *Stille vor dem Sturm*. Here showed that he was not a liberal or a Social Democrat but a conservative who wrestled with how battered West Germany might become a new society based on firm constitutional principles and Christian morality. For a short time he may have thought of Germany's becoming a British-style constitutional monarchy, but once a parliamentary-democratic republic had been created in 1949 he worked for its stabilization and success. This is why his articles in *Stille vor dem Sturm* have been given some space here to present the substance of his postwar ideas. Some of them, such as his hope that the Soviets would allow the reunification of the two Germanies in the later 1950s, were, to be sure, illusory. But others deserve closer attention. They indicate that, if nothing else, Zehrer's notions of politics and society went through a phase that reflected a learning process and a willingness to change. It was only in the mid-1960s that he became more resigned and fatalistic, partly in response to the weakening of his influence within the Springer empire. Afflicted by illness that finally killed him in the summer of 1966, he may have lapsed back into some earlier postures and attitudes. This is where it is possible to establish some continuities, but they were not linear and were interrupted by a period in his life that showed a capacity and willingness to learn and to accept a personal responsibility for the errors of judgment that marked his politics and his journalism in the early 1930s.

4

Hanseatic Journalism
and Its Networks

Newspapers and Politics in Early Postwar West Germany

If the previous four chapters were primarily concerned with the life and work of three prominent Hamburgian journalists as well as my efforts to conceptualize their biographies within a generational framework and, finally, to grapple with the meaning of their anti-Nazism and the direction of their postwar journalism, this chapter turns away from the questions of the freedoms as well as the constraints under which Paul Sethe, Marion Dönhoff, and Hans Zehrer operated as employees of large media corporations after 1945.

Hamburg became one of five media centers in West Germany. Arguably the most important competition arose in the Rhineland, not only because it was a major industrial and commercial region with high population densities but also because it was a stronghold of Catholicism, in contrast to predominantly Protestant Hamburg. Here the *Rheinischer Merkur* became an influential weekly supporting Konrad Adenauer's domestic and foreign policies. The more heavily Protestant region of the Southwest emerged as a third region, with a concentration of more liberal-conservative papers such as the *Stuttgarter Nachrichten* and Eugen Gerstenmaier's weekly *Christ und Welt*. Bavaria was the fourth region, with a mainly Catholic press concentration, although the more liberal *Süddeutsche Zeitung* was also widely read and eventually gained national significance. Finally there was Frankfurt, with the more conservative FAZ, discussed in chapter 1, and the more left-liberal *Frankfurter Rundschau* as well as the left-Catholic monthly *Frankfuter Hefte*.

Like the nascent press as a whole, the newspapers and magazines that were published in the Hanseatic city faced major political and economic challenges, and the ways in which they were overcome provide the larger framework for the biographies of "my" three journalists. However, the shift toward the press in this chapter will not just involve an analysis of the purely structural conditions that the British occupation authorities and their German partners and critics created. Nor, once the Federal Republic had been set up in 1949 and a market economy with strong welfare elements began to unfold, does this chapter examine the dynamics of the West German political economy at large, on which there is a good deal of secondary literature.[1] Rather I shall concentrate on British press policies and five key Hamburgian publishers who either owned the newspapers and magazines or had a major stake in one or two of them.

The papers published in this ancient Hanseatic city represented a mix of a liberal-conservative internationalism, on the one hand, and a Social Democratic press that appealed to leftist working-class readers, on the other. Still, all of them were contributing to the massive reconstruction effort that began straightaway in 1945. But the undertaking was not merely about the revival of the war-torn economy and of a parliamentary-political democracy. Underlying it was always also the recognition of the total destruction that the Nazi regime had left behind, which required a more fundamental effort to rebuild the moral foundations without which the political system would rest on shaky ground. The three journalists whose lives and work have been examined in the previous chapters made important contributions to this renewal, but the publishers and journalists who worked in Hamburg should not be underestimated. In fact, that environment formed the larger context in which Sethe, Dönhoff, and Zehrer were able to develop their ideas of postwar West German society and politics.

To understand the activities and actions of the five key publishers in this picture—Axel Springer, Gerd Bucerius, Rudolf Augstein, John Jahr, and Richard Gruner—it must be remembered that the Basic Law of 1949 guaranteed freedom of expression. For the journalists portrayed in previous chapters this meant that, within the limits of this law and the Criminal Code, they could express their opinions freely. In this respect, West Germany was very different from the Nazi dictatorship that the three journalists and their publishers had lived through. But for journalists who were employees, there were further limits to their freedom of expression. If their publisher disagreed with their views, they could be asked to toe the newspaper owner's line or leave and join an enterprise that was prepared to publish their views. In other words, the basic right rested constitutionally with the entrepreneur and not with the employee.[2] We have already come across these larger realities, especially in the biography of Paul Sethe. He decided to leave the FAZ in 1955 when four of his editor-colleagues were put under pressure by Adenauer and the investors behind the paper. These businessmen quite bluntly declared that Sethe's articles on questions of European integration and of German reunification transgressed the ideological and political framework that they wanted the FAZ to reflect.[3] Since Sethe insisted on the uncensored expression of his divergent opinions, he had no choice but to find another paper that was prepared to publish his views.

He found this paper in Axel Springer's *Die Welt*, but only for as long as Springer agreed with Sethe's positions. When, Springer, after his disastrous visit to Moscow, changed his views on how to deal with the Soviets and their East German satellite in 1958–59, Sethe found himself out of line for the second time. It is in this context that those very bitter sentences must be seen that have already been quoted in two similar and revealing versions. As Sethe put it in 1956, only the person "who is wealthy is [also] free," adding pointedly that this "is not by Karl Marx, but by Paul Sethe."[4] The second statement was no less acerbic: "Press freedom is the freedom of 200 wealthy people to spread their opinions."[5] These quotations must be juxtaposed against a self-confident dictum by Springer, who was then his publisher and hence his boss: "This is all my money, with which I can do whatever I want."[6] Small wonder that when he and Sethe parted ways, the latter told the man who so obviously believed in a paternalistic *Herr-im-Hause* principle that he had been Springer's ally when he first joined *Die Welt*, but that he, Sethe, had "no talent to be a subordinate subject (*Untertan*)."[7] Springer's subsequent softpedaling letter did not move him, and he began to write for *Die Zeit* and *Der Stern*, both publications of which the key owner was Bucerius, who explicitly welcomed Sethe to the circle of journalists in Hamburg's Pressehaus.[8] This is where Sethe finally found his peace of mind. He was at long last given the space that enabled him to express himself freely again on the topics that he felt strongly about and wanted to put his pen to. He also became a mentor of Henri Nannen, who had begun to reconfigure *Der Stern*. It no doubt also helped that conditions in Germany related to issues that were dear to his heart, German unity in particular, had begun to change. The opening toward the East that he had advocated since the early 1950s was slowly becoming a reality.

If this transformation defined the larger constitutional framework of journalism in the Federal Republic after 1949, there was the period 1945–49 to be considered first, in which the British occupation authorities held the reins in their zone. More specifically, they had the right to issue licenses for the publication of newspapers and magazines. Once these had been granted, the newly established papers were kept on a relatively long leash by these authorities. London also decided to establish a newspaper of its own: *Die Welt*. It was funded by the British, but the editor in chief and the editorial staff chosen by them were German. By contrast, the American authorities, having founded their own paper, NZ, in their zone, put American personnel in the key positions.[9] The Americans tended to put in charge refugees from Nazi Germany who were familiar both with the German language and with German cultural and journalistic traditions. But in the US zone there were some in higher positions who, unfamiliar with the milieu and assuming a more punitive stance toward the Germans, were prone to censor the NZ's editors. No less important, the relationship of the latter with their German assistants and readers was necessarily different from that in the British zone. While both Allied papers had large circulations, the NZ was always viewed as an *American* paper by its German readers. *Die Welt*, on the other hand, was composed by native journalists, and the British authorities merely intervened when they believed that their policies were being criticized to a degree that demanded after-the-fact censorship, and even then—as will be seen—they showed a good deal of flexibility.

Of course the German editors could be dismissed at any time, as happened to Hans Zehrer, the first editor in chief, who later claimed that the title of *Die Welt* and also the original design of the paper were based on his ideas.[10] While he stumbled when the British officer in charge of press policy was told of Zehrer's role at the end of the Weimar Republic as editor in chief of *Die Tat*, other journalists who did not have a controversial past or had been persecuted and imprisoned during the Third Reich were found to turn the paper into a widely read daily in the British zone. Accordingly, the printing and marketing of *Die Welt* went fairly smoothly, so that by 1949 it had reached a circulation of just over a million.[11]

The Origins of Axel Springer's Press Empire

By that time, the competition from local and regional papers and magazines that had been granted British licenses had grown considerably. As in other parts of the Western zones of occupation, publishers who had once made their peace with the Nazi regime and had been permitted to print and sell papers until they were forced to close down began to rebuild their businesses. Unless their assets, such as printing plants and buildings, had been destroyed by the war, these publishers would soon apply to the British occupation authorities to be given licenses for their papers. One of the lucky ones in Hamburg was 33-year-old Axel Springer.[12] And he did not have to start from scratch. It was his father, Hinrich, who had built up a successful business publishing books and newspapers during the Weimar Republic. As a member and for a while also the local treasurer of the pro-Republican DDP, he thrived in the urban milieu of Altona, just adjacent to the Hamburgian working-class district of St. Pauli. In 1909 he and a partner had bought the printing firm of Hammerich & Lesser that he used, starting in January 1924, to publish the *Altonaer Bürgerzeitung*, just as the German economy was emerging from the collapse and hyperinflation of the previous year. Eight months later, Hinrich Springer and his associate, Julius Wagener, established the *Altonaer Neueste Nachrichten* (ANN) in the hopes that the paper would be read not only by Altona's bourgeoisie but also by the workers in local industry and the port of Hamburg less than a mile away.

When Springer added two modern rotation presses and expanded his book publishing venture in 1927, the family became quite wealthy and could afford to take a ski vacation in Thuringia in 1929. When the Nazis seized power, the Springers felt no enthusiasm for Hitler, and Hinrich's wife, Ottilie, had no inhibitions against expressing her disgust in front of others so loudly that the family rightly feared her arrest by the Gestapo. With Nazism consolidating, it became a question of economic survival for Hinrich to have the regime's permission to continue publishing the ANN. He succeeded and, following the absorption of Altona into the city state of Hamburg, was able to rename it *Hamburger Neueste Nachrichten* (HNN).[13] It never was an outright Nazi paper, but it was still subject to the new press laws and the vigilant censors in Goebbels's propaganda ministry and the Reich Press Office under Max Amann. Hinrich soldiered on until the war. When Hitler's foreign and military policies escalated into a world conflict, HNN was ordered to close in January 1941. The Springer book publishing continued, though, and, with Hinrich's health deteriorating, his son Axel, born in 1912, began to step into the gap. In his teenage years Axel had, to the dismay of his parents, lived the life of a playboy, leaving school without the *Abitur* certificate and interested mainly in young women and sports cars. He avoided the draft with the help of medical certificates confirming that he suffered from pancreatic problems. Eventually he grew up and began to build a career by learning about modern printing and publishing. After the closure of the HNN he concentrated on the book-publishing arm of Hammerich & Lesser and maneuvered it through the war by producing unpolitical light entertainment.

There is one personal decision that Axel Springer made not entirely freely, when in 1933 he married Martha ("Baby") Meyer, the daughter of the "Aryan" owner of a Hamburgian construction firm, and his wife, Mary, who hailed from the Jewish Seldis clan.[14] After 1939 Mary was deported to Theresienstadt camp, but after a lot of string-pulling by friends and family, she was miraculously discharged. At the time of their marriage in November 1933, the "half-Jewish" daughter Baby had become pregnant with Axel's child. After the child, Barbara, was born in December of that year, the couple stayed together for a while, but the marriage fell apart when Axel became a philanderer. They divorced in September 1938, with Axel admitting to his adultery. It is not clear if he fully realized that Baby, as a "non-Aryan" divorcee, now had to fear anti-Semitic sanctions and internment. Fortunately, she soon remarried Friedrich Funke, another "Aryan," and this liaison survived the war. Nevertheless, Axel's witnessing of the Nazi persecution of the Jews helped turn him into an anti-Nazi. Learning the printing and newspaper-editing trade, he managed Hammerich & Lesser until it was forced to shut down in August 1944. When he applied for a license after the end of the war, the British occupation authorities were happy to give him one. His former Jewish mother-in-law wrote a "whitewash certificate" (aka *Persilschein*) confirming his anti-Nazism, and the rest of his family history also convinced his British interviewers that he should be allowed to revive his father's firm. However, there was another hurdle: his friend John Jahr.

Born in 1900, Jahr had become a member of the Nazi Party, which enabled him to publish books and magazines during the Hitler years.[15] He had met Axel on the North Sea island of Sylt, where they had struck up a friendship and, expecting Germany's defeat, had begun to make plans for the postwar period that relied on their publishing expertise. The trouble was that Jahr, having been a Party member, was refused the required license. However, Axel Springer, having made much of his anti-Nazi attitudes and his longing for a return of the "freedom" that the Allies were now bringing to Germany, also overcame this obstacle and was able to bring Jahr into the growing media company. With the more experienced Jahr at Springer's side, Hammerich & Lesser became the springboard for Springer's meteoric postwar publishing career. He started off with printing brochures and calendars and then discovered radio after Hamburg had become the center of a major wireless station, the Norddeutscher Rundfunk (NDR), soon to be renamed the Nordwestdeutscher Rundfunk, which put out a weekly programming schedule. Taking the *The Listener*, the weekly journal of the British Broadcasting Corporation, as his model, Springer decided to publish a magazine that listed current programs and included articles of general interest to its subscribers. The NDR was only too glad to have another outlet to publicize its features and selections of music. Called *HÖR-ZU!* (with a hectoring exclamation mark), the magazine took off like a rocket.[16] Appearing with an initial imprint of 250,000 in the second quarter of 1947, it sold over one million copies per week by the early 1950s.

Having discovered his vocation, Springer became the driving force behind his firm's subsequent expansion into the intellectual journals business after discovering that there was a strong demand for high-brow discussions of politics and culture. Yet it soon became clear that his *Nordwestdeutsche Hefte*, while sophisticated, would not be a moneymaker. He therefore transformed it into a more popular illustrated magazine, *Kristall.* Owning a daily paper looked even more promising to a budding entrepreneur. At first Springer had plans of reviving the ANN. But competition from dailies that appeared in the morning had become quite stiff in Hamburg by late 1947. There was the *Hamburger Echo*, which was linked to the SPD. The *Hamburger Allgemeine Zeitung* was close to the Christian Democrats, with the *Hamburger Freie Presse* leaning toward the Free Democrats and the *Hamburger Volkszeitung*, a Communist paper. Rumor also had it that the Broscheks, another old publishing family, wanted to republish the time-honored *Hamburger Fremdenblatt.*[17]

However, there was no local paper that came out in the late afternoon, to be read by bourgeois readers in the evenings in the comfort of their homes. Springer decided to move into this gap and in the summer of 1948 laid the foundations of his *Hamburger Abendblatt.*[18] By July 1949 the paper had a circulation of 201,000 and by 1953 sold 332,000 copies, a very respectable number for a local paper. While he had accumulated some capital due to the success of *HÖR-ZU!*, Springer needed additional financing from a bank. The Altona branch of *Vereinsbank*, keen to promote trusted local businesses, lent him the money for the editing, printing, and distribution of the *Abendblatt.* The loan was secured by the income of his radio programming magazine. Running several high-circulation publications meant that Springer also needed buildings, including an office building for a rapidly growing workforce. This time it was Berthold Beitz, the director general of the Hamburg-based IDUNA insurance trust, who approved a loan of no less than 12 million marks. In short, much of the early expansion of Springer's press empire was funded with outside capital. There was still one other promising genre in which he was interested, a monthly that appealed to middle-class women, that is, a "ladies' magazine." He launched it together with his friend John Jahr, who had meanwhile been sufficiently rehabilitated to be given a license jointly with Springer. Springer took 50 percent of the shares of the magazine, called *Constanze,* and the journal attracted many readers among educated women interested not only in fashion but also in features on serious topics of social and cultural concern during the 1950s.[19]

Tireless and with a sharp eye for opportunities in the media world of the West German "miracle years,"[20] Springer spotted two further opportunities. Having visited Britain and studied the methods of Cecil King's successful *Daily Mirror,* he began to conceptualize the *Bild-Zeitung* as a mass-circulation daily that provided little political news but very short articles of general interest to the "ordinary" reader, generously interspersed with photos, especially of sports events and female models in alluring dress. Hamburg had such a paper, the *Hamburger Morgenpost,* which was close to the SPD and appealed to the city's manual workers. Springer concluded that he could to better, so "Bild" appeared in large format with big, sensationalist headlines at the price of a 10-pfennig coin. By September 1953 the originally four-page rag had reached a daily circulation of 1.3 million copies. It was churned out on the latest rotation presses, and the print operation was expanded into the largest print manufacturing facility in Europe, first in Hamburg but soon also in Essen in the densely populated Ruhr region. The distribution network was soon also equal to none.

For Springer there was one final crown jewel to be obtained: a quality daily paper of the kind that the FZ had been during the Weimar Republic, which had the potential of becoming a national paper in competition with the FAZ and would also be read abroad. For a while Springer thought of creating a brand-new daily that, in its planning stage, had the pretentious title of *Excelsior.* But then, he thought, why conceive of a new daily when Hamburg was already the home of *Die Welt,* the daily that, after Zehrer's ouster, the British occupation authorities had built up with the help of Fritz Küstermeier, who had a flawless anti-Nazi record?[21] A member of the SPD, he had worked in the anti-Nazi underground until he was arrested and condemned to spend the next twelve years in prison. Yet, to the amazement of his fellow-editors who joined *Die Welt* with him, he did not harbor any feelings of hatred toward the Germans. Totally devoted to producing an excellent weekday newspaper, he even swallowed the initial stricter supervision by the British, who had invested their pride in this paper. From 1948 onward, a Sunday edition, the *Welt am Sonntag,* was added. Bernhard Menne, who had once edited the *Prager Mittag* and had survived the war in British exile, was appointed as its editor in chief. It was this dual concept of a weekday and a Sunday edition that proved to be a roaring success, reaching a circulation of just over one million in 1949.

However, partly because of increasing competition from West German publishers whose regional dailies were cropping up everywhere, the circulation of *Die Welt* began to decline once the Federal Republic had been founded and Allied licensing came to an end. By 1952, the paper had become a losing venture. Not surprisingly, the British High Commission began to think of selling the newspaper as long as it had not reached the point of bankruptcy.[22] With the founding of the Federal Republic, the British also saw less of a need to own a paper when West Germany was evidently emerging as a fairly stable parliamentary-democratic republic, buttressed by economic prosperity. Consequently, the prospect of the sale of a paper whose total assets were estimated to be around 4.2 million marks attracted a number of publishers, among them Broschek, the Schauberg-Dumont Verlag, which had published the *Kölnische Zeitung* during the Weimar days and, finally, Springer. Following intricate negotiations and backstage maneuvering in which his school friend Eric Blumenfeld, by then a prominent figure in Hamburg's Christian Democratic Union (CDU), as well as Bucerius gave a helping hand, Springer finally came out on top.[23] Suffice it to make three points here. First of all, it was Chancellor Konrad Adenauer who pushed quite hard for Springer to be awarded the prize. With several successful papers under his belt, Springer had the financial and technological capacity to reverse the paper's declining circulation. He also had the ambition to add a quality paper to his stable that had the potential to be read beyond North Germany. Finally, he had an editor in chief, Hans Zehrer, who had been present at the conception of *Die Welt* in 1945–46 and in whom he, having known him from the pre-1945 years and their long walks along the beaches of Sylt, was prepared to put his trust. The agreement was signed on 17 September 1953. The purchase price was 1.3 million marks, and the final cost to Springer came to around 2.7 million marks. He was by now one of the major newspaper publishers in Europe—a man in charge of a media empire who was conscious of his economic and increasingly also his political clout.

Gerd Bucerius: Family Background and Postwar Media and Political Ambitions

The help of Blumenfeld and Bucerius indicates that Springer was not alone in engineering the growth of his empire. Unlike Bucerius, Blumenfeld was not in publishing but was instead a coal merchant who had endured a nightmarish life under Nazism.[24] The son of a Danish mother and a German-Jewish father, he had been deported to Auschwitz at the end of 1942 and assigned to a group charged with removing asphyxiated victims of the Holocaust from the gas chambers. Through various channels his mother had learned about this absolutely awful "job" and, knowing Felix Kersten, Himmler's masseur, asked him to plead with the SS leader to transfer her son. Himmler agreed, and Blumenfeld was sent to Buchenwald concentration camp, but not before a forced sterilization had been performed on him. In the chaos at the end of the war, it was Bucerius who secured Blumenfeld's survival and for a while hid him at his home in Preusserstrasse in the Hamburg suburb of Othmarschen. After 1945 Blumenfeld was not only able to restart his own business but also joined the Christian Democrats, with whose help he gained a seat in the Bundestag in 1949. As a fellow-Hamburgian, he now helped Springer to buy *Die Welt*.

Gerd Bucerius's family was headed by his father, Walter, who, following his legal training, had been working as a civil servant in Hamm, in the eastern Ruhr region, where his son was born in May 1906.[25] He rose to higher positions further West, first in Remscheid and finally in Essen. Having served in World War I as a battalion commander and having earned the Iron Cross First Class, Walter joined Stresemann's DVP and successfully competed for the position of burgomaster in Hanover before transferring to Hamburg to become a director in Hugo Stinnes's shipping trust. Leaving the company upon Stinnes's death in 1924, Walter Bucerius established his own law firm in the city in 1926, with his son following in his footsteps. After receiving his *Abitur*, Gerd spent the next several years pursuing his law studies at Freiburg University. With his exams successfully completed, he undertook his practical training in Hamburg and Berlin, passing his assessor exam in March 1932. In October he married Gretel Goldschmidt, with whom he had fallen in love when he lived as a paying guest with her family in Berlin during his legal training. They moved into a house in Hamburg's Preusserstrasse.

After the Nazis' seizure of power, Walter Bucerius and his son quickly got caught in the net of the regime's anti-Semitic laws. For Gerd his marriage to the Jewish Gretel became a stigma.[26] The introduction of a decree requiring lawyers to show documentary proof of their "Aryan" ancestry put Walter on the spot when a rumor arose that he had Jewish ancestors. He refused to provide the requisite documents and pointed to his stellar service as an officer during World War I. While father and son lost some professional privileges due to the introduction of further discrimination against "non-Aryans" or "Aryans" with Jewish spouses, such as the right to train young lawyers, they, together with their associate Karl Samwer, had plenty of private work to do for clients in North German commerce and industry. Gerd also began research for his dissertation and obtained his doctorate in July 1934.

According to Gerd's biographer, the early years under Hitler were happy ones for him and Gretel.[27] They vacationed together on the Baltic Sea coast, went skiing in Switzerland, and attended a reunion of the Goldschmidt family in fashionable Bad Pyrmont in 1934. Gerd's successful legal practice enabled him to travel to France, Italy, the Netherlands, and Austria. In May 1938 he visited the United States. However, by this time his wife had become increasingly anxious about Nazi persecution; so after the Pogrom of November 1938, her husband insisted that she leave Germany. After another visit to Britain, he found her a job as a domestic servant so that she could leave Hamburg in December of that year. Her mother, who stayed in Germany, was deported to Riga and perished in the East. There is no record of where she was murdered.

Once the war had begun, Gerd Bucerius was drafted into the army and spent two months in military training. But then, instead of being deployed at the front, he was demoted to the "Ersatz Reserve 2" and deemed unworthy to bear arms, probably because of his marriage to Gretel Goldschmidt. Even if there is no documentation of Bucerius's life and views, it seems plausible that he was by now an irreconcilable anti-Nazi who prayed for the defeat of Germany. When his law license was withdrawn, he found a job as manager of the Diago Works, which manufactured pressed-wood panels and was hence classified as a "war-essential" company.[28] The local Nazi economic office pressured him to divorce his wife, now living in Britain. There was an ephemeral threat that he would be drafted into the Wehrmacht, but in the end he only received an order to join the last-ditch *Volkssturm* militia. As Germany sank into chaos, he was ordered to appear before the local Gestapo but was let go. Not surprisingly, he was by now longing for the defeat of Germany. Meanwhile, friends and clients knocked on the door of his house in Preusserstrasse, among them Richard Tüngel, soon to become the editor in chief of *Die Zeit*, the weekly that Bucerius began to publish in February 1946. There also was Erik Blumenfeld, who, after his transfer from Auschwitz to Buchenwald, had escaped to Berlin. Bucerius then learned that he had again been taken into "protective custody" there. As on earlier occasions, Blumenfeld somehow managed to escape again and was at first hidden by a girlfriend in the city before he turned up on Bucerius's doorstep in Hamburg, where he spent the final weeks of the war in hiding.[29]

Given the course of his life under Nazism, Bucerius did not find it difficult to convince the British authorities to allow him to reopen his law practice as early as 1 July 1945. Even more important for his future career, Col. Henry B. Garland, the officer in charge of the press, was prepared to grant him a publisher's license.[30] Next there was Ewald Schmidt di Simoni, who had been a distribution manager at the FZ and later at the *Kölner Stadt-Anzeiger* until the Nazis forced his dismissal because of his Jewish wife. Without a job, he had signed up for the Navy, which turned out to be a blessing for his mother-in-law: when she was to be sent to a camp, a member of his crew who had meanwhile risen to the position of admiral came to the rescue. Learning about the order, he was able to stop the deportation. Wishing to resume a media career, Schmidt di Simoni got a license for a daily newspaper. Finally, there was Richard Tüngel, who had lost his job in 1933 as a civil servant in Hamburg's construction department and subsequently survived as an impoverished writer and screenwriter. In the crazy chaos of postwar Hamburg, it was Garland who connected the three men, along with Lovis Lorenz as the fourth partner.[31] A former editor in chief of *Die Woche*, which had been part of the Scherl publishing empire until 1944, he had worked for the Broschek printing firm. Bucerius had sheltered him, too, in his home in Othmarschen at the end of the war. With Bucerius having inherited some 400,000 marks as well as the parental home and his father's share in the law firm, the four men, whose professional experiences complemented each other quite neatly, began to plan a weekly paper to be entitled *Die Zeit*. Its first issue appeared on 21 February 1946, a mere week after the license had been formally approved.

Next to his publishing, Gerd Bucerius had developed political ambitions and was put in charge of reconstruction in the Hamburg government. Veering toward the SPD at first, but from June 1946 toward the CDU, he remained involved in politics and left the recruitment of staff to his co-founders at *Die Zeit*. The first editor in chief, Ernst Samhaber, did not last for long after he incurred the wrath of the British authorities over undiplomatic remarks relating to their supply of foodstuffs.[32] Tüngel became his successor. In the meantime, Marion Dönhoff had rented a room in the Blumenfelds' home and had joined the editorial staff. By the fall, Ernst Friedlaender, who had returned from his British exile, had been recruited as an op-ed writer. Dönhoff's early contributions to *Die Zeit* have been discussed in chapter 2. The larger point to be made about the paper's editorial team is that none of them was a leftist. Rather the publishers were agreed that the contents would be "German" and national-liberal. Friedlaender, a lieutenant in World War I and before his escape from Nazism a director of the I. G. Farben chemicals trust, had always stood on the political Right.[33] His articles, inevitably perhaps, also took up the question of German guilt, but did so in a more circumspect way than did Tüngel, who became more and more critical of Allied policies and more conservative in his outlook. This made the paper vulnerable to interventions by the British censors. However, even when the criticisms became an irritant to the British, it was Michael Thomas, another German-Jewish refugee, now working in the British administration in Hamburg, who held a protective hand over *Die Zeit* and was prepared to vouch that it was on course politically.

The Acquisition of *Der Stern* and *Die Zeit*

Meanwhile, Gerd Bucerius continued his rise in the CDU. Having gained a seat in the new Bundestag in August 1949 following the first West German elections, he now pitched his tent in Bonn.[34] His divorce from Gretel had gone through in December 1945. Some fifteen months later he married his girlfriend Gertrud after her divorce from Heinrich Ebel had been finalized. Known as "Ebelin," she remained at his side through the many ups and downs of subsequent decades until his death in 1985. Keen to expand his publishing interests, he learned of what looked like a promising opportunity in the spring of 1949: Henri Nannen, whose wartime career has been discussed in the introduction, had, inter alia, begun to publish a youth magazine, *Zick-Zack*.[35] But there was more potential in a richly illustrated magazine, *Der Stern*, which he created and in which he held a 50 percent stake. The other half was owned by the Hannoversche Verlagsgesellschaft, which wanted to sell its shares. Nannen found an investor, Walter Heise, the owner of an electrical goods firm in Duisburg, who allowed him to use his warehouse as the editorial office.

The first issues of *Der Stern*, which appeared in August 1948, shortly after the currency reform, quickly sold over 130,000 copies, with the number rising quickly to 190,000.[36] Learning that Nannen was looking for a further expansion of his successful enterprise and was prepared to move to Hamburg, Schmidt di Simoni brought Bucerius on board, and the two struck a deal with Nannen. In May 1949 he and Bucerius, acting as trustees for *Die Zeit*, acquired 50 percent of Nannen's company and took over *Der Stern*'s lucrative distribution and advertising departments. Nannen moved to Hamburg, into a row of offices in the Pressehaus, next door to *Die Zeit*, and quickly expanded sales of *Der Stern* further. The next step was for Nannen to sell his shares, first to Bucerius and di Simoni. When the latter sold his part, Bucerius was happy to acquire more shares, so eventually he held 87.5 percent, with the remaining 12.5 percet taken up by Richard Gruner, the owner of a large printing firm. Nannen

soon bitterly regretted having sold his stake in the magazine and remained
firmly convinced that Bucerius and his partners had pulled a fast one on him.
As *Der Stern*'s editor in chief, he was now an employee at quite a high salary.
In this role he became a journalist with a genial vision and an enormous drive,
devoting himself totally to the contents and composition of "his" magazine.
Sales rapidly increased to 600,000 by 1952 and later went beyond the million
mark, making Bucerius and his partners wealthy men.[37]

On the other hand, whatever hopes the owners of *Die Zeit* held for its
future, the weekly failed to increase its circulation. By the summer of 1950
it had dropped further to a paltry 70,000 copies. It now proved helpful that
Bucerius had involved himself in high politics and had also become a member
in Hamburg's renowned *Überseeklub* and *Presseklub*.[38] This enabled him to
forge many useful connections. As the paper continued to struggle, Friedlaender, who held 10 percent of the shares, along with Lorenz, also wanted
to bail out. Having bought up their stakes, Bucerius, Schmidt di Simoni, and
Tüngel were left as the owners, but they had to inject fresh funds that the latter two were forced to borrow. Worse, while Bucerius was busy in Bonn politics, his partners simply could not increase the weekly's sales. By November
1950, Brinckmann, Wirtz & Co., the main lender in Hamburg, threatened to
withdraw its credit line. Bucerius scrambled to save the paper. His friend Max
Delev Ketels was prepared to give an advance on ad payments, and Otto A.
Friedrich of the Phoenix Rubber Co. in Hamburg-Harburg, floated a loan
of 10,000 marks. When these funds and others proved insufficient, Bucerius
turned to Robert Pferdmenges, a fellow CDU deputy, powerful Cologne
banker, and close confident of Adenauer. Erhard, whose policies *Die Zeit* had
supported at a critical time of his career as economics minister, was asked to
mediate. After some hesitation, Pferdmenges paved the way for a whopping
450,000-mark loan.[39]

The power Bucerius had accumulated as publisher enabled him to use it in
the first instance against Tüngel as editor in chief of *Die Zeit*, who had adopted
ever more conservative-nationalist editorial policies that undermined the reputation of the weekly. The crunch point was reached when Tüngel decided to
publish Carl Schmitt, the legal theorist who in the 1930s had openly justified
Hitler's "total state." When Marion Dönhoff objected to Schmitt as a contributor, upholding her vow not to allow publication of neo-Nazi ideas, and presented Tüngel with extracts from Schmitt's badly compromised writings, he
scoffed at them. A protagonist of the "Other Germany" of the 1944 resistance,
she resigned her position and went to Britain, where David Astor's *Observer*

took her on.[40] Dissatisfied with other editorial decisions and the right-wing tilt of the editor in chief, Bucerius used his majority in the company to dismiss Tüngel. The latter was outraged and, although he was a minority shareholder, began, with the support Schmidt di Simoni, to sue Bucerius. As is typical of such disputes, it became a long-drawn-out battle that lasted until 1957. After years of haggling, the two sides finally agreed to put their case to a mediating court. In the end, the judges decided that Tüngel and Schmidt di Simoni must sell their shares to Bucerius. In return, Bucerius was to fork out one million marks to each of his two former partners. With his earlier wealth augmented by his 87.5 percent share in *Der Stern*, Bucerius had become not only a wealthy but also a very influential media mogul. In 1959 the Nannen magazine fetched a profit of 1.6 million marks, which rose to 3.6 million by 1960.[41]

All the while, however, Bucerius remained nervous about the success of his papers, even though *Die Zeit*, now led by the former Luftwaffe war propagandist Joseph Müller-Marein as editor in chief and, after her return to Hamburg, by Dönhoff as the key political editor, had been increasing its circulation. Having become more liberal, the paper attracted new readers from among the educated middle classes. It seems to have been his constant business pessimism that now caused Bucerius to look toward Axel Springer with his booming press empire not as a competitor to be outdone but as a partner. To be sure, the two men had known each other since the early postwar years. Both were close to Blumenfeld, and all three had taken their wives on a vacation in the "Kleines Walsertal" to the southeast of Lake Constance in the summer of 1947.[42] It is against this background that Bucerius began to negotiate with Springer about some kind of cooperation and integration of their business interests. But Springer, conscious of his own remarkable success and observing in 1955 Bucerius's endless battle for control with Tüngel and Schmidt di Simoni, lost interest, making Bucerius an outspoken critic of Springer's supposed quest to gain a monopoly position in the newspaper market. He also became a member of a commission, chaired by Eberhard Günther, the head of the Federal Cartel Office, relating to "Press Concentration and its Consequences for Freedom of Opinion," in which he raised the question of "inner press freedom."[43] In February 1960 he had sent Springer a blunt letter accusing him of media imperialism. The latter was not amused, and the two men became fierce opponents.

Still looking for partners, Bucerius reached out to Rudolf Augstein, the third powerful publisher and editor in chief of the Hamburg political weekly *Der Spiegel*, in which John Jahr held a 50 percent stake. Augstein had apparently been toying with the idea of putting all three weeklies under one roof to form an alliance against Springer.[44] When Bucerius heard that Jahr wanted to sell his shares, it was agreed that Bucerius would take Jahr's 50 percent stake in *Der Spiegel*. But the deal collapsed because this time Bucerius came to be vexed by serious doubts. In the end, Augstein increased his share in the magazine to 75 percent, with 25 percent picked up by Gruner, the printer. Bucerius remained the majority owner of *Die Zeit* and *Der Stern*. This time it was Augstein who was left feeling very bitter, all the more so since another of his newspaper projects had also failed; I will tell this story in a moment when I move to the empire of *Der Spiegel* and its rise.

As far as Bucerius was concerned, there were two developments that take me to the end of the 1960s time frame adopted in this book. Faced with Springer's growing power, Bucerius, still worried about setbacks, continued to look for partners. With Augstein out of the picture, there were two other experienced Hamburgian businessmen whom Bucerius had known for many years and who had invested in his empire: Gruner and Jahr. No less important, their interests were neatly complementary. With Springer expanding further into printing and adding magazines to his newspapers, it made sense for Bucerius, Gruner, and Jahr to combine their partially overlapping interests into what on 1 July 1965 became the "Gruner und Jahr" corporation, which included *Der Spiegel*, the ladies' magazine *Constanze*, and *Brigitte*, which had been started for young women, among others. Bucerius's name was deliberately left off the management roster, but he held 28.25 percent of the shares, with Jahr owning 32.25 percent and Gruner 39.5 percent. Since Gruner had always been most focused on the commercial success of his enterprises and Jahr had similarly had little interest in shaping the outlook and mission of *Die Zeit* and *Der Stern*, Bucerius was free to devote himself to the editorial policies of these two publications, though he loved only *Die Zeit*, considering *Der Stern* as the milk cow whose editor in chief Nannen time and again irritated him greatly.[45]

All the while, Bucerius had held onto his seat in the Bonn parliament. But now, after more than ten years in the rough-and-tumble of CDU politics, he decided to resign. It was not just that he was tired of the commute and the many duties that being a deputy carried with it, not to mention the political campaigning and frequent lecture tours. More important, Adenauer and the leadership of his own party had increasingly turned the heat up on him when *Die Zeit* or *Der Stern* published articles that were critical of government or Christian Democrat policies. Throughout the 1950s, this pressure had not been as direct as it had been on the FAZ at the time of Sethe's ouster. Still, when it

came to relations with the East or issues related to the Nazi past, Marion Dönhoff and her colleagues repeatedly incurred the wrath of Adenauer, especially
after Tüngel's conservatism had been replaced by a stronger dose of liberalism
not merely in the paper's cultural and economic pages but also in its political
analyses and commentaries.

In January 1960, Bucerius got into deep waters when he resumed his early
postwar habit of writing an occasional piece in *Die Zeit*. In this case he took
aim at former Nazis in the Adenauer government, in particular at Theodor
Oberländer, the minister for expellees, who had occupied a prominent position in the Ostministerium, which had been involved in the ethnic cleansing
policies of the Hitler regime during World War II. Bucerius urged that this
deeply compromised minister be dismissed from the Federal cabinet.[46] This
demand caused such an outcry in the CDU that its leaders decided to initiate a disciplinary investigation against the publisher. Although the affair went
nowhere, it was a shot across the bow. Two years later, Bucerius faced an even
greater uproar, although this time he was not the author. Instead the Christian
Democrats turned up the heat on the magazine because of an anonymous
article in *Der Stern* titled "Is There Really a Fire in Hell?"[47] Having taken aim
at Catholic doctrine and a dispute between the Jesuits and Dominicans over
this question, which the author felt was undermining the aim of the impending
Vatican Council of creating greater Christian unity, it triggered loud protests.
In an editorial four weeks later, Nannen then poured oil onto the fire when he
linked Catholic positions on the journey of the faithful to another world to its
strict views on marriage and divorce.

The backlash first led Nannen and Bucerius to take responsibility for articles published in the magazine. Nannen added that, while he was unhappy
about the tone of the original article, whose author was now revealed as having
been staff writer Jürgen von Kornatzky, he continued to hope that the Catholic
and Protestant churches would establish a serious dialog among themselves. It
is possible that the scandal might have died down had it not been for a more
general and in fact earlier resentment that the Catholic Church and the CDU
had harbored against *Der Stern*. Over the years Nannen had developed a fine
sense for how to attract a growing readership. Much of what he published
continued to be light entertainment, richly illustrated by photo essays, interspersed with often scantily clad models in suggestive poses. In the eyes of
Church leaders and conservative stalwarts in the CDU the magazine thrived
on pornography, increasingly augmented by contributions that spread leftist
political messages. All this was anathema to the Christian Democrats.

The trouble was that in the view of Bucerius's party colleagues it was not enough for him to take responsibility for the contents of his magazine and to grumble about Nannen's use of risqué photos and provocative political articles.[48] *Der Stern* was by now a political and moral albatross, and Bucerius repeatedly admonished its editor in chief to be less sensationalist. But he also knew that Nannen was indispensable to the magazine's great commercial success. He could not simply get rid of him, even if Gruner and Jahr had supported such a step. In the end, Bucerius resigned from his CDU seat in the Bonn parliament in March 1962 and became a full-time publisher. True, the magazine did not carry with it the kudos of *Die Zeit* and its appeal to West Germany's educated elite readership. Yet, with its circulation reaching several million copies, it offered a steady and welcome flow of revenue. The country's market economy, which Bucerius vigorously defended, provided Bucerius and his family not only with bourgeois comfort, but also—as he put it years later—with freedom. However, he used this freedom as the owner differently from his rival Axel Springer, who, by the late 1950s, had developed firm ideas about the political orientation of his press empire. Accordingly, Springer had surrounded himself with a team of managers who watched over the continued commercial success of his conglomerate and made certain that those who ran the government and West Germany's sprawling bureaucracy would listen to his political agenda. Those who, like Zehrer, still the editor in chief of *Die Welt*, were growing old and resigned or did not support his activism, were—as we saw in chapter 3—marginalized or let go.

Bucerius and the Transformation of His Two Liberal Weeklies

Bucerius had a different perception of his powers as publisher and co-owner of his publications. He would write letters to his editors, call them, or talk to them in the corridors of the *Pressehaus*. He took a special interest in the intellectual development of *Die Zeit* and would join its editorial meetings and participate in the discussions of the contents and layout of the issue at hand. Being himself a rational man and a lawyer, he would reinforce the spirit of a sober exchange of views, at the end of which stood a consensus that preserved the peace and mutual respect among the staff—a spirit that was also axiomatic for the weekly's editor in chief, Müller-Marein, and the increasingly revered Dönhoff, "The Countess." His approach to Nannen and *Der Stern* was more circuitous.

Nannen was generally deemed to be a man who acted spontaneously on his gut feelings and was not easily swayed by rational argument. In light of this, Bucerius kept away from debates among the editors of the magazine. But it seems that Sethe began to move into the position of an elder statesman who dispensed wise counsel to Nannen.

As was mentioned in chapter 1, Sethe had been hired to write for *Der Stern* and *Die Zeit* after his divorce from Springer when the latter had begun to impose his views about the Soviets and the GDR on the editorial orientation of *Die Welt*. While Sethe composed a string of feature articles on historical themes for the *Der Stern* and, apart from looking after the book review section of *Die Zeit*, also commented on current politics during the 1960s up to his death in 1967, he also began a correspondence with Nannen. Unfortunately, only a few letters are to be found in his papers. They date from 1965 and 1966 and have to be seen in the context of a decision that the magazine's editor in chief had been pondering for some time. What had made *Der Stern* such a widely read publication in the 1950s was its peculiar mix of articles supplemented by often sensational and erotic photographs that were part of reports in simple prose on the "tragic" lives of celebrities, political scandals, changing lifestyles, and other things that—as Nannen put it—would be of interest to "Lieschen Müller," that is, to the ordinary, mainly female, reader.[49] Accordingly, the magazine carried many photo features, for example, on Empress Soraya of Persia and other royalty. There were endless stories about Rosemarie Nitribit, a high-class prostitute, and her prominent clients. But the magazine also had increasingly acerbic political content. When Heinrich Lübke was elected Federal president, photos emerged that showed blueprints of makeshift housing in concentration camps in which he, a civil engineer by profession, was said to have been involved. By the early 1960s, government ministers and also Chancellor Adenauer had become the targets of more and more openly political attacks.

However, it would be wrong to assume that Nannen was a negative critic of those in power. He was among the first editors in chief of major periodicals who began to exhort the West Germans to abandon the illusion that the country would ever be reunified within its 1937 borders.[50] Instead he wanted to pave the way for a reconciliation with West Germany's eastern neighbors and with Poland in particular.

He was therefore also an early supporter of Brandt's *Ostpolitik*. Enjoying good contacts with the FDP, he was, from the mid-1960s, also a promoter of a coalition between the Liberals and the Social Democrats that finally came about in 1969. This advocacy for a pragmatic realism notwithstanding, in the early 1960s it was still a matter of finding the right balance between making *Der Stern* a magazine of entertainment and some general educational content supported by rich illustrations, on the one hand, and one with features that were designed to shape political opinion and high politics, on the other. In the mid-1960s Nannen was still struggling with this balance and received advice from various sides on how to proceed. He wanted to be more explicitly political but was still experimenting with how to do this.

It is at this point that Sethe came in as the wise man. In his letter of 9 February 1965 he made a number of points that reveal his thoughts and attitudes towards *Der Stern*.[51] He spoke of his efforts "to participate in the editorial work" of the magazine. In this endeavor, he continued, "I encounter time and again an obstacle that originates in a fundamental difference of opinion about the methods of the political work in an illustrated publication." He added that he would like to talk about this problem with Nannen either in person or at an editorial meeting. All he was trying to do in his letter was to map out a basis for such a discussion. Sethe went on to mention that he had received a number of "interesting letters"—approving as well as critical—in response to the recent "political essays" in *Der Stern*. He then launched into a critique of Nannen's recent innovation of asking politicians to contribute essays on topics of their choice. While agreeing with Nannen's statement that newspapers should be made by journalists and not by politicians, he objected specifically to contributions by Willy Brandt and Franz-Josef Strauss, not because he disliked them but because "their columns are a constant insult to my collective professional pride."

In Sethe's view, *Der Stern's* editors had too much respect for professional politicians and too little esteem for the achievements of their own profession. He had only one explanation for this: that they were suffering from a "collective inferiority complex." It was his carefully considered, though no doubt undiplomatic, view that *Der Stern's* editors merely thought in terms of *Knüller*, namely, stirring headlines and stories that had no more than a momentary impact. These articles would be cited by other papers or in parliament, and that was it. This policy prevented the editors from seeing what could be achieved if the magazine were to set itself the task of reporting over a period of many years, unerringly and uninterruptedly, on really important issues and doing so clearly, comprehensively, and on the basis of its own information-gathering. Where there were corrupt practices to be uncovered in German politics, the editors should rely on careful research, as *Der Spiegel* had encouraged its journalists to do "during its great days" of investigative journalism.

Sethe wanted Nannen to turn toward this type of work, and it may be that he had the *New York Times* in mind as his model of serious journalism. He went on to criticize the handling of interviews in which the interviewers, in Sethe's view, showed "an exaggerated respect" for their subject. It rarely happened, he wrote, that an interview contained anything new or that the interviewer merely made himself the mouthpiece of the politician who had been given a set of questions. In his view, *Der Spiegel* had developed the appropriate model, in which interviewee and interviewers faced each other at the same level and the latter had been preparing themselves very thoroughly in previous weeks. Overall, Sethe believed that a good op-ed piece was more effective than an interview, as a recent article by Nannen on housing policy had demonstrated. Sethe finally favored a well-written report on a press conference by Charles de Gaulle, for example, over an interview with the general. Again Sethe was concerned with the long-term impact of the magazine, which required thorough preparation and persistent reporting. A regular reader of *Der Stern* should within three years have gained a sense that "he knows about de Gaulle all that is worth knowing." This, he believed, was preferable to an "interview that was cited everywhere." Giving another example, Sethe admitted that he had "gained completely new insights" from the magazine's erstwhile "political features on China and Persia." These had been *"much more* valuable" than the interviews with Nikita Khrushchev or Hans Kroll, West Germany's ambassador to Moscow.

Three months later, Sethe wrote another letter to Nannen in which he very much approved of the politicization of illustrated magazines.[52] But he also warned that "a magazine is not an avantgarde paper"; nor does it "have to heed the opinions of the majority." And yet "our tone must be more subdued." He added that whenever "we advance our opinion, we must find a tone that does not offend those who think differently." More worryingly, Sethe had the "uncomfortable feeling" that some editors wanted to use *Der Stern* "in order to open a valve for their party-political fanaticism." He was therefore very glad that Nannen had opposed the idea of transforming the magazine into a "paper of political struggle (*politisches Kampfblatt*)" at the previous day's editorial meeting. Referring to some recent cartoons, Sethe warned that many loyal supporters of the CDU would have been offended by them. Of course, he knew that journalists had "occasionally to step on people's toes." But to do so week after week during an election campaign was not a goal for which it was "worth upsetting thousands of readers." Finally, and in light of continued popular support for the Hallstein Doctrine promulgated to withdraw Bonn's embassies from countries that decided to recognize East Germany,[53] Sethe thought it unwise to agitate too noisily for this policy's abolition. To be sure, he did not want "us to give up our attempts to make visible the outdatedness of this Doctrine"; but its protagonists, who continued to insist on a withdrawal of diplomatic recognition from any foreign country that violated the Doctrine, should not be portrayed as simpletons. What motivated Sethe was the impression that it was dangerous for the magazine's editors to ridicule those who had divergent opinions.

There are a few more letters in which Sethe gave Nannen his views on a variety of specific political issues.[54] But I hope that the role of this veteran journalist as a member of Der Stern's editorial team has been shown sufficiently clearly from the two letters quoted here. That Nannen took his advice seriously emerges from a reply of December 1966 on the occasion of Sethe's birthday.[55] In it he confessed that he had always felt "great inhibitions" during their first conversations, when "a journalistic nouveau riche" had been sitting across from "the doyen of the corps of journalists." Although he had still not quite overcome these inhibitions, on this, Sethe's birthday, apart from sending him his best wishes, Nannen wanted to offer gratitude to Sethe "most cordially" that "you are here and belong to us"—if he were allowed to put it that way. He therefore wished that "you may stay with us for a very long time with your knowledge, your prudence, and your self-doubts, and doubts about us and about everything that is in flux." If this letter is linked to the welcome that Bucerius had extended to Sethe as the publisher of Die Zeit and Der Stern,[56] it is understandable why Sethe felt he had finally found a professional environment in which he could write what he wanted and was able to give strategic advice that was genuinely appreciated.

Rudolf Augstein's Rise and the Role of Der Spiegel in West German Politics

This is also true of the relationship that Sethe developed with the Hamburgian publisher and journalist Rudolf Augstein. To be sure, Sethe never joined the Spiegel empire, but the two men met as neighbors, as they had their homes in the northeastern suburb of Wellingsbüttel, and, time permitting, took walks along the Alster River. Beyond noting this colleagiality, I have included Augstein in this chapter as the third major publisher next to Springer and Bucerius, or as the fifth if Gruner and Jahr are added. As in the cases of Bucerius and

Springer, there was also plenty of personal and professional drama in Augstein's life, including no fewer than four marriages. One further preliminary point has to be made. When describing the personal experiences of Springer and other Hamburgian publishers it became clear how much their lives had become intertwined even before 1945. After the war, life had become even more chaotic, and more than once it was sheer coincidence that they should run into each other, talk to each other, and begin to think of cooperating and combining their business interests or of being competitors. So, while the larger structural conditions—whether under Nazism, the British occupation, or during the boom years of the Federal Republic—must always be borne in mind, there still is plenty of contingency that marked their careers.

Rudolf Augstein was born in Hanover on 5 November 1923 and, unlike Dönhoff, Sethe, and Zehrer, did not experience the collapse of the Weimar Republic and the rise of Nazism as an adult.[57] But his parents—Friedrich, the owner of a small camera factory, and Gertrude Maria, who, having given birth to seven children, was busy raising them—were Catholics. This meant that they were wary of Hitler and his movement. In the late 1920s, Friedrich sold his business at a handsome profit, and this enabled the family to live in some comfort. During the Depression he took up positions as a commercial agent and, in 1938, opened a shop named Photo Augstein. Concerned, like many middle-class parents, to give Rudolf a good education, his parents put him in the strictly Catholic Empress Auguste Viktoria-Gymnasium. This required Rudolf to commute across town to the working-class district of Hanover-Linden, where the environment was even more anti-Nazi. In 1939 this school was merged with the local Realgymnasium, whose pupils were both Catholic and Protestant. Rudolf graduated in 1941 with his *Abitur* certificate in his pocket. In the meantime he had served as an altar boy but had also joined the Hitler Youth (HJ). However, his HJ group was not given a more typical paramilitary training but maintained a puppet theater instead. Rudolf's choices were perhaps typical of the ambiguities that shaped the lives of young people who did not grow up in openly Nazi families.

With school behind him, where had shown some literary talent, Rudolf became interested in journalism and took up an internship at the *Hannoverscher Anzeiger* under Dr. Friedrich Rasche, the editor of the paper's cultural section. Since Rasche was no friend of the Nazis, the internship seems to have reinforced Augstein's reservations about Hitler. And yet the ambiguities continued. In 1941 he recorded in his diary that National Socialism was "an assassination of the spirit." But this remark, which could have landed him in prison, did not prevent him from publishing short pieces not only in Rasche's *Hannoverscher Anzeiger* but also in Goebbels's intellectual journal *Das Reich*. As Germany mobilized for total war in 1942, Augstein was first drafted into the Reich Labor Service and posted to Chelmno (Kulm) on the Vistula north of Torun, apparently to build military installations. After the war he claimed never to have heard about the extermination of Europe's Jews nor of the expulsion of Polish farmers from the region, but his denial may be a case of cognitive dissonance: he did not see what he did not want to see. His next posting was with the Luftgaukommando XI outside Hamburg, but since he was deemed unfit to become a Luftwaffe pilot he was assigned to an artillery unit in Hanover for training. Next he found himself serving with an artillery regiment southeast of Orel near Voronesh on the Don River.

Rudolf was seriously wounded in the arm by shrapnel, and after showing some leadership initiative in his unit, received both the Iron Cross and a decoration for his injuries in silver. Recovering in Zakopane, in the south of Poland, he visited Lemberg/Lvov further east, again allegedly without learning anything about the notorious local ghetto. Never keen to embark on a career as an officer and increasingly pessimistic about a German victory, it was only in March 1945 that he was promoted to lieutenant of the reserve. His experiences in the Third Reich made him a member of the "Generation of '45," as discussed in the introduction. When he was growing up as a teenager under the pressure-cooker ideological atmosphere of those years, his upbringing prevented him from becoming a confirmed National Socialist. But he imbibed the nationalism of the Third Reich inside and outside the Wehrmacht, which stayed with him throughout his life. Disillusioned with the wartime stance of the Vatican, he had also left the Catholic Church and become an atheist. With the Wehrmacht disintegrating, he made his way westward without proper papers. At one point he was picked up by the military police, who were roaming the rear areas to catch "deserters" and executed them without trial, but he was let go. After this lucky escape, he ended up in Hanover and refound his erstwhile mentor Dr. Rasche, who, having convinced the British that he had never been a Nazi, was asked to put together the editorial staff of the *Hannoversches Nachrichtenblatt*, the local paper of the British military government. He was happy to re-employ Augstein after the British cleared him, with Rasche vouching for his anti-Nazi past.

More good luck was on its way. Augstein met John Seymour Chaloner, a British occupation officer who was charged with screening applicants for jobs as journalists.[58] He took a liking to Augstein as he sat in front of him in his tattered Wehrmacht overcoat. Chaloner had two colleagues, Henry Ormond (originally Hans-Ludwig Oettinger), a Weimar judge whom the Nazis had dismissed and who, after a spell in the Dachau concentration camp, had escaped to Britain, and Harry Bohrer, a Czech journalist who had also found refuge in the United Kingdom in 1939. Having fought in the war and now assigned to the building of the zonal press, the three men were keen to establish a weekly that was modeled on Henry Luce's *Time* magazine and offered Augstein a job at their brainchild named, rather unassumingly, *Diese Woche*. Since only Bohrer had journalistic experience, he, for all practical purposes, became its editor in chief and prepared the first issue with Augstein as the editor in charge of German and Allied politics. Hans Toll took over the cultural section. Roman Stempka, who had been a photographer with the Scherl newspaper trust and later with a Wehrmacht propaganda company, was responsible for visual material. The magazine hit the newsstands on 16 November 1946 and immediately published articles critical of British policies. By the fifth issue, this criticism had become so blatant that it caught the attention of the Foreign Office and other British watchdogs. After some bickering and confusion, the order reached Chaloner that *Diese Woche* was to cease publication. However, for some obscure reason, after further negotiations he was given permission to transfer the ownership of the weekly from himself, Bohrer, and Ormond to the Germans on their staff, one of them being Augstein. The trouble was that they now needed a British license, for which the charge was 30,000 marks. Again the three British founders came to the rescue and provided the funds, although it remained unclear where they got the money. Knowing that the first issues of *Diese Woche* had been sold out in no time, Augstein and his associates were optimistic that they had hit a goldmine. Still, the title was rather unattractive, so Augstein renamed the magazine *Der Spiegel*. It quickly became one of the most influential publications of the Federal Republic. By 1948 it sold 65,000 copies per week, increasing to 85,000 in 1949 and to more than 100,000 by 1950.

However, this is not the place to discuss the contents of the new magazine and how Augstein shaped it over the next two decades up to the end of the 1960s. This aspect has been covered extensively in several biographies.[59] Suffice it to mention here that Augstein continued to criticize Allied policies, but this time there was yet another German-Jewish refugee who protected the young firebrand from irate politicians and civil servants in London: Michael Thomas (originally Ulrich Hollaender), the British press officer in Hanover.[60] On the domestic front and much like Dönhoff, Augstein fought for a reconstruction of West Germany in the 1950s that would make a clear break with the Nazi past politically and intellectually. Thus he vigorously argued for the dismissal of refugee minister Theodor Oberländer from Adenauer's Cabinet and advocated for Hans Globke, the secretary of state in the chancellery, who had helped draft the 1935 anti-Semitic Nuremberg Laws, to be sent into early retirement. But there were also contradictions in his writings. While extolling Stauffenberg's 1944 coup as a moral deed, he condemned General Friedrich Paulus and Heinrich Count Einsiedel, who had surrendered to the Red Army at Stalingrad and subsequently worked for the defeat of Hitler on the Soviet side.[61] He took a more lenient attitude toward former Nazis and even higher SS officers, and there were other inconsistencies in Augstein's journalism during the 1950s.[62] However, by 1960 his polemics targeted ever more sharply both Adenauer and Franz-Josef Strauss, his defense minister.

Analyzing Augstein's trajectory not as the editor but as the publisher and co-owner of *Der Spiegel*, we find that there are further parallels with Bucerius and his colleagues. By the early 1950s, irreconcilable differences had arisen between Augstein and his partner Toll.[63] As Augstein put it in the wake of their serious dispute, it was only one person who could give the magazine direction. As a result, Toll was bought out by Augstein, Stempka, and Gerhard Barsch, who had been taken on to look after the commercial side of *Der Spiegel*. The next challenge to the remaining three owners arose when Chaloner, Bohrer, and Ormond, eyeing the success of *Der Spiegel*, claimed that there had been an unwritten "gentlemen's agreement" with them at the time of the transfer of *Diese Woche* to Augstein that each of them would be given 10 percent of the shares.[64] However, since there was no written and signed record of this agreement, Augstein, Stempka, and Barsch refused to redistribute the shares. An illuminating and detailed correspondence about this affair has been reprinted in Brawand's book.[65] With the Germans refusing a deal, the Britons received a token payment in the end. Although Augstein stayed in touch with Chaloner, whose birthday coincided with his own and who nursed nostalgic memories of the difficult beginnings in bombed-out Hanover, the Britons never quite forgave Augstein for his categorical refusal.

It is possible to view this refusal as typical of a hardheaded businessman who was not keen to share the commercial success of the magazine with others. But it seems that Augstein was also aware of the importance of his role as publisher and owner in terms of his constitutional right to shape the ideological and political orientation of his magazine. Just as Springer and Bucerius appreciated the advantages of firm control over the editorial staff, Augstein was no less anxious to secure it. Unlike the three Britons, Stempka and Barsch were the actual shareholders. After helping Augstein fend off the British challenge, they, too, like Toll, were soon bought out. Barsch received 100,000 marks; Stempka got a golden handshake, 150,000 marks. Although Augstein was confident that his strategy would pay off, he, now the sole owner and keen to expand, needed an investor who was prepared to take a larger chunk of the shares but would not meddle in editorial policy. Augstein already knew the ideal partner after he had moved the magazine's offices from provincial Hanover to the rising North German media metropolis of Hamburg: John Jahr.[66] This liberal Hamburgian with a not altogether clean anti-Nazi vest had meanwhile been given a license and had turned *Constanze* into a magazine with a steadily rising circulation. He was not connected to the CDU or the SPD. Instead he tended toward the Free Democratic Party (FDP), the party in which Augstein developed such a strong interest himself that the party put him up for election, and he eventually became a deputy in the Federal parliament. Rather erratically he resigned after only two months to concentrate on the weekly publication of his ever more influential magazine. After this he was perfectly happy for Jahr to take half of the shares against an injection of funds. Augstein now had the journalistic room for maneuver as publisher, while Jahr, as a sleeping partner, was happy with the magazine's continued commercial success.

Augstein certainly used this space in ways that allowed him to practice a much more forceful journalism than his main Hamburgian competitors. Springer, as we have seen, issued no more than broad guidelines to his newspaper editors, especially after his decision in 1958 to steer *Die Welt* and also *Bild-Zeitung* toward a more anti-Communist and anti-GDR crusade. But he left it to the editors in chief and also to newly appointed managers, such as Ernst Cramer, to implement his political vision. He did not participate in the composition and fine-tuning that had to be done day after day. Nor did Bucerius involve himself in the daily chores of editing and last-minute decision-making about contents or headlines. Instead, as we have seen, he attended the editorial meetings of *Die Zeit* when he was in town and also published the occasional article or short commentary.

Augstein, by contrast, took a very proactive role in the composition of every single issue of *Der Spiegel*. He regularly contributed op-ed articles under two pseudonyms: Jens Daniel and Moritz Pfeil. These articles usually contained acid criticisms of politicians and the foreign or domestic policy positions they had taken up, or he commented on various corruption scandals. Except during vacation time or when he was on lecture tours, Augstein missed few editorial meetings at which past, current, and future issues were being discussed. Having written poetry before 1945, he retained a keen interest in fiction and the importance of well-crafted and stylish German. In the early years he read draft articles by his editors and corrected them. When this became too onerous, he joined in the weekly debates with his editors on topics and layout. It did not take long for them to develop a specific *Spiegel* lingo. Once established in Hamburg, the magazine represented serious journalism, though often in rather frivolous and sarcastic prose. It became, as *Le Monde* once put it, the "*enfant terrible de la presse d'outre-Rhin*," to which Augstein, in a speech before the Rhein-Ruhr-Klub of entrepreneurs, once added the observation that "many foul eggs in Germany are not being hatched because there are papers like *Der Spiegel*."[67] Even if they disagreed over the contents of an article, readers often could not but chuckle at the irreverent prose that critiqued a particular issue so brilliantly. In short, Augstein saw himself as part of a team involved in a common enterprise of critical and investigative journalism. Looking back on this teamwork, Augstein once remarked that it would not have been possible for him to run the magazine for forty-six years in autocratic fashion.[68]

By the late 1950s, criticism of Adenauer and his government had become the *basso continuo* of *Der Spiegel*. With the chancellor's socialization going back as far as the Bismarckian period, the problem was viewed by Augstein as a generational one. After all, this was the moment in West Germany's early history when fathers and grandfathers were being reproached for the mistakes that they were said to have made in the final years of the Weimar Republic and at the beginning of the Nazi regime. In this respect Adenauer, who had been born in January 1876 and had been mayor of Cologne during the 1920s, provided a perfect target, and since he had taken the reins of power as chancellor of the Federal Republic in 1949, by the late 1950s, if not before, Augstein thought that the retirement of "*Der Alte*" was overdue. He also opposed the chancellor's exclusive policy of *Westbindung* and urged Bonn to look east toward reconciliation with West Germany's neighbors. Consequently, he rejected the country's integration into the Schuman Plan and later into NATO.[69] When the question came up of how best to counter a Soviet military invasion, he had initially sympathized with Bogislaw von Bonin and his proposals to try to stop the Red Army with conventional tank warfare and the help of armored blocking units along the border.[70]

With NATO members consistently failing to provide the necessary manpower and hardware, Washington began to introduce tactical nuclear weapons into the defensive arsenal of the Western Alliance. Although the Carte Blanche maneuver of 1955 in northern Germany, whose simulated deployment of tactical nuclear weapons had produced unacceptably high civilian casualties, had put a serious question mark behind the viability of this strategy, Strauss, whom Adenauer had made minister of defense in 1956, continued to advocate the stationing of these weapons on West German soil. Some critics, including Augstein, even suspected that Strauss wanted to equip the Bundeswehr with them. As we have seen in chapter 3, this led to protests from West German scientists and students as early as 1957–58. Adenauer remained unmoved, driving Augstein to ever more bitter attacks written in "helpless rage."[71] Perhaps it was due not only to his plan to compete with Springer but also to his wish to increase his capacity to criticize the Federal government that he thought of founding a daily, the *Deutsche Allgemeine Zeitung*, for which he tried to recruit Sethe as editor in chief.[72] When this venture turned out to be too expensive and risky, Sethe was offered a consolation prize of writing for *Der Spiegel*. He did not take the bait and joined the Bucerius publishing house instead, working for *Die Zeit* and *Der Stern*.[73]

The *Spiegel* Affair and Its Consequences

As the debate unfolded, Augstein became convinced that Strauss was no less dangerous than Adenauer and should be made to resign his post. Realizing that this would not be easy on purely political grounds, *Der Spiegel* began to investigate Strauss's the crony system in Bavaria that he had built up as chairman of the Christian Social Union (CSU). Accordingly, the magazine's journalists and researchers were sent south to look into the "Amigo System," through which Strauss distributed favors to friends and family. There was also the *Finanzbau Aktiengesellschaft*, on whose behalf Strauss had written to the Pentagon in connection with the construction of American garrisons in Germany. One of its shareholders was Hans Kapfinger, a family friend and publisher of the *Passauer Neue Presse*.[74] On another occasion, Jochen Becher, the magazine's correspondent in Munich, was sent to Switzerland to scout out Strauss's suspected real estate interests in Ascona. Much was also made of Strauss's gruff treatment of a Bonn traffic policeman who had issued Strauss's driver a ticket for ignoring his hand signals at a busy intersection. In short, to Augstein the defense minister was not just a bully but embodied the authoritarian decision-making of Adenauer's government that *Der Spiegel* kept attacking on several fronts. The aim may also have been to prevent the Bavarian politician from becoming Adenauer's successor, about which plan rumor was rife in the early 1960s.

Not surprisingly, Strauss, increasingly irritated by the attacks on him, thought
of hitting back with the aim of silencing Augstein once and for all. The opportunity for this came in October 1962, when *Der Spiegel* published an article
on the recent "Fallex 62" military exercise.[75] It revealed that NATO was insuf-
ficiently prepared to respond to a Soviet offensive across the East German border. Apparently tactical nuclear weapons had been deployed with horrendous
(simulated) losses. Apart from other flaws, the provision of medical services
for the many "victims" had also been judged to have been totally inadequate.
Fallex 62 had been reported by other papers in rather general terms. However,
Der Spiegel had published details that caused the federal prosecutor's office to
suspect that the magazine had had access to secret information and, by publishing it, had committed treason. Having asked the Defense Ministry for an expert
evaluation, the prosecutor's office concluded that there was sufficient evidence
to open a formal investigation. Learning of this, Strauss informed Adenauer,
who in turn encouraged the defense minister to do whatever he "considered
possible, necessary, and responsible" to pursue the case. Two days after the
publication of the article, he told the chancellor that its contents amounted to
a manifestation of "journalistic terror" against which "energetic measures" must
be taken.[76] On 26 October the prosecutor's office sent a detachment of riot
police and eight detectives to the magazine's editorial offices. They arrested several senior editors and loaded some 17,000 files, 6,000 books, 500,000 photos,
and 10,000 meters of microfilm onto trucks for scrutiny. The doors of the offices
were sealed, so all preparations for the next issue ground to a halt. Augstein,
who had not been in the building, turned himself in after hearing about the
raid. It was then that it was found that Conrad Ahlers, the editor responsible for
the research and composition, was in Spain on vacation. At this point, Strauss
took the matter out of the hands of the prosecutors by illegally calling Hans
Oster, the military attaché in the West German embassy in Madrid, to tell him
to contact the Spanish police and to have Ahlers put in a local prison.

There was an immediate public outcry against the raid and arrests, to which
Adenauer first responded offensively. Encountering reactions of unease even
within his own party, he insisted that there had been an "act of treason."[77] To
him it was "practically certain" that it had been committed "by a man with
power, journalistic power in his hands," adding that this power had put great
responsibility on Augstein's shoulders and that he had betrayed it. Speaking
in the Federal parliament, the chancellor added that the publisher was earning
money from an act of treason. It did not take long before details were being
leaked about the whole operation, causing even Adenauer's own supporters to

throw their arms up in despair. When Strauss had to confess that his telephone calls to Spain had been illegal, people staged protests and asked for his head.[78] The FDP coalition partners were also outraged. Still, the bluntest verdicts appeared in the press, whose freedom was said to be fundamentally threatened by an authoritarian state that had resorted to blunt force and intimidation.

Marion Dönhoff wrote a sharp protest in *Die Zeit*, wondering if those lawyers who had certified the legality of the arrests were in their right minds.[79] Sebastian Haffner, though no friend of Augstein's provocative journalism and invoking his training as a journalist in Britain, argued that if the German public remained silent in the face of such government excesses, he would say good-bye to press freedom, constitutionalism, and democracy in the Federal Republic.[80] The FAZ was reminded of the Third Reich and thought that the government had lost sight of the fact that there were still differences between Germany and the Balkans.[81] It did not take long for commentators to feel confirmed in their anger when the federal prosecutor's office sat on the evidence they had confiscated and did not come forward with any tangible proof from the files that a crime had been committed. By law their accusations had to be duly presented to a court.

Soon the general public became mobilized. Panel discussions were organized about the freedom of the press. Rallies and sit-ins took place in over a hundred cities. Academics and intellectuals signed petitions demanding the release of Augstein and his colleagues and a full special investigation into the entire affair. As the *Spiegel* Affair unfolded, the prosecutors, finding no evidence of criminal behavior by the arrested editors, released them one by one, while others were held without bail. Ahlers was sent home after 51 days, Hans Schmelz after 81 days. The publisher, who had been transferred from Hamburg to a prison in Koblenz, ultimately spent 104 days behind bars. When the judges of the *Bundesgerichtshof* appointed to review the evidence finally prepared their verdict, they found that, while the relevant laws had objectively been violated, the supporting material was insufficient to open trial proceedings. In other words, they did not acquit Augstein and his colleagues; the case was merely shelved, but ultimately the whole affair ended in a humiliating defeat for its instigators and a strange victory for Augstein and *Der Spiegel*. After all, even if the public discussion had highlighted the arrests as a violation of the freedom of the press in general, there was another issue at stake that had been overshadowed by the mass protests.

If these demonstrations had been against the suppression of the freedom of opinion as a constitutional basic right, it was also significant that Augstein, the owner of the magazine, had his freedom of expression violated as the publisher. Worse, he had been incarcerated and the police action had threatened the survival of his enterprise. If more than one issue of the magazine could not appear, the company's losses would mount so quickly that he would face bankruptcy. By 1962, *Der Spiegel* had reached a circulation of some 440,000 copies. This threat was immediately obvious to Augstein, who rightly feared that his life's work was being destroyed in one stroke, the more so since the capital base of the magazine had always been thin and full-page ads were an essential part of its weekly income. Accordingly, the publisher's first reaction was to claim to have been ignorant of the article in question. It then quickly dawned on him that he could not leave his colleagues in the lurch. He decided to stand with them and to direct the management of the crisis. Suspecting that the ulterior purpose of Adenauer's and Strauss's charges had been to silence him politically and to ruin him financially, he gave instructions from his prison cell as to who among the editorial staff would be in charge of what sections of the next issues.

Bucerius and his editors at *Die Zeit* also realized this danger and, together with their colleagues from the *Hamburger Echo*, made their offices, telephones, and other resources available. Christian Kracht, Springer's right-hand man, also offered to help but was whistled back by Axel Springer after *Bild-Zeitung* had adopted the official interpretation of the event.[82] Since Bucerius's papers' offices were in the same building, practical support was quickly arranged, and *Der Spiegel* reappeared after a short hiatus. Its circulation increased considerably over the next few years, and the financial threat evaporated. Like Springer, Bucerius, Gruner, and Jahr, Augstein became a wealthy man.

Augstein, nevertheless, emerged from the crisis deeply traumatized and scarred. There is a photo of him waving from a prison window after his application for release had again been denied in early January 1963. It shows his face in visible distress.[83] Subsequently, *Der Spiegel* and its publisher toned down their aggressive journalism. Adenauer resigned his chancellorship in 1963. Strauss was also forced to leave his ministry and retreated to Bavaria until 1966–67, when he became minister of finance in the CDU/CSU-SPD coalition government that began to reach out to the Soviet Bloc. In this respect Augstein could feel some satisfaction that he had won. Détente between East and West was moving forward, and the danger of a nuclear confrontation with the Soviets had subsided. The path had been cleared for the pursuit of Willy Brandt's policy of "change through rapprochement."[84]

For many contemporaries, a major caesura in the development of the Federal Republic had been reached. The remnants of the authoritarianism of the first half of the twentieth century that had survived in the ministerial bureaucracy and the police and that Adenauer, himself no liberal democrat, had perpetuated and fostered in his government had been pushed back. This was the conclusion of Theo Sommer, the up-and-coming political editor of *Die Zeit*. Looking back on the whole affair, he wrote, "What we experienced in the Pressehaus at the time was the epilog to the German *Obrigkeitsstaat* and the overture to a modern and free German democracy that was thoroughly aired of its *Untertanengeist*."[85] The rules governing the freedom of the press that privileged the owners remained unchanged. But that encouraged Augstein to continue to promote editorial teamwork, and later he even developed a system that gave his employees a share in the ownership of the company. Above all, the younger generation that was now coming along had a different understanding of the freedom of opinion and of tolerance that would survive the storms of the unruly 1970s. If the ouster of Sethe from the FAZ in 1955 had been the first incident to unleash a debate on press freedom, the *Spiegel* Affair represented an even more important turning point that undermined the autocratic traditions of the Adenauer government and fostered firm adherence to the principles enshrined in the Basic Law.

As far as the early postwar decades are concerned, the points made in this chapter about Hamburg's rise as a media center have, I hope, been given sufficient empirical backup. It was not just Sethe, Dönhoff, and Zehrer who wrestled with a Nazi past that had finally ended in 1945 and with what kind of foundations should be laid for West German reconstruction. For Augstein, Bucerius, Springer, and Nannen there were the lessons of the Hitler dictatorship as well as the challenging issues of the country's future domestic politics and its role in Europe. These journalists and publishers also pondered solutions to Germany's postwar division and its relationship with the West as well as with the Soviet Bloc. This is why Hamburg presents such an intriguing story not just in terms of the biographies of three eminent journalists but also as the site where the media wrestled with both the Nazi past and German society's future.

CONCLUSION

Freedom of Expression in the Twentieth and Early Twenty-First Centuries

THE FREEDOM OF expression in the media has preoccupied historians and social scientists for decades, if not centuries. Time and again, this freedom has been called into question or has been undermined by governments and their censors, who have tried to limit or even destroy it. And time and again writers and journalists have given their utmost to insist on the basic right to freely articulate their opinions. They have even put their lives on the line to uphold and restore this basic right wherever and whenever it has been suppressed by autocratic and dictatorial governments, often appearing in democratic guise. Throughout the ages, there has also been the problem of the owners of media empires imposing their views on the writers, journalists, and editors in their employ. Not conforming to the editorial guidelines set by owners has perhaps not been as dangerous as trying to undermine or circumvent government censorship and sanctions, but such opposition could certainly result in dismissal and a journalist's need to find another job with a publisher more tolerant or approving of his or her views.

Germany presents a particularly illuminating object lesson with respect to press freedom and censorship, although no attempt has been made here to trace it back all the way to the early modern period, to the history of eighteenth-century Central European absolutism, or to the government practices adopted in the Bismarckian and Wilhelmine periods except to point out that, while there was no catalog of basic rights enshrined in the German Constitution of 1871 that guaranteed civil liberties, including the freedom of expression, there were times, especially in the 1890s and after the turn of the century, when censorship was handled quite flexibly. Accordingly, it was not so much the censors who brought writers, journalists, and artists to heel. There was a good deal of tolerance, especially in the non-Prussian federal states, which enabled a modern and experimental culture to flourish. However, there was censorship by the owners of print media and also the churches, with the latter being particularly vigilant when it came to questions of religious faith and morality.

The collapse of the Hohenzollern monarchy in 1918 and the ratification of the Weimar Constitution brought fundamental changes in this respect. Next to the promulgation of other basic rights, there was Article 118, whose liberal terms were highlighted in the introduction. If this article provided individual tangible protections against state censorship and also against discrimination in the workplace, this did not mean that the owners had no leverage against their journalists. The basic issue, therefore, was that the freedom to express opinions "freely within the limits of general laws" was limited by the possibility that a journalist would be dismissed and have to find another job if differences of views on editorial policy and content could not be resolved. All this changed again very dramatically when Hitler seized power in Germany, destroyed the Weimar Constitution and its basic liberties, and established a one-party dictatorship in which the free expression of opinions was ultimately even punishable by death.

However, this book has been more than an examination of German journalism under the Nazis. At its core has been an analysis of the professional and personal lives of three influential journalists who belonged to what I have defined as the "Generation of '32." They had been born before 1914, experienced the Weimar Republic as adults, and opposed the Nazi movement in the early 1930s. Yet, when Hitler was appointed Reich chancellor in January 1933, Paul Sethe, Marion Dönhoff, and Hans Zehrer were confronted with the four choices that millions of Germans faced at this time: emigration, underground resistance, joining the Nazi Party and becoming more or less enthusiastic supporters of the "Führer," or withdrawing into "inner emigration." All three chose the last option and between 1933 and 1945 tried to survive materially and intellectually in extremely difficult circumstances. They knew that they lived under the vigilant eye of an increasingly unfree regime that was so ruthless that even their physical survival was at stake. With the Gestapo becoming ever more ubiquitous and repressive, they could be denounced, arrested, and imprisoned at any time and might even be killed.

It seems that Sethe, Dönhoff, and Zehrer believed at first that the Nazi regime could not possibly last for a long time, but when it did and moved toward unleashing a war of aggression and conquest, it became more and more difficult for them to expect a collapse of the Third Reich. Marion Countess Dönhoff, managing her family estate in East Prussia, lived farthest from the centers of power and Nazi persecution. And she did not have to worry about her material existence. In this sense, it was no doubt easiest for her to keep her distance from the regime, while other members of her family made their peace with it and even assumed fairly elevated positions in it. After her brother Heinrich had joined the Wehrmacht and was promptly sent to the front in 1940, the countess was more directly confronted with the realities of Hitler's regime. At first she traveled to Berlin fairly frequently to meet friends, and on another occasion she went East to visit the German ambassador to Moscow. From what little is known, she also talked to him about the future of Soviet-German cooperation. When Hitler's attack on the Soviet Union in June 1941 destroyed any such plans and the war took more and more lives, including her brother's and those of other members of her family, she moved from a position of inner emigration more closely toward active resistance. Having been denounced by a relative, she was fortunate to escape unscathed from her brief arrest in the wake of the failed July 1944 plot to assassinate Hitler, in which several of her friends and also her cousin Heinrich von Lehndorff had participated, for which they were caught, tried, and executed.

Zehrer, meanwhile, lived far away from events in Berlin in his hovel on the island of Sylt, in the North Sea near the Danish border. But without income and with few savings, he began to make compromises with the regime to the extent that he published a successful novel he had written in the late 1930s, which earned him some royalties. He also accepted a paid position with the non-Nazi Stalling publishing house. He, too, therefore maneuvered in a "gray zone" of the inner emigration spectrum, joining the *Schrifttumskammer* out of necessity, but none of the Nazi political organizations. Finally, there is Paul Sethe. Having been forced to leave the *Ohligser Anzeiger* in 1933 and refusing to join the Party, Sethe found a modicum of intellectual shelter and protection from the regime when the *Frankfurter Zeitung* invited him to write and edit its political and military news. At times the line that separated him from outright collaborationism became quite thin. It was the information that he received during his travels about Nazi occupation policies in the East that edged him more and more toward a position in which he would have been prepared to join the active resistance. In the end, he merely appeared on the margins of the 20 July 1944 plot and, unlike his colleague Bartsch, avoided the Gestapo dragnet, largely, it seems, because his name did not appear on any of the lists that Goerdeler had so foolishly drawn up. In the end, all three of these journalists survived the cataclysmic end of the war, though Dönhoff and Sethe more precariously when they had to flee west from East Prussia and Berlin. Zehrer remained untouched on his island near the Danish border. Problems began for him only when in 1946 he ventured from Sylt to Hamburg in search of re-employment as a journalist.

Thenceforth all three wrestled, as writers and intellectuals, with the question not only of how to build a postwar career but also of how to transmit the experiences and insights that they had gained from the previous two decades of German and European history to their fellow-citizens and the international community, horrified by the now certain knowledge of the unprecedented crimes that had been committed in the Nazi-occupied territories and especially in the Holocaust. In an attempt to capture their basic quest, Alexander Gallus and Axel Schildt decided to title their collection of essays on intellectual life in this early period as *Rückblickend in the Zukunft* (Looking backward into the future).[1] There is some plausibility in this title: anthropologists and historians have argued that any society that has undergone a major catastrophe is not in a state of mind to advance toward new goals politically, economically, or culturally. Rather there is a tendency to look into the rearview mirror and try to retrieve those ideas and values of the pre-crisis past that look solid and might serve as the foundation for a fresh start. Sethe, Dönhoff, and Zehrer seem to fit this view. Aware of the total shipwreck that German society had suffered, they did not believe in setting out toward new and unknown societal shores. Knowing that the Nazis had destroyed all moral and ethical standards that the Germans had largely upheld before 1933, the task was to rebuild those standards as a first step.

In the case of Zehrer, who hailed from a Catholic family, the quest to reconstitute postwar society and politics was particularly strongly motivated by his rediscovered faith. There were many other Germans who rejoined the churches as well. Christian values also played a more discreet role in Dönhoff's life, not least since her friends and relatives who had been executed due to their involvement in the July 1944 plot had themselves found consolation in Christianity when they had decided to give their lives for the destruction of the tyrant and his evil regime and prepared to face their executioners. This is why their farewell letters to their families are important in understanding the postwar period. Sethe took a more secular approach to the tasks he saw in front of him but reproached himself for not having been more courageous and more prepared to risk his life before 1945. In short, it is not surprising that all three should have adopted a morally conservative position.

There were nuances, though. Zehrer, holding the most deeply conservative positions, harkened back to his Weimar attitudes of skepticism toward the "masses" and democracy and retained his earlier elitism. The presumed behavior of the German masses under Nazism had merely confirmed him in his views. Accordingly, he also remained the determined anti-Communist he had been since 1919, suspicious of the "proletarian masses." Dönhoff's basic conservatism is also strikingly evidenced in her postwar life and journalism. To be sure, she wanted a modern parliamentary democracy based on the fundamental rights that became enshrined in the West German Basic Law of 1949. She knew that this system needed fostering and that she had to be vigilant against a resurgence of Nazism. For her, West German reconstruction was not possible without a moral foundation that was ultimately rooted in the "Prussian" values that she had grown up with and that had also guided her and her friends in their opposition to Hitler.

With Sethe the situation was even more complex. He had been a Stresemannian liberal-conservative in the Weimar Republic and had then experienced the growing destruction of freedom at the *Ohligser Anzeiger* and the *Frankfurter Zeitung*. Much of his struggle after 1945 was therefore to secure this freedom once and for all, especially the journalist's freedom of expression. This freedom, he felt, was again being denied to him, as it had been under Nazism, during his years as an editor of the FAZ and *Die Welt*. His unhappiness about the pressures that he was under from his publishers, but also from the Adenauer government, caused him to leave both papers. He finally found the freedom had been seeking all the time at *Die Zeit* and *Der Stern* under their owner, Gerd Bucerius.

What last but not least determined the basic conservatism of all three journalists was their deeply ingrained patriotism, which had kept them from emigrating and, after 1945, led them onto a path of advocacy for the reunification of their country. At first their thoughts on this question were still conceived in terms of achieving unity within Germany's 1937 border. But, observing the evolution of international politics during the Cold War, they were realistic enough to appreciate that this goal was becoming increasingly unrealistic. Accordingly, Sethe and Dönhoff came to the support of Brandt's *Ostpolitik*, which was designed to accept the postwar territorial status quo and would, by the same token, pave the way for a reunification of the two postwar German states without the former territories farther East.

However, at least Sethe's and Dönhoff's journalism, and to some extent also Zehrer's, was not merely about securing the freedom of the press in light of the Nazi experience. It was also directed against the authoritarianism that still lingered inside the Adenauer government and its bureaucracy as well as the business community. With a good deal of justification, the first chancellor has been called a "democratic dictator,"[2] and it is certainly striking to see how tightly he tried to coordinate and control press policy. We have witnessed this by analyzing the pressures that Sethe was under in 1955 that forced him to resign from his position with the FAZ. There is also the case of the DPA, whose Social Democrat director, Fritz Saenger, was ousted by the Bonn government in 1959. But at no point did this authoritarianism emerge more crudely than during the *Spiegel* Affair. It is for these reasons that this book bears the title *Journalists between Hitler and Adenauer*, as this was precisely the position in which the three German journalists whose intellectual journeys have been examined in this book, but also Rudolf Augstein and other West German journalists, found themselves.

Ultimately, this study is therefore not just biographical and generational. It revolves around fundamental questions of political choice and of how to react as an ordinary citizen opposed to the rise and seizure of power of a dictatorship—or any authoritarian regime. In this sense this book offers a historical analysis with a very topical political dimension. A look around the globe will show how many journalists have their freedom of expression severely curtailed by government censorship, but also by pressures exerted on them by publishers, political donors, and advertisers. In the United States this question arose even before the rise of President Donald Trump, who publicly declared the media to be enemies. There is also the pressure exerted by the big media corporations, among which Rupert Murdoch's papers and television stations are probably the most glaring examples.

At the same time, the argument can now be heard that the arrival of the Internet and cell phones, and also the expansion of "social media," have promoted freedom of expression in dramatically new ways. The possibilities for voicing and proliferating one's individual opinions have become virtually limitless. Anyone can create his or her own blog, website, or Facebook page and has available a host of other channels of communicating with the rest of the world to spread information about one's favorite topics and causes. Visits and clicks to these sites are instantly recorded, and authors tend to assume that their views are taken seriously, even if the responses to their output are not only affirmative. There is also a movement that tempts those who have written something to market their novel, poetry, or scholarly research without the mediation of a publisher or its editors and peer reviewers. There is no quality control. While fact-checking has grown, it did so because bloggers and tweeters were also free to speak and fake news and alternative "facts" were being spread. Hitherto established knowledge has come to be challenged, and the recipients' "freedom" has become the freedom to pick up from the Internet what they want to hear and believe and to merely confirm their pre-existing prejudices and stereotypes. They live in an echo chamber.

All this looks very "democratic," giving "the people" an allegedly unlimited and open choice. But this advocacy for the world of "freedom" in which we are now said to live tends to overlook one basic issue: it is an illusion to think that this new media world has leveled the playing field. There are, as before, still plenty of people who are "more equal" than others. Notwithstanding the "democracy" of access to digital communication, elite groups continue to have the political tools as well as the wealth that give them superior influence and power. They have the capacity to manipulate those huge numbers of gullible, ignorant, and naïve readers and viewers. Trump, himself a billionaire surrounded by other billionaires and arguably the most powerful politician in the United States, has provided the most glaring proof of what can be done with the skillful use of the new technologies. But there is also ample evidence that all political leaders and their advisors, from the national level all the way down to the localities, are deploying and abusing these technologies, often with disturbing and destructive results, while their "targets" often do not realize that they are being misled and lied to. Of course there are the opinion polls, whose results are now also instantly available. But the question is invariably whether such polls wield any influence on decision-makers or whether they continue to make their political and socioeconomic decisions on the basis of their own prior ideological fixations and material interests. The same question must be asked of wealthy supporters who fund their preferred parties or politicians in the expectation that, once elected, they will gratefully represent their donors' specific interests.

These observations apply not only to the new media, but also to the older ones, such as radio, television, and the print press. At first glance this world is also marked by a huge choice of channels, magazines, and newspapers. Many smaller ones, it is true, had their survival threatened by the popularity of the

Internet. But as long as they exist, they, too, will be confronted with the questions that the journalists at the center of this book were forced to wrestle with, first under Hitler and, after 1945, during the Adenauer years. This is why their life and work provide deep insights into experiences that are as instructive today as they were half a century ago.

ACKNOWLEDGMENTS

GIVEN THE PECULIAR approach taken in this book, I have been fortunate to receive comments and criticisms of its lines of argument from a number of friends and colleagues. My sincere thanks are due to Hermann Count Hatzfeldt, Barbara Sethe (who sadly passed away in 2015) and her family, Axel Schildt, Gunter Hofmann, Norbert Frei, Sari Siegel, Edzard Reuter, Walter Goldstein, Jürgen Kocka, Anne Nelson, Elie Nathans, Mark Tandler, Astrid von Pufendorf, Rainer Hering, Markus Payk, Hans Decker, and Friedrich von Dönhoff. I am also grateful to Axel Schuster and Irene Brauer, whose advice on the Dönhoff Papers was invaluable, as well as Beate Schleicher at the Bundesarchiv Koblenz, Harald Bader of the Mikrofilmarchiv der deutschsprachigen Presse, and Kurt Heydeck and Birgit Bucher at the Berlin Staatsbibliothek. The manuscript benefitted greatly from the experienced and careful editorial work of Amanda Peery and Marilyn Martin. As on many previous occasions, my wife, Marion, was once more the person who patiently listened to the slow evolution of my thoughts on this project, proved a gentle critic of the substance of the book, and also helped to pinpoint its many stylistic infelicities. I am very happy to dedicate this volume to her.

NOTES

Introduction

1. Alice Schwarzer, *Marion Dönhoff: Ein widerständiges Leben* (Cologne, 1996); Klaus Harpprecht, *Die Gräfin: Marion Dönhoff. Eine Biographie* (Reinbek, 2008); Haug von Kuenheim, *Marion Dönhoff* (Reinbek, 1999). Gunter Hofmann of *Die Zeit* is writing a shorter "Deutung" of her life and work in German.

2. See, for example, Karl-Heinz Janssen et al., eds., *Die Zeit: Geschichte einer Wochenseitung, 1946 bis heute* (Munich, 2006), an expanded edition of a volume first published in 1996; Isabell Schreml, *Augstein, Dönhoff, Nannen und Co. Auf den Spuren des Erfolgs einer Journalistengeneration* (Marburg, 2003); Christian Haase and Axel Schildt, *"Die Zeit" und die Bonner Republik: Eine meinungsbildende Wochenzeitung zur Wiederbewaffnung und Wiedervereinigung* (Göttingen, 2008). More generally, Christian Sonntag, *Medienkarrieren: Biographische Studien über Hamburger Nachkriegsjournalisten, 1946–1949* (Munich, 2006).

3. See Ebbo Demant, *Von Schleicher zu Springer: Hans Zehrer also politischer Publizist* (Mainz, 1971). See also pp. 134ff.

4. See, for example, Dirk Moses, *German Intellectuals and the Nazi Past* (New York, 2007).

5. See, for example, Martin Klimke, *The Other Alliance: Student Protest in West Germany and the United States in the Global Sixties* (Princeton, NJ, 2010).

6. See, for example, Rolf Richter, *Kommunikationsfreiheit und Verlegerfreiheit* (Meisenheim/ Pullach, Germany, 1975).

7. See p. 12.

8. Karl Mannheim, "The Problem of Generations," in idem, *Essays in the Sociology of Knowledge* (London, 1959), 276–322. See also, more recently, Julian Marias, *Generations: A Historical Method* (Tuscaloosa, AL, 1970).

9. See Mark Roseman, ed., *Generations in Conflict: Youth Revolt and Generation Formation in Germany, 1770–1968* (Cambridge, UK, 1995).

10. There has been a tendency to relate the issue to a particular date, institution, or prominent politician. See, for example, Robert Wohl, *Generation of 1914* (Cambridge, MA, 1979); Michael Wildt, *Generation des Unbedingten* (Hamburg, 2003), on the members of the SS Reich Security Main Office; "Generation Merkel," cover story of *Der Spiegel*, 10 November 2014, 64–73.

11. No more than three anthologies are mentioned here, whose many contributors give a good indication of the range and scope of this research effort: Jürgen Reulecke, ed., *Generationalität und Lebensgeschichte im 20. Jahrhundert* (Munich, 2003); Ulrike Jureit and Michael

Wildt, eds., *Generationen: Zur Relevanz eines wissenschaftlichen Grundbegriffs* (Hamburg, 2005); Kirsten Garland, Benjamin Möckel, and Daniel Ristau, eds., *Generation und Erwartung: Konstruktionen zwischen Vergangenheit und Zukunft* (Göttingen, 2013).

12. See, for example, Ulrike Jureit, "Generation und Erwartung," in Garland et al., 29.

13. See Garland et al., "Die Erwartung: Neue Perspektiven der Generationsforschung," in idem, 10.

14. A major focus here was on the "Generation of '68" and the conflicts that it unleashed not merely in Germany but also in the United States and all over Europe. See, for example, Martin Klimke, *The Other Alliance: Student Protest in West Germany and the United States in the Global Sixties* (Princeton, NJ, 2010); Axel Schildt and Detlef Siegfrieds, eds., *Between Marx and Coca-Cola: Youth Cultures in Changing European Societies, 1960–1980* (New York, 2006).

15. Dirk Moses, *German Intellectuals and the Nazi Past* (Cambridge, UK, 2007), 7.

16. Christina von Hodenberg, "Politische Generationen und massenmediale Öffentlichkeit: Die '45er' in der Bundesrepublik," in Jureit and Wildt, 266–94.

17. One indication of these perceptions seems to have been the success of Daniel Goldhagen's bestseller *Hitler's Willing Executioners: Ordinary Germans and the Holocaust* (New York, 1996).

18. Friedrich Krause, ed., *Deutsche Innere Emigration* (New York, 1946).

19. Friedrich Krause, "Preface," in ibid., 7.

20. Karl Otto Paetel, "Das Gesicht des innerdeutschen Widerstandes," in Krause, *Deutsche Innere Emigration*, 32–38.

21. Ibid., 35.

22. Ibid.

23. Richard Löwenthal, "Widerstand im totalen Staat," in Richard Löwenthal and Patrick von zur Mühlen, eds., *Widerstand und Verweigerung in Deutschland, 1933–1945* (Bonn, 1984), 60–67. See also Günther Gillessen, *Auf verlorenem Posten* (Berlin 1986), 533.

24. See Peter Steinbach, *Widerstand im Widerstreit: Der Widerstand gegen den Nationalsozialismus in der Erinnerung der Deutschen* (Paderborn, 2001), 64–65.

25. On an application of Primo Levi's concept of the "gray zone" to Holocaust victims, see Sari Siegel, "Treating an Auschwitz Prisoner-Physician: The Case of Dr. Maximilian Samuel," in *Holocaust and Genocide Studies* 28, no. 3 (Winter 2014): 450–81, with thoughtful deliberations on how to conceptualize problems of resistance and collaboration. While the situation of "inner emigrants" was, of course, far less extreme than that of Samuel, the question they had to face was whether they were courageous enough to resist a regime that they knew would result in torture and even death if their attitudes and actions were discovered by the Gestapo.

26. See Paetel's article on "inner emigration" and especially pp. 30 and 38 in the previously mentioned volume edited by Krause referring to Jünger's memorandum, which will be discussed in more detail on pp. 12ff.

27. On Jünger's early career, see, for example, Allan Mitchell, *The Devil's Captain* (New York, 2011), 7ff. See also Ernst Jünger, *In Stahlgewittern: Aus dem Tagebuch eines Stosstruppführers* (Berlin, 1929), English translation *Storm of Steel* (London, 2013). A similar account is in idem, *Wäldchen 125: Eine Chronik aus dem Grabenkämpfen, 1918* (Berlin, 1935), English translation *Copse 125* (New York, 1988).

28. In a quite different mode, see *Der Kampf als inneres Erlebnis* (Berlin, 1922). On Jünger's activities in this period, see also Hans-Peter Schwarz, *Der konservative Anarchist* (Freiburg,

1962); Karl Prümm, *Die Literatur des deutschen Nationalismus der 20er Jahre* (Kronberg i. Ts., 1974).

29. See, for example, Volker R. Berghahn, *Der Stahlhelm, Bund der Frontsoldaten, 1918–1935* (Düsseldorf, 1966); Karl Rohe, *Das Reichsbanner Schwarz-Rot-Gold* (Düsseldorf, 1966), which contains a very good analysis of the larger issues of organizational structures, mentalities, and ideologies of both Republican and anti-Republican veterans' associations.

30. On Jünger's career in the Wehrmacht, see Mitchell, 44ff., and his novel, *Auf den Marmorklippen* (Zurich, 1942), English translation *On the Marble Cliffs* (Norfolk, CT, 1947).

31. On his rather easy-going life and his love affairs in Paris, see Mitchell, 22ff., 79ff.; on the violence around him, the rumor mills, and his fears and insomnia, see ibid., 28f., 37, 45, 58–59.

32. Hannes Heer, "Das Schweigen des Hauptmanns Ernst Jünger: Ernst Jüngers Reise an die Kaukasusfront 1942/43," in Moritz Bassler and Ernst von der Knaap, eds., *Die (k)alte Sachlichkeit: Herkunft und Wirkungen eines Konzepts* (Würzburg, 2004), 97–119. See also Jan Philipp Reemtsma, "'Es schneit der Wind das Ärgste zu': Ernst Jünger im Kaukasus," in idem, *Mord am Strand: Allianzen von Zivilisation und Barbarei* (Hamburg, 1998), 316–46.

43. This was also the attitude of the Kreisau Circle around Helmuth von Moltke. See, for example, Ger van Roon, *German Resistance to Hitler: Count von Moltke and the Kreisau Circle* (New York, 1971). By contrast, Claus von Stauffenberg and the other participants involved in the July 1944 plot wanted to overthrow the regime and replace it with a government that, Hans Mommsen and others have argued, would not have provided a foundation for a parliamentary-democratic republic like the one that emerged from the war in 1949. If the coup failed, they expected it to be proof that Another Germany had in fact existed for which the plotters were prepared to die. On this subject, see pp. 107ff. on the argument between Mommsen and Marion Countess Dönhoff in the 1960s.

34. On the von Stülpnagels', Speidel's, Hofacker's, and Jünger's role in these dramatic events, see Mitchell, 41ff., 48ff.

35. Ernst Jünger, *Der Friede: Ein Wort an die Jugend der Welt* (Zurich, 1949), English translation *The Peace* (Hilldale, IL, 1948).

36. See his Geleitwort to the memorandum in idem, *Sämtliche Werke*, vol. 22: *Späte Arbeiten: Verstreutes; Aus dem Nachlass* (Stuttgart, 2003), 381, and Mitchell, 62, on Jünger's grief when he learned of "Ernstel's" death as late as February, shortly after he had commemorated the anniversary of his own father's passing in early January 1945. He had left Paris long ago, was apparently briefly recruited to the *Volkssturm*, and ended up in the family home in Hanover-Kirchhorst, where his wife, Greta, neé von Jeinsen, was waiting for him.

37. The quote from Jünger is at the head of chapter 3 of the volume by Krause and Paetel, 69. It is undated but probably from the end of the war after the failed 1944 plot.

38. See pp. 134ff., 170ff.

39. See, for example, his *Heliopolis: Rückblick auf eine Stadt* (Tübingen, 1949), and *Gläserne Bienen* (Stuttgart, 1957). But there are also more political writings, such as *Jahre der Okkupation* (Stuttgart, 1958).

40. For a good digest of this scholarship, see Mitchell, 4ff.

41. Daniel Morat, *Von der Tat zur Gelassenheit. Konservatives Denken bei Martin Heidegger, Ernst Jünger und Friedrich Georg Jünger, 1920–1960* (Göttingen, 2007).

42. Georg Friedrich Jünger, "Der Mohn," in Krause, 64–66.

43. Ibid., 46.

44. Margret Boveri, *Wir lügen alle: Eine Hauptstadtzeitung unter Hitler* (Olten, 1965), 713.

45. See, for example, Theodor Heuss-Archiv, ed., *Theodor Heuss: Der Mann, das Wort, die Zeit* (Stuttgart, 1967); Volker R. Berghahn, *America and the Intellectual Cold Wars in Europe* (Princeton, NJ, 2001), 33–34.

46. Boveri, 710ff.

47. See the reference to Meinecke's "patriotic enthusiasm" in Georg G. Iggers, *Deutsche Geschichtswissenschaft* (Munich, 1971), 288. See also Heuss's contribution in Krause and Paetel, 86ff., with a critical assessment of the Nazi past and the question of cooperation with the Western Allies.

48. See, for example, the retrospective admission of the Hamburg industrialist Otto A. Friedrich. He noted in his postwar diaries that he had become a member of the Nazi Party in July 1941 because he could not wish for a German defeat and thought that it would be possible to transform National Socialism "in its European mission." He also hoped that the regime would undergo an "inner purification." See Volker R. Berghahn and Paul J. Friedrich, *Otto A. Friedrich: Ein politischer Unternehmer* (Frankfurt, 1993), 21.

49. Heike B. Görtemaker, *Ein deutsches Leben: Die Geschichte der Margret Boveri, 1900–1975* (Munich, 2005).

50. Ibid., 18ff.

51. Ibid., 32ff.

52. Ibid., 51ff.

53. Ibid., 58ff.

54. Ibid., 68.

55. Ibid., 72.

56. Ibid., 107.

57. Ibid., 85ff., 108ff; Boveri, 236, 344.

58. Görtemaker, 121, 127n.

59. Ibid., 129.

60. Ibid., 130ff.

61. Ibid., 137ff.

62. Ibid., 144ff. and 152, concluding that Boveri's views of the United States have to be seen against the background of Nazi policies of violence and exploitation in Europe. The author thought that in this light Boveri's remarks were "arrogant, even grotesque" when she claimed that European history and philosophy were superior. Her verdict on America could be understood only against the background of the rejection that she had encountered as a "Nazi correspondent" after her arrival there.

63. Görtemaker, 168ff.

64. Ibid., 173ff.

65. Ibid., 199ff., 210ff. See p. 248.

66. Gillessen, 417.

67. Hermann Schreiber, *Henri Nannen: Der Herr vom Stern* (Munich, 2001), 17ff.

68. Ibid., 47ff.

69. Ibid., 97.

70. Ibid., 109.

71. Ibid., 142ff.

72. Ibid., 106.

73. Ibid., 124–25.

Chapter 1

1. Thus Gerd Bucerius to Paul Sethe (PS), 30 April 1963, Sethe Papers (hereafter NLPS), file I. The epithet was used in this case by Bucerius as the publisher of *Der Stern* to express his delight with the arrangement that Henri Nannen, the magazine's editor in chief, had made to recruit Sethe as a contributor and adviser. It should be added that this letter was not written after Sethe's death in 1967, but was a welcome note that he was not merely continuing his work for *Die Zeit* but had committed himself to Bucerius's press empire more broadly. In other words, it was not an obituary, and the welcome "to our neck of the woods (Revier)" seems to have been genuine. On the larger context, see pp. 77ff.

2. See pp. 31ff. and 44ff.

3. See the curriculum vitae that Sethe appended to his published doctoral dissertation, *Die ausgebliebene Seeschlacht: Die englische Flottenführung, 1911–1915* (Bonn, 1932), 139.

4. PS to his sister Herta Sethe, 9 February 1947, NLPS, Correspondence with Herta, Green File. See also Obituary by Dr. Grosse-Dresselhaus, a retired pastor in Halver. The clipping does not give the source and date, but the article seems to have appeared in the local *Allgemeiner Anzeiger* shortly after Sethe's death.

5. Sethe's father, probably by force of circumstance in hard times, also had other jobs, for instance, in real estate, and wanted his son to undergo a commercial training.

6. See the preface to Sethe's dissertation, III–IV. Kern had written about kinship and law in the Middles Ages, but then he compromised himself when he began to write about evolution and "race." See Fritz Kern, *Stammbaum und Artbild der Deutschen und ihrer Verwandten: Ein kultur- und rassengeschichtlicher Vergleich* (Berlin, 1927). The position of *Privatdozent* meant that Hallmann, having earned a second doctorate (*Habilitation*), had the right to give lecture classes and seminars but did not hold a secure academic position and depended on tuition fees related to student numbers.

7. See his *Krügerdepesche und Flottenfrage* (Stuttgart, 1927).

8. Hans Hallmann, *Der Weg zum deutschen Schlachtflottenbau* (Stuttgart, 1933).

9. See Sethe, *Seeschlacht*, also for the following.

10. Julian Corbett, *Naval Operations*, 5 vols. (London, 1919–31); Otto Groos, *Der Krieg in der Nordsee*, first section of *Der Krieg zur See*, 5 vols. (Berlin, 1920–28); Thomas G. Frothingham, *The Naval History of the World War*, 3 vols. (Cambridge, MA, 1925–28).

11. See Sethe, *Seeschlacht*, 34ff., also for the following.

12. See Jonathan Steinberg, *Yesterday's Deterrent: Tirpitz and the Birth of the German Battle Fleet* (London, 1965).

13. See, above all, Alfred Wegener, *The Origin of Continents and Oceans* (New York, 1924).

14. See, for example, Volker R. Berghahn, *Der Tirpitz-Plan: Genesis und Verfall einer innenpolitischen Krisenstrategie unter Wilhelm II* (Düsseldorf, 1971). For different perspectives stressing bureaucratic rivalries, see Patrick Kelly, *Tirpitz and the Imperial German Navy* (Bloomington, IN, 2011), and Dirk Bönker, *Militarism in a Global Age: Naval Ambitions in Germany and*

the United States before World War I (Ithaca, NY, 2012), with a comparative approach. The most recent reassessment of the debate that is critical of the research of Jon Sumida and others on British naval policies as well as of challenges to the work of the 1970s, see Matthew S. Seligmann and Frank Nägler, eds., *The Naval Route to the Abyss: The Anglo-German Naval Race, 1895–1914* (Farnham, UK, 2015).

15. Tirpitz's position in the Reich government had progressively weakened when the failure of his anti-British power-political strategy of 1900 became clear. Between 1912 and 1914 he tried to delay the major war that the German generals were pushing for. Once the war had started, he changed his mind again and advocated an early all-out deployment of the battle fleet in the North Sea.

16. Jonathan Steinberg, "The Copenhagen Complex," in *Journal of Contemporary History* 1, no. 3 (1966): 23–46.

17. See Sethe, *Seeschlacht*, 49ff.

18. See, for example, Alfred T. Paterson, *Jellicoe: A Biography* (New York, 1969).

19. Sethe, *Seeschlacht*, 113.

20. See, for example, Martin Kitchen, *The Silent Dictatorship* (New York, 1976); Francis Carsten, *Revolution in Central Europe, 1918–1919* (Aldershot, UK, 1972).

21. Sethe, *Seeschlacht*, 124ff.

22. Quoted in Hallmann to (Elfriede Sethe), n.d., copy, NLPS, Leitz Organizer, H. He gave the date of Sethe's letter as 2 February 1932.

23. Ibid. This time he gave the date of 11 June 1932.

24. See pp. 44ff., 53ff., 60ff.

25. See Curt Georgi to PS, 13 November 1945, NLPS, Leitz Organizer, G. After 1945, the Allies obliged all adult Germans to undergo de-Nazification. They had to fill out a lengthy questionnaire and appear before a tribunal that judged and classified their former political activities. To get off the hook, defendants frequently submitted letters, for example, from local clergymen, testifying that they had not been confirmed Nazis.

26. Curt Georgi to PS, 13 November 1945, NLPS, Leitz Organizer, G.

27. Thus the masthead of the OA.

28. Figures compiled from Ralf Stremmel, *Politische Plakate, 1870–1960* (Solingen, 1992), 176.

29. For a detailed analysis of election results at the Reich level during the Weimar Republic see, for example, Jürgen Falter et al., eds., *Wahlen und Abstimmungen in der Weimarer Republik: Materialien zum Wahlverhalten, 1919–1933* (Munich, 1986), esp. 67ff. See also Richard F. Hamilton, *Who Voted for Hitler?* (Princeton, NJ, 1982); Thomas Childers, *The Nazi Voter: The Social Foundations of Fascism in Germany, 1919–1933* (Chapel Hill, NC, 1983).

30. See Volker Wünderich, *Arbeiterbewegung und Selbstverwaltung: KPD und Kommunalpolitik in der Weimarer Republik mit dem Beispiel Solingen* (Wuppertal, 1980); Bernd Neufurth, *Solingen 1929–1933: Eine Studie zur Auflösung der Weimarer Republik und der nationalsozialistischen Machtübernahme in einer Kommune* (St. Augustin, Germany, 1984).

31. To save space, the references from Sethe's articles in the OA are given only by the date of publication in the text rather in the endnotes.

32. PS to Brigitte Beer, 10 November 1945, NLPS, file II.

33. See also Sethe's retrospective in *Die Zeit*, 26 November 1965, repr. in Paul Sethe, *In Wasser geschrieben: Porträts, Profile, Prognosen*, ed. Karl Heinz Janssen (Frankfurt, 1968, 9–16).

34. See, for example, Karl Dietrich Bracher, *Die Auflösung der Weimarer Republik*, 3rd ed. (Villingen, Germany, 1960, 287ff.; William L. Patch, *Heinrich Brüning and the Dissolution of the Weimar Republic* (New York, 1998).

35. See pp. 38ff.

36. For a detailed discussion of Schleicher's plans and Gregor Strasser's role in this gambit, see pp. 141ff.

37. On these conversations, see Bracher, 686ff.

38. See the detailed discussion of *Die Tat* in chap. 3, pp. 134ff.

39. The NSDAP gained 39.5 percent of the vote, followed by the SPD, with 30.1 percent, and the KPD, with 11.2 percent. The DVP and DNVP garnered 10.5 per cent in all. See Falter, 96.

40. On Thyssen and heavy industry see, for example, Reinhard Neebe, *Grossindustrie, Staat und NSDAP, 1930–1933* (Göttingen, 1981). On Osthilfe, see, for example, Ian Kershaw, *Hitler*, vol. 1 (1889–1936) (New York, 1998), 416f.; Bruno Bachta, *Die Junker und die Weimarer Republik: Charakter und Bedeutung der Osthilfe in den Jahren 1928–1933* (Berlin, 1959).

41. On the calculations and miscalculations of the Conservatives inside and outside the Hitler cabinet, see, for example, Hermann Beck, *The Fateful Alliance: German Conservatives and the Nazis in 1933* (New York, 2008).

42. See Henry A. Turner, *Hitler's Thirty Days to Power: January 1933* (Reading, MA, 1996).

43. See, for example, Günter Morsch and Agnes Ohm, *Terror in der Provinz Brandenburg: Frühe Konzentrationslager, 1933/34* (Berlin, 2015).

44. See Günter Opitz, *Der Christlich-Soziale Volksdienst* (Düsseldorf 1969).

45. See, for example, Christopher Dillon, *Dachau and the SS: A Schooling in Violence* (Oxford, 2015).

46. See, after years of controversy over whether it was the Nazis who laid the fire rather than Marius van der Lubbe, the recent study by Benjamin Hett, *Burning the Reichstag: An Investigation into the Third Reich's Enduring Mystery* (New York, 2014).

47. Falter, 75.

48. Sethe fell for the rumor that Braun had fled to Switzerland. In fact, Braun had taken his seriously ill wife for treatment and had returned to Germany.

49. See pp. 137ff.

50. DINTA's full title was "Deutsches Institut für technische Arbeitsschulung," and it had been established by Carl Arnhold in the 1920s. Its purpose was to provide professional training for apprentices but also "to instil a spirit of subordination and nationalism." See Timothy W. Mason, "Zur Entstehung des Gesetzes zur Ordnung der nationalen Arbeit vom 20. Januar 1934," in Hans Mommsen et al., eds., *Industrielles System und politische Entwicklung in der Weimarer Republik* (Düsseldorf 1974), 322–51. After 1933, Arnhold obtained the official support of the new regime. DINTA became the "Office of Professional Training and Factory Leadership" and was part of the Nazi Labor Front.

51. See, for example, Beck, 227. Rumors that Oberfohren had been murdered by the Nazis because of his opposition to the New Course were probably false; it seems that he committed suicide because of political pressures on him and because of his growing doubts that allying his DNVP to Hitler had been a terrible mistake. Of course, Sethe made no mention of Oberfohren's death.

52. See pp. 38ff.

53. See, for example, Norbert Frei and Johannes Schmitz, *Journalismus im Dritten Reich* (Munich, 1989); Oron Hale, *Captive Press in the Third Reich* (Princeton, NJ, 1964).

54. Hale, 83ff.

55. See Georgi to PS, 13 November 1945, in which he quoted from Sethe's farewell article that Sethe had published in the OA of 30 December 1933. Georgi added that Sethe had told him earlier that he would like to move to the FZ. There is no evidence on who facilitated his move. According to the commemorative special issue that the postwar intellectual journal *Die Gegenwart* published in 1956 ("Ein Jahrhundert Frankfurter Zeitung begründet von Leopold Sonnemann," 24), Sethe published an article in OA on the FZ's anniversary in the autumn of 1931 in which he highlighted the paper's "lonely position" among the Weimar press. It could be that this opened a channel and that colleagues at the FZ now came to his rescue.

56. Günther Gillessen, *Auf verlorenem Posten: Die Frankfurter Zeitung im Dritten Reich* (Berlin, 1986), 70–71.

57. On the Potempa murders, see, for example, Kershaw, 381ff.

58. See Frei and Schmitz, 11.

59. Gillessen, 8–9.

60. Typed letter fragment, n.d. (end of 1945), NLPS, Correspondence with Herta, Green File.

61. Gillessen, 35. See also Arne Kapitza, "Zwischen Anpassung und Opposition," in *Jahrbuch für Liberalismusforschung* 5 (1993): 69–104; Michael Hepp, ed., *Der geistige Widerstand im Kulturteil der "Frankfurter Zeitung" gegen die Diktatur des totalen Staates* (n.p., 1949).

62. See Hale, 214; Gillessen, 392ff.

63. On IG Farben more generally, see Peter Hayes, *Industry and Ideology: IG Farben in the Nazi Era* (Cambridge 1987). See also Dieter Petzina, *Autarkiepolitik im Dritten Reich* (Stuttgart, 1968).

64. Gillessen, 44ff., 172, 394; Frei and Schmitz, 51.

65. Klaus Hildebrand, *The Foreign Policy of the Third Reich* (Berkeley, 1973); Andreas Hillgruber, *Hitlers Strategie* (Frankfurt, 1965).

66. Gillessen.

67. See, for example, Dagmar Bussiek, *Benno Reifenberg, 1893–1970* (Göttingen, 2011).

68. Gillessen, 42, 198; Hale, 289ff.; Frei and Schmitz, 52.

69. Gillessen, 389.

70. Ibid., 294.

71. Ibid., 430.

72. See Georg G. Iggers, *Deutsche Geschichtswissenschaft* (Munich, 1971), 288, with a reference to Friedrich Meinecke's "patriotic enthusiasm."

73. See Gillessen, 444. See also F. W. Deakin, *The Case of Richard Sorge* (New York, 1966), on Sorge as a double agent.

74. Some of Sethe's papers are held by the Bundesarchiv Koblenz (BAK). They include a collection of his wartime articles, filed under N1471/12. As in the case of the items published in the OA, described earlier, they are not separately end-noted here but can easily be found under the date cited in the text.

75. See, for example, Francis L. Carsten, *Reichswehr and Politics, 1918–1933* (Berkeley, 1966).

76. See Michael Geyer, *Aufrüstung oder Sicherheit? Die Reichswehr in der Krise der Machtpolitik* (Wiesbaden, 1980).

77. Omer Bartov, *The Eastern Front, 1941–1945* (Oxford, 2001).

78. Quoted in Gillessen, 448ff.

79. Ibid., 448f.

80. See Jochen Thies, *Hitler's Plans for Global Domination: Nazi Architecture and Ultimate War Aims* (New York, 2012).

81. On Sybel, see Iggers, 154–55.

82. PS to Häfner, 13 December 1942, NLPS, file I.

83. Astrid von Pufendorf, in *Mut zur Utopie, Otto Klepper—ein Mensch zwischen den Zeiten* (Frankfurt, 2015), 236, cites an article in *Frankfurter Rundschau*. See also note 88.

84. See Frei and Schmitz, 44.

85. Ibid., 101ff.

86. Martin Econ, "Frankfurter Zeitung to End 90 Years of Publication," *New York Times*, 28 August 1943. According to Hale, 286ff., some 500 papers had been closed down in 1941 and another 950 by 1943. Goebbels had proclaimed total war, and this meant total control of the media.

87. Thus *Der Kurier*, 20 June 1946, in BAK, N1471/12.

88. PS to Vacek (Washington), 20 April 1965 (NLPS, Leitz Organizer, X), written after hearing that Klaus Harpprecht wanted to "take aim" at him and Henri Nannen because of their past record. He insisted that he was among twelve FZ editors who were forced to join the VB. He added that he was supposed to become editor in chief of Goerdeler's "government paper" after a successful "uprising" in 1944. He wanted to leave it up to Vacek if he wanted to pass this information on. See also the "Confirmation" that Fritz Saenger wrote after 1945 in support of Sethe's anti-Nazi record, Leitz Organizer, S, with further details on the VB's practices and the pressures that, for example, Rudolf (?) Fischer, a *Ministerialrat* in the government press department, put him under.

89. On the Wehrmachtpropaganda Department (WPr) and its Nazification see, for example, Volker R. Berghahn, "NSDAP und 'Geistige Führung' der Wehrmacht, 1939–1943," *Vierteljahrshefte für Zeitgeschichte* 1 (1969): 17–71.

90. See note 69. This file contains Sethe's pieces not only in the FZ but also in the FA. As in the case of the items published in the OA, they are identified here merely by date of publication and not in the endnotes.

91. See Otto Köhler, *Schreibmaschinentäter: Journalisten unter Hitler—und danach* (Cologne, 1989).

92. PS to "Echo der Zeit" editors, 24 March 1958, NLPS, file I.

93. Janssen.

94. FR, 31 August 1968.

95. On these policies, see, for example, Martin Broszat, *Nationalsozialistische Polenpolitik* (Frankfurt, 1965).

96. PS to Georgi, 25 November 1945, NLPS, Leitz Organizer, G.

97. PS to Herta Sethe, n.d. (1945), NLPS, Correspondence with Herta, Green File. See also Janssen's selection of Sethe's articles, 26ff., 22ff., with postwar portraits of Rundstedt, Erich von Manstein (who issued blatantly racist ethnic cleansing orders) and Friedrich Paulus (who was defeated at Stalingrad). Sethe portrayed Rundstedt as an obedient soldier who would argue with Hitler on purely military-professional grounds and, unceremoniously dismissed more

than once, would devoutly accept another command a few months later. Adding Hindenburg and Ludendorff to Rundstedt's name, he concluded that these three men reflected in a very sad way the slow demise of the top officer corps all the way down to 1945. For a comprehensive survey, see Rolf-Dieter Müller and Gerd R. Ueberschär, eds., *Hitler's War in the East, 1941–1945* (Providence, RI, 1997).

98. See Janssen, 26–28. The article was originally published in *Allgemeine Zeitung* (Mainz) on 1 June 1948.

99. PS to Georgi.

100. Janssen, 27.

101. See Anne Nelson, *Red Orchestra: The Story of the Berlin Underground and the Circle of Friends Who Resisted Hitler* (New York, 2009); Stefan Roloff (with Mario Vigl), *Die Rote Kapelle* (Munich, 2002).

102. PS to Beer, n.d. (end of 1945?), NLPS, Beer Correspondence, file II; PS to Beer, 8 February 1946, in ibid., thanking her for the information that he had passed on to the father.

103. On Klepper, see Roloff, 141ff. On Sethe's changed attitude, see PS to Beer, 28 February 1946, NLPS, Beer Correspondence, file II.

104. Nelson; Roloff.

105. At least in his letter to Beer at the end of 1945, he asked that Scheliha be approached for advice. Working in the German Embassy in Warsaw, the latter had passed on information on SS atrocities to the West. Later he had been in charge of the Polish desk in the Foreign Office Information Department. It is in the Polish context that Sethe must have met Scheliha, who may also have helped organize Sethe's trip to Poland in 1939. See Eckart Conze et al., *Das Amt und die Vergangenheit* (Munich, 2010), 226, 298ff. For further details on his role in the resistance, see Anne Nelson, "Rudolf von Scheliha," in *Widerstand und Auswärtiges Amt*, ed. Jan Erik Schulte and Michael Wala (Berlin, 2013), 35–55.

106. See p. 52.

107. Fritz Bartsch to Elfriede Sethe, 29 June 1967, NLPS, file I, also for the following. This is, of course, a letter written from memory in 1967. But the details are confirmed in accounts that Sethe wrote immediately after the war. See PS to Beer, 13 December 1945, NLPS, Beer Correspondence, file II.

108. Lohse was the deputy of Paul Karl Schmidt in the Foreign Office. While Schmidt was in charge of reporting to Ribbentrop on developments in the domestic and foreign press as well as of influencing the foreign press and directing the domestic press in international matters, Lohse was the liaison between the Foreign Office and the WPr. It seems that he worked with Sethe and may have helped the latter to obtain WPr protection after the shutting down of the FZ. See Conze et al., 147. On the WPr, see note 89 and Volker Berghahn, "Tendances de la 'Wehrmachtpropaganda,'" *Revue d'histoire de la deuxième guerre mondiale*, October 1971, 55–74. The interesting question is whether Ribbentrop, realizing that Germany might lose the war, protected Lohse in order to be able to say that he was not an anti-Semite. Interviewed by Gustave Gilbert, a court-appointed psychiatrist at the Nuremberg Trials, he flatly denied that he made anti-Semitic statements and claimed that he had always thought that the Nazi policy toward the Jews was "madness." See John Weitz, *Hitler's Diplomat* (New York, 1992), 333.

109. PS to "Echo der Zeit" editors, 24 March 1958, NLPS, file I; PS to Vacek, 24 April 1965, NLPS, Leitz Organizer, X–Z.

110. See PS to Georgi, 7 December 1945, NLPS, Leitz Organizer, G.

111. PS to Herta Sethe, 1 February 1946, NLPS, Correspondence with Herta, Green File.

112. PS to Herta Sethe, n.d. (early 1946), in ibid.

113. PS to Beer, 13 December 1945, NPLS, Beer Correspondence, file II. While Sethe approved of assassinating Hitler, one of his colleagues at the FZ took the view "with fanaticism" that "we should rather lose the war, as we would not get rid of the Nazis" by other means. See PS to Herta Sethe, n.d. (fragment), Correspondence with Herta, Green File. This was also the position of the Kreisau Circle around Hellmuth James von Moltke. See Ger von Roon, *German Resistance to Hitler: Count von Moltke and the Kreisau Circle* (New York, 1971).

114. PS to Georgi, 25 November 1945, NLPS, Leitz Organizer, G; PS to Georgi, 7 December 1945, in ibid. It may be that there was also some loose talk about Bartsch's connections with Goerdeler that was quickly stopped. See also PS to Beer, 13 December 1945, NLPS, Beer Correspondence, file II. Overall, the story in Sethe's letters of 1945/46 tallies with what Bartsch wrote to Sethe's widow in 1967 from his perspective.

115. PS to Herta Sethe, 1 February 1946, NLPS, Correspondence with Herta, Green File.

116. PS to Herta Sethe, 24 January 1947, NLPS, Correspondence with Herta, Green File.

117. Ibid. and PS to Herta Sethe, 17 January 1946, NLPS, Correspondence with Herta, Green File; PS to Brigitte Beer, 10 November 1945, NLPS, Beer Correspondence, file II.

118. PS to Herta Sethe, 26 November 1945, NLPS, Correspondence with Herta, Green File.

119. PS to Herta Sethe, 1 February 1946, NLPS, Correspondence with Herta, Green File.

120. PS to Herta Sethe, 2 June 1946, NLPS, Correspondence with Herta, Green File.

121. PS to Herta Sethe, n.d. (fragment), NLPS, Correspondence with Herta, Green File.

122. PS to Herta Sethe, 1 February 1946, NLPS, Correspondence with Herta, Green File.

123. On Schumacher's life, his experiences under Nazism, and his postwar role in the SPD, see Lewis Edinger, *Kurt Schumacher: A Study in Personality and Political Behavior* (Stanford, 1965).

124. PS to Herta Sethe, 1 February 1946, NLPS, Correspondence with Herta, Green File.

125. Ibid.

126. PS to Herta Sethe, n.d. (fragment, with first page missing), NLPS, Correspondence with Herta, Green File.

127. Ibid.

128. PS to Herta Sethe, 14 April 1945, NLPS, Correspondence with Herta, Green File.

129. PS to Beer, 15 November 1945, NLPS, Beer Correspondence, file II.

130. PS to Beer, 30 March 1946, NLPS, Beer Correspondence, file II.

131. PS to Beer, 10 November 1945, NLPS, Beer Correspondence, file II. See also PS to Herta Sethe (?), 6 June 1946, NLPS, Correspondence with Herta, Green File: "I am a pessimist. But I could not have imagined that it could be as bad as this."

132. PS to Herta Sethe, 6 June 1946, NLPS, Correspondence with Herta, Green File.

133. PS to Herta Sethe, n.d. (fragment, 1946?), NLPS, Correspondence with Herta, Green File.

134. See pp. 33f.

135. PS to Beer, 30 March (1946), NLPS, Beer Correspondence, file II.

136. PS to Herta Sethe, 7 December 1946, NLPS, Correspondence with Herta, Green File.

137. PS to Beer, 30 March (1946), NLPS, Beer Correspondence, file II.

138. PS to Herta Sethe, 7 December 1946, Correspondence with Herta, Green File.

139. PS to Herta Sethe, 1 February 1946, NLPS, Correspondence with Herta, Green File.

140. There are frequent references to his efforts to network and raise income for his small family in both the Herta Sethe Green File and the Beer File II. But he also worried about his brother Walther, who had not only held a civil service position in the Third Reich but was also still interned in June 1946. Walther, too, had become disillusioned, but, as his brother wrote to sister Herta on 27 April 1947 (NLPS, Correspondence with Herta, Green File), he was among the "fools" who had "fervently hoped for Hitler's end." By the end of 1947, things were also looking up for him when he was apparently again considered for the position of administrator for the Berleburg district, northeast of Siegen (PS to Herta Sethe, 21 November 1947, NLPS, Correspondence with Herta, Green File).

141. See the clipping on this in *Badische Zeitung*, 10 May 1946, NLPS, Beer Correspondence, file II. Although he would have liked to go to Hamburg (possibly for a position with *Die Welt*, the newspaper that the British authorities were building up at this time), he declined because it was "too dangerous." PS to Herta Sethe, 1 February 1946, NLPS, Correspondence with Herta, Green File. The reason for his reluctance may well have been related to what appeared in the *Rheinische Post* and other papers five weeks later, that is, that Hans Zehrer, whom the British had just appointed editor in chief, had been summarily dismissed when left-wing circles in Hamburg told them about his role as editor of *Die Tat* in 1932–33. See, pp. 134ff.

142. On the origins of the FAZ, see pp. 61ff.

143. On Wehrmacht and civilian opinion at the end of the war, see Wolfram Wette et al., eds., *Das letzte Jahr: Stimmungsberichte der Wehrmachtpropaganda, 1944/45* (Essen, 2001).

144. Dorothea von Meding, *Courageous Hearts: Women and the Anti-Hitler Plot of 1944* (Providence, RI, 1997).

145. PS to Herta Sethe, n.d. (1945), NLPS, Correspondence with Herta, Green File. See also Harold C. Deutsch, *Hitler and his Generals, January-June 1938* (Minneapolis, 1974).

146. Harold C. Deutsch, *Conspiracy against Hitler in the Twilight War,* (Minneapolis, 1978).

147. See p. 53; PS to Herta Sethe, n.d. (1945), NLPS, Correspondence with Herta, Green File.

148. PS to Beer, 28 February 1946, NLPS, Beer Correspondence, file II.

149. Marianne Krell to PS, 18 December 1963, NLPS, Leitz Organizer, K. Krell was Saenger's former secretary.

150. PS to Krell, 9 January 1964, NLPS, Leitz Organizer, K. See also Sethe's portrait of Freisler in Janssen, 21–22.

151. Annedore Leber to PS, 12 February 1946, NLPS, Leitz Organizer, L. On the occasion of the anniversary of the July Plot, Sethe published an article in *Allgemeine Zeitung* (Mainz), 20 July 1948, with portraits not only of Julius Leber but also of Adolf Reichwein, Hermann Maass, and Friedrich Werner von der Schulenburg before Freisler's court; repr. in Janssen, 18–21. On Schulenburg, see chap. 2, pp. 91ff.

152. PS to Herta Sethe, 21 November 1947, NLPS, Correspondence with Herta, Green File; PS to Georgi, 7 December 1945, NLPS, Leitz Organizer, G.

153. PS to Beer, 28 February 1946, NLPS, Beer Correspodencen, file II.

154. Quoted in Gillessen, 69.

155. PS to Georgi, 7 December 1945, NLPS, Leitz Organizer, G.

156. For an insightful analysis of the connections between Welter and a number of business-men interested in founding a conservative newspaper, see Astrid von Pufendorf, *Mut zur Utopie: Otto Klepper—Ein Mensch zwischen den Zeiten* (Frankfurt, 2015), 232ff., also for the following.

157. For more detailed biographies, see Markus Kiefer, *Auf der Suche nach nationaler Identität und Wegen zur deutschen Einheit* (Frankfurt, 1992), 30n.

158. See Rolf Richter, *Kommunikationsfreiheit und Verlegerfreiheit* (Meisenheim, Germany, 1975); Hartmut Soell, "Zum Problem der Freiheit des Journalisten: Aus der Korrespondenz Fritz Erler—Paul Sethe," in *Vierteljahrshefte für Zeitgeschichte* 23 (1975): 91–105.

159. Quoted in Pufendorf, 243.

160. Ibid., 249–50.

161. See, pp. 185ff.

162. See pp. 33f., 65ff. See also Alexander Gallus, *Die Neutralisten* (Düsseldorf, 2001). Interestingly, he signed his early postwar letters to his sister Herta with "Pawel."

163. Quoted in Pufendorf, 258. See also Kiefer, 174–75.

164. See, for example, Robert M. Spaulding, *Osthandel and Ostpolitik: German Foreign Trade Policies in Eastern Europe from Bismarck to Adenauer* (Providence, RI, 1997); Karsten Rudolph, *Die Ostpolitik der deutschen Grossindustrie, 1945–1961* (Frankfurt, 2004).

165. See, for example, Hans Speier, *West German Rearmament and Atomic War* (Evanston, IL, 1957); Gerhard Brandt, *Rüstung und Wirtschaft in der Bundesrepublik* (Witten, 1966). West German industry was initially not particularly enthusiastic about rearmament, and there were also the vexing issues of atomic weapons and what type of military force was to be introduced—professional or drafted. See p. 192n on Bogislaw von Bonin and the FAZ's military expert Adelbert Weinstein.

166. Quoted in Pufendorf, 259.

167. Ibid., 258f–59. On Noack and the Nauheim Circle, see Gallus, 153ff.

168. Pufendorf, 259–60.

169. Ibid., 260.

170. See, for example, Joost Kleuters, *Reunification in West German Party Politics from Westbindung to Ostpolitik* (New York, 2012). Like most other Germans at the time, Sethe, too, at this early stage still thought of reunification in terms of the borders of 1937. Of course American Cold War rhetoric played into this by talking of a rollback of the territorial conquests that the Red Army had made thanks to Hitler, who had refused to stop the war before the Soviets had reached the center of Berlin.

171. The literature on this initiative is extensive, and the question as to whether Stalin was serious about his offer has exercised scholars for decades. See, for example, Rolf Steininger, *Eine vertane Chance* (Berlin, 1985); idem, *The German Question: The Stalin Note of 1952 and the Problem of Reunification* (New York, 1992); Wilfried Loth, *Stalin's Unwanted Child: The Soviet Union, the German Question, and the Founding of the GDR* (New York, 1998); idem, *Die Stalin-Note vom 10. März 1952: Neue Quellen und Analysen* (Munich, 2002).

172. See, for example, Josef Foschepoth, ed., *Adenauer und die deutsche Frage* (Göttingen, 1988); Hans-Peter Schwarz, *Konrad Adenauer, The Statesman, 1952–1967*, vol. 2 (Providence, RI, 1997); Rainer Zitelmann, *Adenauers Gegner: Streiter der Einheit* (Erlangen, 1991).

173. Arnulf Baring, *Aussenpolitik in Adenauers Kanzlerdemokratie* (Munich, 1969), 148–49. The articles and also subsequent ones are reprinted in Janssen, 299ff.: "Die verpassten Gelegenheiten." See also Gallus, 124ff.

174. Gallus, 127–28. See also Kiefer, 104, 120ff., 162–63, 202ff.

175. Baring, 148–49.

176. Quoted in Kiefer, 172ff.

177. Adenauer's Office to PS, 21 April 1952, NLPS, Leitz Organizer, A.

178. See p. 66.

179. See Gallus, 130. See also Paul Noack, "Paul Sethe: Publizistische Opposition gegen Adenauer," in Foschepoth, 235–49.

180. See, for example, Volker R. Berghahn, *America and the Intellectual Cold Wars in Europe* (Princeton, NJ, 2001), 145ff.

181. PS to Henri Nannen, 16 June 1967, NLPS, Leitz Organizer, L. See also PS to Manfred Lauffs and Hans Becker, 10 January 1967, NLPS, Leitz Organizer, L.

182. Kiefer, 256, 370; fragment, dated "October 1955," NLPS, file I.

183. See, for example, Soell, 97ff.

184. See Kiefer, 146–47, 264ff., and Gallus, 115ff., for the positions of Rudolf Augstein and *Der Spiegel*. On Marion Dönhoff's position and *Die Zeit*, see pp. 110ff.

185. Baring, 235, cites a FAZ article by Sethe of 19 December 1952 in which he wrote that, when Adenauer, relying on the counsel of his legal advisers, asked for support of his policy, even his loyal followers had been flabberghasted.

186. For a useful survey of the more recent literature on the 1953 uprising see Jonathan Sperber, "17 June 1953: Revisiting a German Revolution," *German History* 22, no. 4 (2004): 619–43.

187. See Kiefer, 257, 321–22, 586.

188. See the articles in Janssen, 314ff.

189. See Pufendorf, 265.

190. Anton Storch to Adenauer, 16 November 1953, NLPS, file I; memo by?, 16 November (1953), with comment at the top: "Herrn Sethe u. Herrn Hoffmann telefonisch vorgelesen," dated 16 November and initialed "Be" (Beer?), NLPS, file I.

191. Memo by "Dr. H/St (Haffner)," 17 March 1955, NLPS, file I.

192. Albrecht Pickert to Werner G. Hoffmann, 5 August 1955 (copy), NLPS, file I. It is unclear how this copy landed in Sethe's papers, but its being there meant that he was quite well informed on what was going on behind the scenes. Adelbert Weinstein was mentioned as another awkward critic of Adenauer's foreign policy. The letter also contained unsubstantiated rumors about Colonel Bogislaw von Bonin and West Germany's rearmament. See note 210 and p. 65.

193. Albrecht Pickert to Werner G. Hoffmann, 5 August 1955, with comment. See earlier note 165.

194. See Maximilian Kutzner, "Das Wirtschaftsressort der Frankfurther Allgemeinen Zeitung und die Medialisierung der Wirtschaftspolitik in den 1950er Jahren," *Vierteljahrschrift für Sozial- und Wirtschaftsgeschichte* 101, no. 4 (2014): 488–99. See also page "6" of a memo fragment, October 1955, NLPS, file I, in which Sethe is cited as recounting the immediate background to his ouster.

195. Korn was another FZ editor who had learned to write "between the lines" and whom Köhler, 260, had called "a master of language with a backbone with multiple fractures." For a more detailed examination of his biography both before and after 1945, see Marcus M. Payk, "Opportunismus, Kritik und Selbstbehauptung: Der Journalist Karl Korn zwischen den dreissiger und den sechziger Jahren," in Alexander Gallus and Axel Schildt, eds., *Rückblickend in die Zukunft* (Göttingen, 2011), 147–63; Hepp. According to Axel Schildt, in "Im Visier: Die NS-Vergangenheit westdeutscher Intellketueller: Die Enthüllungskampagnen von Kurt Ziesel in der Ära Adenauer," *Vierteljahrshefte für Zeitgeschichte* 64, no. 1 (January 2016), 57ff., Korn also wrote at least one anti-Semitic article in Goebbels's *Das Reich*. It seems that Korn sympathized with Sethe during the 1955 crisis but was sidelined. In January 1957 he replied to a letter written by Sethe, who was planning a retrospective edition of articles written by the FAZ's editorial board. Korn was himself happy to provide his own pieces but felt obliged to ask his colleagues, knowing that he might get some "highly curious reactions." Korn to PS, 17 January 1957, NLPS, Leitz Organizer, K. His colleagues did indeed refuse to cooperate, arguing that the articles merely related to a past constellation and that selected articles would merely give a "deceptive (*schiefes*)" picture. As Payk shows (in "Opportunismus," 158ff.), Korn, at the time still in charge of the FAZ cultural section, increasingly lost influence and was marginalized by his colleagues.

196. Paul Sethe, *In Wasser geschrieben: Porträts, Profile, Prognosen* (Frankfurt 1968), 320–21, with an extract from the article that led to Sethe's resignation from the FAZ editorial board. For further details, see Soell, 105ff.

197. See above p. 70.

198. Ibid, 106.

199. Anton Storch to Konrad Adenauer, 16 November 1953; memo by?, 16 November 1953; and memo, 1953, all in NLPS, file I.

200. Memo by "Dr. H/St. (Haffner)," 17 March 1955, NLPS, file I.

201. See Soell, 105.

202. Ibid., 106.

203. Ibid., 107ff., 204.

204. See also p. 78, with a similar dictum by Sethe when he left *Die Welt* in 1960 after disagreements with publisher and owner Axel Springer.

205. Quoted in Soell, 107.

206. Zehrer to PS, 26 September 1955, NLPS, Leitz Organizer, X–Z.

207. Zehrer to PS, 19 October 1955, NLPS, Leitz Organizer, X–Z.

208. Zehrer to PS, 4 November 1955, NLPS, Leitz Organizer, X–Z.

209. PS to Zehrer, 11 November 1955, NLPS, Leitz Organizer, X–Z. Conscientious as ever, he requested that he be allowed to start his job a day later because of a death in the family. According to the memo fragment, page "6," cited in note 190, other papers also expressed an interest in hiring him.

210. On Weinstein and the larger context of the West German rearmament controversy, see Speier; Gallus, 248–49; Kiefer, 31; Sethe, *Seeschlacht*, 271ff.

211. See Kiefer, 164–65, 202ff., 215ff.

212. *Die Welt*, 11 April 1956.

213. On Pfleiderer and his plan, see Gallus, 85ff.; Kiefer, 368ff. See also Sethe's write-up in Sethe, *Seeschlacht*, 34–35.

214. Karl-Georg Pfleiderer to PS, 18 April 1956, NLPS, Leitz Organizer, P.

215. See the 720-page biography of Springer by Hans-Peter Schwarz, *Axel Springer* (Berlin, 2008), esp. 177ff., 204ff., 251ff. More critical about the Springer empire is Hans Dieter Müller, *Der Springer-Konzern* (Munich, 1968), esp. 185ff.

216. See, for example, James R. Ozinga, *The Rapacki Plan: The 1957 Proposal to Denuclearize Central Europe and Analysis of Its Rejection* (Jefferson, NC, 1989). George F. Kennan, one of America's "elder statesmen," had put forward ideas for a "disengagement" in Europe in his BBC Reith Lectures in the autumn of 1957 that "electrified" Springer. See Schwarz, 260–61.

217. On the trip and its consequences, see Schwarz, 261ff.

218. On the history of the Berlin Wall, see, for example, Norman Gelb, *The Berlin Wall* (London, 1986); Sagi Schaefer, *States of Division* (Oxford, 2014).

219. See Schwarz, 271ff.

220. See pp. 161ff.

221. PS to Springer, 15 January 1959, NLPS, Leitz Organizer, S, also for the following. See also his lecture of 21 May 1957, on The Task of the Publicist, printed in Janssen, 355–56.

222. Formulated in a letter to *Der Spiegel* 19 (1965), repr. in Janssen, 169. On the earlier version of this dictum, see p. 73.

223. Axel Springer to PS, 4 May 1960, NLPS, Leitz Organizer, S.

224. PS to Springer, 30 November 1965, NLPS, Leitz Organizer, S.

225. Augstein to PS, 2 February 1960, NLPS, Leitz Organizer, A.

226. See PS to Beer, 1 August 1960, NLPS, file I.

227. Bucerius to PS, 30 April 1963, NLPS, file I.

228. See the lists in BAK, NLPS, N1471/8.

229. See, for example, Paul Sethe, *Geschichte der Deutschen* (Frankfurt, 1962); idem, *Morgenröte der Gegenwart* (Stuttgart, 1963); idem, *Russische Geschichte* (Frankfurt, 1965); idem, *Schicksalsstuden der Weltgeschichte: Die Aussenpolitik der Grossmächte* (Frankfurt, 1966). The latter study may be taken as a digest of Sethe's views on the course of German history from Bismarck to the 1940s. In the preface he expressed the hope that his book would be read by skilled workers, merchants, engineers, and housewives. But he would be "most proud" if adolescents would be among his readers. Apart from providing history lessons, he also aimed to overcome a frequently found disconnect between the past and the present. And indeed many of his books went through several impressions. Brief mention should finally be made of his study of the French Revolution, *Die grossen Tage: Von Mirabeau zu Bonaparte* (Frankfurt, 1953), in whose preface he sided with the critics of this world-historical event. Here he argued that there had been two revolutions. The first one had broken the chains of the absolute monarchy; the second one had created the "first total state" and had demonstrated to the world "how one breaks the individual in the name of a fanatically believed dogma." He had experienced this himself during the Hitler dictatorship.

230. Fritz Fischer, *Griff nach der Weltmacht* (Düsseldorf, 1961). Although the book was mostly about German aims during the war, Fischer traced these aims back to the pre-1914 period and asserted that territorial expansionism was the reason that Wilhelm II and his entourage had unleashed this conflict in the first place. That argument of continuity put the cat among the pigeons in the West German historical profession, most of whose members were of the older generation and had grown up with the refutation of German responsibility for this catastrophe.

231. The two letters of 27 March 1952 and 20 July 1953 are reprinted in Klaus Schwabe and Rolf Reinhardt, eds., *Gerhard Ritter: Ein politischer Historiker in seinen Briefen* (Boppard, 1984). The letter of 27 July 1953 is cited on 116.

232. Ritter to PS, 17 October 1955, NLPS, Leitz Organizer, R. After Meinecke's death, Ritter was widely deemed to be the doyen of West German historians. Having received his PhD in 1912, having written a dissertation on the Prussian Conservatives under Bismarck, he had fought in World War I and after 1918 begun to write on major figures in German history. His biography of Luther appeared in 1925, of Stein in 1931, and of Gneisenau in 1932. After the Nazi seizure of power, he was among those conservatives who harbored hopes for a national renewal, but, like so many others, became disillusioned. In 1940 he published his *Machtstsaat und Utopie* and joined the early postwar dispute on how far the *"Dämonie der Macht"* was a viable interpretation of Hitler and the Third Reich. Teaching at Freiburg University, he was part of the Freiburg Circle of anti-Nazi professors and was briefly incarcerated after the 1944 plot but survived. After 1945 he delved more deeply into the demonic power argument, publishing another book on this topic in 1947. He then wrote a biography of Goerdeler and his involvement in the conservative Resistance, published in 1954, before he returned to the origins of World War I. In 1956 his sharp critique of the Schlieffen Plan appeared, written against the background of his more fundamental preoccupation with the problem of German militarism. By 1956 he had put out two volumes of this life work, titled *Staatskunst und Kriegshandwerk*. Two more volumes were planned to cover this topic up to 1945, but the Fischer Debate so absorbed him that these two volumes, published between 1964 and 1968, effectively turned into an extended rebuttal of Fischer's interpretation of World War I and did not go beyond 1918. More broadly, he was also opposed to the critical reassessment of Bismarck's policies that Hans-Ulrich Wehler and others began to advance by the late 1960s. They had a broader societal definition of militarism. Ritter saw it essentially as the predominance of military considerations over politics, which he believed to have been the hallmark of the Wilhelmine monarchy. For a full biography, see Christoph Cornelissen, *Gerhard Ritter: Geschichtswissenschaft und Politik im 20. Jahrhundert* (Düsseldorf, 2001). See also Michael Matthiesen, *Gerhard Ritter: Studien zu Leben und Werk bis 1933* (New York, 1993). Several of his books were translated, for example, the four *Staatskunst* volumes under the title *The Sword and the Scepter: Problems of German Militarism* (Coral Gables, FL, 1969ff). Recent evaluations of Ritter's work have taken the view that he was an even more complex historian than earlier interpretations had made out. See Franka Maubach, "Wie es dazu kommen konnte," (in press), 46 pp. See also Samuel Moyn, who in "The First Historian of Human Rights,"*American Historical Review* vol. 116, no. 1 (February 2011): 58–79, argued that Ritter was one of the fathers of the human rights movement after 1945.

233. PS to Ritter, 27 June 1962, NLPS, Leitz Organizer, R.

234. PS, "Als Deutschland nach der Weltmacht griff: Professor Fischers Thesen von der Alleinschuld am Ersten Weltkrieg wird noch viele Dikussionen auslösen," *Die Zeit*, 17 November 1961.

235. *Die Zeit*, 24 November 1961.

236. PS to Ritter, 5 July 1962, NLPS, Leitz Organizer, R. Interestingly enough, he referred to the role that the *Preussische Jahrbücher* had fulfilled in the Imperial period.

237. Quoted by Cornelissen, 603. See also ibid., 604ff., on the moves to withdraw a Goethe Institute subsidy for a lecture tour by Fischer in the United States and the humiliating

backfiring of this plan. See further Ritter to Sethe, 17 October 1961, in Schwabe and Reinhardt, 556ff., with other plans to counter Fischer.

238. See, for example, John A. Moses, *The Politics of Illusion: The Fischer Controversy in German Historiography* (London, 1975). The British-Australian historian Christopher Clark renewed the debate on the occasion of the hundredth anniversary of 1914 with his *The Sleepwalkers* (New York, 2012), arguing that all European governments had stumbled into the abyss. But, inevitably perhaps, there followed a vigorous debate and a scholarly pushback, and it now looks as if the focus is again more on the decision-makers in Berlin and Vienna, with St. Petersburg as a third center that escalated the crisis into war.

239. *Die Zeit*, 5 February 1965. See also Sethe's article in Janssen, 324, on the Rapacki Plan, which ended with the pointed remark that the federal government had opted against pursuing this plan on the basis of the advice of "the military experts." Critical of Adenauer's policy as ever, Sethe cloaked his opposition with an analysis of the situation in July 1914, when military experts had made another bad mistake. Apparently influenced by Ritter's book on the Schlieffen Plan, he viewed the decision of Moltke and Tirpitz as "fateful," even though they were "loyal patriots." But, he continued, "dark clouds" were then gathering around the German people. In it the "disaster" was hidden and through it "the good fortune of the Germans and Europe would crack up."

240. *Die Zeit*, 9 October 1964.

241. Ibid., 5 February 1965. On this volume, see note 232. See also Sethes article in ibid., 1 January 1965, in which he reviewed Karl-Dietrich Erdmann's analysis of Reich chancellor Theobald von Bethmann Hollweg based on the newly discovered diaries of Kurt Riezler, Bethmann's private secretary. This publication led to a renewed controversy, this time between Fischer (who felt Riezler confirmed his perspective on the July Crisis) and Erdmann. It was only later that Bernd Soesemann found out that the crucial pages of the diaries for July 1914 were not the original ones, a fact that Erdmann had neglected to mention in his piece.

242. *Die Zeit*, 13 October 1961.

243. PS to Ritter, 27 June 1962, NLPS, Leitz Organizer, R.

244. See Fischer to PS, 14 February 1967, NLPS, Leitz Organizer, F.

245. I attended this event as a young post-doc from London.

246. This also applied to recent research on the German Revolution of 1918–19 and on the role of Friedrich Ebert. Here he seems to have responded to the research of Peter von Oertzen and Reinhard Rürup, who had argued that the Weimar Republic might have had a better start if Ebert had relied more on the Workers' and Soldiers' Councils for his provisional government instead of forging compromises with the army, the bureaucracy, and big business in the Ebert-Groener and Stinnes-Legien pacts. See PS to Nannen, 16 June 1967, in BAK, N1471/23. The letter was published after Sethe's death in *Der Stern*.

247. Golo Mann to PS, 19 October 1965, NLPS, Leitz Organizer, M. The correspondence between the two men had started in 1964, when Mann drew Sethe's attention to Hermann Rauschning's recent book *Die Revolution des Nihilismus* (Zurich, 1964), which represented the author's interpretation of the Hitler regime. Mann thought that this book was an "enormously important and meritorious" study that might also have gained Sethe's esteem. Mann encouraged him to review it, if possible before Christmas, so that it might be considered during the gift-giving season. There is no space to go into the other correspondence that is less revealing

of Sethe's views than of Mann's, whose books on modern Germany enjoyed a wide readership at the time, though perhaps not so much because of their innovative perspectives as because he was the son of Thomas Mann.

248. See, for example, Angela Stent, *From Embargo to Ostpolitik* (Cambridge, UK, 2002); Peter Bender, *Neue Ostpolitik: Vom Mauerbau zum Moskauer Vertrag* (Munich, 1986).

249. Paul Sethe, *Öffnung nach Osten: Weltpolitische Realitäten zwischen Bonn, Paris und Moskau* (Frankfurt, 1966).

250. *Die Zeit*, 17 July 1964.

251. Ibid., 10 June 1966. Titled "Risse im Widerstand," it focused on Hermann Maass, a Social Democrat colleague of Julius Leber, both of whom Sethe had seen as defendants before Freisler's People's Court when he was sent to the court as an observer. Maas, he reported, had been opposed to Stauffenberg's plan to assassinate Hitler but had nevertheless actively participated in the resistance movement. Still, for Sethe there was a question about the cohesion between its conservative and Social Democrat members. In the meantime, Beck's and Goerdeler's memoranda on their post-coup reconstruction plans had been published. It seems that Sethe's article was written after conversations with Marion Dönhoff, who had become quite agitated over the criticisms that Hans Mommsen and others had recently launched against the political viability of Goerdeler's plans. The latter believed that a modern democratic society could not have been established on the basis of these memoranda. See pp. 107ff. on Dönhoff's reaction.

252. See *Die Zeit*, 5 June 1964 (Profumo), 17 March 1964 (Khrushchev), 2 December 1966 (Soraya).

253. Ibid., 14 July 1961 and 30 June 1967 (Eugen Gerstenmaier), 12 March 1965 (Max Brauer), 14 January 1966 (Rainer Barzel), 11 November 1966 (Herbert Wehner), 29 October 1965 (parliamentarism), 30 June 1966 (federalism), repr. in Sethe, 58ff., 150ff., 170ff., going back to the 1950s.

254. Ibid., 7 October 1960.

255. Ibid., 30 December 1960.

256. Ibid., 24 November 1961.

257. Ibid., 4 February 1966.

258. See p. 83.

259. Barzel to PS, 21 November 1966, NLPS, Leitz Organizer, B.

260. Bahr to PS, 2 May 1967, NLPS, Leitz Organizer, B. On Bahr, his close cooperation, and his strategy of *Wandel durch Annäherung*, see, for example, Gallus, 296ff.

Chapter 2

1. Thus Klaus Harpprecht, *Die Gräfin Dönhoff* (Reinbek, 2008), 11. Names of nobles are given in full for the first time, thereafter with first name and family name or just the first or family name.

2. See pp. 6ff.

3. For fuller biographical details, see Harpprecht; Haug von Kuenheim, *Marion Dönhoff* (Reinbek, 1999), 8ff.; Alice Schwarzer, *Marion Dönhoff: Ein widerständiges Leben* (Cologne, 1996), 43ff., 81ff. All three books contain many illuminating photos of Marion among her friends and colleagues, various members of her family, and East Prussian landscapes. Gunter

Hofmann, who knew her well for many years at *Die Zeit*, is currently writing a biographical "Deutung" of her life.

4. See Monika Wienfort, "Gesellschaftsdamen, Gutsfrauen und Rebellinnen: Adelige Frauen in Deutschland, 1890–1939," in Eckart Conze and Monika Wienfort, eds., *Adel und Moderne: Deutschland im europäischen Vergleich im 19. und 20. Jahrhundert* (Cologne, 2004), 181–203.

5. See Schwarzer, 81ff., 87, with a group portrait of her as the only woman in her senior year.

6. Quoted in Irene Brauer and Friedrich Dönhoff, *Marion Gräfin Dönhoff: Ein Leben in Briefen* (Hamburg, 2009), 15.

7. Ibid., 29.

8. Details in Brauer and Friedrich Dönhoff, 13–14; Harpprecht, 95–96.

9. Discussing my research with titled friends, I was time and again amazed how knowledgeable they were about the aristocracy, indicating to me how this group survived even the defeat of 1945 with its losses of people, land, and property and became once more an influential elite group in West German industry, commerce, and public services, including the Bundeswehr and the Foreign Office, as well as in agriculture and forestry in the Federal Republic despite their losses in Eastern Europe and East Germany.

10. See Schwarzer, 92ff., with a photo of Marion in Switzerland with fellow students, many of whom "thought differently from the Nazis in Germany." See also Kuenheim, 14ff.

11. Brauer and Dönhoff, 55ff.

12. Ibid., 76, 78ff.

13. On the 1940 journey, see Harpprecht, 227. On 1943, see the correspondence in Bucerius School Hamburg, Marion Dönhoff Papers (hereafter MDHH), F48/198–201. I would like to thank Hermann Count Hatzfeldt for giving me access to his aunt's papers.

14. See the exchange in MDHH, F48/202–04, also for the following.

15. On Hitler's strategy in 1940–41 see, for example, Klaus Hildebrand, *The Foreign Policy of the Third Reich* (Berkeley, 1973); Andreas Hillgruber, *Hitlers Strategie: Politik und Kriegführung, 1940–1941* (Frankfurt, 1966).

16. It is interesting to see how the German Foreign Office was trying to help. See the 1987 correspondence between Marion Dönhoff and Ingeborg Fleischhauer in MDHH, F48/206–11. Fleischhauer had researched the Schulenburg story and also found that Schulenburg's *Lebensgefährtin* had been arrested in Mai 1944 and murdered without his being able to do anything. See also pp. 55f. for the account of Paul Sethe's successful effort after 20 July 1944 to enlist the help of a member of the German Foreign Office, who was "half-Jewish" and had been sheltered by his colleagues. This is in contrast to the attitude of many generals: There had been hopes that the appointment of Heinz Guderian to the military *Ehrenhof* that Hitler had set up might make him prepared to be "of use to this or that comrade." But Fabrian von Schlabrendorff (who was dishonorably discharged from the Wehrmacht but acquitted by Freisler's People's Court and therefore survived the war), reported later that this Honor Court did not consider any testimonies of the accused. Instead it relied on Gestapo interrogation files that had been compiled after torture. He added that there was no "glory" in having been on this court. See the undated report that Schlabrendorff attached to his letter to MD, 3 April 1959, in MDHH, F48/213–18. In fact, the responses of the bevy of field marshals and generals provide a very telling account of how far they had allowed themselves to be drawn into a criminal regime and its methods of

warfare. Only one of them, field marshal Erwin von Witzleben, who had lost his command two years earlier, participated in the coup. He was promptly hauled before the People's Court and executed. General Heinrich von Stülpnagel committed suicide (see pp. 13f.), and field marshal Erwin Rommel was forced to shoot himself. See Wolfgang Schieder, "Zwei Generationen im militärischen Widerstand gegen Hitler," in Jürgen Schmädecke and Peter Steinbach, eds., *Der Widerstand gegen den Nationalsozialismus* (Munich, 1986), 436–59, which stresses generational differences that prevented the lower and upper ranks from coalescing. While the percentage of noblemen among the conspirators was high, at 44.9 percent, it was even higher among the generals, at 48.7 percent. See also Detlev Count Schwerin, "Der Weg der 'Jungen Generation' in den Widerstand," in Schmädecke and Steinbach, 460–71, and Marion Dönhoff, "Der Geist Guderians," *Die Zeit*, 23 April 1965. Marion did not directly reproach Guderian for not having participated in the plot, but, in the context of the creation of the West German Bundeswehr, opposed his being made a role model for the new officer corps. She also mentioned that, according to the Kaltenbrunner reports (see note 80), Guderian had not involved himself in the Resistance because it might have required him to commit actions that were directed against his "Führer." At any rate, a week after the failed coup, he issued an order to his general staff officers that thenceforth they must all be "National Socialist Guidance Officers (NSFOs)." On the history of the NSFO, see Volker R. Berghahn, "NSDAP und 'Geistige Führung' der Wehrmacht, 1939–1945," in *Vierteljahrshefte für Zeitgeschichte* 1 (1969): 17–71. On the role of field marshall von Rundstedt, toward whom Marion was later more forgiving, see Harpprecht, 385, while Sethe (see p. 61) took a very critical view of him.

17. See Marion Dönhoff, "Leben und Sterben eines ostpreussischen Edelmannes," in idem, *Namen, die keiner mehr nennt* (Munich, 1964), 67.

18. Ibid., 68f. For the full story of this drama, see also Harpprecht, 294–95.

19. See Schwarzer, 141. See also Jörn Jacob Rohwer and Vera Lehndorff, *Verushka: Mein Leben* (Cologne, 2011); Antje Vollmer, *Doppelleben: Heinrich und Gottliebe von Lehndorff im Widerstand gegen Hitler* (Gütersloh, Germany, 2012).

20. On Christoph's career, see Harpprecht, 224, 263, 301ff.

21. Fürst Ysenburg-Büdingen to MD, 25 June 1979, in MDHH, F49//2/250.

22. See p. 116.

23. MD to Ysenburg-Büdingen, 28 June 1979, in MDHH, F49/2/251.

24. Ysenburg-Büdingen to MD, 5 July 1979, in MDHH, F49/2/252.

25. Rudolf von Thadden, *Trieglaff: Balancing Church and Politics in a Pomeranian World, 1807–1948* (New York, 2013).

26. On the Dohna recruitment, see her testimony in Gordon Craig, "Witness," *New York Review of Books*, 6 December 1990, 3–7; Harpprecht, 283, 298–99.

27. See Harpprecht, 286ff.

28. Bogislav hailed from the Dönhoff-Krafftshagen line and had joined the Nazis in March 1932. Pursuing a diplomatic career, he was consul general in Bombay before returning to Germany. Notorious for his Nazi sympathies and, as "Pucky" pointed out, under the influence of his wife, he seems to have been rather an unpleasant man who repeatedly sued the Dönhoffs at Friedrichstein, but always lost. See ibid., 155, 197.

29. Kuenheim, 33f. See also pp. 93f.

30. Quoted in Craig.

31. See pp. 90ff.

32. Craig, 4.

33. If her position in the 1930s had been one of "inner emigration," by the second half of the war she saw herself, like Sethe, as moving to a position of "active resistance." Hans and Sophie Scholl presumably also fall in this category, although their leaflets called for "passive resistance." See the text of the lecture Marion gave at Oxford University in October 1985, reprinted in Irene Brauer and Friedrich Dönhoff, eds., *Marion Gräfin Dönhoff: Zeichen ihrer Zeit; Ein Lesebuch* (Zurich, 2012), 443. See also Franka Geyken, *Wir standen nicht abseits: Frauen im Widerstand gegen Hitler* (Munich, 2014).

34. Schwarzer, 143.

35. For details, see Brauer and Dönhoff, 92ff.; Kuenheim, 38ff.; Harpprecht, 311ff. See also more generally Stefan Aust and Stephan Burgdorff, eds., *Die Flucht* (Stuttgart, 2002). As millions were moving West, life in the cities also collapsed due to the impact of Allied bombing. See, for example, Wolfram Wette et al., eds., *Das letzte halbe Jahr: Stimmungsberichte der Wehrmachtpropaganda* (Essen, 2001); Jörg Friedrich, *Der Brand: Deutschland im Bombenkrieg, 1940–1945* (Munich, 2003).

36. Marion Dönhoff, "In Memoriam 20. Juli 1944," passim. Fritz Stern was kind enough to lend me his original copy. It was republished in 1980 by the Forschungsgemeinschaft 20. Juli with a foreword by the association's president, Rüdiger von Voss. Stern appended a brief note pointing out that there is no mention in this account of Auschwitz or other camps. Although Marion knew about the murder of Jews in the rear areas by the Einsatzgruppen, the Wehrmacht, and police units, she later insisted that she did not hear about the camps and the gas chambers. Rumors about the fate of the Jews had been circulating before the end of the war and can be found in the volume edited by Wette et al. But they were rumors, and to many in Germany and also in the West they seemed incredible, partly because what we know now for certain was still beyond the horizon of our human experience, as the historian Walter Laqueur once remarked. The Dönhoff document is also reprinted in Rüdiger von Voss and Günther Neske, eds., *Der 20. Juli: Annäherung an den geschichtlichen Augenblick* (Pfullingen, 1984), 37–57.

37. On Blumenfeld, who was "half-Jewish," see Frank Bajohr, *Hanseat und Grenzgänger: Erik Blumenfeld. Eine politischen Biografie* (Göttingen, 2010). See also p. 193.

38. "Totengedenken 1946," *Die Zeit*, 21 March 1946. The German notion of *Mensch* was in general use at this time. It is gender-neutral and has been taken into the English language as such, connoting more than a (male) "man."

39. On the role of the theologians see, for example, John Moses, *The Reluctant Revolutionary Dietrich Bonhoeffer's Collision with Prusso-German History* (New York, 2009); Charles Marsh, *Strange Glory: A Life of Dietrich Bonhoeffer* (New York, 2014).

40. Quoted in Brauer and Dönhoff, 104.

41. John Conway, *The Nazi Persecution of the Churches, 1933–1945* (London, 1968); Werner Koch, "Widerstand der Bekennenden Kirche?" in Richard Albrecht et al., eds., *Widerstand und Exil, 1933–1945* (Frankfurt, 1980), 97–111; Ger van Roon, "Der katholische Widerstand," in Albrecht et al., 112–26; Richard Steigmann-Gall, *The Holy Reich* (New York, 2003); Gordon Zahn, *German Catholics and Hitler's Wars* (Notre Dame, IN), 1989.

42. *Die Zeit*, 18 July 1946, repr. in Brauer and Dönhoff, 30–34.

43. *Die Zeit*, 3 October 1946.

44. "Hände weg!" (Hands off!), *Die Zeit*, 16 January 1947.

45. Ibid.; Hans Bernd Gisevius, *Bis zum bitteren Ende* (Zurich, 1946), English translation, *To the Bitter End* (Boston, 1947).

46. See Gisevius's own story in his *Bis zum bitteren Ende*, and, for example, *Hitler's Chief Spy: The Wilhelm Canaris Mystery* (London, 2005).

47. Originally working for the criminal police, during World War II Nebe took command of the SS *Einsatzgruppe B*, responsible for the murder of some forty thousand Jewish men, women, and children in the Soviet Union. Returning to Berlin from this gruesome assignment, he continued to work for the Reich Criminal Office and joined the anti-Nazi resistance. Having passed on information about those SS liquidation squads to Hans Oster in Canaris's *Abwehr*, he was arrested and executed. See Ronald Rathert, *Verbrechen und Verschwörung: Arthur Nebe; Kripochef des Dritten Reiches* (Munster, 2001). Schacht had been president of the Reichsbank during the Weimar days but stayed on after 1933 and also acted as Hitler's economics minister from 1934 until he was dismissed when he disagreed with the regime's stepped-up rearmament program and its reckless financing. See, for example, John Weitz, *Hitler's Banker*, Boston 1997; Heinz Pentzlin, *Hjalmar Schacht: Leben und Wirken einer umstrittenen Persönlichkeit*, Vienna 1980. Put on trial as a major war criminal at Nuremberg after 1945, he was acquitted on all counts and lived in retirement until his death in 1970. Schacht wrote to Dönhoff asking her for details of her criticism of Gisevius. He added that he had not always agreed with Gisevius's views. For him the question was whether his account of events was accurate. Hjalmar Schacht to MD, 9 February 1947, in MDHH, F48/182. There is no evidence of a reply, and she may well not have written one.

48. Canaris had transferred Gisevius to the German general consulate in Switzerland and had used this position to pass on secret information to Allen Dulles, the local resident of the OSS, the American intelligence service. Returning to Germany in 1944, Gisevius was interrogated but released. Fearing renewed arrest after the failed coup, he went into hiding before managing to escape to Switzerland.

49. On Ernst von Weizsäcker and his trial see, for example, Eckart Conze et al., *Das Amt und die Vergangenheit: Deutsche Diplomaten im Dritten Reich und in der Bundesrepublik* (Munich, 2010); Marion Thielenhaus, *Zwischen Anpassung und Widerstand: Die politischen Aktivitäten der Beamtengruppe um Ernst von Weizsäcker im Auswärtigen Amt* (Paderborn, 1984). Having sided with him and his father, she later formed a strong friendship with Richard. See MD to Weizsäcker (April 1995) in MDHH, F49/2/150, with a good summary of their many conversation about Ostpolitik, democracy, the brutalization of daily life, and basic ethical values. See also their cooperation relating to the founding of the Aspen Institute Berlin on pp. 119f.

50. See, for example, her articles "Die Zeit ist abgelaufen," *Die Zeit*, 13 July 1950, about the Nuremberg Trials and their end, and "Kriegsverbrechen und Völkerrecht," *Die Zeit*, 23 November 1950. See also p. 101. See further her book *Foe into Friend: Makers of the New Germany from Konrad Adenauer to Helmut Schmidt* (New York, 1982), with a first chapter titled "Who Are the Germans?" Her critical attitudes toward the occupation policies of the Allies must probably be seen in the larger context of the early editorial orientation of *Die Zeit*, which was openly conservative-nationalist. See pp. 116f. See also Norbert Frei, "Als die deutsche Volksseele kochte," in *Süddeutsche Zeitung*, 5 November 2013.

51. See, for example, Anna J. Merritt and Richard L. Merritt, eds., *Public Opinion in Occupied Germany: The OMGUS Surveys, 1945–1949* (Urbana-Champaign, IL: 1970; idem, eds., *Public Opinion in Semi-sovereign Germany: The HICOG Surveys, 1949–1955* (Urbana-Champaign 1980); Elisabeth Noelle-Neumann, *The Germans: Public Opinion Polls, 1949–1966* (Bonn, 1967). All three books contain rich sources on West German opinion. See also Ian Kershaw, *Der NS-Staat* (Reinbek, 1994), 267–315: "Widerstand ohne das Volk." For the discrimination against the widows and children of the men of 20 July, see Dorothee von Meding, *Courageous Hearts: Women and the Anti-Hitler Plot of 1944* (Providence, 1997).

52. Marion Dönhoff, "Eugen Gerstenmaier," *Die Zeit*, 17 August 1950.

53. Idem, "Das Bild des Menschen," *Die Zeit*, 23 July 1953.

54. See also, Ger van Roon, *German Resistance to Hitler: Helmuth Count von Moltke and the Kreisau Circle* (New York, 1971); Helmuth James von Moltke, *Letters to Freya, 1939–1945* (New York, 1990).

55. See also Günther Weisenborn, ed., *Der lautlose Widerstand: Bericht über die Widerstandbewegung des deutschen Volkes* (Hamburg, 1953), with many statistics of executions and accounts of both elite and popular resistance.

56. One of the first studies on local working-class resistance is Erich Matthias, ed., *Widerstand gegen den Nationalsozialismus in Mannheim* (Mannheim, 1984), with accounts of the logistical difficulties of resistance and interviews with the widows of executed Social Democrats and Communists.

57. The reassessment of the Communist resistance and especially of the Red Orchestra Group came much later, after the end of the Cold War. See, for example, Stefan Roloff, *Die Rote Kapelle* (Munich, 2002); Anne Nelson, *Red Orchestra: The Story of the Berlin Underground and the Circle of Friends Who Resisted Hitler* (New York: 2009).

58. Marion Dönhoff, "Das Gewissen steht auf," *Die Zeit*, 15 July 1954.

59. Annedore Leber, *Das Gewissen steht auf* (Berlin, 1954, 1968), English translation *The Conscience in Revolt: Portraits of the German Resistance, 1933–1945* (Mainz 1994).

60. See, for example, Detlef Graf von Schwerin, *"Dann sind's die besten Köpfe, die man henkt": Die junge Generation im deutschen Widerstand* (Munich, 1991, 1994). The generational aspect of the conservative military resistance is no doubt important. See also note 16.

61. "Der 20. Juli," *Die Zeit*, 15 July 1954. It was not written by Dönhoff, but she no doubt stood behind the review.

62. Marion Dönhoff, "In Flensburg diskutieren Schüler den 20. Juli," *Die Zeit*, 15 March 1956.

63. While the roles of Yorck, Leber, and Schulenburg have already been mentioned, Helmuth Stieff provides another example of the journey that many conservative officers took. An anti-Republican in the Reichswehr during the early 1930s, he continued to serve after 1933 and rose to the position of general by 1942, when he joined the Resistance. What drove him were the atrocities committed in Poland in 1939–40 in the rear areas by SS contingents and later the strategic and tactical mistakes made outside Moscow in 1941-42.

64. On Rothfels, see Jan Eckel, *Hans Rothfels: Eine intellektuelle Biografie im 20. Jahrhundert* (Göttingen 2005).

65. See, for example, Ingo Haar, "'Volksgeschichte' und das Königsberger Milieu," in Hartmut Lehmann and Otto G. Oechsle, eds., *Nationalsozialismus in den Kulturwissenschaften*, vol. 1, Göttingen 2002, 169–209; Jan E. Dunkhase, *Werner Conze: Ein deutscher Historiker* (Göttingen,

2010); Eduard Mühle, *Für Volk und den deutschen Osten: Der Historiker Hermann Aubin und die deutsche Ostforschung* (Düsseldorf, 2005); Michael Burleigh, *Germany Turns Eastwards: A Study of Ostforschung in the Third Reich* (Cambridge, UK, 1988).

66. Hilldale, IL, 1948. The publisher was the right-wing Regnery & Co.

67. On Trott zu Solz, see, for example, Henry Malone, *Adam Trott zu Solz: Werdegang eines Verschwörers, 1909–1938* (Berlin, 1986); Giles MacDonogh, *A Good German: Adam Trott zu Solz* (New York, 1989). Subsequent research has been skeptical about the chances of this initiative. After all, Chamberlain had very scant information about the 1938 conspiracy. Its member belonged to the conservative-nationalists, about whom the British government had unhappy memories dating back as far as the pre-1914 period. So connecting with them seemed less plausible than continuing to negotiate with the actual Hitler government in power. See Harold C. Deutsch, *Hitler and His Generals: The Hidden Crisis, January-June 1938* (Minneapolis, 1973); Karl Rohe, ed., *Die Westmächte und das Dritte Reich, 1933–1939* (Paderborn, 1982), with a number of essays that pinpoint the British dilemma in 1938.

68. Rothfels was not the only scholar to characterize Hitler in this way and to speak of *Dämonie der Macht* as a way of defining the essence of the Hitler regime.

69. See also Marion Dönhoff, "Es fehlt nicht an Vorbildern," *Die Zeit*, 17 July 1964, with references to Trott and Moltke.

70. MD to Dürrenmatt, 20 July 1984, in MDHH, F43/1. It may be that what she had in mind was Carl Zuckmayer's dramatization of the role of Admiral Canaris, "Des Teufels General," which was also made into a movie.

71. Dürrenmatt to MD, 16 August 1984, in MDHH, F43/1.

72. Ibid., F42/1; Bucerius to MD, 21 July 1984, in MDHH, F42/1.

73. MD to Kohut, July 1978, in MDHH, F45/2/315.

74. See pp. 96ff.

75. There is now a growing body of research on how families coped with the massive human losses of the Nazi period and also on the situation of returning POWs, especially from the Soviet Union, in the 1950s. See, for example, see Frank Biess, *Homecomings: Returning POWs and the Legacies of Defeat in Postwar Germany* (Princeton, NJ, 2006).

76. See Kurt P. Tauber, *Beyond Eagle and Swastika*, 2 vols. (Middletown, CT, 1967).

77. Ibid., vol. 1, 344ff.

78. Von dem Bussche to MD, 21 May 1951, in MDHH, F42/2.

79. Marion Dönhoff, "Protest gegen eine Publikation," *Die Zeit*, 20 October 1961, with the text of her letters to Seewald.

80. Reichssicherheitshauptamt, ed., *Spiegelbild einer Verschwörung* (Stuttgart, 1961). The lack of an introduction and also of a carefully edited and footnoted text was remedied much later by Hans-Adolf Jacobsen, ed., *Opposition gegen Hitler und der Staatsstreich vom 20. Juli 1944 in der SD-Berichterstattung* (Stuttgart, 1989).

81. See Theo Sommer, "Hitlers Held," *Die Zeit*, 28 July 1963.

82. Hans Mommsen, "Gesellschaftsbild und Verfassungspläne des deutschen Widerstandes," in Walter Schmitthenner and Hans Buchheim, eds., *Der deutsche Widerstand gegen Hitler* (Cologne, 1966), 73–167; Hermann Graml, "Die aussenpolitischen Vorstellungen des deutschen Widerstandes," in *Der deutsche Widerstand gegen Hitler*, 15–72. See also Peter Steinbach, *Widerstand im Widerstreit: Der Widerstand gegen den Nationalsozialismus in der Erinnerung*

der Deutschen (Paderborn, 2001); Gerd R. Überschär, ed., *Der 20. Juli: Das andere Deutschland in der Vergangenheitspolitik nach 1945* (Berlin, 1998).

83. Ian Kershaw, *The Nazi Dictatorship: Problems and Perspectives of Interpretation* (London, 1993), 154–55.

84. Returning to his criticism in *Süddeutsche Zeitung* on 21 Juli 1999, Mommsen tried to be more nuanced in his discussion of the motives of the individual plotters. In many cases he nevertheless pointed to their social anti-Semitism and their quest for the "moral reconstitution of the nation."

85. Klemens von Klemperer, *German Resistance against Hitler: The Search for Allies Abroad* (New York, 1993).

86. MD to Klemperer, 13 July 1987, in MDHH, F45/2/176.

87. Ibid.

88. MD to Sternberger, 6 August 1984, in MDHH, F49/1/13.

89. Repr. in Brauer and Dönhoff, 441–54.

90. Eckart Conze, "Der Aufstand des preussischen Adels," *Vierteljahrshefte für Zeitgeschichte* 51, no. 4 (October 2003): 483–508.

91. An expression coined by sociologist and friend Ralf Dahrendorf in Dahrendorf to MD, 1 November 1979, in MDHH, F43/1/60. He continued that it was spearheaded by "the Protestant Mafia" of Hamburg. On this aspect, see chap. 4, pp. 183ff.

92. Repr. in Brauer and Dönhoff, 109.

93. Thus Conze, 489–90. See also her article "Es fehlt nicht an Vorbildern," *Die Zeit,* 17 July 1964, written on the occasion of the twentieth anniversary of the 1944 plot.

94. Körber to MD, 13 September 1988, in MDHH, F45/2/281.

95. Dönhoff, with the four essays mentioned here on 37–52, 73–84, 87–139, and 61–70.

96. See Celia Applegate, *A Nation of Provincials: The German Idea of* Heimat (Berkeley, 1990); Marita Kraus, "Heimat—Begriff und Erfahrung," in *Heimat, liebe Heimat,* ed. Hermann Haarmann (Berlin, 2004), 11–27, arguing that the term is personal and not abstract. It is an inseparable part of one's personality and can therefore not be lost. Nor is it purely local or bound to geographic borders (12). She quotes a Jewish refugee from Bremen (19), who after the war spoke of a "longing for the grey skies" of the North German city.

97. See the account of her intellectual journey toward reconciliation and her own thoughts on the subject of Heimat and loss in Kuenheim, 94ff. See also her article "Menschen im Abteil," *Die Zeit,* 14 September 1947, on a railway journey and an exchange with a young Polish traveler who also felt a longing for home (*Heimweh*). She also reports on other travelers, their small worlds, and their quests to rebuild their ordinary lives.

98. See, for example, Klaus J. Bade, ed., *Neue Heimat im Westen: Vertriebene, Flüchtlinge, Aussiedler* (Münster, 1990).

99. See, for example, Richard H. Immermann, ed., *John Foster Dulles and the Diplomacy of the Cold War* (Princeton, NJ) 1990.

100. See pp. 65ff. The debate has rumbled on into this century. See, for example, Gerd Meyer, *Die sowjetische Deutschlandpolitik im Jahre 1952* (Stuttgart 1970); Rolf Steininger, *Die vertane Chance* (Berlin, 1985), whose title gave his argument away; idem, *The German Question: The Stalin Note of 1952 and the Problem of German Reunification* (New York, 1990); Wilfried Loth, *Die Stalin-Note vom 10. März 1952: Neue Quellen und Analysen* (Munich, 2002); Kundra Schoppmann, *Die Stalin-Note vom 10. März 1952* (Munich, 2013).

101. Marion Dönhoff, "Fünf Minuten vor Zwölf," *Die Zeit*, 19 June 1952.

102. On 1953, see, for example, Arnulf Baring, *Uprising in East Germany* (Ithaca, NY, 1972); Christian Ostermann, *The United States, the East German Uprising, and the Limits of Rollback* (Washington, 1994); Carole Fink et al., eds., *1956: European and Global Perspectives* (Leipzig, 2006).

103. See, for example, Melanie Ilic and Jeremy Smith, *Soviet State and Society under Nikita Khrushchev* (New York, 2009); Volker R. Berghahn, *America and the Intellectual Cold Wars in Europe* (Princeton, NJ, 2001), 178ff.

104. See, for example, Hans-Peter Schwarz, "Journey into the Unknown," in idem, *Konrad Adenauer*, vol. 2 (New York, 1995), 164–76.

105. Marion Dönhoff, "Moskau zweigleisig," *Die Zeit*, 25 August 1955; idem, "Heimkehrer-Stopp," *Die Zeit*, 10 November 1955.

106. Dönhoff, "Bilanz: Stärke oder Entspannung," *Die Zeit*, 27 October 1955.

107. Dönhoff, "Doppelgleisig fahren," *Die Zeit*, 2 August 1956.

108. Dönhoff, "Nach Moskau fahren oder nicht? *Die Zeit*, 27 September 1956.

109. Dönhoff, "Michel gegen Michel," *Die Zeit*, 17 January 1957.

110. Dönhoff, "Entscheidung für Jahrzehnte," *Die Zeit*, 6 June 1957.

111. Dönhoff, "Reden und Rüsten," *Die Zeit*, 26 December 1957.

112. Dönhoff, "Die Schwäche des Guten," *Die Zeit*, 9 January 1958.

113. See pp. 158ff.

114. Kuenheim, 41f.

115. See Schöllgen.

116. See, for example, Arnulf Baring, *Machtwechsel: Die Ära Brandt-Scheel* (Stuttgart, 1982).

117. Marion Dönhoff, "Stichwort Oder-Neisse," *Die Zeit*, 17 April 1959.

118. Dönhoff, "Unser Draht nach Warschau," *Die Zeit*, 5 October 1962.

119. Dönhoff, "Versöhnung—ja, Verzicht—nein," *Die Zeit*, 4 September 1964.

120. Dönhoff, "Ein schwarzer Tag," *Die Zeit*, 1 February 1963; Dönhoff, "Warnung vor de Gaulle," *Die Zeit*, 15 February 1963.

121. Dönhoff, "Ostpolitik mit de Gaulle," *Die Zeit*, 3 December 1965.

122. Dönhoff, "Wie neu ist die neue Ostpolitik?" *Die Zeit*, 7 April 1967.

123. Brandt to MD, 6 March 1958, in MDHH, F42/2.

124. MD to Brandt, 4 January 1967, in MDHH, F42/2.

125. Scheel to MD, 28 February 1973, in MDHH, F48.

126. See, for example, Baring.

127. See notes 23 and 24 for full references to this correspondence.

128. Repr. in Brauer and Dönhoff, 111–16.

129. See the correspondence in MDHH, F42/1, F42/2, F45/1, F46/2, F49/1. Her relationship with David Astor is intriguing. As will be explained pp. 116f., when she fell out with Richard Tüngel, who had asked Carl Schmitt to write for *Die Zeit*, Astor hired her for his Sunday paper, *The Observer*. However, they had known each other several years earlier and, according to Harpprecht (393ff.), became close friends. There is still a lot of mystery about Marion Dönhoff's private life, especially since she confessed to having had several suitors, but she never married.

130. See note 52.

131. See, for example, Tauber.

132. See, for example, Eric Weitz, *Creating German Communism, 1890–1990* (Princeton, NJ, 1997); Carl-Heinz Böttcher, *Eine neue KPD?* (Cologne, 1968), 17ff.

133. See pp. 170f.

134. See Henning Hansen, *Die Sozialistische Reichspartei: Aufstieg und Scheitern eines rechtsextremen Partei* (Düsseldorf, 2007); Manfred Jenke, *Verschwörung von Rechts?* (Berlin, 1961), 48ff.

135. Tauber, 119ff.; Jenke, 161ff.

136. Marion Dönhoff, "Vertanes Erbe: Am Tag ein Adler, des Nachts eine Eule, das ist die FDP," *Die Zeit*, 1 December 1955.

137. Dönhoff, "Zerfall der bürgerlichen Mitte," *Die Zeit*, 17 May 1951.

138. Dönhoff, "Nichts dazu gelernt," *Die Zeit*, 4 December 1952. See also Jenke, 199ff.

139. Dönhoff, "Die bösen Deutschen," *Die Zeit*, 13 February 1959.

140. Dönhoff, "Sechs Herrenmenschen," *Die Zeit*, 8 July 1954.

141. Dönhoff, "Antwort an Ziesel," *Die Zeit*, 9 August 1963; Dönhoff, "Ziesel, Strauss und die Bundeswehr," *Die Zeit*, 3 July 1964. For a comprehensive analysis of Ziesel's biography and postwar activities, see Axel Schildt, "Im Visier: Die NS-Vergangenheit westdeutscher Intellektueller; Die Enthüllungskampagnen von Kurt Ziesel in der Ära Adenauer," in *Vierteljahrshefte für Zeitgeschichte* 64, no. 1 (January 2016): 37–68, esp. 39ff and 66–67.

142. Schmid to MD, 14 June 1955, in MDHH, F48/181. On the CCF, see Berghahn; Peter Coleman, *The Liberal Conspiracy* (New York, 1989); Pierre Grémion, *L'intelligence de l'anticommunisme* (Paris, 1995); Michael Hochgeschwender, *Freiheit in der Offensive?* (Cologne, 1996); Frances S. Saunders, *The Cultural Cold War* (New York, 2000). See also Carlo Schmid, *Erinnerungen* (Bern, Switzerland, 1979).

143. Marion Dönhoff, "Wo stehen wir und wohin steuern wir?" *Die Zeit*, 24 June 1960.

144. See Berghahn, 230–76.

145. Ibid., 276–83. The friendship between Stone and Dönhoff became close during the 1980s. See Stone to MD, 4 November 1987, in MDHH, F49/1.

146. See pp. 211ff.

147. See pp. 87ff.

148. Marion Dönhoff, "Preussens Erben," *Die Zeit*, 26 January 1962.

149. Dönhoff, "Bis zum letzten Mann," *Die Zeit*, 13 May 1954.

150. Dönhoff, "Vorbild Preussen?," *Die Zeit*, 17 February 1967.

151. Dönhoff Dönhoff, "Erst kommt das Geld—dann die Moral," in *Die Zeit*, 3 May 1989.

152. Dönhoff, "Eine Gesellschaft ohne moralische Massstäbe gerät in Gefahr," *Die Zeit*, 2 March 1993, repr. in Schwarzer, 287–89.

153. Dönhoff, "Zivilisiert den Kapitalismus," in Brauer and Dönhoff, 478–84.

154. Dönhoff, "Zwölf Thesen gegen die Masslosigkeit," in Brauer and Dönhoff, 472–77.

155. Michael Schaller, *Ronald Reagan* (New York, 2011); Judith Stein, *The Pivotal Decade* (New Haven, CT, 2010).

156. MD to Schmidt, 27 August 1982, in MDHH, F48/116.

157. Stone to MD, 27 September 1989, in MDHH, F49/1/56.

158. For Stone's biography, see Berghahn, 3–51.

159. Bertram to MD, 2 December 1998, in MDHH, F42/1. See also p. 121. On the historical roots of this attitude, see Hartmut Berghoff, "Adel und Industriekapitalismus in Deutschen Kaiserreich- Abstossungskräfte und Annäherungstendenzen zweiter Lebenswelten," in Heinz

Reif, *Adel und Bürgertum in Deutschland* (Berlin, 2000), 270: "Put in Marxist terminology, being did not determine the consciousness of the aristocracy, but its consciousness always withdrew upon itself and ignored the transformation of the environment. What contributed to this inner emigration were above all the educational patterns of aristocratic parental homes and the esprit de corps of elitist regiments." See also p. 97 her first postwar essay.

160. On Christoph, see Brauer and Dönhoff, 269. See also Marion Dönhoff, "Der 30. Januar," *Die Zeit*, 29 January 1953.

161. Marion Dönhoff, "Das Ende der Konservativen," *Die Zeit*, 6 July 1960. And again her critique of capitalism: a nation that merely keeps the economy going will "perish without spirit and soul."

162. See, for example, Hermann Beck, *The Fateful Alliance: German Conservatives and the Nazis in 1933* (New York, 2008).

163. See pp. 93ff. As a family friend observed about her upbringing in East Prussia, she had been "the most Prussian" among her siblings. See Schwarzer, 50.

Chapter 3

1. Quoted in Michael Stürmer, *Koalition und Opposition in der Weimarer Republik, 1924–1928* (Düsseldorf, 1967), 251. For the troubled early years of the Weimar Republic, see, for example, Volker R. Berghahn, *Modern Germany: Society, Economy and Politics in the Twentieth Century* (New York, 1987), 67ff.

2. See, for example, Mary Nolan, *Visions of Modernity* (New York, 1994); William C. Mc-Neil, *American Money and the Weimar Republic* (New York, 1986); Jon Jacobson, *Locarno Diplomacy* (Princeton, NJ, 1971).

3. On Hitler, see, for example, Richard J. Evans, *The Coming of the Third Reich* (New York, 2004), 195ff.

4. See, for example, Eric Weitz, *Creating Communism: 1880–1990* (Princeton, NJ) 1997.

5. See, for example, Berghahn, 92ff.

6. For the best study on Hindenburg, see Wolfram Pyta, *Hindenburg: Herrschaft zwischen Hohenzollern und Hitler* (Munich, 2007).

7. Martin Kitchen, *The Silent Dictatorship* (New York, 1974).

8. See, for example, Francis L. Carsten, *Revolution in Central Europe, 1918–1919* (Aldershot, UK, 1972).

9. Pyta, 403–18.

10. Ibid.

11. See, for example, Martin Broszat, *Hitler and the Collapse of the Weimar Republic* (New York, 1987); Karl Dietrich Bracher, *Die Auflösung der Weimarer Republik* (Villingen, Germany, 1955), 287ff.

12. Ebbo Demant, *Hans Zehrer als politischer Publizist: Von Schleicher zu Springer* (Mainz, 1971), 9ff.

13. See Kurt Mottok to HZ, 1 September 1966, in Bundesarchiv Koblenz (BAK), NL Zehrer, N311/16, fol. 1. For the following biographical data, see also the special edition *Sonderdruck Hans Zehrer für Mitarbeiter, aber auch Nachrichten aus dem Verlagshaus* (Berlin: Springer-Verlag, 20 September 1966).

14. On Mannheim, see his "The Problem of Generations" in idem, *Essays in the Sociology of Knowledge* (London, 1959), 276–322.

15. On Pareto, see, for example, Raymond Aron, *Main Currents of Sociological Thought 2: Durkheim, Pareto, Weber* (Harmondsworth, UK, 1970), esp. 155ff.

16. See Redaktion "Die Welt" to New Tork Times, Bad Godesberg Office, 7 September 1966, in BAK, NL Zehrer, N311/13, fol. 1.

17. Demant, 13; Edith Hanke and Gangolf Hübinger, "Von der 'Tat'-Gemeinde zum 'Tat'-Kreis: Die Entwicklung einer Kulturzeitschrift," in *Versammlungsort Moderner Geister: Der Eugen Diederichs Verlag—Aufbruch ins Jahrhundert der Extreme*, ed. Gangolf Hübinger (Munich, 1996), 299–334. *Die Tat* was founded in 1909, and Diederichs took it over in 1912. At that point it had the subtitle, "A Social-Religious Monthly," which was changed several times, however. See also Kurt Sontheimer, "Der Tat-Kreis," *Vierteljahrhefte für Zeitgeschichte* 7, no. 4 (July 1969): 229–60; Walter Struve, "Hans Zehrer as a Neoconservative Elite Theorist," *American Historical Review* 70, no. 4 (July 1965): 1035–57.

18. The September 1931 issue of *Die Tat* still listed Dr. Cornelius Bergmann as editor in chief; by November 1931, it was Zehrer. But he had contributed to the journal since 1930, if not before. In August and September of 1931, *Die Tat* had published two unsigned articles ("Wohin treiben wir? Weltuntergangsstimmung," 329–54, and "Kapitulation oder kämpfen?" 409–28) that appear to have been written by the new editor. The November issue (p. 679) also reprinted a piece from the 9 October edition of *Berliner Tageblatt*, the Berlin sister paper of *Vossische*, noting that Zehrer had been working on the editorial staff of the latter until 1 October. The paper added that Zehrer had now joined the Black Front and had spoken at a conference organized by Otto Strasser, the front's leader, at Lauenstein Castle. Replying to this news the next day in a letter to Theodor Wolff, Zehrer denied having hooked up with the "revolutionary National Socialists" and having made a presentation at the castle. He added that he welcomed criticism of *Die Tat* and of himself as the editor that was based on fact and demanded a correction in Wolff's paper. The following page contained an appeal to the readers of *Die Tat*. It reported that circles had been formed in various places to talk about the journal's articles and to seek active cooperation. The publication would thenceforth also assume a more active role. Developments in the country required stricter coordination of like-minded people in the hope that, as the Weimar "system" collapsed, they would facilitate renewal. Some of these circles had become so large that they should be more closely integrated, but should not become rallying points for political and economic special interests. Those who felt akin to *Die Tat* were urged to send their own addresses and also those of existing Tat Circles. The aim was to gain the support of all those who had read recent issues with approval and to advance the journal's work in practice. See also the retrospective remark by Paul Sethe (in *Die Zeit*, 2 September 1966, quoted in Demant, 71): "It was at this time that one often met young people on trains who were reading the 'Tat'; almost always these were people with intelligent [and] pensive faces."

19. *Die Tat* 23, no. 8 (November 1931), 674–75.

20. See Volker R. Berghahn, "Die Harzburger Front und die Kandidatur Hindenburgs für die Präsidentschaftswahlen 1932," *Vierteljahrshefte für Zeitgeschichte* 1 (1965): 64–82.

21. Hans Zehrer, "Die eigentliche Aufgabe: Die Angst vor der Wirklichkeit," *Die Tat* 23, no. 10 (January 1932): 777–800. See also idem, "Deutschlands Weg im Engpass," *Die Tat* 23, no. 11 (February 1932), 857–73.

22. See Pyta, 645ff.

23. Ibid., 701ff.

24. Ibid., 715ff.

25. Hans Zehrer, "Der Sinn der Krise: Das Ziel; Die neue Volksgemeinschaft," *Die Tat* 23, no. 12 (March 1932), 937–57.

26. Zehrer, "Die Frühjahrsoffensive: Politik und Charakter,"*Die Tat* 24, no. 1 (April 1932): 1–14; idem, "Die Dritte Front. Die Revolution des Stimmzettels," *Die Tat* 24, no. 2 (May 1932): 97–120.

27. "H.Z.," no title, *Die Tat* (May 1932): 183.

28. Hans Zehrer, "Der Entscheidung entgegen: Brünings hundert Meter," *Die Tat*, no. 3 (June 1932): 193–203. In the July issue of *Die Tat* (vol. 24, no. 4, 341–47), "H.Z." published a relatively brief piece titled "Die neuen Herren" that appeared before the election on July 31. He was critical of Brüning's successor, Franz von Papen, who was not legitimated at all by the "will of the people." He warned that relying on the "power of the bayonets" could not be the foundation of the Papen government and mentioned War Minister Schleicher, who was also anxious to avoid using the Reichswehr in domestic conflict. He did not expect the NSDAP to gain much over 40 percent of the vote. If no right-wing government could be formed by including the Center Party, fresh elections should be held. See also the *Glosse*, signed "H." [= Hans Zehrer?] on the role of the Reichswehr. What had to be avoided was for the more promising possibilities concerning the future of the country to be blocked by its military deployment at home.

29. Hans Zehrer, "Revolution oder Restauration? Drei Elemente des Staates," *Die Tat* 24, no. 5 (August 1932): 353–93. Similarly, his article titled "An der Wende! Die Revolution des Stimmzettels ist beendet," *Die Tat* 24, no. 6 (September 1932): 433–51, repeated that there was a great yearning for social justice extending from Strasser across the Christian trade unions to the Social Democrats and Communists. It was no longer impossible to think of a consensus among Schleicher, Strasser, and Adam Stegerwald, the leader of the Christian union movement. The "national" and "social" movements were coming more closely together. It was thus not sufficient just to rely on the powers of the president. Connections with the Social Democrats and the regional associations must also be made. While an economic council would represent the economic interests in a corporatist fashion, Hindenburg might also consider setting up a permanent presidential council.

30. See Demant, 93ff.; Sontheimer, 248ff.

31. Henning Grund, *Preussenschlag und Staatsgerichtshof im Jahre 1932* (Baden-Baden, 1976); Wolfgang Benz and Immanuel Geiss, *Staatsstreich gegen Preussen: 20. Juli 1932* (Düsseldorf, 1982).

32. Pyta, 733.

33. See, for example, Peter D. Stachura, *Gregor Strasser and the Rise of Nazism* (London, 1983), 101ff., also for the following.

34. Axel Schildt, *Militärdiktatur mit Massenbasis? Die Querfrontkonzeption in der Reichswehrführung um General Schleicher am Ende der Weimarer Republik* (Frankfurt, 1981); Pyta, 769ff.; Ian Kershaw, *Hitler, 1889–1036: Hubris* (New York, 1999), 393ff.; Klemens von Klemperer, *Konservative Bewegungen zwischen Kaiserreich und Nationalsozialismus* (Munich, n.d. [1957–58]); Thilo Vogelsang, *Kurt von Schleicher: Ein General als Politiker* (Göttingen, 1965), 83ff.

35. See, for example, Henry A. Turner, *Thirty Days to Power: January 1933* (Reading, MA, 1996); Pyta, 791ff.

36. See, for example, Karl Dietrich Bracher, Wolfgang Sauer, and Gerhard Schulz, *Die nationalsozialistische Machtergreifung* (Cologne, 1960); Hermann Beck, *The Fateful Alliance: German Conservatives and the Nazis in 1933* (New York, 2008).

37. Turner.

38. Hans Zehrer, "Deutschland ohne Hindenburg: Die politische Prognose," *Die Tat* 24, no. 9 (December 1932): 721–29.

39. His successor was Giselher Wirsing, who, once a sympathizer of Gregor Strasser, had made his peace with Hitler after January 1933. It may have been that he was an informer for Himmler's Security Service (SD). By November 1938 he had risen to the rank of SS-Hauptsturmführer (Captain) and, apart from continuing to publish *Die Tat*, in 1939 renamed *Das XX. Jahrhundert*, became editor in chief of the Nazi newspaper *Münchener Neueste Nachrichten*. He lectured on anti-Semitism and published a fiercely anti-American book, *Der masslose Kontinent*, in 1943. And yet it seems that his elevated position within the regime enabled him to protect Zehrer at the time of the June 1934 purge and later. On their postwar relationship, see note 85.

40. Anon. [Hans Zehrer?], "Die Aufgaben der Armee," *Die Tat* 24, no. 12 (March 1933): 1033–41.

41. "a" [Hans Zehrer?], "Schleicher und Strasser," *Die Tat* 24, no. 12 (March 1933): 1067–68.

42. Hans Zehrer, "Autoritär oder was sonst? Um die Nachfolge des Reichspräsidenten," *Die Tat* 24, no. 12 (March 1933): 1024–33.

43. Hans Thomas, "Das Ende des 'Fortschritts,'" *Die Tat* 25, no. 5 (August 1933): 353–64.

44. Hans Zehrer, "Die Revolution von rechts: Der Kampf zwischen Staat und Volk," *Die Tat* 25, no. 1 (April 1933): 1–16.

45. Ursula Bier-Hauser to HZ, 14 May 1963; Hans Zehrer's Statement relating to Bier's dismissal, 21 May 1963; and Ursula (Bier-)Hauser to HZ, 25 May 1965, all in BAK, NLHZ, 311/22, fol. 1.

46. Zehrer's Statement.

47. Jung was a "Young Conservative" adviser to Vice Chancellor von Papen. He had written about the development of the Hitler regime in quite critical terms. See *Roshan Magub, Edgar Julius Jung, Right-Wing Enemy of the Nazis: A Political Biography* (Rochester, NY, 2017). Papen was also arrested, but released. Considering that Schleicher and Major General Ferdinand von Bredow, another trusted comrade, had been murdered, some senior officers pressed War Minister Werner von Blomberg to demand an explanation and rehabilitation. But since the Reichswehr had provided logistical support for the bloodbath, the leadership put out a shameful statement to the effect that the two officers' honor had not been violated because they had fallen on a battlefield onto which their fate had led them. They had become embroiled in purely political power struggles and had taken paths that had been viewed as hostile to the government and had resulted in fateful consequences. There had been no change of position on this both within the government and the officer corps; nor would it now be possible. Shortly after Hindenburg's death on 2 August 1934, the officer corps took a personal oath to Hitler, who in his speeches after the Roehm Purge had been spreading the lie that the SA leadership but also Schleicher wanted to topple his government and had hence committed treason. See, for example, Thilo Vogelsang, 102ff.

48. Thus Paul Sethe, "Das war Hans Zehrer: Ein Wanderer zwischen den politischen Welten," *Die Zeit*, 2 September 1966.

49. Ludwig von Kobyletzki recalled this remark by Zehrer. See his letter to HZ, 22 June 1964, in BAK, NLHZ, 311/10, fol. 1.

50. The book was published in 1938 by Ullstein. See BAK, NLHZ, 311/26, fol. 1, with a copy of the pre-publication agreement between Ullstein and Zehrer, 5 November 1937, which also included book, translation, and film rights and an agreement that he would submit his next three novels to the publishers. The preface to the postwar republication revealed his mood during the mid-1930s. Hans Thomas, it reported, had written this book "during the most severe depression of his life." This is why it became "a light and funny book." It was written "when he did not have anything left to live on and no prospect of earning something." But ultimately he "earned ten times more than his income from his serious books will ever be."

51. The film rights were acquired by the Tobis Company for 8,000 marks. See HZ to Soschka (Deutsches Druckhaus Tempelhof), 5 January 1949, in BAK, NLHZ, 311/26, fol. 1; idem to Soschka, 12 September 1950, in BAK, NLHZ, 311/26, fol. 1, with the remark that the movie had done poorly.

52. HZ to Soschka, 25 August 1948, in BAK, NLHZ, 311/26, fol. 1.

53. See the special edition *Hans Zehrer für Mitarbeiter*. See also Stalling Verlag to Freyberg ("Welt"), 25 August 1966, in BAK, NLHZ, 311/13, fol. 1.

54. The letter is quoted, together with others to his wife, in Demant, 141.

55. Sofia Schleehahn to Editors of *Die Welt*, 29 August 1966, in BAK, NLHZ, 311/14, fol. 1.

56. Hans Zehrer, *Der Mensch in dieser Welt* (Reinbek, 1948), English translation, *Man in This World* (New York, 1955). The word *Mensch* in the German title should be borne in mind as being more gender-neutral than "Der Mann in dieser Welt." See Lilje's introduction, ix.

57. Lilje's introduction to *Der Mensch in dieser Welt*, ix.

58. Dorothy Thompson to Ernst Rowohlt (copy), 12 May 1950, in BAK, NLHZ, 311/25, fol. 1. In the same place, see also correspondence relating to a French translation. During that same year, Zehrer, apparently convinced of the importance of his work and still looking for ways to boost his income, approached Rowohlt about the publication of a second volume. When the latter hesitated, he told him that he would try to find another publisher. HZ to Ernst Rowohlt, 25 April 1950, in BAK, NLHZ, 311/25, fol. 1. Apart from *Percy auf Abwegen* and *Der Mensch in dieser Weit*, also published also as a paperback, in August 1951 Zehrer signed a contract for a novel to be titled *Der General*, with a delivery date of 15 January 1952. It was apparently never published, but judging from the title it was designed to be a dramatization of Schleicher. See the documents in BAK, NLHZ, 311/24, fol. 1.

59. Zehrer, 44ff.

60. See, for example, Kurt Sontheimer, *Antidemokratisches Denken in der Weimarer Republik* (Munich, 1968); Klemperer; Armin Mohler, *Die konservative Revolution in Deutschland, 1918–1932* (Stuttgart, 1950.

61. See, for example, Randall Hansen, *Disobeying Hitler* (London, 2014), 19.

62. On Catholicism in the Nazi period after 1945, see, for example, Günther Lewy, *The Catholic Church and Nazi Germany* (New York, 1964).

63. Dietrich Bonhoeffer and Martin Niemoeller were among the most prominent pastors. See pp. 99ff.

64. On Protestantism in the Third Reich and after 1945, see, for example, Doris Bergen, *The German Christian Movement in the Third Reich* (Chapel Hill, NC, 1996).

65. See p. 188.

66. Lilje had originally been favorably disposed toward Hitler but soon distanced himself and founded the "Jungreformatorische Bewegung," which developed links to the confessing church. Later he gave pastoral support to the conservative Resistance, which led to his arrest and trial after the failed July 1944 plot. He survived and became a major voice in the postwar evangelical church and was a cosignatory to the Stuttgart admission to German guilt of October 1945. See Hans Uden, *Hanns Lilje: Bischof der Öffentlichkeit* (Hanover, 1998). See also Matthew Hockenos, *A Church Divided: German Protestants Confront the Nazi Past* (Bloomington: Indiana University Press, 2004).

67. See pp. 149f.

68. The Americans adopted a different approach by founding *Die Neue Zeitung* (NZ) as the newspaper in their zone, staffed at the top by their own journalists. See Jessica Gienow-Hecht, *Transmission Impossible: American Journalism as Cultural Diplomacy in Postwar Germany, 1945–1955* (Baton Rouge, LA, 1999); Dominique Herbet, *Die Neue Zeitung: Un Journal Américain pour la Population Allemande, 1945–1949* (Villeneuve-d'Ascq, France, 1997).

69. See Demant, 154ff.

70. Rowohlt's agreement with Zehrer, 9 July 1947, in BAK, NLHZ, 311/25, fol. 1.

71. Rowohlt to HZ, n.d. (1925?), in BAK, NLHZ, 311/25, fol. 1.

72. Rowohlt to HZ, 17 February 1948, in BAK, NLHZ, 311/25, fol. 1.

73. Ibid.

74. HZ to Deutsches Druckhaus Tempelhof, 2 August 1948, in BAK, NLHZ, 311/26, fol. 1.

75. HZ to Soschka, 25 August 1948, in BAK, NLHZ, 311/25, fol. 1.

76. Soschka to HZ, 2 January 1952, in BAK, NLHZ, 311/25, fol. 1.

77. HZ to Soschka, 24 January 1952, in BAK, NLHZ, 311/25, fol. 1. In the meantime, the Druckhaus had again become part of the Ullstein-Verlag.

78. See Film Contract Company to HZ, 1 December 1959, in BAK, NLHZ, 311/25, fol. 1; Wolfgang Steinhardt of Arthur Brauner's CCC-Film to HZ, 5 January 1959, in BAK, NLHZ, 311/25, fol. 1; Ullstein Verlag to HZ, 26 February 1964, in BAK, NLHZ, 311/25, fol. 1.

79. Zehrer, *Man in This World.*

80. See, Hans-Peter Schwarz, *Axel Springer: Die Biografie* (Berlin, 2008), 177ff.

81. See BAK, NLHZ, 311/17, fol. 1, with a cutting of Jürgen Tern's article "Zehrer zum Abschied," in FAZ, n.d. (summer 1966). He referred to the war years when Zehrer met with young Springer for walks on the dunes of Sylt and introduced him to politics and newspaper publishing.

82. Copy in BAK, NLHA, 311/13, fol. 1.

83. See Schwarz, 209ff.; Demant, 176ff.; Hans Dieter Müller, *Der Springer-Konzern* (Munich, 1968), 159ff.

84. See also p. 140.

85. See Giselher Wirsing to HZ, 12 January 1965, in BAK, NLHZ, 311/23, fol. 1., in which he expressed fear that the Holtzbrincks, the owners of *Christ & Welt*, were looking for a buyer of the weekly. While the paper's sales rose later that year, Wirsing worried about the long-term prospects and the pressures by the large media corporations. Later that year they corresponded about Armin Mohler, Ernst Jünger's very conservative erstwhile private secretary, as an op-ed writer for both papers. Addressing each other as "dear Wirsing" and "dear Zehrer" and still on

"Sie" terms, they extended cordial greetings to their respective wives at the end. HZ to Giselher Wirsing, 16 August 1965, in BAK, NLHZ, 311/21, fol. 1; Wirsing to HZ, 31 August 1965, in
BAK, NLHZ, 311/21, fol. 1. In September they spent a "nice evening" together. See HZ Diary,
1964–65, entry for 13 September 1965, Handschriften 133, Staatsbibliothek Berlin (Stabi). (I
would like to thank Antje Bammer, Zehrer's niece, for her permission and her sister's to use
this volume of the diary.) However, Wirsing did not attend Zehrer's funeral because of a cold
and merely wrote that he wished to "shake [his widow's] hand." See Giselher Wirsing to Erika
Zehrer, 26 August 1966, in BAK, NLHZ, 311/16, fol. 1.

86. See pp. 65ff.

87. See Demant, 178.

88. See pp. 170ff.

89. See, for example, Volker Berghahn, *America and the Intellectual Cold Wars in Europe*
(Princeton, NJ, 2001), 143ff.

90. See, for example, Hans-Peter Schwarz, *Konrad Adenauer*, vol. 2 (Providence, RI, 1997),
164ff.

91. See Schwarz, 222.

92. Ibid., 254.

93. Ibid., 252f. See also Friedrich Zimmermann to HZ, 28 May 1957, in BAK/NLHZ,
311/23, fol. 1, with very interesting insights into Blankenhorn's thinking and the tensions
among Adenauer's advisers.

94. See Gerhard Wettig, ed., *Chruschtschows Westpolitik, 1955–1964* (Oldenburg, 2015).

95. For details on this disastrous trip, see Schwarz, 262ff.; Demant, 184ff.

96. See Schwarz, 279ff.

97. Ibid., 297–98.

98. See pp. 135f.

99. HZ to Springer, 29 May 1960, in BAK, NLHZ, 311/23, fol. 1.

100. HZ to Springer, 17 October 1963, in BAK, NLHZ, 311/23, fol. 1.

101. See Demant, 208.

102. Ibid., 197.

103. HZ to "Dear Cramer," 10 January 1965, in BAK, NLHZ, fol. 1. See also Demant, 206.

104. See Schwarz, 355ff.

105. See Cramer to HZ, 28 January 1965, in BAK, NLHZ, 311/23, fol. 1, with a retrospective
on the new "command structure."

106. M. Becker's expert evaluation, 5 October 1964, in BAK, NLHZ, 311/23, fol. 1; Heinz P.
Karpinski's evaluation, 6 October 1964, in BAK, NLHZ, 311/23, fol. 1.

107. For details on the Brandt issue, see Cramer to HZ, 28 January 1965; Cramer to Willy
Brandt, 28 January 1965, expressing his delight with Brandt's article; and HZ to Ernst Cramer,
25 January 1965, all in BAK, NLHZ, 311/23, fol. 1.

108. HZ to Cramer, 25 January 1965, in BAK, NLHZ, 311/23, fol. 1.

109. Cramer to HZ, 28 January 1965, in BAK, NLHZ, 311/23, fol. 1.

110. HZ to Springer, 29 January 1965, in BAK, NLHZ, 311/23, fol. 1.

111. Cramer to Heinz Barth, 8 December 1964, in BAK, NLHZ, 311/31, fol. 1. Six months
earlier Barth had questioned Wallenberg's decision to send Lothar Ruehl as the military correspondent to Paris. Barth promptly raised the question of the division of labor between the two.

It was just another reflection of the crisis of *Die Welt* and the jockeying for influence among Springer's "team."

112. See account in HZ to Springer, 22 September 1965, in BAK, NLHZ, 311/23, fol. 1.

113. See his diary entries from the autumn of 1964 in Staatsbibliothek Berlin, Handschriften 133.

114. Several entries for February 1965 in Staatsbibliothek Berlin, Handschriften 133.

115. Entries for 24 April and 22 September in Staatsbibliothek Berlin, Handschriften 133.

116. Entries for 5 March, 30 March, 25 August in Staatsbibliothek Berlin, Handschriften 133.

117. Entries for 21 April and 25 August in Staatsbibliothek Berlin, Handschriften 133.

118. Entry for 7 May 1965 in Staatsbibliothek Berlin, Handschriften 133: "Die Ratten verlassen das sinkende Schiff." One reason seems to have been that Cramer helped move the papers into more and more conservative waters by attracting right-wingers such as Mohler. A study of Cramer's intellectual journey would also have to deal with his willingness to condone the work of former Nazis. When Heinz Galinski, one of the leaders of the West German Jewish community, complained that *Die Welt's* cartoonist Hicks had published an anti-Semitic cartoon in 1944, Cramer replied that this event from his past was known when Hicks joined the Springer Corporation. He had repented and had done his best to provide restitution through his recent drawings. Cramer added that, when deciding to work again in Germany, he realized that he would be surrounded by people who had collaborated with the Nazis, whether they were forced or did so voluntarily or with abhorrence. But if they had changed and had not been involved in crimes, cooperation with them made sense to him. He had seen Hicks's "disgusting drawings," but *Die Welt* had done right to give him a chance. Galinski might find this "too Christian," but it was also very deeply ingrained in "Jewish thought." See Cramer to Heinz Galinski, 1 April 1965, in BAK, NLHZ, 311/34, fol. 1.

119. Entry for 21 February 1965, HZ Diaries, in Staatsbibliothek Berlin, Handschriften 133.

120. Various entries for March 1965, in Staatsbibliothek Berlin, Handschriften 133. The subsequent account, covering May 1965 to the spring of 1966, is based on the continuation of Zehrer's diary, still in the possession of Antje Brammer. Again I would like to thank her and her sister for putting this second volume at my disposal and for allowing me to cite from it.

121. See Demant, 211.

122. Ibid., 212ff.

123. Zehrer, *Man in This World.*

124. See pp. 153ff.

125. See Maximilian Terhalle, *Deutschnational in Weimar: Die politische Biographie des Reichstagsabgeordneten Otto Schmidt (Hannover), 1888–1971* (Cologne, 2009).

126. Ibid., 389ff.

127. See Hans Ewers to HZ, 22 June 1964, in BAK, NLHZ, 311/10, fol. 1, in which he recalled meeting Zehrer at Schmidt-Hannover's villa on Sylt to discuss Schmidt's manifesto. The document, he added, was designed to define the spirit and objectives of a future policy of "the smashed fatherland" on a nonsocialist and noncollectivist basis. Looking back, Ewers was saddened that nothing tangible had come of this effort.

128. See pp. 155f.

129. Zehrer, *Stille vor dem Sturm,* 207–11.

130. Ibid., 181–86.

131. Ibid., 186–90.

132. See pp. 134ff.

133. Zehrer, *Stille vor dem Sturm*, 195–99.

134. Ibid., 199–203.

135. Ibid., 7–8.

136. Ibid., 11–16.

137. See Samuel Huntington, *Clash of Civilizations and the Remaking of World Order* (New York, 1996).

138. Zehrer, *Stille vor dem Sturm*, 16–20.

139. See p. 154.

140. Zehrer, *Stille vor dem Sturm*, 20–25. Francis Fukuyama, *The End of History and the Last Man* (New York, 1992).

141. Stille, 25–28.

142. Ibid., 33–37.

143. Ibid., 37–43.

144. Ibid.

145. Ibid., 46–53.

146. Ibid., 50–55.

147. Ibid., 55–58

148. Ibid., 61–73.

149. Ibid., 78–82.

150. Ibid., 82–86.

151. Ibid., 86–90.

152. Ibid., 120–24.

153. Ibid., 156–60.

154. Ibid., 160ff.

155. Ibid., 134–38.

156. Demant, 217ff.

Chapter 4

1. See, for example, Alan Kramer, *The West German Economy, 1945–1955* (Oxford, 1989); Detlef Junker, ed., *Die USA und Deutschland im Zeitalter des Kalten Krieges, 1945–1968* (Stuttgart, 2001), 401ff.

2. See, for example, Rolf Richter, *Kommunikationsfreiheit = Verlegerfreiheit: Zur Kommunikationspolitik der Zeitungsverleger in der Bundesrepublik Deutschland, 1945–1969* (Meisenheim, Germany, 1975).

3. See, pp. 63ff.

4. See, p. 73.

5. See, p. 78.

6. Quoted in Hans-Peter Schwarz, *Axel Springer: Die Biografie* (Berlin, 2008), 308.

7. Ibid., 365.

8. Axel Springer to PS, 4 May 1960, NLPS, file I.

9. See Jessica Gienow-Hecht, *Transmission Impossible: American Journalism as Cultural Diplomacy in Postwar Germany, 1945–1955* (Baton Rouge, LA, 1999); Harold J. Hurwitz, *Die Stunde Null in der deutschen Presse: Die amerikanische Pressepolitik in Deutschland, 1945–1949* (Cologne, 1972); Hans-Dietrich Fischer, *Reeducations- und Pressepolitik unter britischem Besatzungsstatut: Die Zonenzeitung "Die Welt," 1946–1950* (Düsseldorf, 1978); Nicholas Pronay and Keith Wilson, eds., *The Political Reeducation of Germany and Her Allies after World War Two* (London, 1985); Karl Christian Führer, *Medienmetropole Hamburg* (Munich, 2008).

10. See Fischer, 49ff.

11. See Ebbo Demant, *Hans Zehrer: Von Schleicher zu Springer* (Mainz, 1971), 148ff., 162ff.

12. On the early life of Axel Springer and his family, see Schwarz, 17ff.

13. Ibid., 59ff.

14. Ibid., 55ff.

15. Ibid., 81.

16. Ibid., 111ff.

17. See, for example, Frances Rosenfeld, "The Anglo-German Encounter in Occupied Hamburg, 1945–1950," PhD dissertation, Columbia University, New York, 2006; Hans Dreckmann, *Hamburg nach der Kapitulation: Erinnerungen an 1945–1949* (Hamburg, 1970); Michael Ahrens, *Die Briten in Hamburg* (Munich, 2011); Jan Heitmann, *Das Ende des Zweiten Weltkrieges in Hamburg* (Frankfurt, 1990).

18. See Schwarz, 129ff.

19. Ibid., 124.

20. Hanna Schissler, ed., *The Miracle Years: A Cultural History of West Germany, 1949–1968* (Princeton, NJ, 2001). See, for example, Gudrun Kruip, *Das "Welt"-"Bild" des Axel Springer* (Munich, 1999); Hans Dieter Müller, *Der Springer-Konzern* (Munich, 1968), 73ff. ("ein deutsches Massenblatt: *Bild*"); Claus Jacobi, *Der Verleger Axel Springer* (Munich, 2005).

21. See, for example, Fischer, 61ff.

22. See ibid., 135ff.; Schwarz, 177ff.

23. Schwarz, 184ff., with many intriguing details on the wheeling and dealing surrounding the sale and the help that Springer got, especially from Adenauer and other CDU politicians.

24. See the biography by Frank Bajohr, *Hanseat und Grenzgänger: Erik Blumenfeld; Eine politische Biographie* (Gottingen, 2010).

25. On the history of the Bucerius family, see Ralf Dahrendorf, *Liberal und unabhängig: Gerd Bucerius und seine Zeit* (Munich, 2000), 11ff.

26. Ibid., 31ff.

27. Ibid., 34ff.

28. Ibid., 45ff.

29. Ibid., 52–53.

30. Ibid., 57ff.

31. Ibid., 67ff.

32. Ibid., 92ff.

33. Ibid., 93–94.

34. Ibid., 63ff.

35. See pp. 191f.

36. See Hermann Schreiber, *Henri Nannen: Der Herr vom Stern* (Munich, 2001), 220ff.

37. Ibid., 237ff.

38. On Bucerius's career, see Dahrendorf, 73ff., 126ff.

39. For details of this drama, with the rescue operation by Pferdmenges and others, as well as the ensuing seven years of "warfare" with his partners, see ibid., 95ff.

40. See, for example, Klaus Happrecht, *Die Gräfin Marion Dönhoff. Eine Biographie* (Reinbek, 2008), 435ff., which includes her move to London. On Dönhoff's earlier relationship with David Astor, see p. 253n. See also Jeremy Lewis, *David Astor: A Life in Print* (London, 2016).

41. See Dahrendorf, 121.

42. See the vacation photo, in ibid., 64(f).

43. See Schreiber, 298.

44. See Dahrendorf, 165ff.

45. Ibid., 124, 176ff.

46. Ibid., 144–45, 156.

47. Ibid., 146ff.; Schreiber, 303ff.

48. Schreiber, 305–6, 308ff.

49. Ibid., 283ff.

50. See Juliane Gräfin von Schwerin, *Henri Nannen: Der Stern und die Ostpolitik der sozialliberalen Koalition* (Hamburg, 2000), 63ff., with a comprehensive analysis.

51. PS to Nannen, 9 February 1965, NLPS, Leitz Organizer, N. This is a carbon copy of this letter, but it is crossed out with a red pencil. It seems that the letter was not sent and its message was presented by Sethe at an editorial conference instead.

52. Sethe to Nannen, 9 April 1965, NLPS, Leitz Organizer, N. This letter seems to have been sent. The date is added in red pencil at the top.

53. On this controversial issue, see, for example, William G. Gray, *Germany's Cold War: The Global Campaign to Isolate East Germany, 1949–1969* (Chapel Hill, NC, 2003).

54. In NLPS, Leitz Organizer, N.

55. Nannen to Sethe, 12 December 1966, ibid.

56. Bucerius to PS, 30 April 1963, NLPS, file I

57. See, for example, Leo Brawand, *Rudolf Augstein* (Düsseldorf, 1995); Otto Köhler, *Rudolf Augstein: Ein Leben für Deutschland* (Munich, 2002); Peter Merseburger, *Rudolf Augstein: Biographie* (Munich, 2007), and also for the following about his career up to 1945.

58. Brawand, 88ff.

59. See note 57.

60. See Michael Thomas, *Deutschland, England über alles: Rückkehr als Besatzungsoffizier* (Berlin, 1984), esp. 226ff.

61. Merseburger, 171–72, 116–17.

62. Ibid., 177ff.

63. Brawand, 121ff.

64. Ibid., 107ff.

65. Ibid., 257ff.

66. Ibid., 111.

67. Quoted in Merseburger, 201 and 169. Merseburger provides an illuminating analysis of the journalism of *Der Spiegel* and the acerbic lead articles that Augsein regularly published under the pseudonyms of "Jens Daniel" and "Moritz Pfeil."

68. Augstein as cited in Brawand, 71.

69. See Brawand, 121.

70. See p. 240n, and Merseburger, 192f.

71. Quoted in Merseburger, 217.

72. Ibid., 235–36.

73. Rudolf Augstein to PS, 2 February 1960, NLPS, Leitz Organizer, A.

74. On this affair see Brawand, 141; Merseburger, 237.

75. See Brawand, 131ff.; Merseburger, 213ff.; David Schoenbaum, *The Spiegel Affair* (Garden City, NY, 1968); Martin Doerry and Hauke Janssen, *Die SPIEGEL-Affäre* (Munich, 2013). The removal of Fritz Saenger as head of the Deutsche Presse Agentur (DPA) is also to be seen as an instance of the Adenauer government's coordinating press policies in an authoritarian fashion. For several years Adenauer had "encouraged the waging of a long guerilla war campaign within the DPA to have [the Social Democrat] Saenger removed which was finally successful in 1959." Following Sethe's ouster from the FAZ in 1955, this sequel "neatly symbolized both the desire of the predominantly conservative-orientated publishers to be 'Herr im Hause' . . . and the entrenchment of the 'CDU state' during the first two decades of the Federal Republic." Thus wrote Peter J. Humphreys in *Media and Media Policy in West Germany* (New York, 1990), 63. See also H. W. Gross, *Die Deutsche Pressagentur* (Frankfurt, 1982), 110–11.

76. Quoted in Merseburger, 250.

77. Ibid., 264.

78. Ibid., 365–66.

79. Marion Dönhoff, "Ihr Seid mir schöne Juristen," *Die Zeit*, 9 November 1962.

80. Quoted in Merseburger, 266.

81. Quoted in Brawand, 141.

82. See Merseburger, 255–56.

83. Ibid., 276.

84. "Wandel durch Annäherung"—a famous concept of Ostpolitik, apparently coined by Brandt confidant Egon Bahr.

85. Quoted in Merseburger, 267.

Conclusion

1. Alexander Gallus and Axel Schildt, eds., *Rückblickend in the Zukunft: Politische Öffentlichkeit und intellektuelle Positionen in Deutschland um 1950 und 1930* (Göttingen, 2011).

2. Charles Wighton, *Adenauer: Democratic Dictator* (London, 1963)

SELECT BIBLIOGRAPHY

Applegate, Celia. *A Nation of Provincials: The German Idea of Heimat*. Berkeley, 1990.

Baring, Arnulf. *Machtwechsel*. Stuttgart, 1980.

Beck, Hermann. *The Fateful Alliance*. New York, 2008.

Berghahn, Volker. *Modern Germany*. Cambridge, 1982.

———. *America and the Intellectual Cold Wars in Europe*. Princeton, 2001.

Berghahn, Volker, Paul Friedrich, and Otto A. Friedrich. *Ein politischer Unternehmer*. Frankfurt, 1993.

Brawand, Leo. *Rudolf Augstein*. Düsseldorf, 1995.

Cornelissen, Christoph. *Gerhard Ritter*. Düsseldorf, 2001.

Dahrendorf, Ralf. *Liberal und unabhängig: Gerd Bucerius und seine Zeit*. Munich, 2000.

Demant, Ebbo. *Von Schleicher zu Springer: Hans Zehrer als politischer Publizist*. Mainz, 1971.

Dönhoff, Marion. *Namen, die keiner mehr nennt*. Munich, 1964.

———. *Foe into Friend*. New York, 1982.

Edinger, Lewis. *Kurt Schumacher*. Stanford, 1965.

Frei, Norbert, and Johannes Schütz. *Journalismus im Dritten Reich*. Munich, 1989.

Führer, Karl-Christian. *Medienmetropole Hamburg*. Munich, 2008.

Gienow-Hecht, Jessica. *Transmission Impossible*. Baton Rouge, 1999.

Gillessen, Günther. *Auf verlorenem Posten*. Berlin, 1986.

Görtemaker, Heike. *Ein deutsches Leben: Die Geschichte der Margret Boveri, 1900–1975*. Munich, 2005.

Hale, Oron. *Captive Press in the Third Reich*. Princeton, 1964.

Hamilton, Richard F. *Who Voted for Hitler?* Princeton, 1982.

Hansen, Randall. *Disobeying Hitler*. London, 2014.

Harpprecht, Klaus. *Die Gräfin Dönhoff*. Reinbek, 2008.

Heydekamp, Peter. *Media and Media Policy in West Germany*. New York, 1990.

Kershaw, Ian. *The Nazi Dictatorship*. London, 1993.

Kiefer, Markus. *Auf der Suche nach nationaler Identität und Wegen zur deutschen Einheit*. Frankfurt, 1992.

Kleuters, Joost. *Reunification in West German Party Politics from Westbindung to Ostpolitik*. New York, 2012.

Klimke, Martin. *The Other Alliance*. Princeton, 2010.

Köhler, Otto. *Schreibtischtäter*. Cologne, 1989.

Merseburger, Peter. *Rudolf Augstein*. Munich, 2007.

Mitchell, Allan. *The Devil's Captain*. New York, 2011.

Moses, Dirk. *German Intellectuals and the Nazi Past*. Cambridge, 2007.

Nathans, Eli. *Peter von Zahn's Cold War Broadcasts to West Germany*. Basingstoke, England, 2017.

Nelson, Anne. *Red Orchestra*. New York, 2009.

Pronay, Nicholas, and Keith Wilson, eds. *The Political Reeducation of Germany and Her Allies after World War II*. London, 1985.

Richter, Rudolf. *Kommunikationsfreiheit und Verlegerfreiheit*. Mannheim, 1975.

Schissler, Hanna, ed., *The Miracle Years*. Princeton, 2001.

Schoenbaum, David. *The Spiegel Affair*. Garden City, NJ, 1968.

Schreiber, Hermann. *Henri Nannen*. Munich 2001.

Schwarz, Hans-Peter. *Konrad Adenauer*. Vol. 2. Providence, RI, 1997.

———. *Axel Springer*. Berlin, 2008.

Schwarzer, Alice. *Marion Dönhoff*. Cologne, 1996.

Sethe, Paul. *In Wasser geschrieben*. Frankfurt, 1966.

Sontheimer, Kurt. *Antidemokratisches Denken in der Weimarer Republik*. Munich, 1968.

Spaulding, Robert M. *Osthandel and Ostpolitik*. Providence, RI, 1997.

Stachura, Peter. *Gregor Strasser and the Rise of Nazism*. London, 1983.

Steigmann-Gall, Richard. *The Holy Reich*. New York, 2003.

Steinberg, Jonathan. *Yesterday's Deterrent*. London, 1965.

Steininger, Rolf. *The German Question*. New York, 1990.

Stent, Angela. *From Embargo to Ostpolitik*. Cambridge, 2002.

Tauber, Kurt P. *Beyond Eagle and Swastika*. 2 vols. Middletown, CT, 1967.

Terhalle, Maximilian. *Deutschnationalismus in Weimar*. Cologne, 2009.

Turner, Henry A. *Thirty Days to Power: January 1933*. Reading, MA, 1996.

Van Roon, Ger. *The German Resistance to Hitler*. New York, 1971.

Von Meding, Dorothee. *Courageous Hearts*. Providence, RI, 1997.

Von Pufendorf, Astrid. *Mut zur Utopie*. Frankfurt, 2015.

Wighton, Carles. *Adenauer: Democratic Dictator*. London, 1963.

Zehrer, Hans. *Man in this World*. New York, 1955.

INDEX